P9-CQL-233

MEMBERS
OF THE CLUB

MEMBERS OF THE CLUB

THE COMING OF AGE OF EXECUTIVE WOMEN

DAWN-MARIE DRISCOLL

and

CAROL R. GOLDBERG

THE FREE PRESS
A Division of Macmillan, Inc.
NEW YORK

Maxwell Macmillan Canada
TORONTO

Maxwell Macmillan International
NEW YORK OXFORD SINGAPORE SYDNEY

Copyright © 1993 by Dawn-Marie Driscoll and Carol R. Goldberg
All rights reserved. No part of this book may be reproduced
or transmitted in any form or by any means, electronic or
mechanical, including photocopying, recording, or by any
information storage and retrieval system, without permission
in writing from the Publisher.

The Free Press
A Division of Macmillan, Inc.
866 Third Avenue, New York, N. Y. 10022

Maxwell Macmillan Canada, Inc.
1200 Eglinton Avenue East
Suite 200
Don Mills, Ontario M3C 3N1

Macmillan, Inc. is part of the Maxwell Communication
Group of Companies.

Printed in the United States of America

printing number
1 2 3 4 5 6 7 8 9 10

Library of Congress Cataloging-in-Publication Data
Driscoll, Dawn-Marie.
    Members of the club: the coming of age of executive women /
Dawn-Marie Driscoll and Carol R. Goldberg.
        p. cm.
    Includes index.
    ISBN 0–02–908065–7
    1. Women executives. I. Goldberg, Carol R. II. Title.
HD6054.4.U6D75 1993
331.4'816584—dc20   93–25796
                                                          CIP

3 2280 00876 3559

For Norman Marcus and Avram Goldberg

CONTENTS

ACKNOWLEDGMENTS

Being a coauthor is a dynamic experience, with one person pushing, the other pulling; each challenging the other, each uplifting the other at critical moments. Yet this book is not our story alone. The real driving force came from the women whose stories we tell and whose thoughts we share. This constant prodding, cajoling, calling, and exalting became a part of the process. "Listen to this," one would say from across the country, and regale us with a recent incident. "This is the only thing I've ever read that tells the truth about executive women," said another, after reviewing a chapter excerpt.

We owe a large debt to the women who were willing to talk honestly and openly with us, sharing their anecdotes and strategies. The book had its origins with the formation of the Women's Economic Forum in Boston, and the businesswomen in that group were the core that supported us throughout. They encouraged us, read early drafts, challenged ideas, and added new ones. As the size of the group expanded, becoming the Massachusetts Women's Forum and a chapter of the International Women's Forum, our circle of thoughtful business and professional colleagues expanded globally. To all of them we are especially grateful.

We run a risk in mentioning individual names in an acknowledgment, knowing that to omit some may appear to diminish their contribution. For that reason, we will not list all of the women (and men) who spoke to us and made significant contributions of time and insight. We treasure the friendship of those who agreed to be named in the book—identifying them makes their experiences more immediate and real. But the contributions of those who asked not to be identified are no less valuable. While we may have changed some names and career or city identifications to meet their wishes, they will recognize their words and thoughts. We owe them a thank-you as well.

Writing a book is an arduous process, as every first-time author discovers. For that reason we must acknowledge several women in particular who helped in its creation. Harvard University vice president and general counsel Margaret H. Marshall, Harvard Business School professor Rosabeth Moss Kanter, and former Harvard dean of education Patricia Albjerg Graham wrote thoughtful recommendations on our behalf, urging the Bunting Institute at Radcliffe College to accept two businesswomen as 1990–91 Visitors-in-Residence. Director Florence Ladd and her advisers must have been persuaded by three such eminent recommenders, because she welcomed us to her distinguished company of women at the Bunting and encouraged us every step of the way. She never failed to offer just the right word of support or ask the critical question when we needed it.

The Bunting Institute is a special place, a gathering of women scholars from many fields and from around the world. On our first day we left the orientation slightly bewildered, wondering if we would ever understand the esoteric research projects that our fellow sisters were undertaking. Our project was pretty pragmatic stuff in comparison to theirs. But week after week we became immersed in the world of interdisciplinary studies and the dynamic of the gatherings enhanced our work. We could not have imagined the degree to which so many of our Bunting sisters would contribute to our work and we thank them for it. We are particularly indebted to the late law professor Mary Jo Frug and saddened that she could not have read our final product.

Our Bunting Institute project became a book because of the careful attention of our agent, Jill Kneerim of the Palmer and Dodge Agency, who knew how to capture random thoughts and help shape them into a proposal. She advised us to choose an editor rather than a publisher and we listened to her. Susan Arellano liked our ideas even before she moved to The Free Press, and our manuscript became a better book with her critical hand on its pages. We didn't know there were editors still around like Susan, who actually worked with authors, questioned their statements, improved their copy. There is and we found her. We are very fortunate.

Throughout the process, we were inspired by our children, Christopher Marcus, Deborah Goldberg, and Joshua Goldberg. We wrote the book in large part because we hope to leave them and our grandchildren a fairer and more secure economic world.

Lastly, we love and profoundly admire our husbands, Norman Marcus and Avram Goldberg, who from the very beginning have advocated the goals of feminism. They are our severest editors and critics and our best friends. They have made us sharper thinkers and better writers and have sustained us throughout with their enthusiasm and humor. This book is for them, our partners.

INTRODUCTION

We are both insiders. We always have been and probably always will be.

This book represents two adult lifetimes in the making. Between us, we have nearly sixty years of experience in the business and professional world, and our career paths were nearly parallel in their dedication to feminist activity. Both tracks intersect with this book, culminating valuable years of exploring and discussing the strategies that businesswomen can use to improve the economic and social status of all women.

To understand how this book evolved, it helps to know where we started.

Carol entered Jackson College, Medford, Mass., in 1949, interrupting her undergraduate education when she married in 1950. She was ahead of her time in working part-time in fashion retailing, even when her children were born. She received her B.A. degree in 1955, and when her family figured out that she was serious about working, they suggested she join the family supermarket business—with no promise of advancement. From then on there was no turning back. She climbed the ladder, holding a variety of positions in The Stop & Shop Companies, a multibillion-dollar supermarket and department store chain. With only a few short breaks (if one considers the Advanced Management Program at Harvard Business School a break) she ended her career with Stop & Shop as president and chief operating officer in 1989. Now she is president of Avcar Group Ltd., a marketing and consulting firm, and serves on the board of directors of several national companies.

After more than thirty years in the corporate world, Carol has a long string of "first female" here and "only woman" there. She is accustomed to that and not impressed. Rather, Carol is more concerned about the women who are coming along and the opportunities they will find in today's workplace when the expectations for them are different than those she faced as a young executive.

Dawn-Marie graduated as an English major from Regis College, in Weston, Massachusetts. She feels that attending an all-women's college was critical to her later success. She was one of only a few females in her law school class in the early seventies, a minority percentage whom she encountered again in the halls of the Massachusetts State House where she started work as a Graduate Legislative Fellow. She continued in the public sector, as an attorney for the Massachusetts State Senate, and also taught law school courses on sex discrimination, a new and exciting topic for young lawyers at the time. In 1978 she moved into the private sector, working for more than a decade as vice president of corporate affairs and general counsel of Filene's, the Boston-based department store chain.

During her years in the business community, Dawn-Marie was also often the "only" or the "first" woman in a variety of prestigious civic, business, and professional organizations. After Filene's she became a partner at Palmer & Dodge, a large Boston law firm. Now, like Carol, she serves as a corporate director and consultant. She often speaks to organizations on issues relating to women in business and the professions and has worn the "role model" insignia, although she and Carol know that counseling individual career women is only minimally effective and efficient in making a major impact on the economic advancement of all women.

Carol and Dawn-Marie had known each other for years. When the opportunity came along to share a joint appointment as Visitors-in-Residence at the Mary Ingraham Bunting Institute at Radcliffe College, where a select number of women scholars pursue their chosen projects for a year, they jumped at the chance. They could not refuse the rare gift of working in that unique environment, studying issues they had been discussing together for years. Their goal? As insiders, to provide some answers to the question women were asking, "What strategies can I use to get to a position of leadership and influence," and that corporations, law firms, and other professional institutions and organizations were asking, "What can we do to attract, retain, and promote talented women."

THE PROJECT . . . AND THE ISSUES WE PURSUED

Our project at the Bunting Institute was prompted by anecdotes we were hearing concerning senior-level women who had reached and remained at the top of their businesses or professions, and about others who left their corporations and businesses for other pursuits. Many were "in transition"; others, although working successfully, were mentally looking ahead to the next stage of their lives. We wondered if there was a trend in the isolated stories we heard even though we knew that individual accounts of life at the top from those who left were colored by the specter of a declining economy, corporate restructurings, belt tightenings, and consolidations. Yet questions remained. Were women using these new developments as opportunities to start new careers, or were they being forced out? Were men at the top "circling the wagons," letting few women into the power structure? Was the power base at the top hospitable toward women only in good times, when there were enough rewards to go around for everyone? Or was this a time of dynamic change, full of opportunities for women who had developed leadership skills and were now ready to lead the economic community? We knew many women who were now well ensconced at the top, who had mastered difficult issues and had made it into the power structure of their economic world, finding the effort worthwhile.

As businesswomen with a close circle of female peers, we spoke frequently with other women about what we were all observing. All of us had found unprecedented personal and professional success, and felt a profound commitment to those women who were coming along behind us. Invariably our care and concern for the economic community in which we played an important role led us to conclude that the businesses and professions in which we were involved needed this talent pool of capable women managers in the coming decade. How could the economy flourish if capable women were blocked from leadership roles at the top, or worse, chose to leave for more receptive opportunities? More important, how could we convince those who were leading our organizations to attract and retain women as leaders? Finally, we felt it was most critical to give women a clear picture of what life at the top is like, to share with them what other women are saying and doing, and to describe the possibilities that lie ahead for women. For women who are tempted to ask "Is it worth it?" or "What's the point of working inside the system?," the voices of senior female executives whose experiences we describe ring loud and clear as a positive message to all.

The core of our Bunting project and this resulting book focuses on women at the senior levels of our professions. We began our project with some preconceptions, but first we chose to listen. In the beginning, the hundreds of voices and stories were discordant. Executive vice presidents, chairmen, presidents, managing partners, and other top female executives of traditional companies and professions shared their thoughts and experiences. "Time" is the issue, said one. "Playing golf," said another. "Changing the culture and values" is the opportunity, agreed many. Before long, a common theme was apparent: the need for women to tell each other how to achieve the power and influence that would allow them to make a difference for other women at all economic levels.

The executive vice president of a Chicago bank said it well. "A light bulb went off in my head one day," she said to us. "For many of us who had no role models, we just worked extremely hard. Like Cinderella, we could go to the ball only if we worked like a dog all day. Well, our male peers are already at the ball. Women are just as smart, or in some cases smarter, but it's the men who are off getting their names in the paper, doing the strategic planning, meeting with the governor because the women are back in the office doing the work.

"We've got to stop and change gears," she said, "and tell each other how it works. My professional goal now is to work less hard but to make more of an impact. And we've got to tell the younger women not to repeat our mistakes and not to give up. They've got to learn the trick of working smarter, not harder, earlier in the game."

In the last few decades, women told us, they learned and integrated male-directed values of dress and behavior, but too often ended up as the power behind the throne, not beside or on it. These women even earned the same credentials as men, hoping to make their way to the top using the same techniques that made their male peers captains of industry. So what went wrong? Why, after more than fifteen years of doing "the right thing," did women find little consolation in business magazine cover stories that tried to explain "Why Women Still Don't Hit the Top?"

We believe that neither the American economy nor the women who work in it can afford to agree with naysayers who try to rationalize this sorry situation from behind a cloak of negative stereotypes: Women are underpaid, overworked, stressed, single, and isolated; in positions of prominence but no power. This description does not fit the women we know, many of whom hold senior positions in a variety of companies and professional firms and exercise power in leadership roles. Admittedly few in number, they have made it in a "man's world." We believe if more women are to progress to leadership roles, and if American businesses and professions want to move more of them up to the highest levels, we all must understand and confront the real challenges these women have faced.

Therefore, this is a critical moment for women in the business world to do one of two things. They can allow the popular backlash against feminism and assertive women to silence them, negating the hard-earned gains of older women and discouraging younger women from pursuing careers in the economic world. After all, speaking out about one's personal history and acknowledging social as well as economic goals involve risk. It's always easier for successful women to quietly and gracefully assimilate into the male-dominated environment they became accustomed to, and let the next generation of working women figure out how to make it for themselves.

Or, by sharing information and personal stories, they can help other women achieve important posts in the nation's corporations and business institutions, assume leadership positions in key industry and civic organizations, and begin the third stage of the modern-day women's movement: partnership feminism, with its goal of economic empowerment for all citizens.

The business and professional women we spoke with across the country cited only one answer: Women must help other women become leaders in the economic world. It is high time that senior executive women tell their stories, they said, so that younger women don't fall prey to the negativism of the popular press. Rather than simply revealing themselves as role models, senior executive women are now speaking clearly about *how* they did it, *why* they did it, and *what* they are doing now that they are in positions of power and influence. To them, the whole point of making the effort is to set and shape the agenda and impact outcomes, not just carry out the plans men make.

It became increasingly apparent to us that a number of women holding responsible senior positions in corporations and professions had learned important lessons about how to confront issues and overcome barriers. They are members of an exclusive group, participating in the decisions affecting the direction of the American economy in the coming decade. They are role models for younger women behind them in the workplace. Their experiences are magnified in importance, for what these women at senior levels are thinking, discussing, and concerned about reflects the talent pool that their industries and professions will find in the 90s. We thought it was time to share their thoughts and experiences, hopefully to inspire more women to claim their place as leaders in the economic world with confidence and determination.

MEMBERS
OF THE CLUB

CHAPTER ONE

OPENING THE CLUBHOUSE DOOR

This book is about women who have made it in business and the professions and how they will lead the next stage of the women's movement. As seasoned executives, they have overcome obstacles and are showing other women how they can do it, too. But reaching the senior level is not enough; these executives are using their leverage in the economic community to bring about change, thereby proving the effort to reach the top was worthwhile. They are members of The Club, that elite group of chief executive officers, partners, investors, and leaders in the economic community whose influence greatly exceeds its numbers.

No less an organizational guru than Tom Peters, who defined excellence for American business and industry in the 1980s, proclaimed that the business world of the 1990s will be dominated by women. In an article for a popular women's magazine, Peters went so far as to proclaim that "the time has come for men on the move to learn to play women's games."

We hope that neither sex will continue to indulge in game-playing, but we think Mr. Peters may be on the right track. The sheer statistics about the critical mass of women in the workplace, many of them now moving into decision-making roles, makes his thesis compelling:

- 45 percent of the civilian work force are women, an estimated 54 million workers
- over 40 percent of those graduating from college with degrees in business or mathematics are women, as are those graduating from law

school with J.D.s; 34 percent of M.B.A. degrees awarded in 1990 went to women

- nearly 6.1 million women are employed as executives, administrators, and managers
- women now hold over 41 percent of all managerial positions, up from 32 percent in 1983

Statistics such as these attest to the vast pool of women qualified to lead many of America's businesses and corporations. Yet women are still glaringly underrepresented at the uppermost level of corporations, law firms, and other professional enterprises. Less than 5 percent of the nearly 6,000 directors of 500 large companies surveyed by the magazine *Executive Search Review* were women, and 285 of the companies had no women board members. In the public sector, historically more hospitable to women, the top jobs are still reserved for men, with women holding only 31.3 percent of the high-level state and local jobs in 1990 and only 10 percent of senior federal posts. Closed out of many top jobs and professions, women are still not making as much money as men. In 1990 the median annual income for women was $20,656, just 71 percent of the $28,843 median income for men, a ratio better than the 60 percent figure in 1975 but still lagging. An average female college graduate today earns less than a male high school graduate, and a female high school graduate earns less than a male high school dropout.

It is tempting to make a connection between the few women of senior status and the fact that women are starting their own businesses at a rate four times faster than the overall average of new business starts. They now own 30 percent of all American companies, a statistic that may be fine in the pure realm of entrepreneurship, but an ominous one for the traditional male-dominated corporate and business world that would seem to need all the help it can get these days.

Statistics such as these are popularly used to prove the existence of a "glass ceiling," but we have tried to avoid the term wherever possible. We believe the origin of the image lies with women who enjoyed an early and easy entry into the business world and then moved ahead rapidly into middle-management positions. Their experiences differed from the earlier generation of women who had difficulty entering and met barriers at every level. This younger group arrived at middle-management levels together with men and then realized their male peers were moving up at a faster pace than they were. Some dropped out of the race or changed direction. Others became frustrated and crashed into what they saw as an invisible barrier to female advancement, and called it the glass ceiling.

However, the successful women of both generations with whom we talked faced these issues pragmatically. The older women who had difficulties with access and no expectations of advancement were practical in judging the real world and worked strategies around barriers. Many younger women with impressive educational credentials had higher expectations and were eagerly sought after. Some initially denied there were any barriers to their advancement, but even if they later discovered them, they developed effective strategies for personal success. They did not deny the existence of a glass ceiling, but neither did they accept it as inevitable. The glass ceiling did not become a reason or defense for failure for either group.

The career and life cycles for many of these women were similar. Even if they entered into the world of work with lowered expectations or a diminished sense of their own abilities, they worked hard and progressed nicely, achieving increased status and responsibilities. But even many of those who encountered nothing but success early on distinctly recalled an "Ohhhhhh . . . *no!*" moment when they realized they had encountered a new dynamic impacting their effectiveness and power at higher levels.

Rejecting the notion that they had hit a glass ceiling, these women used a different image to describe what impacted their progress as they moved along in their careers: the comfort zone. Unlike the imagery of the glass ceiling, which conveys a mental picture of an invisible, impenetrable barrier that is specifically placed above a woman's head by a conspiratorial cabal of male executives, the "zone" is simply a safe haven for those who belong there. A glass ceiling is mean; you can see through it but you can't get above it. Those who operate in a comfort zone are neither malevolent nor biased; understandably, they are just doing what is comfortable, usual, and habitual.

One woman described the two this way: "At my former engineering company, the senior executives had no interest or intention of promoting women. They didn't want them present in their councils of power; they didn't value women's opinions; they didn't believe clients wanted to deal with women as peers; they didn't think women could manage large projects; they didn't want women on the board of the company; and they didn't care. I saw the glass ceiling very early on and left.

"However, in my present company," she said, "senior management gives a lot of lip service to the importance of advancing women. The company has one woman on its board. They try to recruit women and are honestly bewildered when any of us leave. I believe they want to do the right thing, but they just don't get it yet. The corporate environment still telegraphs subtle messages to the women that the men are 'us' and the women are 'them.' The men in the office go out and golf with clients on Wednesdays, never asking us if we would like to come along. The men decide which one of them will represent our company at the chamber's annual dinner, and if one of them can't make it, no one goes. The men rant and rave about a lousy subcontractor, but if one of us were to behave that way, we'd be ostracized. The men act as if this is their own company and we are here by their acquiescence. There is no partnership, no sense of ownership or complete inclusion yet."

Penetrating and changing the comfort zone so that it welcomes all executives is a challenge, but a necessary one if women are to reach maximum effectiveness. The bad news is that the zone creates a culture (and in some cases, a set of professional rules) that impacts most negatively on women, excluding them from arenas of corporate, civic, and economic power. The good news is that the comfort zone is not immutable, and the ways to move into it are, surprisingly, available to all.

Senior executive women are telling other women—and the corporations and businesses that employ them—that the keys to success in combating the comfort zone are not exclusively hard work and excellent performance but rainmaking (generating revenues, clients, and profits), visibility, and relationships—as we will hear in Chapters 2, 4, and 5. These women moved ahead by understanding and using power, particularly the collaborative power of other women forged in the wide range of professional networking groups described in Chapter 8. They've all faced social and cultural barriers, even discrimination, but they've dealt with them and worked around them, as we learn in Chapters 6 and 7.

These executive women acknowledge that men and women are different, but instead of muting these differences, they understand and use them, as they explain in Chapter 3. They are feminine and family-oriented and have never thought that they had to sacrifice relationships, outside interests, or pleasure to succeed. Now that they are at the pinnacle of their careers, they are embarked on new challenges, including working in an international economy, serving as corporate directors, leading their own corporations and industries, and influencing their own economic communities.

Having broken through the comfort zone, top women executives are emerging as leaders in many professions and industries, using their personal power currency to improve the social and economic climate for other women and their families. This, they conclude, is the real definition of the success of women in the business and professional world: the ability to stamp the imprint of women on the business community and make a difference in the lives of others.

To do so requires women to pierce the comfort zone and become participants in the most powerful institutions in their communities, where they can interact with influential economic leaders. We call that being members of The Club.

THE CLUB

The Club is not an institution that can be found in the telephone book, nor does it have a list of members. No single definition precisely fits The Club, but we know it when we see it. Business leaders in any city in the United States could name the most influential individuals in their community, and the profiles of the members of each list would be nearly identical. Some would describe The Club as an inner circle of male senior-level executives and professionals, all of whom know each other, many of whom have shared past experiences in school, the military, or their companies. But we think that definition is too limited. Club members are not necessarily the lavishly paid executives who move effortlessly from corporation to corporation, for in some cities, faceless executives slide in and out of town, barely making an impact. Nor are Club members necessarily just chief executive officers of their companies. Some may be retired, self-employed, or prominent in their own realm. However, the majority of Club members are business and economic leaders whose activities affect how others think and work.

In our view, in every community a handful of prominent individuals influences the intersection of public and private policy decisions. Often primarily businesspeople, The Club may be the mayor's "kitchen cabinet"; officers of the local chamber of commerce, real estate board, or local economic development authority; or all of the above. Club members sit on the boards of directors of the most prominent nonprofit institutions such as United Way as well as the city's cultural organizations. They serve on corporate boards. They allocate resources and influence government officials. Club members initiate public/private partnerships and help mold public and industrial policy. Some may run for office; many contribute heavily to local elected officials.

Those on the outside may see The Club as strictly a men's hut, "a place of taboo, a repository of arcane and secret lore." That description is now usually reserved for the few remaining private clubs that offer male members warped refuge from the real world. The Club does not bar women, although in many cities relatively few participate; it is open to opinion leaders without regard to gender, title, or status.

In Dallas, for example, the power center has shifted. "The old boys used to control the town," said a Dallas woman who heads her own company, "but now that the traditional industries such as energy, petroleum, and real estate have been hit hard by the economy, some of them have gone bankrupt or left town. This provides a great opportunity for a new group of leaders to exert influence."

The Dallas City Council, the Dallas Citizens' Council, and such prestigious institutions as the Dallas Symphony and the Susan G. Komen Breast Cancer Foundation are among the influential organizations where Club members are found, and more women are participating as equal partners with men. "Unlike cities such as Atlanta, where women are still known as Mrs. So-and-So, and few care about public policy, in Dallas, women have their own separate identity from their husbands, and are known for their own accomplishments," another executive woman noted. "If it weren't for women like them, we wouldn't have Ann Richards as governor of Texas and Kay Bailey Hutchinson as U.S. senator. The women got together and said to the men, 'I've given money to your candidates for years, now you give to mine.' Economically powerful women are now becoming members of The Club in Dallas and using those positions of prominence to get things done."

In Boston, The Club is also shifting, thanks to economic restructuring of the business community. Years ago, The Club would have been identified primarily as "The Vault," "a semi-secret group of thirty top business leaders who meet regularly to discuss and help chart the city's economic and political future," according to the Boston Urban Study Group, authors of the popular and irreverent citizen's guide *Who Rules Boston?*. Membership in the Vault was accorded by position: the heads of the city's major corporations, as well as the heads of the city's few business associations. "Working behind the scenes, the Vault exercises considerable raw power to influence political decisions and direct economic resources," the guide revealed.

Other business institutions, such as the Boston Municipal Research Bureau, the Massachusetts Taxpayers Foundation, and the Greater Boston Real Estate Board, were similar to the Vault and revealed a similar membership. Club members in Boston were also traditionally found among the trustees and directors of the city's leading cultural institutions, including the Museum of Fine Arts, the Boston Symphony Orchestra, WGBH, and the Opera Company of Boston—understandably so, as these institutions sought to broaden their funding bases. Boston's social service sector provided a similar picture. Hospital boards of trustees, college and university boards, and even the United Way board were drawn from the same powerful circle of directors of banks, insurance companies, corporations, and real estate firms that control Boston's other major institutions.

But now The Club has changed, even in Boston, a city never known to accept change easily. As the economic power of the city's major corporations declined, and some even disappeared thanks to corporate restructuring forced by the 1990 recession, the power of the Vault ebbed. As in other cities, corporate leaders were forced to pay more attention to their own businesses, and less attention to civic affairs. Even well before this time, enlightened corporate leaders made a conscious effort to broaden and diversify the boards of directors of several of the city's important business boards, and businesswomen progressed through officer positions to chair several important business associations. The increasingly diverse United Way board of directors elected its first female chairman, and when its executive director retired, the board chose a black female as his successor.

Dallas and Boston are not unique cases. Joining The Club in the 1990s is so surprisingly simple that some women may not know they qualify. Not just chief executive officers, but lawyers, stockbrokers, architects, hospital administrators, former public officials, and management consultants are members of The Club. They are often women who have risen through the ranks of their businesses and professions—not necessarily to the top—who have the energy to become visible beyond the confines of their jobs and the confidence to contribute in a predominantly male environment. The common ground they share with Club members is a desire and willingness to work on behalf of local and national issues, and the ability to wield and leverage power. It is the strategic exercise of this power, these women state, that will translate into improved economic status for all women in the community.

Clearly, the ability to bring money or raise money carries clout with Club members. Money is power—an obvious observation but one that needs restating for some women who think they deserve a seat at The Club table without commanding the same economic resources others do. Yet money is only part of the story. Public visibility gained by representing her employer or industry trade association or through prominence in her own profession or volunteer activities also earns acceptance. And as with any other group dynamic, style and the ability to get along with others count.

Naturally, if a woman represents a major local employer she will probably be seen as more influential than an entrepreneur from a small business or a community volunteer. But that isn't a gender issue. That's life. As one executive said, "Women have more power when they speak from a big picture point of view than as an individual. Then they are depersonalized; they come with power that represents more than just their own voice." Because most powerful members of The Club work in large, male-created and -dominated institutions, we have limited most of the stories in this book to women who have succeeded in those environments. While many of their observations and ideas are applicable to women working in other areas, these businesses generally provide a more direct route to The Club, making it critical that women working in those institutions succeed.

Membership in The Club rarely happens overnight. Patience, energy, and perseverance are required.

Women across the country got a good look at one Club during the Clarence Thomas–Anita Hill hearings, as fourteen white males, members of the U.S. Senate, deliberated the choice of a Supreme Court Justice. The televised proceedings were good theater, but what really counted was going on off-camera: the vote tallies, the arguments, the decisions about whom to call as witnesses and when. Businesswomen know that the same informal alliances and interactions are happening back home. Outcomes are rarely influenced at city council or legislative hearings; that's the theater. The important decisions about the future of a community are made by Club members over breakfast in the best hotels, at board of directors' meetings, on the golf course, from one car phone to another. Quietly and hidden from public view, real estate developments are planned, executive directors of key organizations are chosen, legislation is supported or opposed, and candidates are favored with a private meeting. Women must be in that community power loop if they are to influence economic events.

The economic debacle of the eighties and the bleak prospects for the nineties have given women a new sense of urgency. Time is getting short to begin to move women into top positions. Women may now hold a greater number of "manager" jobs, but there are still few at the senior levels. A 1991 study by the Fund for the Feminist Majority showed that only 2.6 percent of the corporate officers employed at the nation's largest companies were women. At the current rate of increase in executive women, it will take until the year 2466—over 450 years—to reach equality with executive men, according to the Fund.

Women can't wait that long to claim equality in the corporate office rolls. Neither can the nation's economy or the women and children across the country who are sinking lower into poverty. Understandably, executive women could get discouraged if they believed the bleak numbers. The answer is to forget about titles and percentages and concentrate on placing women in key positions of economic power.

Just two examples help tell the story. Most senior-level judges are recruited from those who have become partners in major law firms, from the highly demanding field of academic law, or from positions of prominence in major bar associations and other professional activities. To succeed in these fields of law requires the greatest time and effort at approximately the same time many female lawyers are the busiest with family responsibilities. Those chosen, therefore, are apt to be men and, according to Professor Susan Okin of Brandeis University, would seem to be the least well informed to make decisions about such family-sensitive matters as parental notification for abortion, wife-battering, and the impoverishment of women and children by divorce. She calls it a "systematically built-in absence of mothers . . . from high-level political decisions."

The situation is not much better in many realms of the business community, where the peer pressure to conform to the free-market, less-government-regulation, no-more-taxes party line is intense. The dynamic of how many business organizations function results in decisions often being made by group-think or by a small circle of individuals among whom diverse points of view are unwelcome. For example, Robert Allen, chairman of American Telegram & Telegraph Co. is also head of human resources for the Business Roundtable, a national group of chief executive officers and one of the leading "Clubs" of influential policymakers. In 1990 the group opposed the civil rights bill, supporting the Bush administration's position. But when Allen and a few other executives decided to sit down with civil rights leaders to exchange views, the Roundtable was immediately criticized by administration officials, and *Wall Street Journal* columnist Paul Gigot suggested that Allen was being duped by civil rights leaders. Allen backed off.

The conservative press and other business leaders monitor executives who stray too far from the free-market ideology, criticizing such firms as General Mills Corp. and DuPont Co. for giving to the Children's Defense Fund or the National Audubon Society, and the Bank of Boston for donating to the League of Women Voters education fund. Rather than take the heat from their peers, some corporate executives prefer to let their trade associations and national organizations articulate policy. The key question for executive women is whether the presence of more of them in business associations such as Allen's Roundtable would change the dynamic and, ultimately, the outcome. It may take a critical mass of women in key positions of leadership to change the picture.

We talked with hundreds of senior executive women across the country who are not only successful in their business or profession, but who are members of The Club, wielding influence in their communities on behalf of women and their families. We uncovered important common themes among the women who are assuming leadership roles, which we will explore in detail in later chapters. But as we listened to women articulate why they attached such importance to the idea that by their senior status they could help women at all levels, one subject became pervasive. Invariably, whether or not they chose to use the word *feminist* as a self-identification, they endorsed principles held by many feminists and insisted there was little conflict between the goals of feminism and the principles of capitalism.

The conflicting image of feminists in executive suites makes some women smile. As the president of a large commercial real estate company said, "In the sixties I was outside the gate, marching and protesting the establishment. Today I *am* the establishment!" She is not the only prominent businesswoman to note that irony, although few would express it openly to male colleagues around the conference room table. But examining feminism in the context of the business world is central to understanding how intelligent, activist women not only eagerly seek and find fulfillment through leadership roles in the economic community, but also how they use their positions to effect positive changes.

In addition to the fact that early feminists are now in their forties and older, ready for leadership positions in the private sector, there is another reason to look at the convergence of feminism and the business world. It may explain the lack of women in senior positions, or the presumed ambivalence some women feel in striving for them. Many younger women feel the moral quality of what they are doing with their lives is as important as the amount of money they bring in. If these women don't understand that there are many feminists who are working hard to effect change from senior positions within the capitalist system, they won't envision themselves in that role, too.

After speaking to a women's business organization in which Dawn-Marie Driscoll described the activities of other feminist business leaders in her peer group, she received a letter from a suburban commercial real estate vice president who had been in the audience.

"Most days I feel like a freak of nature," the broker wrote. "It was like a blood transfusion to hear the stories about what some women are doing behind the scenes. Since I rarely get the opportunity to work with high-powered women, I assumed that they didn't really exist. . . . Whew! What a relief to learn that you and your colleagues are out there and are thriving."

Dawn-Marie was surprised. If this young professional woman didn't think feminism and a successful career in the traditional business world were compatible, how many more could there be out there like her? Undoubtedly there are a number of other businesswomen who care deeply about equality but don't believe that a woman can call herself a capitalist and a feminist at the same time. Yet many businesswomen agree with our definition of "feminists" as women who share past experiences of segregation and subordination, now engaged in a common effort to help all women have choices and achieve goals. The top executive women we interviewed across the country now have seen this ambivalence among younger women often enough to conclude that they are not doing a very good job getting the word out about active feminists in business and the professions.

In the course of our study we encountered women like Susan Kiler,* senior vice president of a national insurance company, who, at thirty-seven, was one of three female elected officers of her 12,000-employee company.

"I've never thought of myself as a feminist," she said. "I guess I am just too young. I came here right out of business school in the late seventies. Twelve years later, I'm still getting promoted, taking responsibility for more areas of the company. I've never experienced discrimination along the way, and so I never found the old battles of feminists relevant. In fact, I've been promoted much faster than I would have guessed. And I absolutely *do* want to be CEO someday!

"But I'm not totally naive," she continued. "Now that I'm at the top, I can't help but notice that there is something going on. Not discrimination, but I do believe the battles that women have to fight are more subtle. The men at the top are so macho. They seem absolutely content working with other men just like them. Some days I want to scream, wondering what I'm doing here."

THE F WORD

Susan was struggling with her notion of what it means to be a woman in the upper ranks of her corporation, fighting the comfort zone. She was gradually realizing that although executive women had fought earlier battles to open some career doors for her, she was the one now actually on the front lines of senior management. But like many other women of her generation, she is a late-blooming feminist, isolated in her capitalist environment. She may not have experienced the blatant sex discrimination that older executive women encountered, but neither does she find the term

*Throughout the book, an asterisk indicates that we have changed the name of the woman quoted—and in some cases the name of her company and city—at her request.

femi-Nazi amusing. At this critical stage of her professional life, she is dealing with emerging questions of identity and values.

She is not alone. The late feminist legal scholar Mary Jo Frug once challenged her students by asking "Is Madonna a feminist?" Thinking about Madonna's hypersexed on and off stage persona strains one's serious definition of feminism. When considered in the light of achieving goals and making choices, however, the answer becomes clear that Madonna is indeed a feminist. This forces us to abandon stereotypes about what feminists look and sound like.

In the context of the business world, the term *feminist* can be risky because it can conjure up stale visions of muscular women marching in T-shirts and sturdy shoes yelling political slogans. Contemporary stereotypes portray the superfemale of today dressed in power suits, Ferragamo shoes, and Rolex watches—an image just as negative as the bra burners of the seventies. One female general counsel of a Fortune 500 company in New York feels that the new corporate twist on the modern feminine mystique is as pejorative as the older one, no better than an economic Barbie Doll.

If that is what modern feminism really is, some women want no part of it. In a 1989 poll of college women conducted by R. H. Bruskin Associates, only 16 percent considered themselves feminists, although 95 percent agreed that men and women should receive equal pay for equal work and 90 percent said they believed sexism still existed. Studies of executive women are not that much different. In one comprehensive survey published in 1987, only 40 percent of those polled considered themselves feminists, a fact that blatantly contradicted their stands on major feminist issues.

But many executive women who are feminists are now willing to stand up and be counted. Like Professor Frug's students who came to see Madonna as a feminist, they realized the image a woman conveys may only partially reveal her true self. Just because a woman appears to be a consummate senior executive, those who proclaim themselves to be the gatekeepers of true feminism should not count them out. As Frug argued, images are not necessarily reality; they can be constructed and deconstructed by whoever is drawing the picture. Madonna has drawn her own picture to further her objectives as a professional performer and to shape the image that comes across to her audience. But she has made the choice and is clearly in charge. So, too, many senior executive women, whether they accept the designation as feminists or not, act on feminist principles and by their example are motivating other women to join them in flexing their economic muscle.

Feminists of all stripes—gender feminists, radical or cultural feminists, socialist feminists, and others—have been striving for decades to move women into positions of equality and influence, using strategies as diverse as lawsuits and legislation to curriculum reform. But the most effective change agent may be the basic and widespread economic power of women. Those in senior executive positions already have power. Other women leverage their power from outside the business community by helping others achieve their goals. There is great potential for women's economic influence to be felt in economic circles, but their clout is still to come. Whether businesswomen like Susan Kiler will seize the moment is now up to them.

Since the early seventies, graduate professional schools have sent an increasing percentage of women from their classrooms into the "pipeline." Many of these women are now experienced enough for senior management positions. But in the last twenty years, not as many women have reached the upper ranks of their corporations or professions as their numbers might dictate. The reasons are not entirely conclusive. Males who deny the existence of a glass ceiling or comfort zone say women still haven't spent the requisite number of years working. Those who believe in a glass ceiling see a generation of older male executives conspiring to bar those who do not look, act, and sound like them. And those who don't know whether or not a glass ceiling exists say there are few jobs at the top of the corporate pyramid and therefore the competition for everyone is fierce, regardless of gender. In an environment of fierce competition, those in the zone win.

All of this may be true. But we have one more view of the problem. We have observed that in some women latent feminism sneaks up and overcomes desire and ambition. Thinking the two values can't coexist, these women return to that which they value most highly—the ability to be free to define themselves, instead of having their identity constantly defined for them by their corporate culture comfort zone and their male peers. The stories usually contain the same basic plot line: women reach senior management levels, partnership rank, or equivalent, and then leave to start their own business, accept a government service position, or pursue a long-standing and totally different dream. The business community loses their talent at a critical moment. How does this happen?

Many of the women in the pipeline were, at their core, feminists. Choosing paths other than teaching, social work, or nursing, they went to law or business schools or entered executive training programs that eagerly sought them out in the sixties and seventies because they were smart and ambitious. When they joined traditional businesses and professions, they checked their feminism at the door, thinking it was irrelevant or unwelcome. They honed their professional talent under the tutelage of experienced mentors, focusing on developing skills and earning good performance reviews, promotions, and salary increases. Early in their careers they had little reason to philosophize about the meaning of work, little insight into life at the top of the pyramid, and little time to question how they were spending their time. Their focus was on the here and now, with a vision that doing well would earn advancement.

However, as these women approach senior levels, their responsibilities and breadth of vision have changed. They are at a chronological age and job level when it is not unusual to question one's life's work. Like the anecdote about the middle-aged man who asked, "Who was that twenty-one-year-old kid who decided I wanted to be a dentist?" these women have also begun to examine the substance of the careers they chose one or two decades earlier. They are lawyers who appreciate the billings that accrue from defending a corporate client in a sex discrimination case, or retailers who understand why the Christmas catalog is geared to convince primarily female charge card consumers to spend 15 percent more this year than last. However, their feminist instincts suggest there are now more compelling ways that their positions near or at the top of the economic ladder can benefit society.

As executive women become less willing to subordinate their own values to those of the workplace and wonder how feminism can be relevant to senior management, it is critical for capitalist feminists like those profiled in this book to reveal themselves. Otherwise, lurking ambivalence may lead executive women to rationalize why they don't need to seek the top chairs. We have heard the disguised comments, such as: "What more do I have to prove?" "This is not what I want to do anymore," "It's not important. It's not me." Such comments may camouflage a basic uneasiness about how feminism can be compatible with the business world.

These women do not shrink from difficult decisions; rather, they look for a connection between the reality of the business world and the opportunity to make a positive difference. It is this balance in personal values that some women in the business world have been missing and think impossible to find.

We found women across the country who had achieved membership in The Club and who were willing to share their stories so that others could benefit. These highly successful women are energized by both their professional challenges and the opportunities they found to improve the economic status of others in their community. Many of them concentrated on their careers first, but they didn't hesitate to step into leadership roles when the time was right. They are feminists and businesswomen. Here are the stories of two such leaders of The Club who took very different routes to the top: Sally Berger in Chicago, who developed her personal power first and then focused on how to use it in the private sector, and Diane Capstaff in Boston, who found a challenging corporate environment and challenged herself to accept every opportunity it presented.

SALLY BERGER: POWER PLAY

Sally Berger, partner and national director of health care practice development for Ernst & Young, the national accounting and consulting firm, proves that the personal power currency developed from rainmaking, visibility, and relationships can be more important for women in gaining membership in The Club than the most prestigious credentials, honors, and blue-chip professional experience.

Berger's office on the thirty-sixth floor of Chicago's IBM Plaza is as large as many apartments, with floor to ceiling windows, a small dining table, comfortable couches, and three walls full of framed photographs, citations, awards, and personal letters from presidents, ambassadors, and celebrities from all over the world. Sally, an elegantly dressed blond, unhesitatingly welcomes visitors while fielding phone calls and questions from two assistants.

"I had my first paid job at age forty," Sally recounted. "My business is getting business for the firm, placing the firm before its clientele in a professional manner."

Sally's dramatic rise to success began with tragedy, the death of two children from cystic fibrosis. Married to Miles Berger, a successful businessman, Sally was the perfect corporate wife who never dreamed of a personal career as a senior executive in a national firm. She turned her grief into therapeutic action, volunteering to raise money by accepting the cochairmanship of a year-long fund-raising effort for the Michael Reese Hospital and Medical Center in Chicago. As a corporate wife, she called on over 500 executives of major corporations for contributions, and in 1973 raised $1.5 million, six times the amount raised during any previous campaign.

"People give money to people, not causes," Sally said. "I just asked people I knew to introduce me to people they knew."

In short order, Sally was appointed a trustee of the medical center, and began serving on many hospital committees, including the executive committee. She also began writing "Trustees Forum," a monthly feature for her hospital magazine, in which she discussed health care policy issues from the perspective of a trustee and interviewed doctors on the medical staff on their particular expertise.

Fund-raising skills are transferable, and Sally understood the connection between the delivery of community health care and the power of those who make public policy decisions. In 1975 she served as chief executive and administrative officer of the nonpartisan citizens' committee "For Chicago" to reelect the late mayor Richard J. Daley. Under her leadership, the committee membership grew from 28 to a total of 25,000, with 5,000 active volunteers operating 12 neighborhood offices.

Sally's growing leadership skills did not go unnoticed. She was appointed the first chairman of the Chicago Commission for Health Planning and Resources Development, presiding over a thirty-member board and coordinating its activities with the professional staff.

"In that job, I met every head of every hospital," Sally said, explaining the commission's mandate to assure equal access to quality health care at reasonable rates. "They had to come and deal with us for what they wanted." Using her old fund-raising techniques, Sally collected cards, notes, and invitations, jotting on each one how and where she had met the person, and filed them in a shoe box.

More names were added, as Sally accepted speaking engagements from California to Florida, and the governor appointed her to the State of Illinois Statewide Health Coordinating Council. In 1977, Secretary of

Health, Education and Welfare Joseph Califano, Jr., appointed her to the National Council on Health Planning and Development. At its first meeting, she was elected the chairman, and served simultaneously on her local, state, and national health planning agencies. Awards rolled in, from the American Jewish Committee to the International Organization of Women Executives, and her shoe box full of names grew.

At that point, Sally knew she had an expertise, and wanted a job. She met with a partner of the national accounting firm that had done consulting work for the Chicago health care commission, and showed him her shoe box.

"I can develop more health care business for you," she said. "But I need to be a partner in the firm. I need to be presented as a peer to the clients I am trying to attract." The local partner, knowing of Sally's reputation and contacts, was enthusiastic, but the corporate headquarters in New York was not. Bringing someone in from the outside as a partner was not an everyday event and so their answer was no.

Sally was disappointed but not discouraged. In 1980 she accepted a position as senior vice president of Amherst Associates, Inc., a leading financial consulting and computer company in the health care industry and soon landed a $3 million consulting contract.

"I just did the same thing I did in fund-raising," Sally said. "People give business to people, not to firms. I knew one of the founders of the company and he arranged the meeting."

Sally continued to attend national conventions and health care meetings, speaking, meeting, and greeting old acquaintances and new contacts. As she continued developing new relationships to facilitate business, her company grew, and was acquired by another company. Sally enhanced her own national visibility in the health care field by writing columns and articles about health care management and interviewing chairmen of hospital boards around the country. In turn, she was the subject of many feature stories in publications ranging from her local Chicago newspapers to McCalls magazine. She also kept in touch with the accounting firm.

Sally continued doing well, landing an attractive $10 million contract for her company. At this time the thinking at Ernst & Young had begun to change. The professional firms were all getting very competitive in their approach to attracting new business and to the credit of Ernst & Young's vision and leadership, its management saw an opportunity to meld the firm's technical expertise with this unusual talent. They offered Sally a partnership and asked her to be the national director of the health care practice development, and they set about to create an environment in which she could grow.

Visibility and personal power are still an integral part of Sally's practice development activities: speaking, writing columns and newsletters, and hosting a national television program on health care issues. Building relationships is a key part of rainmaking, or business development, she said.

"Women have to work much harder at visibility, at bringing in business, to overcome our handicaps. Of course, I can invite some guys golfing if I want, because it's my club. But most women can't. And we don't sit in taverns with guys. So we have to use the fact that we're a woman for our advantage. When I walk in a room, eighty percent of the men kiss me. I like them. I like people. People is what this business is all about. Whether it's raising money for politicians, helping somebody with a personal problem, or featuring a hospital chief executive on my television show, I develop personal connections with people. Men don't do that. Oh, sure, they have their own version, but I like to keep relationships going. It's more than a business deal."

Sally is powerful and successful in her field, but she doesn't hesitate to use her personal power to help others to be successful as well. For example, her articles are often written jointly by Sally and a health care partner. Sally takes partners with her to meet potential clients, and includes them in events.

"Some of my partners don't want to concede that business getting is something women can do," Sally said with a grin. "So we do it together."

Sally combines the dramatic effect of her femininity with her understanding of how personal relationships can cement business relationships. She makes every new acquaintance a friend. Some women may look at Sally's success and dismiss it, saying she started with advantages other women didn't have, including a successful husband and a comfort level with The Club's social circle. But they are missing the personal dynamic that Sally brings to her work, an approach to the business world that any woman can copy.

Sally's story is unusual but instructive for women in all businesses and professions. Instinctively, perhaps, Sally Berger understood what many women never learn: the importance of personal power to advance a career and move women into positions of influence. Sally has successfully combined a personal interest in health care with a dynamic career, first by influencing the public health care agenda, and then by using her expertise to develop business for her firm.

Many women don't understand the potential clout of personal power, because they approach The Club from the opposite direction. They think they will be powerful only later, after they earn credentials, work hard invisibly, advance quietly, and then begin to hold positions on community and civic boards. It is at that point that they will finally influence public policy issues they care about.

Take, for example, Anne,* a career banker in Cleveland. She first tiptoed into the large community when she volunteered to help in her bank's annual United Way drive. The bank linked up with a local child-care agency, and Anne visited its executive director and staff. Then Anne accepted her boss's suggestion to serve on the allocations committee for United Way, as a community volunteer. Several years later, Anne was nominated to serve on the board of directors of United Way, and when she suggested forming a special task force on child care, she was appointed chairman. Anne selected a diverse group of Cleveland community and business leaders to serve with her, and a year later, the board of United Way approved a multimillion-dollar allocation to a unique Child Care Initiative Fund, to triple the number of affordable child-care spots for working parents.

Anne gradually came to realize how her personal power and corporate clout could make a difference on issues she cared about while Sally Berger showed how to influence public policy early in her career. Some women who have been solely focused on their work environment are jolted into action by specific events, and then eagerly plunge into activities outside of work.

For Camille,* a television producer in Hollywood, the Clarence Thomas–Anita Hill hearings were a wake-up call to action. "I've never been involved much in issues," she said. "My own career has been too hectic. But I've decided to use all my professional skills to help Congresswoman Barbara Boxer in her campaign for United States Senate. I see now that we need more women in the Senate, and women who live in California just can't leave it up to chance that Boxer will get elected. We have to make it happen."

If Anne, Camille, and Sally were to get together, we know they would say the same thing to business and professional women: The earlier in your career you understand and use power, the more successful you'll be.

What is power? Some women will recoil from the term, equating it with a white male's deal-making, aggressive, competitive quest for riches and insincere flattery. But executive women across the country showed that their definition of power is quite different.

Power implies money, but it does not take a lot of money to have power. The importance of money to power is, in one woman's view, "the ability to give it away." A woman who earns $60,000 and freely funds candidates, causes, and efforts of those she supports has more power than a woman who earns $250,000 and spends it all on clothes, house, and vacations.

Sally Berger gained power early in her rise to fame by raising money for her hospital. She commanded respect and admiration for her ability to bring in revenues, just as the rainmaker who brings in major clients or customers is often the most powerful executive in the professional suite. Similarly, a woman who makes the decisions about allocating the financial resources of her corporation, whether she is the general counsel who chooses which outside law firms to hire or the vice president of public affairs who dispenses charitable contributions, comes to any conference table with extra power accorded to her by virtue of her position. (The opposite is also true. A woman who does not have the authority to make a decision about contributing money "without checking back at the office" is a powerless participant in any gathering.)

Power is access to resources. Simply knowing and being able to access those with money, information, and support is power. Sally's shoe box and her being on a first-name basis with the city's most prominent elected officials made her powerful in her own right. She shows that an up-to-date Rolodex of powerful individuals (increasingly, other female friends) who will not only return her phone call but do what she requests is power.

Sally is on the phone from morning to night. She knows that part of her power is her ability to get cooperation from others, just as she willingly extends herself when she is called upon to do a task or favor.

Information or expertise conveys power. An ability to do a job, solve a problem, or lead others to the answer is power, whether or not the person holds a powerful position. Anne's in-depth knowledge of her city's child-care issues and resources gave her power in community circles, and

Camille's expertise in the techniques of television made her a powerful volunteer in her local election campaign.

Every woman has some knowledge or contact that gives her power, but not enough women think to let others know how powerful they are. Too often women hide their expertise, friends, or experience, thinking it inappropriate or unseemly. But in the business world, there are appropriate ways of communicating power. Photographs on the wall, like those in Sally's office, make a statement without a word being spoken.

Marilyn Mitton* hinted to a co-worker at her real estate development company that her recent election as chairman of her city's economic and development council would provide a good marketing opportunity for her firm. He agreed, suggested to the president that the company host a reception in her honor, and invited clients, community opinion leaders, and the press. Meanwhile, Marilyn contacted her own circle of friends, personally requesting that they make a special effort to attend. At the crowded reception, as the president greeted hundreds of guests, elected officials, and potential clients, he murmured to Marilyn, "I had no idea you knew so many prominent people!" The president and every guest at the reception realized that Marilyn was powerful.

Power is the ability to reward. While this often involves money and corporate perks, in other instances, simple recognition, attention, and knowing what truly motivates someone else can be just as effective. When Sally Berger walks into a room and greets individuals, they have her total and complete attention, and she makes them feel as if they are the most important persons in the world at that moment. She listens intently to what they are saying, and remembers it. Sally's personality exudes positive reinforcement, confidence, and intensity.

Power also comes from the ability to generate fear and awe, or the unspoken threat to punish; that's why litigators from a federal agency have built-in clout, even if they are earning one quarter of the salary of their defense attorney opponents, and why the publisher of a newspaper is always perceived as powerful, whether or not he or she would use that power to achieve any hidden agendas. Women who hold such jobs and are uncomfortable thinking about power may miss the built-in leverage these positions provide. On the other hand, women who are not themselves in positions of power can still strategize together about how to achieve power together.

"When something happens to one of us, we share the story," one woman said of her close-knit group of female business leaders. "Invariably someone in the group comes up with a counterpunch she can deliver. We don't get mad, we just get even."

Sally Berger's story illustrates another important aspect of power. Many women think power and clout come from a particular position, and therefore they focus on the promotion, title, or salary level, feeling diminished if they don't receive it. While it is true that, at first blush, a title indicates a degree of importance, it does not always follow that the individual holding the title is either respected or powerful. Women are better advised to concentrate on developing their personal reputation and self-confidence than a position; the position may very well follow, as it did for Sally.

We've seen how Sally developed her career, building on the power she gained in each activity and position. But what about the women who hold jobs that aren't particularly powerful? What are they supposed to do?

The same thing: just show up, advises Harvard Business School professor Rosabeth Moss Kanter. Be there.

"I can't tell you how often I talk to young women who miss things because they're feeling a little sick or they have too much work to do and say, 'Well, my presence isn't that important. It will go on without me.' It's not true. Unless you're there, involved, showing up, unless you say to yourself that nothing that happens in the world will be as good unless I'm there, will you ever attain the kind of power that will help you lead and shape the world the way you want to shape it," Kanter said.

Sally Berger showed up. While it is true that at her first hospital fundraising meeting "Wanda Denner, Executive Vice President of Worldwide Conglomerate" might have commanded more attention because of her perceived clout, with the resources at her command, the first time she does not show up, or follow through, her power is diminished. Sally showed her clout by her action. Real power resides in those like Sally who are admired for their personal traits, their honesty and integrity, their charisma, their follow through, their leadership ability, and, ultimately, their "star" quality.

This star quality is not insignificant. Kanter insists that power makes an individual more attractive ("the Henry Kissinger syndrome"), and there is no reason why the connection between attractiveness and power need be a male domain. Senior executive women like Sally Berger have their self-esteem and femininity well in hand; they know that having and using power enhances their status. If they are perceived as powerful, they are less often treated as second class.

Every woman can develop some degree of star quality even if she is not yet at a senior level. A dynamic personality and reputation for attention to others develops by habits as simple as making each office visitor feel unique, returning phone calls the same day, or remembering and noting details about individuals on their business cards.

One president of a real estate company shared her ideas about how women should act to enhance their star quality: "Assume you are at the top level and present yourself that way. Act like you are powerful, and you will be treated that way." It is a concept that applies to the manager of the mailroom as well as to the senior vice president.

Women like Sally Berger refute popular theories that women fear power because the power that accompanies senior status is one of isolation and loneliness. Certainly, life at the top of corporations or institutions can be isolating, particularly for those constantly on display. If life there is isolating, and few relationships are possible if one is to retain an image of power and authority, do women hesitate to claim the top positions because of a fear of that isolation? And is isolation a necessary condition of power, as some claim?

Absolutely not, answer senior executive women. They have no fear of success, as described by former Radcliffe College president Matina S. Horner. They are not worried about their competence and prominence eroding their notions of femininity. Nor do they suffer anxiety when their achievement in the business world arises from competition against others. Like Sally, they have found that success in the business world need not be a zero-sum game.

Nor is their power bound by limits ("if I have it, you don't"). There has been a resistance to women in power perhaps because of the assumption that in many cultures, there is only so much power to go around. In bureaucratic organizations that are proscribed by boundaries, levels, rules of behavior, and incremental attainment of status and outward signs of hierarchy, "giving" power to a woman means that some man may have less.

Women, however, have a different view of power. First, they don't let others "give" it to them by virtue of a title or other indicators of status. They know they can be powerful on their own. Second, they believe in the philosophy that is slowly reaching some corporate suites: The more power you have, the less you should use, and the more others should also become powerful. Regal, rigid lines of authority are giving way to collegial, democratic behavior. Sally Berger doesn't worry which partner in her office "gets the credit" for bringing in business. She gladly facilitates the ability of everyone to attract more clients to Ernst & Young.

Sally's understanding and use of personal power obliterate a persistent stereotype about women, no doubt coming from those who equate femininity with powerlessness. They view women acting submissively to men, trying not to offend men in power in order to enhance their own attractiveness and conclude these women are powerless because they are not dominant. They confuse power with aggressiveness. Those who are threatened by powerful and accomplished women perpetuate the myth to keep women at a distance and assuage their own distress.

But being powerful does not mean acting macho. Power gets things done, a notion that plays to women's strengths at achieving results through harmony. Women are often good negotiators, working through a process independent of the problems involved. They concentrate on preserving relationships, in contrast to many men who are more concerned with winning and losing than a compromised outcome that would benefit both sides.

The myth of powerlessness in women also persists because of the confusion between managerial ability (competence) and leadership ability (power). Corporate executives see women *thinking* smart, performing tasks well, but they don't observe them *acting* smart, strategizing and leading. In choosing potential candidates for top managerial positions, leadership capabilities win out over managerial or technical ability all the time. At the most senior levels, corporate and professional chieftains want actors and leaders, not thinkers and clerks. Senior executives expect technical competence in managers at the middle levels. At the top of their business, the competence they need is leadership. If they don't believe women will seize and use power, how can they trust them to lead?

Women who want to influence the economic agenda of their community by assuming leadership positions in its key institutions must practice using power. Many will find they do it naturally.

A 1990 study of men and women in the American corporation conducted by Russell Reynolds Associates Inc., a national search firm, confirmed what many women already know: Women in both staff and line positions are more likely to be leader-style executives (visionary, initiatory, charismatic, innovative, and strategic) than their male counterparts.

These results aren't startling, although Russell Reynolds called it a "surprising finding." We have already observed that women are good leaders, but the women we know are both strong leaders and sensitive to those they're leading.

The myth of powerlessness in women persists because of the refusal to see power and sensitivity as compatible qualities. But as more businesses see the benefits of empowering employees (already a strategic element of companies delivering superior customer service) they will turn toward a new definition of power and acknowledge that women excel at it.

DIANE CAPSTAFF:
SHATTERING CORPORATE MYTHS

John Hancock, the Boston-based international financial services firm, is one corporation that recognizes the value of women to an organization. Like Sally Berger, Diane Capstaff has progressed to a senior place in the business world, although she has taken a more traditional path. The words *glass ceiling* do not enter her vocabulary, as she describes her own personal history. An astute observer of the corporate world, Diane knows that barriers and obstacles to advancement prevail in all cultures, but her strategy, like that of many other women, was to work through them. Focusing on the existence of a glass ceiling keeps many women powerless. Being motivated and preparing for opportunities that might come along moves many women like Diane directly to The Club.

Twenty years after she joined John Hancock, Diane Capstaff became its highest-ranking female executive and a member of its Management Committee. As executive vice president for Corporate Operations, she manages a staff of 1,300 people and a budget of more than $100 million, ensuring that Hancock's 18,000 employees are trained, reviewed, and promoted, and have the computers, information systems, and real estate facilities they need to perform their jobs in locations around the world.

"I came to Boston as a change after working in New York City," Diane recalled. "When I interviewed at John Hancock, I told them that I would only stay a year. That was twenty years ago."

John Hancock was able to keep Diane interested, moving her from assignments in personnel to corporate operations. After she directed the Office of the Future, concentrating on automation and productivity improvements, she received a key assignment as staff to the president and chairman of the company. Staff, a key job? What about the old rule that staff jobs are dead ends, and that line jobs are important?

"That job was key because I learned so much about the whole company. We set priorities for implementing new ventures, products, and services. Of course, working for the president and chairman was good exposure. They were two men that believed that people advance, not gender. They also felt that staff positions were among the hardest line jobs a person could have because you have to get something done using your personal power, influence, and credibility, not your position or the fact that the people you are trying to motivate report directly to you. Staff jobs are important leadership positions," Diane said.

"Line jobs are also critical. Five years later the company assigned me to head up a critical segment of our group insurance business, including sales and administration. This division had a thousand employees and a budget of $65 million, and I ran Human Resources for the company at the same time. I had never been in sales before, and our group had a very successful year. We worked hard, and saw real fruition to our efforts. It was a great experience."

John Hancock believes in developing all its employees to the best of their abilities. The company doesn't want anyone to be obsolete. Education plays a key role. "We offer technical and management courses during the day. After hours, the company pays for employees to get degrees in programming, law, and M.B.A.—practically whatever our employees are interested in. For me, an M.B.A. was important to keep up to date with business theories."

With her education and business experience in hand, Diane used her leadership skills outside the company, often an important part of executive development. In the town of Winchester, she assisted the Board of Selectmen with its executive search for a superintendent of schools, a town manager, a director of public works, and a town controller. Hancock asked her to coordinate its long-standing partnership program between the company and Boston's English High School, and as Diane began to represent the company in many of Boston's business and civic activities, she became known and respected by her corporate peers, members of The Club.

Diane's span of influence continued to grow. The board of trustees of a prestigious Boston museum asked her to assist in its search for a museum director. Diane became an influential member in one of The Club's most important city organizations, the Boston Private Industry Council. This business-led, nonprofit organization helps Boston residents overcome employment barriers, develop marketable skills, and obtain jobs. It is held in high regard by community activists, business leaders, and city and state elected officials. In 1984, Diane was elected its president.

"Community assignments are not required for success at John Hancock," Diane admitted. "They are optional. However, we do believe they are important developmentally. These activities give you a balanced life and a broader pespective, and they develop important skills for managing staff, understanding budgets, and leading peers from outside your own company. I think it's frightening that some corporations concentrate on developing specialists in their own industry, and then when these individuals get to the top of the house, they are not broad enough. When you're at the top, you must deal with a wide range of groups and issues. Community activities and different job assignments help you to do that effectively."

Fifty-billion-dollar companies like John Hancock do not promote someone to executive vice president if he or she has not performed well and demonstrated broad-based leadership qualities. John Hancock believes in advancing both women and minorities; it is not tokenism. Women such as Diane Capstaff have succeeded on merit. Many senior executive women Diane's age and older first appeared in the business and professional world in the late sixties and early seventies, when there was pressure to include them. Doors opened and they rushed through. Now they are partners in law firms and heads of corporations, having made it to the top on their own merits. Many corporations have put practices in place to ensure the progress made during the past twenty to thirty years continues.

"John Hancock's work force is sixty-two percent female," Diane said. "Our senior management group goes off site for two days a year to do nothing but work on succession planning and map out the key jobs for the future for both genders and all ethnic groups. We want all our people to succeed."

But unlike Diane, who wasn't afraid to take on new positions and run the risk of failure, some women don't always take the initiative to succeed, preferring to leave their professional development in the hands of those who give them assignments.

Gail Weber, senior vice president of The New England, the Boston-based insurance company, believes a lack of living role models is one reason why more women do not openly press for advancement in corporations. "When I interview new executives in our corporation, I frequently ask them about the significant influences—role models—in their developing years. Invariably, the men always mention someone they knew—a coach, a teacher, a priest. Women, I found, use fictional characters, or women they have heard about but don't know. Our problem was that we weren't able to identify with any real-life female role models, so we didn't see ourselves in nontraditional roles, particularly roles of influence and power in the business world. As a result, if we were ambitious, we considered looking around outside the corporation for our next opportunity."

Diane cites many role models—her father, professors, her husband, many people at work—who offered different points of view and support at different stages of her career. "I feel fortunate to have had role models who gave me positive examples of how to manage work and family. One significant role model always told me to work on the things that I felt were important—a lesson that I've taken to heart and has helped me be successful," Diane said.

Women who are at the critical point of deciding whether they want to strive for top positions look up to the women who have made it. They must believe that the Diane Capstaffs of the world are just like them, and followed no hidden ways up or through the organizations available to only a chosen few. Corporations that want to attract more women to senior management must demystify top positions and show they are achievable, not insurmountable.

The same principles that worked twenty years ago for Diane are still working, and the best companies look for executive talent without regard to gender. Diane's advice to women is to find the right industry or company and then seek out the assignments that build on past knowledge and experience.

"Take what you know and keep adding to it. Accept assignments that will stretch and complement your knowledge. Learn as much as you can.

This is the best way to grow and make sure you are ready when opportunity arises," Diane said.

Some women tend to believe that corporate institutions are rigid because they are large. In many large companies, procedures and policies are necessary to manage the vast number of employees that in some cases is larger than the population of small countries. Size does not imply that these companies do not accommodate the needs of individual employees or their families.

Diane has played a significant role in bringing family-centered programs and policies to John Hancock. As a senior manager, she has been able to voice the concerns of many women and families and help spur the company to action.

In seeking corporate cultures that are flexible, women must look behind the company name and scrutinize the human qualities of the management team. At John Hancock and many other companies, senior management sets the tone and climate for all employees. Many companies, including large ones, are now breaking into smaller work units and divisions, delegating decision making to local managers who can be more entrepreneurial about where and when the work gets done, and where they find talent. These local managers have few preconceived ideas about ability or work styles and are often blind to gender distinctions.

While it is often risky to generalize about professions or industries, younger industries such as the software field have a reputation for being flexible employers. With less time for a rigid corporate culture to develop, entrepreneurial behavior and individual life-styles flourish in an atmosphere of acceptance.

But older, traditional professions may also surprise women. Insurance, banking, and law can be just as welcoming to women as a dynamic high-technology start-up. While John Hancock is still a hierarchical organization, executives such as Diane Capstaff are trying hard to make the organization flatter and build more cross-departmental teams. "We often spot a talented person who emerges with a great reputation from these team work groups," Diane said. "She might have been lost in her pyramid, but the exposure to others outside of her direct supervisory group showcased her potential. We use these new organizational structures to uncover talent in all levels of the company."

Diane dispenses with the fallacy that women lack technical expertise to succeed in the corporate world. While many women of Diane's generation entered the work force with often nothing more than a liberal arts degree, statistical studies for the U.S. Department of Labor and graduate school enrollments attest to women's qualifications today. Law, medicine, and business schools report female enrollment of close to 50 percent, while longitudinal studies of women's academic performance, such as Clifford Adelman's "Women at Thirtysomething," show that women won more scholarships, completed degrees faster, and had higher grade-point averages than their male peers.

The "velvet ghetto" jobs of human resources and public relations for women are quickly disappearing, as more women are seeking the important "make it or sell it" jobs of engineering, manufacturing, finance, marketing, and sales—the career areas that lead to senior management positions.

"We have many capable, talented women in key management and staff positions. In a few years they will be leading the company. I may be the first woman to make it to the John Hancock Management Committee, but there are many more women right behind me," Diane said.

Fortunately, the numbers of men with limited cultural expectations of women are diminishing rapidly as more women like Diane assume leadership positions in business. Furthermore, many younger men who are now ready to replace their predecessors have a different personal history of relationships with women. They have lived in coed dorms, studied with women, perhaps served in the Peace Corps with them, and entered corporate training programs alongside them. Their female classmates and coworkers will no longer tolerate the myth of stereotypes. As Diane surveys the personnel needs of her corporation in the next century, this is good news. She knows Hancock will need all the talent it can attract to compete internationally.

Sally Berger and Diane Capstaff live in different cities, and took different routes to the top of their professions. Sally, a community volunteer, never expected to be a partner in a national accounting firm. Diane, a psychology major from George Washington University, never expected to be one of the senior managers in a $50 billion financial services company. The two women work in different industries, but despite their unique stories, they share many similarities with each other and with hundreds of other senior women across the country.

Both felt right from the beginning that they had options. This attitude was critical in their eventual success. Other women in their shoes might have felt trapped by their geographical limitations, by responsibilities for children or spouses, or by a self-limiting but false view of the possibilities open to them. But openness to varied experiences gave Sally, Diane, and others like them the ability to try new challenges, and the freedom to fail.

Neither of them set out to find career success, but it came as a by-product of rewarding work. Sally and Diane said yes—yes to challenging assignments, yes to an unexpected opportunity, and yes to positions of leadership in community organizations. With each step, their personal power grew, the rewards became greater, and the work more fun.

They were focused on the job at hand, not because the position carried a particular salary level or status, but because they wanted to be as effective as possible at the time. This focus gave them the freedom to stretch their abilities and experiences.

Sally and Diane also clearly understood the complexity of their industries and the myriad factors that contribute to profits. When it came to dollars and cents, they were as oriented to the bottom line as any of their male peers. In this, they had uncovered a key factor in their later success.

CHAPTER TWO

RAINMAKING

The Entry to The Club

The failure to generate business has prevented women from catapulting to the top.
> —Rita Hauser, partner, Stroock, Stroock and Lavan,
> New York City

O ne of the toughest challenges for senior executives, male or female, is to keep revenues and new business coming in the door and to increase market share and profits. Those who attract paying clients and directly improve the bottom line get high marks, and women have to be as good at "rainmaking" as men if they are going to be powerful members of The Club.

In all fields, including law, contracting, accounting, consulting, architecture, and engineering, among others, senior managers must continually expand their client base while servicing existing clients, helping them figure out what they need and then deliver it. At the same time they must fend off external competitors. Financial institutions seek commercial loans and transaction fees. Manufacturers, retailers, restaurateurs, stockbrokers, and travel agents fight to improve their market share, increase customer loyalty, and respond to new tastes and trends. Newspapers and television networks court the patronage of advertisers. Even in the world of medicine, the ability to attract the large research grants that help pay the overhead determines who attains senior status. Success or failure often depends upon skill at generating new clients or sales, or in some cases, the discovery of new connections between market needs and solutions.

The term *rainmaking* is widely used to describe this business-generating skill. It evokes an image of showering or bestowing new clients upon a business. Like storm clouds over parched California, those who can make rain are revered for their life-giving properties. It is they who sustain the company.

Top-level women across the country continually cited rainmaking as one of the most important issues facing executive women today—and not the existence of a glass ceiling or intense competition for a decreasing number of corporate positions. The complex issue of rainmaking goes to the heart of the dilemma about stereotypes concerning women, and attacks the question of whether women can be as successful as men at top-level jobs. Business executives disagree about the impact of gender differences and whether the way women are culturally socialized makes it harder for them to ask for business, to clinch the deal, or to be aggressive about taking risks to increase profits. We are told business is primarily given by male chief executive officers, purchasing managers, and senior executives to other men. Will these men continue to prefer to give their business to other men, even as more women rise in the business world? We are told women can't put in the time and effort that is necessary to be a successful business generator, assuming the travel, golf, civic, and business commitments that are often required. Is it a false perception that women lack success at rainmaking because there are few women who do it well? Does a small number make this a self-fulfilling prophecy? Are we blinded to the numbers of men who are not successful business generators because they blend in with the pack?

In tough economic times, rainmaking is more than critical; often it determines which top executives keep their jobs. In the 1980s, companies and professions became accustomed to charging high fees and attracting easy business, thanks to the financial excesses of Wall Street and the lending policies of the nation's financial institutions. There was less pressure on women to generate business when most of it walked in the door. In the reactionary climate of the nineties, however, rainmaking is not only more highly valued, it is the deciding survival factor. In addition to short-term cost-cutting measures, layoffs, and restructuring, companies that hope to survive must generate sufficient business to support their remaining employees.

Private law practice tells the tale. The unofficial macho slogan at Boston's large law firm, Hale and Dorr, is: "You eat what you kill"; the more business a lawyer brings in, the higher his income. Even former New York City mayor Ed Koch, now a partner at Robinson, Silverman, Pearce, Aronsohn & Berman, knows his job is to "hustle up new clients" for the firm. Those who watch "L.A. Law" on television and think Susan Dey and Jill Eikenberry lead challenging lives should remember Abby, the character played by Michele Greene, who was denied partnership status at McKenzie Brackman because she was not a rainmaker.

As the economy worsens and pressures to generate business become more intense, or as industries experience increasing domestic and foreign competition, this picture is repeated in other professions. At KPMG Peat Marwick, the international accounting firm, where annual partner salaries range as high as a million dollars, partners at the lower end of the salary scale have a fragile tenure. In 1991, Peat decided to dismiss almost one sixth of its partners, responding to a lag in per-partner revenues and a high number of partners compared to the rest of the professional staff. At First Eastern Bank Corporation of Wilkes-Barre, Pennsylvania, Vice President Karen Richards had to sell twice as many municipal bonds in 1990 as she did in 1985 to make the same profit.

To see how revenues affect both the bottom line and the careers of top executives, consider a typical law firm of fifty partners and one hundred associates. Each associate, at an average salary of $80,000, will be expected to produce a minimum of 1,950 billable hours of work per year. Forty hours of actual billable time may translate into seventy or more work hours in most firms. The billable time is charged to clients at $150/hour, with each associate generating $292,500 per year in billings. With two associates per partner, each partner is responsible for producing $585,000 of work for associates to bill, plus billing his own time at $275/hour, with an expected billing rate of 1,650 hours a year. (These are fewer hours than associates because partners also have to manage the firm and find potential clients, all nonbillable time.) Total average revenues per partner in this firm are $1,038,750. At a 63 percent overhead rate for expenses for associate and secretarial salaries and the like, the per partner profit is $384,338. Depending on the spread, or ratio, of the highest salary to the lowest, new young partners might earn $135,000, while rainmakers, who bring in several million dollars' worth of business a year, will command salaries of several times that amount.

This picture assumes that each of the fifty partners can bring in more than a million dollars of business per year, that the hourly standard is attained, and that all clients pay their bills. If twenty of the fifty partners produce revenues averaging only $500,000 per partner, all the partners face a pay cut of more than 50 percent, as the per-partner profit average drops to $168,837. Only a firm with a number of significant rainmakers can afford to keep going if 40 percent of its partners don't produce to standard. With many law firms hiring an equal number of male and female associates, economically savvy partners are looking ahead a decade or two and wondering if the female contingent will carry its weight in per-partner revenues.

In other profit-making organizations, the picture is similar. In large retail store chains, senior management appointments rarely go to support staff but to executives in line positions who manage and control profit-making departments. There are two primary career tracks for advancement in retail, both considered line. One career track is through merchandising departments that control product procurement, promotion, pricing, and markdowns, and the other is through field or store operations that create sales revenues and manage personnel and operating expenses. These line executives have the power and responsibility to control expenses, thereby directly leveraging sales.

Key retail staff executives in finance, legal services, human resources, and computer technology, although important, are rarely considered candidates for chief executive officer in retail operations. Although some senior people in these positions are influential in their own realms, they simply do not have the power or track record to translate increased sales into increased profits. In the retailing business, where profit margins range from 2 to 10 percent, every additional dollar of sales that can add a dollar of profit is precious. Conversely, because most expenses in retailing are fixed, even a slight drop in sales is perilous. The retailing czars are those who can generate healthy sales and profits by their merchandising and marketing skills.

At Bloomingdale's in New York City, smart merchandisers unveiled a series of designer rooms on the fifth floor of the flagship store, enhancing the store's home furnishings department and luring customers up on escalators past each floor's new offerings. All of the rooms carried a unique theme, and changed periodically during the year, attracting repeat visitors. The result was the highest sales per square foot in the department store industry for the aging 59th Street location. At Stop & Shop Supermarkets, Carol Goldberg and her executive team created the concept of the "superstore," putting supermarket and drugstore merchandise under one roof. In these new stores, double the size of regular supermarkets, higher gross margin general merchandise sat next to perishable grocery items. The cost of running the store was lower ("aspirin lasts longer than flowers," Carol said) and the stores were much more profitable than the traditional supermarkets.

In some industries, positions of influence and power go to those who can navigate the tricky path to market, where the product, once launched, will generate several hundred million dollars each year. For example, in biotechnology, the route from the laboratory to the pharmacy shelf takes six to ten years and the average drug costs $220 million to develop. If the drug does not receive its approvals, the investment is lost. If it is successful, the drug makes the executives who manage the entire process the most powerful in their companies. "The knowledge base that is needed to bring a drug to market is extensive," said Alison Taunton-Rigby, former senior vice president of Genzyme Corporation. "You are working with a large, often changing team of individuals, from scientists to manufacturers and marketers, over a period of several years. The process is complicated and high risk."

In other businesses, the route to revenues may involve a balance of policy negotiations, marketing skills, customer identification, and adjustments to the business climate. The lumber business, for example, is threatened by a decline in housing starts, by increasing competition from other building materials, and by conservation groups, which want vast tracts of forest lands transferred from logging companies to the National Forest Service. Further restrictions on logging will increase the price for lumber, narrow profit margins, and decrease demand while making competing products more attractive. Credit for generating business may go to the executive who can unravel these complex issues, not those who simply add a few more lumber yards to the client roster.

The rewards are great for successful rainmakers. The top positions, salaries, stock options, perquisites, and prestige go to those who bring in the business. At some Wall Street financial service firms, partner salaries can be a million dollars or more. In addition to salary, partners receive a generous budget to remodel offices, all-expense-paid memberships at private clubs, and twenty-four-hour car service on demand. Furthermore, as in re-tailing, the route to the chairman's office in many companies runs directly from a sales vice presidency or other top revenue-producing positions. The best office, the highest salary, the key business community memberships, the support resources, and the ability to control where the company spends its money reside with the executive who is responsible for sales and profits.

What is the ultimate point of having a high salary, the corner office, the seat at the table, and the power that rainmaking brings? Simply to be in a position to change the rules of the game when necessary. If business institutions and the larger economic community can benefit by the values, ideas, and information that women bring to the table, women must be in positions not only to suggest change, but to make it happen. Real change is instituted in The Club, and the most respected route to that sphere of influence is by success at rainmaking.

WOMEN AS RAINMAKERS

This major barometer of achievement—individual contributions to sales and profit—is not often recognized by women, especially not early in their careers. Many women feel that if they simply work hard at their assigned tasks they will be noticed and rewarded—a formula for advancement that worked for them through their schooling. Once they reach senior levels, however, rainmaking is an issue that hits them squarely between the eyes.

"Let me tell you why rainmaking skills are important," says Catherine Atwater,* the senior vice president of an international consulting firm and the managing partner of one of its biggest offices in the country. We were talking in her spacious executive suite in Chicago. The room's Turk-ish rug, chintz-covered couches, and profusion of fresh flowers in crystal vases attested to Catherine's taste and success.

"Men know instinctively why bringing in business is important, but women need to be reminded. This is something that women at the top cannot overemphasize to other women who want to reach senior levels.

"First of all, you'll be judged on it. When we decide to make someone a vice president in our business, it is partly based on past performance and

---

*An asterisk denotes that we have changed the name of the woman quoted, and in some cases the name of her company and its location as well.

partly on what we view as their potential. Can they bring in and keep the business? Our pay is based on that, and at the partner level, you know how everyone else is doing."

Catherine paused to pick up a Limoges cup and saucer from a silver tray and pour coffee.

"Second, at that level, it is everyone's job," she continued. "It is hard to be a good rainmaker. There is no way around it; the ability to attract business is an extraordinary quality, based on a subtle combination of personality, experience, trust, and relationships with others. There are probably one or two at the most in our firm who are whizzes, but *everyone* has to do it to some extent. That's the point. Everyone has to do it, and women are no exception."

Women like Catherine Atwater have earned places at the policy-making table. They control their professional environments and their careers and, like professional baseball players with .350 batting averages, are in demand. They are attractive candidates for higher positions, from managing law partners and cabinet posts to chief executive officer and corporate director. Even if they decline these overtures, savvy women know that their power is enhanced simply by being asked. When their name appears in the newspaper as a potential candidate, or when male members of The Club discuss them favorably, their power quotient goes up.

Women who have achieved impressive levels of success in their fields are forthrightly discussing the importance of rainmaking and, in some cases, refuting bad or simplistic advice they were given earlier in their careers. Some women recall being figuratively patted on the head and told not to worry about it. Now, however, women are as interested in being successful rainmakers as their male peers, but are concerned to read stories such as one in the *National Law Journal*, where 85 percent of respondents in one survey said it was more difficult for women to bring in business than it was for men, in part because it is harder for women to break into predominantly male client circles. While this may be true, women like Jane Macon, a partner at Fulbright & Jaworski in Texas, contend that women can bring in business if they get out there and use proven techniques that work for men. "This isn't a gender issue. There are plenty of men who think that if they do good work, business will walk in the door. Well, this isn't the sixties any more. That just isn't true."

The answer to the question is critical, for many women feel that if they can't or won't generate business, bring in referrals or make deals with predominantly male business-givers, perhaps the corporate and professional suites will never entirely welcome women at the senior management level. The stakes in business are too high and the risks too great for purely sex-based egalitarianism.

Margaret Marshall, a former law firm partner and past president of the Boston Bar Association, states candidly that higher percentages of women partners in firms can be an economic liability, unless they learn to recruit clients. When women realize the importance of generating new business and, with the help of their companies or firms, develop skill at it, they will be as successful as the men. Otherwise, rainmaking may well be the one insurmountable hurdle that keeps otherwise talented women from reaching the top position in their business, or jolts them from that position in perilous economic times.

Not every career path requires rainmaking as an essential skill. An accountant who joins a large corporation and progresses to chief financial officer has different measures of success along the way from an accountant who joins a private firm and hopes to be made partner one day. The senior vice president for human resources at an international financial services company is not judged on the sales generated by the company's various product lines, nor is the chief operating officer of a bank promoted on the basis of the new business generated in the bank's trust department. Some companies, because of the nature of their business, do not rely upon traditional rainmaking to put profits on the bottom line. For example, the chairman of a public utility company whose revenue-raising ability depends on convincing public utility commissions about the fairness of the proposed rate increases has no need for rainmaking skills.

But women who want to minimize failure and make the most of their professional abilities should scrutinize their own career options carefully. Too many women have gone into law, accounting, and other "service" professions thinking they were professions only, not recognizing that they are businesses with a bottom line. It is clear that most businesses and professions want executives at the most senior levels of policy and management who have demonstrated successful business-generating skills somewhere along the way. Lack of those skills creates a ceiling for executives, whether they are men or women.

FINDER OR BINDER?

Once a woman has chosen a business track or profession where success will depend on rainmaking, she has two rainmaking options: In business language, they are called finders and binders. Finders, those who discover and secure new markets and clients, have been and will be the most acclaimed of the rainmakers. Senior women who are after the shortest, most direct route to The Club tend to choose the finder path. Binders, those who service and retain existing clients, follow the axiom that it is most profitable to keep existing customers satisfied than to find new ones. Many women have found the binder role to be less stressful.

A woman who hopes to be a successful rainmaker by binding someone else's "finds" must choose her corporate environment carefully. Many businesses emphasize getting repeat business and developing loyal customers on the theory that it is not until you develop the resale that you generate a revenue stream. Is the task to develop a loyal customer base of those who will keep returning to you for office supplies or machine parts? Or is the business based on onetime, individual transactions? The strategy of a car dealer is quite different from that of a stockbroker, but in most businesses, there is a place for the binder, although he or she will generally be less valued than the original "finder."

"I can think of a few women who have become quite successful as binders," says Alice Lewis,* an accountant in New York City. "But doing this involves a strategy as carefully cultivated as being a rainmaker yourself. First, you have to be as good as—no, not just as good as—better than your male peers. Second, you have to be good at marketing yourself internally, instead of externally. In an accounting firm, for example, the big rainmakers have to get to know you, and know how good you can be with their clients. That involves careful mentor-picking, careful department-picking, and careful assignment-picking. And finally, you have to develop a sponsor and hope that nothing happens to him or her, for it is that person who will keep tossing the business to you, knowing that you will service it carefully to the benefit of you both. Eventually you will become the binder, that inherited link or contact point between your firm and the client."

Many women have found that binding a client is a service they enjoy and one that enhances their own job satisfaction. They do particularly well in forging ongoing relationships with their client contacts by promptly returning client calls, solving their problems, and assembling professional teams for client projects. Attentive and diligent, they earn clients' enduring loyalty for their employers. Judith Cook* is a partner at a large accounting firm in Tampa, Florida, where she enjoys a substantial health care practice representing hospitals, health maintenance organizations, and other health care providers. She doesn't hesitate to give her home phone number to clients, saying that when an important financial or tax issue arises, "the CFO often needs to talk to me right away. I'm always available by phone for them." Clients are pleased with such personal service, and Judith receives credit for retaining their loyalty. As a part-time partner and the mother of three young children, she does not have time to bring many clients to the firm.

Binding, or retaining existing clients, is an important skill in businesses with a reputation for excellent client retention. Florence Crawford,* managing director of a national advertising agency in New York City, explains:

"A good long-standing client is gold for us, and senior executives who forge personal relations with such clients are our stars. A good client is a leader in his particular industry—a quality name. Since advertising agencies generally do not represent competitors, you naturally seek the best client in each class. A good client is also one you can do good creative work for, because that builds your reputation and brings in other clients. A good client is not only a source of growing revenues but an important reference to others, who seek you out after watching its advertising success.

"So even though we don't use the term *rainmaking* in advertising, we do bind, and perhaps that is why women have been generally more successful in advertising than in other fields. After all, when a client is buying an advertising agency, he's buying the people in the room. The people in the room convey who we are and what we can do. This is a relationship business. Our executives must have superlative personal skills—part silver tongue, part showmanship.

"When a client leaves, it's not because the job is done, or the assignment completed. Generally it's because the relationship isn't working any more—and that's not good. So we love our client binders!"

PLAN A CAREER PATH EARLY

Too often, women fail as rainmakers not because of an inherent inability to generate business, but because they did not analyze their careers early enough to plan successful strategies. It is never too early for a woman to start thinking about whether a particular field requires rainmaking skills, and if so, what training and career moves will enhance those skills. Strategic planning early on can avoid substantial disappointment later.

"Did you ever notice that women have a tendency to just fall into jobs?" asks Anne Anthony,* a litigation partner and bar association president in Seattle. "We like the job we're in, but maybe we'll take the next opportunity that comes along because it also seems interesting. There's no plan and we don't carry along our prior associations and experiences to the next position. Then, when we reach a level where we're expected to bring in business, we're not prepared.

"Instead," Anne continues, "women need to make connections as they go along, and keep building on the past. Our lives have to look like a pyramid, rather than like slightly overlapping concentric circles. Successful men seem to know this instinctively. They know that their teammate on their soccer team in prep school is now the CEO of XYZ computer firm in Palo Alto. They don't hesitate to trade on that connection. Do women use their contacts like that? Not often."

Anne Anthony figured it out, but seldom does anyone ever tell a woman, early in her career, that her success at the highest levels of an organization will almost always be based on her ability to attract business. The director of training and development for a large New York law firm explained why her firm did not even include a segment on rainmaking in its training program. "We don't want to scare new associates by having them worry about that yet," she said. Presumably, male associates got the hint as children when they watched their fathers socialize with potential clients on the golf course or in the locker room. If not, their mentor-partners show them the ropes. For many women, any hints they pick up come too late.

"I worked so hard, doing what I thought was acceptable," one forty-five-year-old woman accountant told us. "I put in long hours, and became the expert in several areas of the tax code. I didn't even have to look up the answers in the book. Now I've been passed over for partner twice, and the firm is about to lay off some accountants because business is down. I may be one of them. I had no idea until it was too late that I should have been outside the office all those years, learning to bring in business like the men. That's what counts in the end."

Recognizing the importance of rainmaking early in a career gives women a head start in developing this skill. "I was insulated for ten years in government service and another ten years as the executive of a large department store chain before I heard the term *rainmaking* used by lawyers in private practice," Dawn-Marie says. "Those who learn about it late in their careers are playing catch-up to those who have been living and breathing it since college. On the other hand, I realized I knew something about it, even if I hadn't heard the term, when I was asked to speak on a legal panel about how to attract clients. As general counsel of a $500 million corporation, I knew firsthand the criteria I used in choosing outside counsel."

Carol recalls her start in retailing in 1955 when she was working as a trousseau coordinator for Joseph Magnin department store in San Francisco, and summoned up enough courage to decline a promotion to bridal buyer.

"The last thing I wanted to do was to go to manufacturers and just write order slips for bridal dresses. I knew that I wanted to stay in retailing, and I knew that the traditional path for women was through the buying office. But somehow, at that moment, when I had a chance to make one of my earliest career decisions, I sensed instinctively that the person who controlled the layout and operation of the store was responsible for generating sales, controlling expenses, and producing profits. I wanted to be *that* person. How did I know? I didn't really. Somehow I just followed my instincts and my observations that those at the top had gone up through the line.

"I was faced with that issue again many years later," Carol said. "I had been working for several years in our corporate marketing department at Stop & Shop, and even though I was earning national recognition for our private label packing and new store design concepts, it didn't count much inside the company. The only thing that counted was line. So, in 1967, I started planning a career move. It took me two years, but at age thirty-eight I went back to school, to the Advanced Management Program at Harvard Business School, and then when I came back to the company, I first negotiated my way into a lower-level line job in the department store division. Then a year later I was back in the supermarket company as vice president and general manager of a division of eighty-eight food stores. That turned out to be a very important career move. I doubt I would have been selected president of The Stop & Shop Companies if I hadn't had extensive line experience."

Time and time again, women told us they were slow to learn how important rainmaking is to their success. In one graduate school after another the "how to" of mustering clients is rarely mentioned. Therefore, many women tend to concentrate more on learning their jobs. They excel at assigned tasks instead of developing the skills and relationships that are so important to generating business.

When women are pressed for time, it is easy for them to resent the time that is required to develop relationships, both inside and outside the office. But most business-givers are interested in executives as people first, and only secondarily in their skills and abilities. As Sally Berger said, "People give to people, not to causes or companies." A mentor who is considering passing on an important client to a potential successor cares more about how his successor will treat the client, and less about his or her graduate school transcript.

Women also suffer from a lack of role models who are rainmakers. If few women are publicly touted as good business-getters, this lack of recognition, coupled with most women's reluctance to boast about their achievements, results in fewer women grasping the how and why of rainmaking. Obtaining and retaining clients is less important than other skills women bring to the workplace; success belongs to those who do good work, these women believe. They are wrong, and the sooner women reorder their priorities to include rainmaking at the top of the list, the more successful these women will be.

The American Institute of Certified Public Accounting (AICPA) points out in its study of women in the accounting profession:

> In general, women seem less aware than men of the necessary qualifications for advancement to top-level positions. Although both male and female panelists identified the same personal traits required for success in an organization—technical competence, commitment, willingness to work hard, good interpersonal and management skills, leadership char-

acteristics—female panelists noted that women do not always understand the importance of more subtle criteria, such as visibility within the organization, the benefits of a mentor, and the importance of presenting a successful self-image.

. . . women often believe that good performance alone will gain recognition, whereas men understand that performing well is simply one factor in career advancement.

RISK-TAKING PAYS OFF

In addition to learning early the importance of rainmaking, women would do well to become risk-takers. Aggressively going after sales and increased profits usually involves risk of some type, and the greater the risk, the greater the reward.

One risk-taker is Deborah Sinay, vice president/general sales manager at the Hearst-owned WCVB-TV in Boston. Deborah has risen to the top of her profession in broadcast sales, a managerial position traditionally dominated by men. She proves the point that not only can women bring in business, but they can also supervise a staff (of twenty-nine) and administer the station's enormous sales efforts (with an annual budget of $60 million, the station's net revenues are estimated at $110 million). In addition to all of this, this mother of two young children was elected by her professional peers to chair the prestigious Advertising Club of Greater Boston, a 1,700-member trade association for the local advertising and communications industries, and then elected president of the New England Broadcast Association.

"On an even playing field, women do just fine bringing in business. They are thorough, directed, and work well with the clients," she said. "When I first came to the station we had a few male salesmen in the department who were adequate, but they weren't very well trained," Deborah recalled. "We were just becoming computerized, so I took a big leap. I instituted enough training in computers, statistics, and everything else that our salespeople need to know to land the business. We also talk a lot among ourselves. Women are not hesitant to find out what they need to do the job. There is no such thing as a dumb question in my department. Now we're the top revenue-producing station in our market."

Jane Carter,* the chief operating officer of a multibillion-dollar bank in Los Angeles, provides another view on the importance of risk-taking: "Today, I'm afraid, success in the financial world for women involves two critical factors besides knowledge of the business. The first is the ability to take risks and the second is a successful track record that demonstrates that ability. Whether in portfolio management, currency trading, or complex financial lending, making money in this business depends on risk-taking. A starting point for women is to see and accept demanding jobs in which they can try out their skills, and bring home some victories. I'd advise young women coming along to look for those risk-taking jobs and departments, and try them out. That's the best route to the top of any financial institution."

Jane acknowledges that risk-taking is easier said than done. "Let's face it, women have been culturalized to smooth things over. Men don't have to do that. But from the time we were little, we were always making things nice, easing rather than disrupting. So men put women in the make-it-nice-jobs. Jobs that involve risks aren't for women, because men haven't seen women *behave* that way. And then when they do, men don't like these women. They come across as tough, bold, fearless, aggressive—traits which some men view as negative in a woman. It's a problem that women help solve only by demanding chances at those jobs, and then succeeding."

NETWORKING WORKS

While Jane Carter sees risk-taking as one important ingredient in the rainmaking mix, she doesn't see the road to success stopping there. Networking is another major component. "The days of business walking into the bank are over," she said. "A friend of mine who is CFO for a major consumer product company said he gets so many calls in a week from potential bankers that he simply won't take them any more; he wants to know the person he does business with. So women have to network. *This* is what matters. *This* is the driving force."

Although networking has been described by one woman as "hanging around with people you don't know or don't like," hard work in its pursuit has rewards. When Dawn-Marie was general counsel of Filene's, the New England department store chain, she often had occasion to hire outside law firms to handle an expanding work load. Her secrets about how she chose outside counsel held no surprises. Quality of legal work was not a paramount issue, because she assumed that she would receive high-quality work from any of the major law firms in town. She started with people she knew and respected, never giving business to someone she didn't know. This personal relationship with the lawyers she chose assured her of their ability to handle the case or assign it to the best person in their firm. She simply would not choose a stranger.

Women who attend seminars devoted to instruction in the fine art of rainmaking dutifully write down "network" in their notes, promising themselves to call three acquaintances for lunch and join one civic group. But being known and knowing people is more than a routine activity. It is an attitude and a state of mind, a positive commitment to frequent social interaction. It is difficult to become an extrovert halfway into one's career; most successful rainmakers begin socializing with potential contacts much earlier. It is also difficult to network if women are distracted by family, financial worries, or personal insecurities. There is no formula for successful networking, but it does require a certain zest and enthusiasm for putting people together.

Many women meet other people happily, enjoying their company, but some do not think of this activity as business development. "There are two types of women who join groups," Jane Macon commented. "Those who network for business, and the 'touchy-feely' types. The second group never makes the connection."

The opportunities for women to network are vast, ranging from professional associations and alumni groups, to chambers of commerce and community, religious or sports organizations. Some women belong to a choral group or have a share in a ski house, but never think to discuss business or find out what their peers do for a living. Worse, many women downplay their own accomplishments and expertise, even in response to a simple question in a social setting.

"Women should develop a four-sentence paragraph that rounds out the picture of what they do and elevates their professional standing," advised Anne Anthony, the Seattle lawyer. "They should practice it on their dog, their family, and their college roommate. After a while, it should be as natural as saying their name."

"Don't simply say, 'I'm a lawyer' and think that even this sentence is boastful. It's not good enough. Instead, say, 'I work in the corporate department of a large Seattle law firm handling intellectual property and trademark problems for computer software companies. This area of law is changing all the time, and getting more complex as the industry is maturing, particularly with international issues. It's an area that fascinates me.'"

Anne starts her day with 7:00 A.M. breakfast meetings, serves on the governor's judicial nominating panel, and frequently entertains as part of her professional life. She is twice married, and has no children of her own, although she enjoys her husband's grandchildren and her own nieces and nephews.

"I received my first lesson in visibility early in my career," she recalled. "I was handling my first major trial and entered the courtroom the first day. The judge looked at my opposing counsel and said, 'Good morning, George.' Then he looked at me and said, 'Would counsel please introduce herself?' I vowed at that moment to reverse that pattern so judges would know *me* when I walked into courtrooms. Now I know every judge on the state and federal level, many of whom I've helped get there. But it's been a long-term strategy.

"Being well known and visible is hard work," she admits. "There aren't enough hours in the day, and if you have conflicting pressures at home, work-related outside activities are often the ones to go. But you can't ignore them. This isn't brain surgery after all; it is just good common sense." Anne offers a few tips to help women achieve greater visibility. "Join your professional association. Volunteer for committees. Chair a committee. Run for office. Become an officer. Become president. Write articles. Give panels and presentations for your professional education organization. Serve on the task forces when asked. Serve on nonprofit boards. And speak up with authority when asked what you do!"

DEVELOP PERSONAL RELATIONSHIPS

Networking to increase visibility is just the first step. Developing personal relationships is what will eventually bring in clients, particularly in those businesses that are not strictly price competitive or competence competitive. If the element of service is at all part of the equation, the business may just as likely be given to friends instead of strangers.

If a woman is hard at work at her desk all day, how does she foster relationships that will lead to future business? For many women, the answer is a social life that is an extension of the workday. Being accessible to other people involves breakfasts, lunches, and, for some, evening activities. But relationships can be built by phone contact as well. "I think of myself as a telephone operator," said Eleanor Morgan,* a Detroit utility executive and chamber of commerce director. "All day long I'm on the phone or meeting people, making connections for them with other executives or community leaders I know in the city. I'm the common element for all of them and that's fine. I enjoy putting people, ideas, causes, and business connections together."

Relationship issues can be tricky for women if men are usually the ones who give them the business. Florence Crawford's advertising agency has been unusually successful in retaining its large client base while attracting new business. She describes a comfort zone within which the willingness of men to give business to women varies by the individual: "Even in advertising, which is a good business for women to work in, there is a comfort level between the client and whomever he or she can work with. It is hard for women to develop and maintain a relationship with male clients. It's not that women can't play golf, or go to professional football games. It's the whole male locker room environment. I call it 'the camaraderie issue.'"

By acting professionally, women executives are dealing with tricky relationship problems head-on. Kaye Ferriter, a partner at Coopers & Lybrand, the national accounting firm, says rainmaking is easier for women at national firms, whose clients look for a large, well-respected name. "Leads often come in because of our name and reputation," she explains. "And here, individuals have more support in the process of seeking clients. Obviously, in smaller firms, women face relationship issues. But it will get better simply as women extend their careers. People who formerly worked for one company or organization will get promoted or change jobs and then work for another, providing contacts for new business. It works for men, and it will work for women."

Catherine Atwater, a management consultant, agrees that women can succeed at generating business, particularly as the business culture relies less on the old-boy network. "There has been a shift in our business," she says, "and I expect in others. Ten years ago, business depended on who you knew. Now, almost every piece of major business is bid out, and you are competing for the job. You have to be good. This is where other issues like style, personality, presentation, and self-confidence show up. On the one hand, it is easier for women, because now we can get a foot in the door. On the other hand, there is more competition. You must beat out the competition in every aspect. The corporate executives must be comfortable with you, with your understanding of their business, and with your approach to solving their problem. They want to feel that you will do a good job for them. That is why landing the business is only one part of the equation. After that, the client has to be serviced, and serviced well. You can't simply delegate the assignment and mentally check out on the project."

How does she accomplish all this?

"Slowly and methodically," Catherine confides. "I was fortunate in that I was grandfathered by the firm and allowed to retain my seat as the corporate director of several large national corporations. The firm no longer allows that. But those associations allowed me to meet a number of CEOs and other directors from all over the country, so I am fairly well known by now. Contacts alone don't win you the job; expertise, ability, and client trust are important. But the fact that I am known in corporate circles gets us in the door."

Once in the door, women must project self-confidence and be able to talk to anyone in any setting. Sharon Mitchell,* a partner in an accounting firm in Washington, D.C., shares her secrets in the art of client conversation. "With men, I generally talk about sports. I've met few men who can't sustain a conversation about sports, even on the most superficial level. So I read the sports page every morning.

"With women, surprisingly, it's a little more difficult. The fact that we are both women doesn't automatically give us common interests. So I look at the wall in her office. If she has pictures of children or family, I'm all set. If she doesn't, I can usually start with the weather or the traffic, or if it is close to a vacation season I find out if she has made any vacation plans. If I'm really stumped, I can seize upon some local issue, without trying to guess her position. 'Are you as glad as I am that the election is over?' worked this past week! I couldn't have guessed what candidate she supported, but it gave me the opening to find out. But all of this is a learned skill. Men have told me they have trouble talking to women they have just met, and want hints on how to make small talk prior to plunging into business. I've suggested some of this, and it seems to work."

Despite their inroads into the old-boy network, women encounter occasional inevitable disappointments.

Diane Dean,* managing partner of an architectural firm in Baltimore, Maryland, has developed antennae to notice when the old-boy odds are against her: "We had been invited to make a presentation for a major new hospital building," she explains. "It was a big job, but we had done buildings like this before; in fact, I had landed the past jobs. The building committee of the hospital had interviewed six firms. I studied the composition of the committee carefully. There were a few women trustees, a couple of administrators, and some outside supporters of the hospital—men who had financial or real estate experience. One of the committee members was a major contractor, and I discovered that the hospital had hired him as their construction supervisor.

"The presentation went well and the feedback I received from our liaison on the committee was good. A few days later I heard the committee had narrowed the competition to two bidders—our firm and one other. Needless to say, when the other firm won the job I was sorely disappointed.

"But the story doesn't end there. A short time later I had another project with the firm that won the job. One day I was at their offices, talking to one of their partners. He mentioned in passing another project his company was working on, in conjunction with the same fellow who was the construction supervisor on the hospital building.

"I thought it was more than coincidence that the supervisor's name popped up again. Is it possible that he influenced the committee to hire that firm for the hospital job. If so, was it illegal? Of course not. Unethical? Of course not. He wanted a level of comfort with people he knew and had worked with before, as would I. I probably would have done the same thing, but it's tough to come so close and lose out in the end to the old-boy network."

Diane explains how she dealt with the disappointment, knowing full well that she and her colleagues had worked hard to do a good job, and convinced that they were better than the firm that was chosen. "I try not to take it personally. I put it behind me and get pumped up for the next chance to bid, the next presentation. I know we did well and came close. We impressed the committee. We'll get the next one."

Jane Macon of Texas says that the way to get into the network with the boys is to just do it. "I don't mind being a hands-on-type of lawyer," she said. "I get a lot of referrals from project-type people. I meet the engineers right on the job site, and the other guys who are working on the job. We work as a team and they know they can call me night or day, as soon as they run into the least little problem, and long before the job shuts down. I get a good rapport going with the guys who are building the project. By the time the question of legal representation gets to the general counsel, I'm likely to be recommended by the project people. The general counsel knows he can rely on the quality of Fulbright and Jaworski's legal work. Working for a nationally known firm is a big plus for women and minorities. You don't have to worry about validating your own credibility each time.

"I also get a lot of business traveling on airplanes. Let's face it, who else sits in first class except businesspeople? Most of my clients are men, and I work hard at client loyalty. I'm available for them. If I know a client is coming into town, I call them and buy them a drink or dinner. Even if they're not free, they know I tried," she said.

"And I don't forget that clients are people, not companies. People have problems, too, and if you quietly solve their problems, they'll be grateful. My clients can call me at any time, and they do; after all, it's always on a weekend that your teenage kid gets arrested for drunken driving, right?"

In her professional life, Jane constantly uses the "five magic words" that many women use naturally, without thinking of them as a key ingredient in rainmaking success. Saying "How can I help you?" is a wonderfully easy way for women to cement personal relationships. The answer may be to bring the listener a new client, to look over his wife's résumé or to help him meet a certain member of The Club. But having heard the question, it is more likely than not that the listener will then say, "Now, how can I help you?"

DEVELOP A SPECIALTY

Another strategy for women who want to be successful rainmakers is to develop a specialty or professional niche that puts them in demand. The opportunity to become a specialist may arise at any time. For example, a woman may develop a new product for her company early in her career, thereby becoming the expert on it. For others, expertise comes from a stint in academia. Two examples are Dr. Marina Whitman, who became vice

president at General Motors after holding an academic post as an economist, and Matina Horner, the former president of Radcliffe College, who
became executive vice president at TIAA/CREF, the pension fund for
most of the nation's colleges and universities. Government appointments
can polish expertise. Paula Gold made a successful career shift from her
post as secretary of consumer affairs and business regulation in Massachusetts to executive positions as senior vice president at New England Elec-
tric Systems, a regulated utility, and vice president at Plymouth Rock As-
surance Corporation, an insurance company. In most cases, being a
specialist involves speaking or publishing in the particular field of expertise, a platform from which referrals often materialize.

Attorney Margaret Marshall thinks specialization is a good strategy on
the road to generating business referrals. "Be an expert, so others don't see
you as a woman but as an expert in something specific. I know one woman
who was an expert in airport siting issues. Another drafted and promul-
gated the rules on a new and obscure part of the tax code for the Internal
Revenue Service, and later built a lucrative referral practice."

Women who generate significant business through a specialty caution
other women to choose their specialty carefully. So-called power special-
ties, though male-dominated, generate power business. For example, rate-
making economists or lawyers for telecommunications companies can
command much higher fees than those earned by personal financial planners and divorce lawyers, because the clients are willing and able to pay
and the stakes are high. Architects who build world-class concert halls or
office towers command higher fees than those who remodel homes.

When referrals from professional peers are the primary basis for generating business, careful strategizing is called for. "Women must be perceived
as tough enough to handle someone else's client but respectful enough not
to steal the client," Marshall cautioned. "The trick is to service the client
so well as to make an admirer of the referring professional as well as the
client. A practice built this way leads to more and more referrals."

Florence Crawford explained why women who are specialists in the
advertising business offer a case in point. "Women who have done their
homework, speak confidently, and make a good presentation invariably
gain the respect of their clients. Women experts are listened to.

"Advertising is a good profession for women because it has easy and
open access," Florence continued. "It depends less on credentials, such as

where you went to college, whether you made law review or Phi Beta Kappa, or what your social and class credentials are. It's simply a job you learn by doing. If you are good, you will get ahead. If you are not, you won't. And then becoming a specialist, or expert, with a good track record will put you in demand."

Being known as a specialist allows women to develop business by concentrating on referrals from their professional peers. In some fields, however, referrals can come directly from the general public, allowing women to be successful without necessarily depending on referrals from a closed society of competitors that is difficult to penetrate. Women must work hard to generate the visibility and name recognition that produces clients who seek them out by name, but it is a strategy that has worked well for many.

Women who target and develop their own client base can give superior service and can ignore their competitors. "Financial services can be an equal opportunity profession," said one stockbroker in Tulsa. "After all, sales are nondiscriminatory. If you produce and service your clients well, you get the same rewards. And it is better now that the compensation system has changed. Your pay is based on assets under management, not commissions from transactions. That way there is less of an incentive to churn accounts, which the men always did more than women anyway. I think women are more concerned about their clients. We take time with them. Maybe too much time. But I think that in the end we keep more accounts. The men in my office won't spend time with a new customer, explaining things. When a man gets a call, he'll just say, 'I'll send you a brochure.' I want to make sure the potential client understands what I am recommending. So I've developed a good client base of customers who want my level of service."

Dr. Susan M. Love, director of the Center for Breast Disease at UCLA Medical School, is a professional who has developed such a national client base that while she was in Boston the Faulkner Breast Center expanded greatly to meet the demand of surgery patients seeking the type of care she and her colleagues delivered. Even before her move to Faulkner, Dr. Love quickly became known by women as a physician who didn't automatically recommend a mastectomy for women facing breast cancer. She helped her patients make their own decisions, empowering them to be part of the healing process. Dr. Love is famous for demystifying breast cancer and giving a level of personal care and attention to her patients that is markedly different from the expected medical model. She also received wide media attention for her campaign to get breast cancer information to consumers and for her subsequent *Dr. Susan Love's Breast Book.*

Dynamic, outspoken, and warm, Dr. Love is a hit with the media, and is not afraid to use her popularity and expertise to forward an agenda for national research on women's health. Whether she is on Ted Koppel's "Nightline" show (tossing gilt Ping-Pong balls and suggesting men remove the tissue in their testicles and replace it with the balls so they'd be free from worry about testicular cancer) or featured in newspaper and magazine articles women read and share ("Operating with Love"), Dr. Love is aware of the power she wields. A flood of business is a side benefit. "I have patients from all over the country," she said, "who have asked their own physicians to give them a referral to me, because they have heard of me and the Breast Center. But in most cases their physicians did not initiate the referral themselves; it came directly from the patient."

ATTRACTING THE BUSINESS OF WOMEN

Susan Love has a natural base of women clients in her business, but other women have found that as more women understand the importance of rain-making, they seek out women to patronize and make referrals. Jane Macon recalled one of many such instances in her career. "I knew the president of a major real estate analysis firm from our association in the 'old-girl network' of the Committee of 200 and the International Women's Forum, who was made president of a major real estate firm in London and New York with properties across the country. When she looked at what they were doing in Texas, she said, 'Why are we using that firm?' She called me right up and I've been representing them ever since. We did that one real quick."

A woman can take advantage of her unique position in a male-dominated environment not only by making a name for herself but by zeroing in on obtaining the business of other women executives. As more and more women become general counsel, chief financial officer, or vice president of human resources at corporations or agencies, they look for the presence of senior women in the companies they patronize as one indication of how the company values women. This alone is a compelling reason for women to be selected as part of any company's business development team. The picture of senior-level women in progressive professional firms interacting with female clients is worth a thousand words.

Lucia Bearse,* a well-known lawyer who specializes in employment contract work for high-technology companies in Los Angeles, has used her visibility to develop a reputation with clients. When working with outside firms she is alert to the absence or presence of women. "You never know who will be on the other side, and it is just good common sense to try to make as many positive points of contact as possible. In my experience, the female senior executives of our clients are always looking for the presence or absence of a female lawyer. I know I always like to see a woman on the other side.

"As chairman of the board of directors of a large nonprofit institution, I was recently invited, along with three other officers, to a lunch given by the senior executive of one of our city's largest banks. The lunch was held in the bank's private dining room, usually reserved for power lunches with major clients, but this was planned as a social occasion.

"The very smart thing that the bank did was to invite their highest-ranking woman to attend the lunch, along with two of her male colleagues. I was pleased to see another woman there, and I put that bit of thoughtfulness in the bank's positive column. If I had an occasion to use the bank in the future, I would certainly call the woman I met so that she would get credit for the referral.

"I have to admit," Lucia adds, "that when I staff a litigation matter, I try to balance it with male associates. Rarely do I present an all-female team to a client. Not that it would be negative per se, but I am aware of those points of contact on the other side."

Does this mean that an all-male team would lose business because it didn't include a woman?

"Probably not," she admits. "But if a company has good women they'd be crazy not to include them."

Florence Crawford disagrees, "I've seen it happen in advertising, much to my secret delight. A major subsidiary of a consumer product company decided to change advertising agencies, and invited three major advertising firms to make presentations. On the scheduled date, six men from one advertising company showed up at the corporate headquarters to make their pitch, and found themselves giving it in front of a six-member, all-female team from the company! They didn't get the job."

Women are serious about helping each other become successful, as across the country they gather on a regular basis to discuss business and make referrals. "Women giving business to women" has become a rallying cry, as women identify other women they can do business with. Some women's organizations have published books and directories listing local women-owned firms for easy reference. The Tulsa (Oklahoma) Women's Foundation publishes an Honor Roll of Tulsa Women in Business, highlighting businesses as diverse as Louise Gillam Interior Lighting Company, a forty-six-year-old company, to neurological surgeon Dr. Marilynn E. Lins and optometrist Dr. Carol Lynne Sweet.

North Shore Women in Business, an independent women's business organization of more than 300 members in northeast Massachusetts, includes women who work for large traditional companies as well as those who own their own business. Its former executive director, Georgina Keefe-Feldman, describes its membership: "We have bankers, chiropractors, insurance agents, piano teachers, and lawyers. Many of our members work for large companies and firms, and we know it is just as important for those women to be successful business generators as it is for a woman who owns her own firm. We all share the same objectives: to get the word out about women in business and to bring them the business."

Some women, like Phyllis Swersky, former executive vice president of A.I. Corp., a Boston-area software and expert systems company, give business to other women as a matter of course. "I've been trying to reach you all day!" she said to Dawn-Marie, her voice cracking over her car phone. "We need to change accountants at A.I. Corp. What women do we know at the major firms who we can call to get credit for coming in to bid for our business?"

Directing business to women is not always easy, but as women are more aware of the economic power they wield, they are asking sharp questions about the presence of women in companies and firms.

"I can't do much inside the firm to promote women or push for women partners," said Irene Heath,* a Seattle accountant. "If I started to do that I'd be completely ineffective in the other things I'm trying to get done within the firm. But I do look for opportunities to remind clients about how powerful they can be. If a *client* says, 'I'm disappointed not to see any women on our accounting team,' the firm would jump through hoops to find them and satisfy that client if it could. The message would be much stronger."

Florine Frank,* operating president of a worldwide manufacturing company, agreed, but was cautionary. "I have tried that when I am the client. One consulting firm came in to make a presentation to us and I asked them how many female managers they had and would any be working on our account. But I have to be very careful. For one thing, we have strict rules about how we give out contracts to prevent favoritism. Second, there are only so many times I can 'go to the well' about women's issues in the company. I have to save my moments for the ones that count. If this were my own business, it would be easier. But my bottom line is that I do it whenever and wherever I can. What's the point of being successful if we can't use our power to help other women be successful?"

Women understand how "getting credit" for bringing in business works in various professions and know that a woman doesn't actually have to have a woman as lawyer, accountant, or pension fund manager, as long as a woman gets the credit for bringing the client in the door. The individual executive who "originates" the matter is the person who knows the client and matches the client with the appropriate service provider or contact within the firm or business. The originator need not *do* any actual work at all—her male partner, customer service representative, or colleague may perform the service or complete the deal. But the woman who originates it receives the most credit in the internal allocation of credits and rewards.

In some companies, even outside directors are expected to be rainmakers. "Our chairman kept a list of each director and how many new commercial business clients he or she had referred to the chief lending officer," said a former bank director. "I felt the pressure to introduce my contacts to the bank if I wanted to continue on the board. He made it quite clear that in his eyes, to represent the bank to the outside world and help him bring in business was part of our role as a director."

These factors—choosing a career path early, taking risks, networking, developing personal relationships with clients, developing a specialty, and attracting the business of other women—are worth careful study from prospective rainmakers. Few women can afford to bypass any of them. The game is tough enough when all the rules have been formulated by men. But the playing field is not entirely uneven. When brainpower alone is the measure, well-educated women compete equally with their well-educated male colleagues. In business situations where skill and expertise count the most, they do just fine. Traditional female conditioning—those repeated admonitions to do well in school, to prepare and produce tirelessly, to work hard and reap rewards later—may even given them an edge up in their careers. The distance successful business women have traveled suggests how much farther they may go. Today, talented businesswomen are directing policy from the company executive's office, having earned those positions as influential rainmakers.

THE FUTURE: CHANGING THE RULES

Success at rainmaking is not just a means to a new Mercedes, additional stock options, or tenure in a prestigious job. Few senior executive women are motivated merely by the ability to purchase new toys, impressed by the size of their offices or stretch limousines, or content with seniority and a title. Many women seek power and influence that accompanies a reputation for business generation for other reasons as well.

Women across the country have told us that they are frustrated and antagonistic about a system of incentives that rewards individual achievement when the system is stacked against them and a system of scoring that reinforces competition—despite having succeeded in this game themselves. How much more productive and less stressful would the challenge of rainmaking be if the rules were modified to ensure success for all who worked hard instead of just glory and credit for a few? These top executive women are challenged to develop a way of doing business that adds a system in which everyone can flourish in an atmosphere of creative interdependence in addition to recognizing the superstars.

This requires changes in rules, in policy, in carrots and sticks. It first requires that women who have proven themselves to be successful rainmakers step into policy-making roles.

But these women accept the hard work that goes with the endeavor and are excited by the opportunity to make their influence felt. They see the direct connection between successful rainmaking and proximity to the power base. As one consultant said, "There are two rainmakers in my firm who bring in enough business for everybody. It really wasn't expected that I would bring in business, but now that I don't have young kids any more, I feel I should be a 'grown up' consultant and bring in business. It makes no sense to abdicate the top spots to men. I want that top spot now."

These successful women rainmakers are clear about what they would change. For example, they know that "keeping score" of who puts the most points on the board is a male competitive model that sometimes works against bringing harmony and economic success to the overall institution and ignores the contributions of others who work for a common goal. At worst, disputes about who gets the rewards can be a major distraction that not only splits firms apart but drives good talent—men and women—away.

"This notion of the who-gets-the-credit game, and petty office jealousies drove me crazy," said Susan Perrel,* a former Wall Street municipal financier. "Wall Street was the original old-boy network, where they simply did not want women to play in their backyard. Well, I was willing to stay there to learn, but in no way was I going to stay in those conditions.

"On my second day in the office, a very smooth rainmaker who played power games with the best of them came in the office and pointed at me. 'Hey, you,' he called. I looked around, to see if maybe he was calling someone else. No, he was looking at me. I couldn't imagine what he wanted.

"'I hear you're from ———,' he said, referring to my former home state where I had been a cabinet secretary in state government.

"'That's right,' I replied, curious as to where the conversation was heading.

"'Well, do you know Mr. X?' he asked, naming a current powerful cabinet secretary.

"'Yes, I do,' I answered, thinking how lucky I was that he had named one of my friends. Mr. X was a career public official, and someone who had been in state government for a long time. He had been very nice to me during the transition from my administration to the one in which he now serves, and we had stayed in contact. The young rainmaker challenged me to set up an appointment for him with Mr. X.

"I knew it would be easy and I was pleased to be able to show some success on my first week at work. I called Mr. X who was delighted to hear from me and most receptive to meeting with me and my colleague.

"When I told the rainmaker, he was silent, clearly surprised. He had not been able to get through to him (an experience common to many), and simply had assumed that no one could, including me. It also began to dawn on me that he wasn't all that happy that I had arranged an appointment; women weren't supposed to show him up. Perhaps I had stepped on his toes? I dismissed the thought because, after all, we were all here to bring in business for the firm, right?

"The next day, however, a supervisor in the office approached me. 'You had no authority to make that appointment,' he thundered. 'Break it!' I was totally confused by what was happening. 'I can't,' I protested. 'Besides, I was simply doing what I was told.' How was I supposed to know that I wasn't to help out the rainmaker? 'I can't break the appointment,' I continued. 'Appointments with Mr. X are simply too hard to get; he's booked up weeks in advance. You simply *don't* break an appointment with him. Even though he is a personal friend, I'd never get another one.'

"I stewed over these developments, and so did others in the office but for different reasons. They clearly didn't want a first-year associate—no matter what his or her background, age, or experience—going out and getting clients, particularly if it embarrassed rainmakers who weren't able to get the appointment themselves. So I ended up going on the appointment myself. Mr. X and I had lunch, and I told him the whole story. His reaction was simple and swift: 'Get yourself out of there. You're too smart for them.'

"Well, I stayed for a while, and confounded them more by bringing in business my first year. They had given me a pro bono project to do on behalf of a nonprofit agency because no one else wanted it. I did it, and excelled. I kept in contact with the group, which, shortly after, received a large appropriation from the state. They came to me as a paying client to do a financial analysis for them. My firm couldn't believe it. Once again, I had broken the rules.

"The short end of a long story? I stayed eight years, and learned all I could, knowing all along that I wasn't going to stay in that environment. I left and started my own firm, and in six months I have more business than my new partners and I can handle. We do first-quality work, without regard to the fees we charge. We share the profits, without regard to 'who gets credit' for this or that. We all do the work. I work hard, and earn as much money as I can, but my life-style is my own. The reward of not being on Wall Street, with the pressure to do deals simply to do deals, is my own moral center. I simply will not do a deal for a client that I think is economically and financially bad for them, even if it means losing the fee.

"Of the women who were ahead of me on Wall Street, not one is left. It is a catch-22 situation: You can't get the resources unless you lead a team, and you can't bring in business without the resources, and you can't lead a team unless you bring in business. I was smarter than a lot of the men there and had to beg for an analyst to help me on projects!"

Susan's story is not unusual. Talented women are leaving corporate and professional America to start their own businesses not because they can't succeed in fulfilling the task of rainmaking at their former companies, but precisely because they don't care for the male-created rules of the game.

Attorney Lucia Bearse had another story to tell. "I was once approached by a major corporate client to do a big job. I was delighted, and circulated the usual memo to see if there were any conflicts with any of my partners who may be representing the opposing party. If there were, the firm would not have been able to take the matter unless it had the consent of both sides.

"Much to my surprise, one of my partners called me and said, 'I have a problem with your new client. I represent one of his major competitors.'

"'But not on this matter,' I answered. 'The competitor is not involved.'

"'No,' he said, 'but my client wouldn't like it if you represented his competitor in any dealings.'

"'Well, that's too bad,' I replied, 'because if there is no legal conflict, I'm going to pursue it. I obviously won't discuss my client's business with you and I know you respect the same confidences of your client.'

"My male partner, who was protecting his client base, took the matter to the firm's conflicts committee and won this dispute. I appealed to the executive committee and still lost. One of my other partners later told me that this partner is very jealous of any new business that would threaten him in any way, particularly if they make his clients nervous. He is very worried about losing them so he fights a lot of matters, but loses most. The bottom line is that he found it easy to fight a woman, once he lined up the conflicts committee and the executive committee against me. After all, what does it matter to them if a female partner is not successful in bringing in business? They don't expect me to be, anyway."

Protecting turf. Taking credit. Stealing clients. The old-boy network. Women who are successful business generators have also dealt with these obstacles, but they have done so with an eye to the future, when there will be more women in senior management, serving on the executive, management, and policy committees. They do not deny that sales, revenues, and new clients are the lifeblood of all profit-making organizations, but the importance of these elements can be repositioned. Many men agree with women who see that generating sales does not have to be linked to characteristics of aggression, competitiveness, and performance tests. Rainmaking goals can also be achieved through teamwork, sharing resources and power and reinforcing relationships—skills that are natural for many women and reflect their personal values. Then, instead of trying to adapt to a male model of business culture late in their educational development and business-orientation period, women will be using their own strengths to match the needs of their professional lives, achieving a higher level of career and personal satisfaction.

As we explore in the next chapter, there are differences in working styles between some men and women, described in a shorthand fashion as "task-oriented" and "people-oriented." Despite the two approaches, many executive women feel that the most effective managerial style is an androgynous one that integrates both styles. Many rainmaking environments, however, structure measures of achievement and rewards around a task or goal model, in which doing the deal, earning the fee, landing the account, increasing the rate of return, and getting credit supercedes rewarding collaborative efforts and long-term productivity or simply doing what's right for the customer. These structures, with the compensation formulas that accompany them, are viewed as anachronistic by many women and, perhaps surprisingly, by some men as well.

The heart of the issue was best stated by Sandra Watson,* a successful employee benefits consultant. "Where do we go from here?" she asked. "Are we going to go through the glass ceiling or is it time to rebuild the house? I'm not sure, in retrospect, that the current house is built for women."

This startling comment came from a woman who was the epitome of professional success earned in the male tradition. She is a highly paid, well-known partner in a broad-based financial services firm, who had chaired all of the important association committees in her area of specialty, had served on national committees, and was a noted speaker who had developed a dynamic and far-flung practice. She was already a very visible specialist when many women were just discovering there were careers in her field. She was a role model for many of them, accomplished in her work and exuding confidence. Because she had succeeded, was it not possible and worthwhile for other women to try to follow her career path? Surprisingly, her attitude belied the feelings she had about the way business is done in male-dominated business cultures.

"The real issue around rainmaking is the connection between it and the values we bring to our job. Hustling for business is required, obviously, if firms are to remain profitable. But some women feel that hustling for business so we can all be richer this year than we were last year is simply not worth it. Our own value system of what we think is important doesn't match the reality of why we're doing this.

"But if success at rainmaking allows us to reach positions of power where we can change things, then *that* is worth all the effort. Because I do think women's values are different than men's. For example, it's time to reexamine the way we structure and reward each other," she said. "If we have women at the top of management committees in firms we can raise the issue of revenues generated, hours of work, and salaries. I'd like women to begin to ask, in the executive committees and compensation committees, if the top executives in the firm are satisfied with making $150,000 or $200,000 instead of twice that amount. I think we should begin to impose the view that life-style and professional satisfaction are more important than the extra $100,000. After all, we all make *enough* money."

She added, smiling, "Who among us is brave enough to raise the question?"

Sandra was not alone in questioning the status quo of high salaries and the hours required to generate them. Doris Cook* is a senior woman partner at a large law firm. Close to retirement, she is the dean of women lawyers in her city, having started her practice part-time, in the sixties, before any major firm had a policy about part-time lawyers. She worked part-time while her children were young, and because she was one of very few women in legal practice in her city, her firm didn't worry about "setting a precedent" or establishing policy when they allowed her the privilege. "We're doing it for Doris, after all."

Looking back on her career, Doris reflected on the climate in the law firm of the nineties. "The partners were debating our part-time policy, and they forgot that I wouldn't have been among them had they not extended that arrangement to me, years ago! You know, I had to remind this firm recently about its history, what it had stood for.

"But I'm afraid now, because of the pressures of economics, we are getting away from some of the values we had in past years."

Doris paused, and looked out of her thirty-fifth-floor window at the office towers around her. "You know, she said, "this city wasn't built overnight and women's careers aren't made overnight. I'm concerned—can women sustain the tremendous amount of time and effort that is required? Will their partners, peers, or employers give them the luxury of the long view? Can they take the time to work out a specialty or a niche, develop their reputation, write and speak and gradually make a contribution to their profession and their community, if the payoff doesn't begin to show up until they are more mature than their successful male peers? That's the question. How long will we let women take to be 'successful'? Because 'success' for women like me includes a balanced life. The smart firms will wait, because the return on their investment is there."

Sandra, Doris, and other women have raised good questions. How will women *really* benefit once they have power? What are their assumptions about life at the top and what are their goals and values? They may find that many of them are working more for professional and personal satisfaction than simply for more money. Necessarily, then, attitudes about bringing in business and the very structure of their workplace will change from those assumptions.

Enlightened leaders of business and the professions will seek out these women now, because they are voicing values that will be demanded by the work force of the future. First, businesses must take the necessary steps to ensure that every female executive has as much opportunity to bring in business as her male peers. They must eliminate haphazard policies or intentional obstacles that limit a woman's rainmaking potential and drive away the female talent that all businesses need to be successful. Women will gravitate to employers who move women into policymaking roles and explore new methods and incentives for rainmaking. It is not axiomatic that all such businesses are started or owned by women. Traditional companies that recognize the rainmaking strengths of women, and see the benefits of the growing movement among women to bring business to other women, will be ahead of their snoozing competition.

Finally, at the top of the most inclusionary companies, both men and women can begin to reexamine the whole structure of business generation. The scorekeeping, emotional detachment, aggressiveness, and autonomy involved in individual rainmaking might be complemented by a system that includes cooperation, involvement, credit-sharing, caring, responsiveness, a sense of community, and attention to mission.

The strategies might not change, but the dynamics of how they are implemented might well be different. For example, women will still want to focus on the requirements of rainmaking early in their career, but in those tentative early years of personal career growth and learning from others, some women may more easily adapt to a rainmaking model that is based on cooperation and mentoring. As they develop a style that works best for them, they may end up with an individual approach or they may prefer a partnership with others. But with years to practice in an environment that accommodates many models for achievement, in the long run women will be more successful.

The same is true for the strategy of risk-taking. Some independent, self-assured women will prefer to take risks on their own, but others may prefer to neutralize the individual risk by finding a way to share it with others and also share the rewards. One way is not necessarily better than another as long as the bottom line benefits from the effort. Too many business leaders, however, are stuck in place with one strategy of identifying and attracting clients, one way of training executives, and one formula for assigning rainmaking credit. Their method may have worked in the past, but positioning businesses for future profitability requires that executives constantly reexamine their old assumptions and habits and try new approaches. Their women executives may present new rainmaking ideas that add value and profits to the old models.

Executive women consistently cite rainmaking as a critical factor in the improvement of the country's economic growth and in earning membership in The Club. They also believe that when more women are in a position to make policy regarding rainmaking, the business and professional world may look different. The old-girl network of sharing success strategies, business generation, and referrals will be the first stage in making it happen. Structural change must be the next step, leading to greater productivity and profit.

CHAPTER THREE

VIVE LA DIFFÉRENCE?

Now, honey, we're going to choose off the menu,
but don't you go ordering one of those *salads*,
now—we want a red meat senator!
— Colorado rancher, hosting U.S. Senate
candidate Josie Heath for lunch

Julia Simons,* senior vice president of one of the world's largest public relations firms, paused thoughtfully before she answered a question about the differences between men and women at the top of her firm. We were having dinner in one of Washington, D.C.'s, most elegant restaurants, and the second U.S. senator-turned-lobbyist had just stopped by the table to acknowledge her.

"Even at senior levels, women are still expected to be the worker bees," she said. "Men expect we'll bring everything to closure. We are always the ones that finish the job, do the project, the presentation, excellently, while they are off someplace, doing something else with other members of The Club. They know that we are back in the office, doing the work, doing it well. They think that if they put women in senior management, who will do the work? Men *do* look at women differently—even at the top—and I'm not sure how we break out of it."

Julia had put her finger on a nagging problem. Women look and are different from men. The physical differences are obvious, but differences in women's early socialization, adult values and perspective, and approach

---

*An asterisk denotes that we have changed the name of the woman quoted, and in some cases the name of her company and its location as well.

to their career are less obvious. This does not mean all women act or work differently than men, but most have had the experience of being treated differently. This presents a critical question for women and their employers: Are there valid reasons why women's differences impact on their ability to become members of The Club—or is the problem one of cultural and social expectations?

Julia, who had never married and as a result had modeled her working style on the male work ethic of Washington, D.C., reflected on her own career rise and concluded that the question of differences has validity. "I think women have the same goals as men: money and power. Power is a big issue for women. You *do* have to be highly competitive and have a sense of control.

"But I also do think women question professional life more. Their life is not their work. Life is richer than work. The 'relating' part of life is as important. Therefore women are never fully satisfied with just the energy they devote to work, in the absence of other things. It's our socialization. Men get all filled up with work. Women don't. Look at Washington, D.C. This is a very 'work' city. Even play is work. I work all the time, but I find I need time out, to step away from the unrelenting, male-dominated work culture of this town."

Julia would never express these opinions in mixed company; after all, she has succeeded in a high-pressure environment where few women are considered equals by male Club members. Julia is sensitive to the cultural roles of men and women in Washington. "There's a lot of 'romancing' in this job," Julia explained. "You have to soothe the male ego and be charming. You never want to threaten them, even as you're reaching for more power yourself."

Julia and other top-level executive women know that acknowledging women's differences in the workplace is risky. Suggesting structural changes in rules and culture to accommodate a diversity of work styles is simply not done. Most men have a vested interest in maintaining the status quo; after all, that is how they rose to the top. They understand the rules of the game and the dimensions of the playing field. If changed, they might not only lose out, but they may open up spots for players who were never in contention before. So their defenses go up, and new ideas are discouraged. If it's too tough for the women to handle, let them get out of the game, they say. At that point, many women who have succeeded by understanding and working in male-created cultures concede. Although women may manage differently, and try to establish a distinct culture once they are in The Club, they'll do it quietly.

Executive women do not talk out loud about gender differences because the stakes for acceptance are too high. Instead, the discussion is left to journalists and academics. In executive suites, issues of childbearing, femininity, socialization, psychological makeup, institutional mores, and career theory are politely ignored, or everyone just agrees to resolve them on male terms. This is not surprising, because women know that the concept of "difference" raises the specter of hierarchy in which one gender is "less" and another "more." Furthermore, the words sound jarring even when we verbalize the concept that women are different (raising the presumption that women should be treated differently). In an era in which all discrimination is suspect, it is certainly unacceptable to say that blacks, Jews, or Italians are different, and therefore workplace structures must change for them. Rather than sound sexist themselves, executive women tiptoe around the issue of gender, deciding to assimilate.

"I don't know if women executives are different than men," said a senior vice president of human resources in an international financial services company. "I'd certainly never express that point of view here on the fortieth floor. But I can tell you this. I can cite many instances in which I've been the only woman in a meeting and a decision was being made collectively by the rest of the group that I strongly disagreed with. I've argued forcefully, made the others stop and defer the decision and I usually could talk them out of it later on. I know I've brought a different perspective to the discussion and I've made a difference on many issues. But I have to assume that a self-confident man with my value system and point of view would have done the same."

Executive women may be reluctant to proclaim that they manage differently, but journalists and academics who have studied and written about the traits of women who have risen to top executive ranks have solved the problem of hierarchy by extolling women's managerial styles and concluding that "different" may mean better.

Sally Helgesen is a journalist who studied the working styles of four top executive women. Helgesen's aim was to retrace a 1968 study of male executives, examining what managers do all day. She concluded that female managers operated most effectively by being in the middle of things, communicating, listening, empowering others to act. She coined the phrase "web of inclusion" to describe how women create an alternative structure to the traditional command-and-control. Helgesen's concept mirrors that of Anne Jardim, dean of Simmons Graduate School of Management, who used the term *centrarchies* to describe the circlelike organization women favor.

University of California professor Judy B. Rosener concluded that a second wave of executive women is rejecting the old rules that governed pioneering women's route to the top. These modern executive women are creating a different path to the top, "succeeding because of—not in spite of—certain characteristics generally considered to be 'feminine' and inappropriate in leaders."

Rosener's 1990 study of International Women's Forum members, published in the *Harvard Business Review*, examined the leadership style of successful women—an "interactive" model, in which women worked to have positive interactions with others. The "women encourage participation, share power and information, enhance other people's self-worth, and get others excited about their work." This leadership style, Rosener concluded, emerged because of the socialization and career paths taken by these women. Rosener later reveals what may be equally important: Most of the women surveyed worked for medium-sized, fast-growing companies or organizations, suggesting that traditional, large-scale companies may not have been as receptive to this new female leadership style.

We're not convinced that extolling a particular managerial style as "feminine" is helpful in moving women into positions of economic power. Management theories that favor less authority at the top and a more participatory style have been around for a long time. As Carol noted when asked to comment on the Rosener study, "I do agree that this participative style comes more naturally to women. But male-oriented cultures as diverse as Japanese companies or Levi-Strauss seem to have perfected the art of participatory management."

Dr. Mildred S. Myers, senior lecturer at Carnegie Mellon's Graduate School of Industrial Administration, states that the majority of studies of managers in actual work situations have found no significant differences between men and women. The debate about women's managerial style occurs, she said, because of deeply entrenched perceptions and attitudes rooted in societal values, not in actual experiences.

Many executive women also dismiss the relevance of gender generalizations. "I'm not sure about the notion of a male style of leadership or management versus a female style," said Marilyn Swartz Lloyd, president of Beacon Management Company. "What is much more important is the culture of the organization you're in. I was in the public sector before switching to a private, family-owned company. I never noticed any real differences between men and women, but I did notice cultural differences. Some companies are team-oriented, some are competitive, some are highly visible, vocal, and others have a quieter style of leadership. You have to figure that all out to be successful."

The truth is that distinctions between how men and women project management and leadership qualities are narrowing. The real problem lies with the fact that, as a female New York banker stated, "There is a very narrow band of 'acceptable' behavior, which is a blend of men's and women's values." In an increasingly diverse work force, this narrow band must expand for both men and women, and for the ultimate productivity of American businesses. The American white male mode of operating in a business culture is not the only right way, as anyone who has done business overseas can attest.

The question of gender difference is a complex one, but many executive women agreed on two points: physical differences matter, and social and cultural differences can be understood and overcome.

PHYSICAL DIFFERENCES ARE SKIN DEEP

Even though we are uncomfortable with what sounds like sexism, we cannot ignore the fact that there are biological differences between men and women that do not apply to differences among blacks, Jews, or Italians. Women have children and men do not. On that issue, most professional women say the distinction of motherhood ends several months after giving birth, although in some workplaces, cultural biases last longer.

"After each of my three children were born, I came right back to work and was just as productive as ever," said a West Coast computer company executive vice president. "But I couldn't ignore the uneasiness of our company president, who was a husband in a traditional marriage. He obviously thought that it was terrible I wasn't home with my children even though he appreciated my contributions to the company. He just couldn't resolve it in his own mind."

At least this executive didn't say anything overt, unlike in past incidents that women cite. Carol has never forgotten her own story of accusatory questioning, symbolic of how men controlled the culture of her own family's company.

"I was interviewing for a new job with an executive in the company. His boss was in the room but wasn't saying much. The executive asked me a number of questions about my experience, and then said, 'What will you do if you get pregnant?'

"I was so stunned at the question that all I could do was give him a matter-of-fact, production-line answer: 'If I get pregnant it will take nine months and then I'll have a baby,' I replied. The ball was in his court. His boss left the room suddenly—to keep from laughing, I later found out. I obviously won points with my nonemotional answer, and I got the job.

The fact that women have children is obvious and many executive women said that if they take a matter-of-fact attitude toward childbirth, that factor alone has little or no impact on how they are perceived at work. What is more frustrating to mothers and nonmothers alike are ingrained stereotypes based on their biological differences that give rise to comments like those uttered by Gen. Robert H. Barrow. In a move some women saw as denying them the chance to earn promotions and become members of The Military Club, Barrow argued that women should not be allowed into combat. "Death. Dying. It's . . . uncivilized! And women *can't do it!* Nor should they even be thought of as doing it. The requirements of strength and endurance render them *unable* to do it. And I may be old-fashioned, but I think the very nature of women disqualifies them from doing it. Women give life. Sustain life. Nurture life. They don't *take* it."

The field of combat is not far from the world of noisy manufacturing plants, dirty construction sites, or dark and smoky international airport meetings in Moscow or Cairo. Stereotypes based on biological differences (or more precisely, prejudices) continue to keep women from critical business arenas.

Some women fear that biologists are now adding fuel to the fire over stereotyped gender differences. Despite the fact that almost every branch of the life sciences is now eagerly studying biological differences between the sexes, including issues of brain size and cognitive skills, the differences are statistically so small as to be meaningless. So we won't penalize men yet for being less intuitive than women because we know little about the impact of gender differences on outcomes.

Top executive women told us there are only two biological distinctions between men and women that count, but they more accurately describe them as issues of power and not gender. These two are the fact that women look different from men and they are generally not as strong as men. These differences do not affect all business environments equally, but they are certainly present.

The fact that a woman wears a skirt and can't get a man into a half nelson doesn't disqualify her for senior executive status, of course. The problem with these differences is subliminal, in perceptions, attitudes, and reactions. Executive women raise physical differences as issues because at one time or another they have had to face them and decide how to handle them.

"Everytime something like this comes up I think I'm the only one who has experienced it," said Julia Simons, describing an incident in which it was assumed she was the secretary taking notes and not the senior executive present at a meeting. "It's only after I talk with other executive women that I discover they've been through it too. Then we all regale each other with replaying the incidents and bemoaning 'what I should have done.' Well, next time we'll be better prepared."

The first barrier most women experience is visual. Women look different than men, making them immediately visible as "something other," not unlike blacks or Asians. Unless they take on a Yentl-like disguise and pretend to be men and go undercover in a man's world, the minute they walk into a room they are considered by some to be secondary. This is why some female reporters and writers use their initials instead of their first name and why other women insist on titles of address to reinforce their status. Women know they are always being sized up. Is she fat? Is she single? Is she attractive? Does she know anything? How did she get here? How shall I address her? Or worse, "since she's only a woman, she can't be the most important one here, and I'll spend my time talking to someone else."

Carol recalled one such instance as she was riding on a corporate jet to Greenbriar, to attend an annual retreat of selected retailing and food product chief executive officers being held at the exclusive resort hotel. The high-level junket brought together an exclusive group of corporate leaders and their spouses for three days of seminars that featured prominent national figures such as Henry Kissinger and Alexander Haig, along with a healthy dose of golf, tennis, and socializing.

As president of the multi-billion-dollar Stop & Shop Companies, Carol was invited to travel on the Nabisco corporate jet with her husband, the CEO of Stop & Shop. She took a seat next to a former banking executive, who was recently hired by RJR Nabisco to run its tobacco company.

"I said hello to him, and noted that he had a huge notebook in his lap—the statistical analysis book on the tobacco company prepared by KKR, the financiers that had bought Nabisco. Our company had just been bought by KKR, so I was intimately familiar with the overwhelming mass of data they produce," she said.

"I leaned over his shoulder and said, 'I see you're on the Team Nabisco chapter.' I was going to save him a lot of time and trouble and tell him where to concentrate in the book. I knew what it was like to come in and try to absorb a tremendous amount of information. As a member of The Club who'd been through it, I knew how KKR presented things. I could tell him just where to look, and suggest how I'd attack some easy areas, to be a hero early.

"Well, he must have been taken aback by what he thought was female aggressiveness. He clearly didn't want to talk to me, and got up from his seat, saying he'd like to introduce me to his wife. As he started to walk down the aisle of the plane, I said, 'Fine, but I'm not through talking to you about that book.'

"In two minutes he was back in his seat. Someone in the back of the plane had clued him in to the fact that I wasn't just a corporate spouse, that I was one of his biggest customers. He obviously had no idea who I was, and I can see why, since he was new to the company. But he started to listen carefully when I made a few more suggestions about the data book!"

Business settings where women have a professional reason for their presence are easier locations in which to overcome negative stereotypes than social settings. In many social gatherings, even the most powerful executive women are treated in a condescending manner, as having status only as the companion of a more powerful man.

"My husband and I were invited to spend five days cruising the Nile with six other couples," a senior-level Seattle investment banker recalled. "The men were all senior corporate executives or international financiers, and they totally ignored me, even though the group was small in number. I could have done Far East and Pacific Rim business with each one of them, but it was impossible to engage them in business conversation despite the fact that they were engaged in it throughout the trip. I finally gave up and just enjoyed the scenery."

"On the last day, one man did ask about my business," she recalled. "Evidently his wife told him that I was president of the Seattle Economic Club and had handled complex international transactions for companies like his. But they all saw me as 'someone's wife' and that's all—even though another man told me by the end of the trip he knew every man intimately and had planned to do future business with each one of them. For them, it wasn't just a vacation, but I was not in their sights. They thought only the men were worth talking to."

Women who are ignored or devalued by members of The Club because of their sex suggest the solution depends on the setting. In a business environment, she can insist upon respect and recognition, enlisting the help of a male partner, if necessary. In a social situation, the answers are: Remember it. Don't get mad. Get even. Or forget it.

When executive women who have been ignored rise to prominence in the business community, some may have a chance to turn the tables on those who have ignored them, because the difference in the way women look is not a one-way street. Few male business executives realize the extent to which women size up their environment, instinctively counting the number of other women in a room. Women repeatedly look for other women on the board, on the masthead, on the team making the presentation and understand that such pictures reflect more than just the unconscious habits of those who assembled the group. Those who are viewing an all-male group (or all-anything), whether it be on a conference panel, masthead, or board of directors, often find themselves fighting feelings of frustration and anger. This single picture "generates a sense of nobodiness" as one woman said, automatically placing those who are excluded in the category of outsider, unimportant, or subordinate. At the most human, subconscious level, then, a tension arises, as spectators struggle to process the message or character of the group with impartiality and ignore the subliminal signal that the spectators do not matter.

Dawn-Marie was invited to give a speech one summer at a major AT&T/Bell Laboratories facility on "The Myth of the Glass Ceiling." She walked into the large auditorium and noticed a row of photographs along one wall, solemn portraits of past plant managers. The all-white male lineup was striking—a megamessage, she told the audience. "If I were a female executive at this facility and wanted to assess my chances of moving ahead, this room sends me a not-so-subtle signal that the glass ceiling lives," she told the mixed audience. "If I were plant manager and wanted to convince a diverse work force that there was equal opportunity for all, I'd replace these photographs with pictures of men and women interacting together and with clients out in the field. The megamessage about inclusiveness would change instantly, without one word being spoken," she suggested.

The visual message companies send about who is valued is loud and clear to women and minorities, but not all corporate executives understand the power of the signal. They miss the visual impact of biological differences, a shorthand way women keep score.

"Let's all call a press conference on the front steps. We can assemble all the leading women in town to cut our charge cards in half in front of the cameras," one angry stockbroker suggested to a female lawyer. Their favorite retail store had just gone public after a successful leveraged buyout, making its top executives multimillionaires. The women didn't begrudge the chain its success; they supported its growth enthusiastically, spending thousands of dollars there annually. They cheered when the leveraged buyout saved it from a corporate raider; they were ready to buy its stock three years later.

But they were stunned and then furious when they read the prospectus and discovered that the company had no women on its board of directors, despite making its profits from female customers and employing a primarily female work force.

"I know the chairman and the president," said a former retailing executive. "They're not doing this deliberately, I'm sure. They probably didn't realize how it would come across."

"That's the problem," retorted the stockbroker. "Men look at women and think 'lesser' or 'unnecessary.' Women look at a lineup of men and think 'excluded.' It's nothing short of insulting to the thousands of women in this town who helped make them successful."

Not all men are oblivious to how a company's image comes across. Some men are now flagging the megamessage that companies send with an all (usually white) male lineup.

Dawn-Marie was selected to join the search committee to nominate the next president of a major human service agency upon the retirement of its incumbent head. The committee, comprised of several directors, balanced corporate executives and community leaders, as well as the past and present chairmen of the board.

At its first meeting, the committee decided to hire a national executive search firm to help it uncover the very best individuals for this once-in-a-decade chance to choose an important community leader. The salary was well into six figures, and the size of the agency guaranteed that excellent national candidates would apply. The search process itself was a unique opportunity to send a strong signal to the entire community about the diversity of the agency, and the committee was seriously committed to including women and minorities as candidates for the position.

The group quickly settled on two search firms, but Dawn-Marie requested that a third be added to the list. She served on another board with its local managing director, and was impressed with him. She secretly hoped that his firm would win the assignment but she knew the firm first needed a chance to be considered by the committee.

The week before the scheduled interview, each member of the committee received a package of information from the search firm, including its glossy annual report. When Dawn-Marie opened it and looked through it, her heart sank, but she was silent.

Unfortunately, one of her male committee members was not. Just before the firm's delegation arrived for the interview, he held up the two-page photo spread of the firm's national board of directors for the rest of the committee to see. "What's wrong with this picture?" he asked. The all-white male lineup in the annual report spoke for itself. Dawn-Marie knew that there was little the search firm representatives could say in the interview to convince the committee that they understood why and how to do a serious search for women and minority candidates. They didn't get the assignment.

PHYSICAL DIFFERENCES: DANGER ZONE

Obviously, differences between men and women are not just visual or subtle. They are physical, and men and women are not equal in physical strength or their ability to withstand attack. Former governor Madeleine Kunin of Vermont was asked to compare her semester at Harvard's Kennedy School of Government with her appointment as Radcliffe College's Distinguished Fellow in Public Policy at the Bunting Institute. The Bunting, the country's first and largest multidisciplinary think tank for women, was specifically designed as a supportive climate for female scholars.

"It's like the difference between testosterone and estrogen," Kunin said.

The Kennedy School is not inherently a dangerous place for women, but Kunin's simile expresses the caution many women instinctively feel in even the most innocuous male-dominated environments, and why executive women raise their vulnerability to violence as the other biological difference that matters. "Women lead their lives in fear of violence," said Dr. Carol Nadelson of Boston, the first woman president of the American Psychiatric Association. "Men never do. They don't know what it is like."

Issues around violence are extremely complex, but they are basic to gender differences. Women believe that violence is inextricably bound up with the masculine sense of self, even though most men do not behave that way. But the fact that men have the capacity to be violent is enough to make many women naturally fearful. Women also express violence, but often as a defensive response to situations that make them fearful rather than as an offensive approach to a weaker person. It is the difference in experience and perception of violence in society that relates to one's gender, not necessarily the behavior itself.

Few male corporate executives are that violent, of course. They exemplify good manners, and may be particularly chivalrous to women. But by the same token, few men are afraid of physical harm and therefore are not as conscious of the role that violence against women plays in American society, including the business world.

Many executive women do not relax easily in new situations, having learned to be on guard against the unknown. Is the parking lot empty? Is the general area around the hotel considered safe? Can she go out to a meeting or dinner alone or with a male business acquaintance? Can she jog in the morning? If a stranger approaches her, what should her response be? Even if she appears calm and pleasant on the outside, she is alert and suspicious inside. There is no foolproof way to distinguish a man who will harm a woman from one who will not, and it is just her gender that may make her a victim. Women have reason to be cautious. C. Everett Koop, the former surgeon general, has identified violence against women as the number one health problem for American women, causing more injuries than automobile accidents, muggings, and rapes combined.

Koop may be in a class by himself in understanding violence as an ever-present, nagging threat to women, but a male lobbyist in Texas related how his own consciousness was raised on the issue. "It was about four-thirty on a Friday afternoon, and I went in the basement entrance of the state capital building," he said. "I stepped in the elevator next to a woman I had never seen before, and I ignored her, but I sensed she stiffened when I got in the elevator with her. We were the only two in the elevator.

"We rode up to the fourth floor together in silence, and I let her step off first. She walked a little faster then I did, but I followed her down the empty hall, past closed or empty offices. I suddenly realized how much heavier my footsteps sounded, coming after her, and I noticed she picked up her pace a little.

"There was no one around, and at the intersection of the corridors, by the governor's office, she turned right. So did I, sounding as if I were deliberately stalking after her. The corridor we were walking led to a dead end except for emergency stair exits. The speaker's office is the last office on the right, and by the time she got there, she pulled the door open fast and rushed in. I followed her; as it happened, we both had appointments there, but when I saw her flushed face, I knew I must have scared the daylights out of her. Believe me, until that moment, I had no idea how I must have come across to her. And here I am, harmless! But I suddenly realized what women go through all the time."

We think the lobbyist is an unusually sensitive man, which is one reason he has a cadre of close female friends in the business and political world. More often we heard stories like that of Marjorie Stevenson,* newly appointed vice president of a major teaching hospital and medical center.

"I was attending my second meeting of the management committee and we were reviewing capital budget requests for the coming year. The vice president of operations listed his priorities, and then quickly ran through his secondary list. When he skimmed over upgraded lighting for the parking garage, my eyes caught those of the vice president of nursing, the only other woman on the committee. We had the same reaction, and spoke up at once. That expenditure was a top priority for us, and we finally convinced the others around the table that our staff, patients, and visitors would consider it a priority as well. But if we hadn't been there, and presented our arguments forcefully, I'm not sure it would have occurred to the others that lighting was so important."

Marjorie Stevenson and other executive women have used their positions to sensitize business peers and change workplace policies to improve the general climate of safety for women. As the numbers of working women and their influence increase, workplaces, hotels, and other public environments may become less dangerous for all and social tolerance for violence against women may decrease.

Women's sensitivity to threats of violence is only partially based on biological differences that make them generally smaller, weaker, and less able to defend themselves against attack. Women's socialization and life experience may account for traits of caution, dependence, and passivity, which are found more often in women than in men and which impact their later achievement in the business world. Most women were raised differently than their male peers; they are trying hard not to let it matter.

SHORTCHANGING GIRLS, SHORTCHANGING BUSINESS

Top executive women can look back at their own socialization and pinpoint with accuracy those defining moments that stacked the deck against them. These women who have succeeded in male-dominated business cultures stress the need for women to remember and overcome early acculturation. It is bad enough when others treat women differently, but for women to perpetuate their own handicaps is worse.

Leslie Mardenborough, vice president of human resources for the *New York Times,* had to work hard to overcome early socialization that created barriers of unrelenting self-doubt.

"I was guilty of a subtle behavior of sending off signals that I wasn't confident because I wasn't competent. I was doing that to myself. Even when I was promoted, I thought there was something wrong with the picture. I felt I wasn't the most competent because I didn't *know everything that everyone else collectively knew.*"

Why did Mardenborough feel she had to be perfect and know everything to succeed, whereas a man who won a similar promotion might very well see the promotion as an affirmation of his own self-worth? The socialization process starts early. Adults respond differently to male and female children, as any woman who has picked up a crying toddler can attest. Boys are encouraged to be independent and girls are comforted. Passivity and dependence in girls are not negative traits; aggression and separation are applauded in boys. A girl's self-esteem lessens as she grows older, while a boy's confidence rises. Even the most well meaning parents who attempt to balance the social culture, putting dolls in boys' hands and trucks in girls' hands, find themselves up against peer pressure and the mores of the playground and schoolyard.

As one gender sensitive mother recalls, "At Halloween, when my daughter was eight, I tried to encourage her to be Robin Hood or the captain of a ship, or even the devil; but she would be satisfied with nothing less than the frilliest ballerina tutu. I'm sure it was her revenge on her feminist mother!"

From preadolescence on, young girls have an exaggerated notion of the importance of being liked. The behavior of "good girl" works for them, as they bring home rewards from school, summer camp, and church for behaving in deferential and sweet ways. The attributes of caregiver, nurturer, and peacemaker are learned early, practiced on dolls and friends, and reinforced in books. Being nice is more important than achieving other goals, especially if the latter requires competition and aggressive behavior. Achievement for girls often means being well behaved and perfect in everything.

Leslie Mardenborough is working hard to recognize the effect of these social behaviors on her own career. "One issue that derails male and female executives," Mardenborough said, "is failing to respond to feedback. I received some important feedback from a friend who berated me for not accepting friendship. I've always been the one who helped. I'm not the one who asks for help, because that would be giving up control. So I'm working on this!"

Dr. Nadelson explains why overcoming these early socializations are important in the business world. "The so-called feminine characteristics of responsiveness, accommodation, and nurturance make it difficult for many women to assume and project authority. They may feel uncomfortable about relinquishing these traits or allowing the emergence of others that have been characterized as masculine. Conflict is generated between their needs for competence and success and the comfort of a socially sanctioned role and style, despite its lack of fit or reward."

Nadelson's observation about the conflict between how society tells women to act and how it receives female voices of authority is critical to understand if women are to be visible in The Club, as the next chapter reveals. But Nadelson also zeroes in on a basic career dilemma for many women: How hard should they push to get ahead if being liked by men is important to their female psyche?

Many executive women who have joined The Club ranks said they were blessed with a family that reinforced achievement and ignored gender stereotypes.

"When I was growing up, I never heard the difference between boys and girls," said Therese Maloney, executive vice president of the Liberty Mutual Insurance Company. "We were always told, 'You are a Maloney.' That's where we got our self-esteem. Maloneys were good in math. Maloneys excelled in school," Therese recalled.

"I was also a good listener at dinner conversations. My dad was born in 1880. He had two female cousins; one was the treasurer of the World Peace Foundation, and the other was a key executive in a wool import business. When they'd come to dinner at our house on Sunday, he'd say to one, 'So, what's going on in the world?' and to the other, 'So, how is business?' Their opinions mattered to him, and I grew up knowing that women could have opinions on such topics."

Unfortunately, even the Therese Maloneys of the world who were not handicapped by their own upbringing find themselves on the receiving end of gender stereotypes and slurs due to the socialization of others. Women who entered the business and professional world in the late sixties and early seventies all have stories of facing discrimination, exclusion, or odd treatment, usually at the hands of men. For example, Dr. Matina S. Horner, former president of Radcliffe College, recalls her first lecture as a new member of the Harvard faculty in 1971:

"I was then one of four women on the 793-member Faculty of Arts and Sciences at Harvard. There was one woman on the tenured faculty in a position reserved for the woman appointed to the Radcliffe Zemurray Professorship. The ratio of men to women in the undergraduate student body was four to one versus today's 1.3 to one. There were virtually no women in high administrative positions. At the end of that lecture about a dozen young Harvard men came up to me to explain that they had no intention of taking psychology but wanted to see 'what it felt like to be lectured at by a woman and to see if a woman could be articulate.' It was a rather stunning experience to realize that the articulateness of all womanhood was on trial by the success or failure of my first lecture as a professor at Harvard."

While the business and professional world has welcomed more women to its ranks in the two decades since Horner's psychology lecture, gender stereotypes still persist.

"Our bank was selling off one of its most profitable divisions," said the executive vice president to whom the division reported. "We had made the decision to sell on purely economic terms, but the new owners were from outside the state and hundreds of jobs would be lost. All of the senior management team supported the decision, but we were mindful of the emotional and political effect it would have when it was announced to the public.

"The president of the division and I were discussing this in the presence of one of our investment bankers from a large Wall Street firm. He was a typical young 'Master-of-the-Universe' type, who had little sympathy for the workers. While my job certainly wasn't at stake, he turned to me and said, 'Don't worry, you can always just open a dress boutique.'

"I couldn't think of an appropriate response in time, so I let it pass. But if I had been a black career banker twice his age, I suspect he wouldn't have told me I could always just go open a watermelon stand. The truth is that it is more acceptable to be sexist than racist in the business world."

Taboos against overt racism are firmly in place in the business and professional world, but misunderstandings about how to treat women are still widespread. It is probably not an exaggeration to say that every senior executive woman has experienced a sexist comment, slur, or condescending form of address in her career. While none of them rises to the level of sex discrimination, they certainly occur because of gender differences and the cultural stereotyping or prejudices of the one who expresses them. Most women, however, like the banker dealing with the executive from Wall Street, let such remarks pass.

"I hate to let it go, but I usually do," said an appeals court judge in California. "There is a relationship between language and social thought, and sexist language helps to perpetuate a sexist society. But I save my public rebukes of my colleagues and peers for those times that really count and try to let the rest slide. I think women have to be careful not to appear too sensitive or fragile. Sometimes I'll try to use humor and turn it around, but on the 'small stuff' I don't go around embarrassing people. And in the scheme of things, I can't honestly say it bothers me *that* much."

What is interesting, however, is how many women of her professional stature have remembered the sexist incidents in their past, even to the precise detail of where they were, who else was in the room, and how they felt. To them, at their core, these stories are not just minor annoyances. They are important because women who are now in leadership positions in many economic institutions have shared these experiences in common, histories and stories that are not shared by men.

Many of these women began working in the business world battling the establishment for equal rights, correcting inequalities that kept them out, or enduring unusual scrutiny or snappy comments merely because of their gender. They began their careers in an era that perpetuated the "good girl" standard. They were protected from achievement and the energizing fulfillment that many men experience in a career for their own good, they were told.

One California court finally got it right, invalidating a state law prohibiting women from tending bar, saying, "The pedestal upon which women have been placed has all too often, upon closer inspection, been revealed as a cage." It was just two decades ago that courts started to strike down barriers that kept women from such nontraditional jobs, airlines were prohibited from firing female flight attendants based on their age or marital status, and women finally could become Rhodes Scholars, astronauts, and Episcopal bishops.

Understandably, the male peers of today's executive women simply cannot relate to the experience of women whose qualifications, initiative, dedication, and personal family plans were once called into question at various stages in their careers.

Sally Frame Kasaks, chairman and chief executive officer of Ann Taylor, remembers applying for a bank loan early in her career as a retailer. "Women couldn't get credit in those days without our husband's or father's signature. I was furious and vowed to be financially independent from that day on."

Like Kasaks, women who have lived through these experiences have not forgotten these incidents, nor the pervasive impact that socialization has on both men and women.

INSTITUTIONAL ROADBLOCKS

Socialization that sanctions only certain roles or behavior for women, and a culture that reinforces these limitations, are only one side of the "difference" equation. The very way that our business and professional world is structured sometimes impacts negatively on women. A corporation's physical surroundings and status symbols, age bias, lack of mentoring, hidden promotional criteria, and the corporate culture itself are all factors that must be reexamined to understand their effect on both sexes.

This is not to say that all business structures are inherently wrong; in many instances, the rules and culture serve valid purposes, and it is women who must adapt to them. The requirement of line experience or rainmaking success for senior management positions makes sense. In other instances, however, factors within the workplace serve only to perpetuate the status quo and make it difficult for women to advance, such as a refusal to try staff executives in line jobs or to allow flexibility in career paths. Businesses that are content to rely upon just half of the power, talent, and brains of the country don't have to think about institutional roadblocks. Businesses that want to attract and retain the best talent must look hard at issues they may have ignored.

Some institutional barriers are so obvious that women feel excluded right from the beginning, when they walk into the lobby of the company's office building. Alice Friedman, chairman of the architecture department at Wellesley College, explained: "The concept of tall office buildings as an example of power and hierarchy is an argument at various levels of symbolism: the skyscraper as phallic substitute, an analogy for hierarchy, and the association of both of those with patriarchy."

These environmental concepts are subtle but real. From churches to private clubs, women have experienced how our environment reinforces the separation of individuals, and the dominance of one group over another. Often, architecture and interior design serve to reinforce existing power relations, usually that of men over women.

When an executive woman who works on the thirty-sixth floor emerges from the elevator, she may feel more at home, depending on the internal structure of the offices. Offices often emanate out from a conference room, and those who work there feel comfortable going among them. But if she is a visitor, calling on executives, she may walk off the elevator to face another barrier. Usually she will face a woman, guarding and ministering to the needs of a male group. Her role is to keep others from having access to those in power. A male visitor may automatically feel superior to the female receptionist, assuming she is there to minister to him too, and not be put off. But not all women will feel that way.

The trappings of the office environment also send megamessages. Portraits of male company founders and primarily male sporting scenes portrayed in paintings or photographs convey a different image than quilts hung on the walls and plants. Alice Friedman suggest that a deliberate strategy of combining a work environment with the qualities of a private environment works best to convey an atmosphere of inclusion.

Friedman warns, "Even within a space that is theoretically open to you, there can be a division. For example, in a faculty club of a university or in an executive dining room, there may be a designated table for individuals to sit at if they have not planned to meet anyone. But if every day the only ones who sit there are older male senior executives or chaired faculty, there is no way a woman would feel that it was her place too."

The resilient future senior executive officer has made it past the receptionist, however, and she is now in the executive suite, perhaps for a job interview. It is here she may test another institutional barrier: a rigid notion of what a female executive looks like. Her age may now impact upon her future success in a way that a man's age would not.

Many companies and professions welcome young women into their employee ranks. "A man will give an attractive woman a chance," said one psychologist, "but not when she gets a few gray hairs. Then she looks too much like his mother, especially if she comes across as tough. It's called transference."

But how many institutions will be as willing to hire an entry-level executive, first-year associate, or college instructor at age forty, forty-five, or fifty? The candidate may have twenty to thirty productive years ahead, but many institutions won't consider her because she doesn't fit their image of a new executive. Some men may find themselves in the same situation, but there are fewer men who are entering the workplace for the first time in middle age, with only parenting or community experience on their résumé.

The age question is not just an idle inquiry. It impacts greatly on women, because of the differences in the life cycles of men and women. Some women may very well be starting the best years of their lives at forty. Many become more assured, aggressive, and enthusiastic about taking risks as they get older, having thrown off the cloak of insecurity and self-doubt left festering at younger years. A woman of mid-adulthood is often most challenged and energetic, particularly since in many cases the demands of her children and her spouse's career obligations may be behind her.

Two factors—early socialization that diminish her self-confidence as a young adult, and family responsibilities that become her priority—directly impact upon how she measures up to her male peers. She may look equal on paper at age twenty-two, but is it any wonder that, at thirty, thirty-five, or forty, men have surpassed her? Many women don't care about the age at which they restart a dynamic career. They are not out to keep score with men their own age. But companies and professions are not as forgiving or flexible. Institutional structures and prejudices are partially to blame. In academia, for example, a professor must generally be reviewed for tenure within six to eight years after a first teaching post. There is rarely an opportunity to keep on working; a professor without tenure is "up or out." In the private practice of law, even those law firms that allow associates to go "off track" for a few years generally require that partnership decisions be made within ten years of an associate's hire. As in academia, nonpartners are usually out.

The same scrutiny is required in the corporate world. How many companies actively seek "older" women and are willing to invest the training and supervision that will produce a talented and seasoned executive? It is often easier to make assumptions about what these women will do (quit, get tired of working, follow their retired spouse to the golf course, lose interest). But many women's lives do not lay out neatly along a traditional corporate or professional model of entry-level training program at twenty-four, first vice presidency at thirty-four, and senior executive status at forty-four. A supremely confident, well-educated, and mature female candidate may want to begin a career at forty-four, after her family responsibilities or a first career are over.

The corporate world hasn't really understood the relationship between being a highly successful career woman and a successful parent, suggested one corporate lawyer who entered law school after teaching high school for ten years. "Can you start a career today at age forty?" she asked. "In 1975, women could enter professions late, be trained, and have a successful career. Because of a growing economy and particularly the presence of affirmative action lawsuits and initiatives, many professional schools and companies opened their doors wide to find more women. They welcomed homemakers, schoolteachers, and social workers who wanted a start at a new career. Now, in part because of the shrinking of management levels, neither men nor women can do that."

Catherine Atwater, the international management consultant, expressed her frustration watching a close friend try to knock down corporate doors.

"My own company recruits just on business school campuses and I see how limiting that can be. I know for a fact that women can enter the work force at an older age and be productive. One of my close friends from college was divorced at age fifty. She went back to a fine private university for some tough finance courses, and then started interviewing. She called on many of her social peers, senior captains of industry, who were polite but patronizing. They simply didn't see her in the role of an entry-level executive.

"Finally I suggested she ignore all her male contemporaries and interview with an aggressive forty-year-old male she hoped to work for. I knew they'd be impressed with how serious and mature she was, and they were. She got a good job with an international office product manufacturer, went back and got her M.B.A. at night, and is a success story at age sixty. But it was needlessly difficult for her, and a number of companies missed out on a very good manager."

Unlike Catherine's friend, some younger women have found easy entry into the business and professional world only to find that institutional structures are barriers to advancement once they get there. We are able to understand why this happens, thanks to the pioneering work of psychologists who challenged the male model of adulthood as the mature and correct one. It is not enough to state that girls are socialized differently than boys, and that by the time they are adults they should be able to overcome this handicap. We also have to acknowledge—tiptoeing through gender generalizations about an entire sex—that a significant body of research in the last decade makes a case that gender development leads to differing personality traits and moral perspectives in adult women. These are not biases that must be reprogrammed to a male model; they are authentic on their own, and their effect in the business and professional world is real.

In her book, *In a Different Voice*, Harvard professor Carol Gilligan argued that men and women approach and resolve situations of moral conflict differently; women value relationships, empathy, and caring more then hierarchy, rights, and rules. "The sequence of women's moral judgment proceeds from an initial concern with survival to a focus on goodness and finally to a reflective understanding of care as the most adequate guide to the resolution of conflicts in human relationships," Gilligan wrote.

While not all psychologists agree with Gilligan's theory, for many executive women, this difference between a "care perspective" and a "justice perspective" explains why many of them experience the same set of circumstances differently than their male peers, and may have an equally valid viewpoint to express.

"Every significant disagreement I've had with our senior executive group involves the treatment of employees," a Los Angeles high-technology executive related. "On business goals and strategies we agree, and we even agree about tough decisions like terminations or plant closings. But how it's done, and how people are handled, have provoked major fights. Luckily, I've prevailed. They see no problem with approving a capital expenditure to refurbish the executive dining room or restripe the parking lot the same week we announce that eight hundred employees will be laid off. I suggested we spend the money on outplacement counseling instead. You know, sometimes they just don't think."

This concern for others and the preservation of relationships creates a conflict for some women who have chosen a profession in which strict rules and adversarial procedures dominate the resolution of conflict. Because of the separate development routes taken by men and women, and the social environment in which they work and live, women approach the business world with a set of values, vision, and understanding that may not conform to the male-designed workplace culture. "Most boys gain a vision suited for a world of advocacy, stoic detachment, autonomy and suspension of emotional judgment. Girls' development usually instills sensitivity to others' feelings, cooperation, involvement and contextual understanding," concluded two Harvard researchers in a study of men and women lawyers. Another study of reasons why men and women left the law profession revealed that many women reflected "a general ethos of hyper-masculine legal culture," leaving such firms "because the only other choice was to adopt these values as their own."

Some theorists see the definition of women as wives and mothers as explaining other major differences between men and women. Women's sense of self is being able to maintain a connection to others and the world, psychologists argue. Women live in a private, more domestic world of relationships where "Who are you?" is answered by "wife, mother, friend." On the other hand, men value separation, living in a public world of occupational identity ("I am a banker, doctor, lawyer, CEO").

But some executive women disagree with those who state that relationships are paramount to women because of their unique ability to mother and their concern with family. Sally Berger describes this concern with relationships as a different style that women have in dealing with others and exercising power.

"Women shouldn't behave like men; they don't have to in order to exercise power. I'm a host on a television show. The thing I do best is to take care of my guests. I make them comfortable. There are two ways to treat a guest: make them shake in their boots and be awed by someone else who has power and control over them at that moment, or it can be the other way. I find that it's very natural for women to take care of guests and there is a certain power you can exercise in making people feel good about themselves and comfortable in your hands."

But the implication of this research is profound for an American business world in which the ideals of individualism, status, singular achievement, and competition are paramount. It would be a mistake for American business to promote only women who fit the male model and ignore the rest, much the way psychologists stubbornly acknowledged and heard only one gender's voice until recently.

Businesses that seek the talent of both genders will reexamine their own culture, from top to bottom, to see if gender differences affect what women strive for and what they achieve. The glass ceiling may just turn out to be nothing more than a misfit between a male-created business culture and the psychological development and life experiences of adult

women who work there. Some executive women are not convinced that
the differences between men and women are biologically or psychologically based, or that a sufficient number of women fit the patterns to make
any generalizations accurate. In this, they are like the question of how many
Zen Buddhists does it take to change a light bulb? (Answer, two, one to
change it and one not to change it.) There are two natures in every individual. Like the Zen Buddhist, an executive is male and not male, female and not
female. Therefore the behavior, experience, and sociological environment of
women as well as men warrant attention by corporate executives who are
making a sincere attempt to understand and accommodate diversity.

The very question of titles illustrates the issue. Many women are socialized to achieve vicariously through others, and to contribute to their
success, as Professor Rosener noted. The importance they place on relationships outweighs the status accorded to them. As Julia Simons* said,
women do not necessarily find their sole self-identity at work, regardless of
their corporate title. Men who hold occupational status as the sole mark of
esteem therefore may view women who are blasé about titles as ambivalent about their careers, when that may not be the case at all.

Carol unknowingly acted out this precise scenario in 1963, not understanding the importance of titles. "I was director of advertising, and I was
having difficulty getting people in the company to respond to my direction, even getting out the weekly newspaper ad," she said. "My boss, who
was the president of the supermarket division, wanted to promote me to be
vice president of advertising and sales promotion. I thought he was telling
me that I couldn't get my job done without a title, and that the quality of
my work wasn't good. I was too naive to know that when you join executive ranks, people look at your title. The day after my promotion was announced, everyone was more cooperative. Boy, did I learn a lesson!"

Women who are unimpressed with titles feel that they are in many
cases a false measure of achievement, and therefore are reluctant to accord
the proper amount of deference to a title when the person holding it is
undeserving. They see right through the facade. But men use titles to tell
who the players are, just as they rely on rules to regulate the marketplace
game.

Gilligan's explanation of women's concern for caring and relational
responsibilities may help explain the frustration many executive women
feel when confronted with rules that make little sense, or rules for the sake

of rules. Rules in some cases are unyielding structures that do nothing to enhance productivity or take into account situations of men and women with families. These rules make it difficult for some women to advance in their professions, adding to their frustration and resulting in a loss of talent for American business and institutions. In these cases, women argue, rules are only a means of enforcing the dominance of one individual over another and do little to achieve the objectives of the parties.

One judge discussed her frustration with rules of the court system that are enforced for her but ignored for others. "I'm a single parent of two young children, and the chief justice knows it. When I was first appointed to the bench, I was assigned to a court near my home town, and that was fine. But then the chief switched me to a court fifty miles away. I can't drop off my kids at school until eight-thirty, and judges are expected to show up at nine, even though sessions don't usually start until ten. The clerks in the court complained around that I was always late, so of course the chief heard about it. Now I have a reputation as 'that woman who can't get to court on time.' Of course there are plenty of male judges who also show up late, or worse, take off for the afternoon at one o'clock, but the chief has ignored them for years. Rules are just convenient for when he wants to use them."

The conflict between adherence to unbending professional standards (with its unrelenting deference to hierarchy and status) and a human concern for moral choices plagues women who must keep proving their allegiance to rules set by others. Arlene Fitch* is a manufacturing executive in Detroit who never forgot one unpleasant incident at a former company.

"I had an appalling boss, and was asked to do something I felt was unethical and illegal: lie about a black employee that he didn't want to promote. I refused. He said, 'Are you willing to stake your career on this guy?' I said, 'My career doesn't depend on him or you or this job.' After that, whenever anything came up, he always said, 'Oh, I forgot, you don't care about your career.'" Her determination to take a moral stand regarding an employee instead of siding with her supervisor may not be unique to her gender, but it is the kind of story we heard frequently from executive women.

Adherence to informal rules can be just as important as stated rules in helping women pass the tests of career advancement, but without a guide, many women miss them. Worse, in a culture of rigid rules and behavioral norms, some women don't even realize they've missed them. "When I started in the bank it was like learning to dance with a new partner," an executive vice president said. "I watched how men behaved, and paid attention to who spoke when.

"I also figured out I was paying attention to the wrong things," she said. "For example, I would get all worked up about our annual performance reviews. I took them at face value and honestly believed for a long time that my performance as measured against agreed-upon goals for the prior year would determine my advancement. That was only partially true. What was equally important was how I got along with everyone and whether I was perceived as loyal to the chairman and the present group in command. I had to show, in as many ways as possible, that I was a full-fledged, enthusiastic member of the team. *That* was a rule that no one told me. Once I was on the team, my assignments got better, I supervised a larger group of people, and I added some line responsibilities to my staff functions. But none of that happened because I met my numerical goals of last year."

While the guidance of other executive women and, occasionally, a male peer, can help ease the entry into the business and professional world for women, sadly, most women have to go it alone. They are up against a world of rules, informal or otherwise, deference to dominance, and a culture of self-promotion. Some women find these jarring aspects of the business culture grating against their own innate values. This discomfort is bound to have an impact on how women succeed in male-dominated environments. For example, if it is true, as Dr. Nadelson suggests, that women are reluctant to boast of their own achievements, preferring to help others be successful, how well do women fare in annual performance reviews, which are structured to measure individual achievement? It is the exceptional company that not only recognizes teamwork but rates individual contributions to the overall team. Matching evaluation processes to a female style of professional achievement that favors preserving relationships over individual scorekeeping is not just theoretical fodder for psychologists and journalists. It may be one key to the door of The Corporate Club.

Another key is the criteria companies and institutions use in evaluating executives or in establishing qualifications for promotion or appointment. The "criteria factor" is often the battleground between male-created business cultures and the very qualities that make women different from men.

One female scholar called it the "too game," by which women are excluded from serious consideration for top jobs. They are dismissed for having a quality that men regard as negative but would be acceptable in a man (my "right" is your "wrong").

"One women brought a multimillion-dollar grant to her institution, but when the chair of her department opened up, she didn't get the job. They gave it to a guy. She was told she is 'too difficult' and 'too hard to get along with.' There aren't male department chairs who aren't hard to get along with and difficult?" she asked.

"The flip side of 'too' is 'enough.' They'll say she is 'not enough of a leader' or 'she's not tough enough.' The answer is that women have to get themselves in positions of power where they can influence the process, on the search committees or in senior management. Then they have to question the criteria. What does 'leadership skills' mean, after all? It usually means something different to men than it does to women."

A woman who serves on the board of directors of a large health maintenance organization said the pleasure of "being a grownup" was the opportunity to open her mouth at board meetings about criteria. "We had hired a search firm to find our next chief executive officer," she said, "and they had come to the board meeting with their proposed job description, a five-page enumeration of the qualities they were looking for. It was obvious to me they had written it for a candidate they had already identified. If that was the case, I wanted it clear from the beginning how he was going to answer to me, so I said, 'Where in this writeup is a requirement of the person's commitment to diversity, at all levels of the organization?' There was a thunderous silence, but I waited. After some shuffling, the others agreed it must be a part of the criteria."

Joan Burke, executive resource officer of the John Hancock Company, believes that companies can solve the "too" or "enough" problem by making sure that women get the experience and feedback they need early enough in their career. Burke's chief responsibility at Hancock is to act as an inside-the-company search firm, monitoring high-potential candidates among 1,200 of the company's 8,000 home-office grade-A-level executives. She makes sure there are no glass ceilings or glass walls inside Hancock to derail women and minorities.

"I lay the tracks for the fast trackers," she said, explaining how Hancock helps prepare its best executives for The Club inside Hancock. Its senior officer level includes only 14 percent women, but because Burke's high-potential group is 40 percent female, she predicts many more will be ready for senior management positions.

"We look for a proven track record and superb managerial skills," Burke said. "Our job is to make sure that executives have a chance to get those experiences and that they get honest feedback. We make sure they get exposure to senior management, specialized training, outside board assignments, and the best academic programs we can find. We move them into job assignments where they can show us what they can do."

Burke is sensitive about how difficult it is for some women to make it to the top levels at Hancock, particularly if they are not prepared to take charge of their own development, and seek out the variety of professional assistance Burke's office can offer.

Hancock is a particularly good culture for women, as Diane Capstaff discovered. Not all companies are as serious about being gender-blind to talent. From the outside, however, it is difficult to pierce through the veil of acceptable equal opportunity numbers and discern the real environment. Sometimes the only window inside a company is to talk to other women in the industry, women who have worked for the company in the past, or members of women's professional networking organizations who may have built bridges to company executives. The presence of women in top management and women on the board of directors is sometimes a good indication, but not the only one.

Some companies tout the number of women in top management ranks, but the reality is entirely different. A retired male New York broadcasting executive recalled with embarrassment how his company made the numbers look good. "We gave vice president titles to women who were in corporate communications, publicity, and even the librarian, and we congratulated ourselves on having women at the senior executive levels. But the truth is we'd never let any women into sales, engineering, or programming."

In companies in which entrenched men dominate the powerful departments and bar entry to women, the "criteria" and "culture" barriers are still formidable. Barbara Heard,* senior vice president of one of the nation's largest financial service companies, sees it firsthand.

"It is amazing to look at how corporations hire people at the top level. The more talented people go by the wayside if they don't fit in. 'Chemistry' is important. The boys think they need someone who takes orders. Working with people you like and respect is the equivalent of good working culture and chemistry. I never confronted the question of what to do if someone says, 'I simply don't like her because she's a woman.' Executives are too sophisticated to say *that*, but I know what the code words are when it's simply a matter of chemistry. 'No teamwork' are the words they will use instead to reject someone. It means the same."

Chemistry among top executives sets the culture in the organization, and often women don't fit. It takes a healthy dose of stoic resolve to work well in those environments, particularly when a woman is isolated as the most senior female executive. The temptation to leave may be great, but women who have stuck it out insist change can happen.

"I believe women are different from many senior executive men, and our approach to relationships and dealing with people will win out over time," said a banker who had survived the collapse of her institution, once led by an aggressive egomaniac.

"At the bank, people all down the line were very nasty because the CEO was nasty and confrontational. He would yell, call names, and take no prisoners. I worked for a CEO clone, but I was determined to hold my ground with him. One day he yelled at someone who worked for me, and I told him, 'You won't do that again. If you have a problem, see me first.'

"He did it again, so I went into his office and sweetly said, 'Is there anything I can do for you?' He said, 'Why?' I said, 'Because you are overloaded and tense.' Then it dawned on him. He said, 'I did it again.'

"Then, before I went on vacation, I sat down with him to talk about how he'd deal with my people while I was gone. I told him they were nervous about my going away, and why. When I came back, he was pleased because he'd behaved—just like a child.

"The tone starts at the top," she said. "A new CEO can change the tone of the bank in an instant. It happened here, after the regulators and the board got rid of our former guy. The old attitude was to 'kiss up to the chairman and kick ass to the staff to get what you want.' Not anymore."

An advertising executive listened to this story and realized that the attention women pay to relationships in the workplace is not unique to one industry. Executive women can use their power to change the culture in many places, as she herself had done. "You know, women in top positions really are role models for how relationships must work in the office," she said. "I remember one point when two peers reported to me, a man and a woman. One day the man yelled at the woman in the hallway. I'm ordinarily very calm, but when I heard about it, I 'lost it.' I called him in and told him in the strongest tones I've ever used, 'You'll never do that again.' He changed his behavior fast, and it didn't take long for the story to filter down through the company."

In ways that matter in the business world, men and women are different. This does not necessarily mean that men must change or women must change. We are confident that the business and professional world will rapidly accommodate many different styles of work and an increasingly diverse work force. But women cannot rely on the popular business media to present a diverse picture. Businesswomen are still largely invisible to the outside world, hindering their acceptance in The Club.

CHAPTER FOUR

DEVELOPING PERSONAL CURRENCY

"I could tell the writer had a preconceived negative point of view about my life. On the day of the
interview, I was on an all-time high. I had just
finished our successful initial public offering, and
even my kids were excited about it. . . . I had just
had a great vacation break—but the writer refused to portray a happy, well-adjusted executive
woman who loves her work!

—Phyllis Swersky, former executive
vice president, A.I. Corp.

M any women have already learned how increasing their name recognition among opinion leaders can enhance their power in their own business or
profession. It is often an important ingredient in success at rainmaking.

Reputational visibility within the larger business and civic community
is also a key strategy to moving women into The Club. To wield power and
influence in The Club, a woman must first be known as an individual who
deserves to be there. Because of her personal or professional power, she
cannot be ignored. We call this quotient of power *personal currency*.

Personal currency includes three factors working together: physical
demeanor and presence, a persuasive communication style, and a strategic
understanding of how to work with the media to achieve specific goals, as
the following stories of women in The Club reveal.

The notion that visibility is a key ingredient in developing personal
currency for women is as basic as Economics 101, but many women resist

the lesson. We understand why. Visibility involves putting yourself out there, into the limelight, or allowing yourself to be positioned there. Visibility involves risk. Women are not accustomed to boasting, recoiling from it. Women prefer to talk to further personal interaction with others, not to claim attention or to impart information.

Micho Spring, a president in the Sawyer Miller Group, remembers her early reluctance in dealing with the press, and looks back on it with wry amusement. A corporate communications specialist, Spring has great credibility with the press, and is often quoted in the newspaper on business and community issues. She is a regular commentator on one of Boston's most popular Sunday morning public affairs programs. But she didn't start out with a warm relationship with reporters; her first press exposure was traumatic.

"I was working as executive assistant to Boston's mayor Kevin White, and I had just been promoted to deputy mayor," Micho recalled. "George Regan, his press secretary, told me that *Boston Magazine* wanted to do a story on me. I told him, 'No way.' I knew that the mayor hated publicity about anyone on his staff; after all, he was the one who had to run for reelection, not any of us. George told me it would be the cover story, and I kept saying no.

"Finally George wore me down, after promising me the photographer would only use black and white film, so they couldn't use it on the cover. I figured at that point I had resisted long enough, and it was George's call. So I gave the interview, but when I went to comb my hair, the photographer switched cameras on me and took a color picture. I ended up on the cover *and* inside the magazine."

Micho gasped when she saw the story. "Maria del Rosario Fernandez was one of the children waving flags in the streets on the day of Fidel Castro's triumphal entry into Havana from the Sierra Maestra in 1959," the story began. But by 1980, Micho was "the most influential woman in the city," "brilliant, gracious, enthusiastic, indefatigable, resilient, spunky and devious." Former city aides were unstinting in their praise of her. "She knows how to tap resources, to build alliances, and to weave networks. She moves with grace among all kinds of communities," one gushed. She's "more powerful than any other aide," said another.

That story started the press attention on Micho, most of which she felt was terrible. "They portrayed me as 'Madame Defarge,'" she said. "But I also found that my power currency inside the hall went up as a result of the *Boston Magazine* piece."

Micho Spring was on the map in Boston, and so was her career. After Kevin White's terms as mayor ended, his deputy mayor for policy management was avidly sought by the private sector. She became president and chief executive officer of a new telecommunications company, a member of the editorial board of a local television station, a director and then chairman of the board of the United Way, a director and member of the executive committee of a major teaching hospital, a trustee of both the New England Aquarium and a local community college, and a director of a major retailing chain. When the telecommunications company was sold, Spring started another company, specializing in communications strategies for large corporate clients.

"To show you the power of the press," Micho said, "after I left public office I went down to the tax assessor's office to pay my taxes. The clerk behind the counter said, 'Oh, so you're Micho Spring! You're so small! I thought you would be huge!'

"I ran into the photographer for *Boston Magazine* years later," Micho recalled. "She apologized for tricking me with the switch in cameras but I said, 'In retrospect, you might have done me a great favor.'"

Visibility is often what makes the difference between dramatic professional success and average achievement. Substance and achievement are valuable, but they are less valuable if only a supervisor knows about them. Even traditional corporate managers and staff executives within corporations should seek to develop the personal reputation that business-seeking professionals strive for as a matter of course.

Micho Spring is not the only woman to discover how visibility can help a career. Carol recalls her first taste of publicity: "In the sixties, I was the boss's daughter and the wife of the boss's son-in-law. I had few professional credentials of my own inside the supermarket company until our trade press did a story on my operating style and called me 'the secret weapon at Stop and Shop.' My credibility inside improved right away."

Public visibility of a top executive can enhance employee loyalty and morale with a company or professional organization. Motivating employees requires business leaders to expose their own personalities and values to scrutiny. Executives with strong convictions, forceful personalities, and visible expressions of concern for people are respected—sometimes re-vered—by their employees. These are executives who have had experi-ence in exposing their personal and human side to others. In a communi-cations era of "up close and personals," corporate executives realize the traditional cloak of corporate anonymity is no longer effective in achiev-ing internal or external goals.

The use of visibility and publicity often extends below the executive ranks. Federal Express, Nordstrom's, and other enlightened companies have institutionalized public displays honoring employees who have given unusual service or performed extraordinarily well. These employees are widely touted as "heroes." Women who want to lead these companies and employees must also be seen as public figures. Like college presidents, reli-gious leaders, or politicians, they must learn to project authority and char-acter to a wide range of constituencies: the investment community, em-ployees, clients and customers, the business press, board members, and public officials.

There is no more important time to call upon these women who have reserves of positive public reputation than in the time of a corpo-rate crisis. Executives who must lead corporations in times of stress must be willing to show their personal integrity, community concern, accomplishments, and even their vulnerabilities, and rely upon their public stature to project their message. Professor Rosabeth Moss Kanter of the Harvard Business School calls this "reputational capital" and Carol has seen how it works firsthand. When Carol's company was the target of a takeover threat, the local business pages did not hesitate to take sides, extolling the history of her family's personal involvement over decades as civic and charitable leaders. Her reputation as an ac-tive, caring, and involved executive made the story of the takeover fight more than an ordinary Wall Street corporate battle. Because her employees, customers, and the press knew her family story so inti-mately, they had a personal interest in the outcome.

Similarly, when Johnson & Johnson faced its Tylenol poisoning scare, its chief executive officer, James Burke, got high marks for immediately appearing on television, as a man in charge, concerned, and contrite. No one doubted his values: personal safety outweighed loss of profits on the product and even the risk of falling stock prices. In the end, Johnson & Johnson and its shareholders benefited from his public leadership.

Contrast the public relations disaster that befell Exxon after the *Valdez* oil spill. Exxon's chairman Lawrence G. Rawl had developed a style and reputation as a low-key manager who preferred to delegate authority to others. No mortal sin there. But had he been as well known as Lee Iacocca of Chrysler or David Kearns of Xerox, he might have had some currency that would have helped him face the biggest crisis in his career. He may have even developed instincts that would have prompted him to respond more quickly to the disaster, with comments more sensitive than just blaming Coast Guard and Alaska officials for cleanup delays. As Dow Corning and other companies join the list of those taking a public battering for poor executive leadership in a crisis, top executive women know they could do a better job.

Excellence in tough times is not demonstrated just by managers of one sex, of course. But company executives who have performed poorly in times of crisis have often come from environments characterized by arrogance, insularity, and inbreeding, in many cases cultures that also accept few women at the top. Corporate cultures noted for values of open communication, diverse points of view, integrity, and concern for a broad range of stakeholders—values many executive women cite as important—are often those that can adapt quickly to changing circumstances and external events.

Visibility is not only a positive factor for professional success or enhancing corporate leadership. It is also a good insurance policy when unexpected events happen that stall or derail a career. At the moment when women need personal power and leverage to deal with a difficult working environment, public visibility is a secret weapon that works.

"I was the most senior woman at the bank," Isabelle Engel* told us. "I was a well-known name and face in town with the business community, and I served on several civic boards. When the new management came in, they decided they wanted their own boys at the top. They started by taking away areas of responsibility, then my car, then my staff. They didn't touch my salary or title, but I knew what was going on."

Isabelle tried negotiating a generous settlement package, including bonuses and stock she had been promised would accrue in later years. The chairman played dumb, ignoring her polite attempts to start a frank conversation about her situation. Finally, she hired a tough litigator to negotiate for her.

---

*An asterisk denotes that we have changed the name of the woman quoted, and in some cases the name of her company and its location as well.

"The final arrow in my bow was publicity. I let my lawyer threaten that I would file a lawsuit, and when I did, I'd go public to the business press. They were more afraid of that than anything," she said.

"They've held me up as a role model for women in the company, and they knew I had allies all over the city who would descend on the board and other senior managers on my behalf. They didn't want a public mess. But they just weren't sure enough of me to figure out whether I'd stay a good girl and be quiet, or whether I'd tell my story. I kept them guessing. But this only worked because I was so well known. If I were invisible, I wouldn't rate much attention in the press."

In communities across the country, executive women such as Micho Spring and Isabelle Engel have discovered the power of visibility and are using it effectively. But not all executive women have reached their level of understanding. Some feel it is not feminine or do not yet have the self-confidence to aggressively seek visibility. We believe the reverse is true: The combination of a dynamic personal style and visibility is what makes executive women most effective.

FIRST IMPRESSIONS COUNT

It's too bad that we have to start a chapter on personal currency and visibility with the bold assertion that confidence and style matter, but they do. We say that it's too bad because in the all-perfect world, women and men would be accepted and respected for their intelligence, energy, and contributions, not on how they also project themselves. But it is a simple fact that to be effective in The Club and to change its culture, women must first reach key positions in The Club. The route to membership requires developing effective personal currency in the existing culture, which is still rife with bias. People are like books, where the cover presents an image of what's inside, and dictates how we are perceived by others. It may be startling to mix the power of feminism with gentle persuasion, but first we are seen and judged, rather than known and judged. Life in the business and professional world is not unlike our earlier days of boy-meets-girl, where first impressions count. "She's terrific" was a much better introduction to a blind date than "she's so smart."

"Tell young women that you can be a nonthreatening feminist!" one senior executive pleaded with us. "I used to love to surprise men who complimented me on my dress and later asked, 'You're not one of those feminist types, are you?' I'd answer, 'Of course I am. This is what a feminist looks like!'"

Heresy? No, it's life. And women who want to be effective members of The Club must understand the power of their own persuasiveness.

There are two initial reasons to pay attention to first impressions as a strategy for effective leadership in The Club. First, charisma is a powerful force that is valued by both men and women in our culture. Second, we must confront the retreat from feminism because of its negative, countercultural images. To recapture feminism, we must recognize and then embrace the many qualities that the public world values.

Many women who are in senior-level positions in business and the professions were the girls of the fifties and sixties, the feminists of the sixties and seventies, and the business executives of the seventies and eighties. To understand why positive charisma is important to them, we only have to look back at their formative years. They were raised to keep up appearances in a time that sociologist Wini Breines calls "the sexualization of the popular culture in a postwar consumer society." Girdles, Breck shampoo ads, hoop skirts, pierced ears, and Doris Day cheerleader sweaters projected a white suburban life-style for girls in which romance was the only achievement that mattered, and marriage was the goal. Many girls who grew up in those times had no idea that their adulthood would be spent working in corporate boardrooms, courtrooms, or hospital operating rooms. Today, these women laugh at the fashion magazine stereotypes, but they don't abandon the image-making easily. They know that conformity to good taste and the prevailing culture is important, if only to gain access to the culture to change it.

This preoccupation with the female as an object of attractiveness (and therefore an object for romance) is ingrained in American images. Americans revere the fictional picture of a woman as a desirable companion, a caring parent, and a careful consumer. From the 1942 advertisement for Palmolive soap, in which a blond woman with beatific eyes lifted skyward says "I pledge myself to guard every bit of Beauty that he cherishes in me" to the 1991 advertisement portraying two female friends, one gushing to the other, "He's crazy about my kid. And he drinks Johnny Walker Red," women are portrayed in their relation to men. Even the advertisements that acknowledge that women work pander to a woman's personal style. The Charlie (perfume) woman has one hand clutching a briefcase and another patting the rump of her companion in his power suit and tie. Hanes features real professional women in its ads for stockings; does the pitch imply that a woman can be a success and have pretty legs at the same time, or is the implication that perhaps it was her pretty legs that won her professional success?

It's not news that attractive women sell on Madison Avenue. But a woman who projects self-confidence and achievement also sells in corporate boardrooms. Just as there are few captains of industry whose shirttails are hanging over a paunchy stomach and scuffed shoes, there are few women in The Club who look and whine like Roseanne Arnold. In a few workplaces, merit may be rewarded, and personal style is less relevant. But they are few in number, regrettably. Effectiveness in The Club demands a personal dynamism that commands attention, respect, and admiration. This is true both for men as well as women, of course, but because women are more visible they must meet a higher standard of scrutiny.

We know that women won't be taken seriously unless they project an image that coincides with what society expects. It may be wrong, but it is reality. It is no different for presidential candidates or television news anchors; when individuals are seeking to influence the public, the public has to stop and listen to them. To command attention from the public, they must present an effective image and demeanor.

"I'd call it 'presence,'" said a New York retailing executive. "It took me a while to understand its effectiveness, but I learned it by watching another woman. When I was a young junior retailing executive in Chicago, the most senior woman in our company, Miss Carey, was close to retirement age. She was a commanding figure: big boned, tall, with a distinctive style of dress and huge jewelry and the slightest Southern accent. She had started in retailing in the forties, and for many decades was the only woman executive in our company and the only visible woman in the Chicago business community. *Everyone* knew Miss Carey.

"Early on, I dismissed her. I looked at her and assumed she was the stereotypical Queen Bee who had survived as the only woman in a male business environment by bonding with the men around her, but who had little interest or understanding of what young women in the sixties and seventies were thinking about. After a while, I came to understand the reason she was so effective, and I developed a real affection for her. When you entered her office, she always rose to her full height to greet you, called you by name, and looked you straight in the eye with her full attention. For the time you were there, she made you feel like you were the most important person in the world to her—if not the *only* person. She listened intently to what you said, and by the time you left, she had made you feel very special. She had 'presence' in spades. I've always tried to emulate her ever since."

Many executive women have learned that they are most effective when they let their personal style of dress help them express both good taste and individual presence. They no longer need the corporate security blanket of serious gray or blue suits and tailored blouses, and few follow the changing fashion dictates of Seventh Avenue. They have the confidence to dress in whatever way makes them feel good. They are in control of the message they want to send. One bank executive vice president recalled how she learned that a dose of femininity could be effective and please herself at the same time:

"I usually wore my most conservative suit to board meetings where I was scheduled to make a presentation," she said. "At one meeting, however, I wore a pretty silk dress, and I received several compliments on it. I noticed that the board members smiled at me more, and seemed to pay more attention to me. I think they relaxed and decided that because they were looking at an attractive picture, they were in more of a receptive frame of mind to acknowledge what I was saying. I always wore a dress after that."

Let's face it. Women like to feel secure and comfortable at work. We have more self-confidence when we know we look good. The fashion industry reports a rise in individual expression, even in the most conservative executive suites. Cashmere, colorful knits and silks, scarves, pins, and ensembles have replaced the most boring wardrobe. At one bank board meeting, twelve men filed in with dark gray suits, and the three women showed up all wearing red jackets. The chairman took his seat and said, "Would anyone like to guess what the power color is today?"

"I like dressing up," said a very attractive chief operating officer of a major bank. "I love clothes, and I like experimenting to see what looks best on me. I know I do a better job when I look good, and those who work around me like it. It's an advantage to look and act feminine, one that I have used over the years most effectively. I'd recommend it to all women who want to get ahead! Not that it replaces performance or genuine achievement, but it gives you a head start."

Executive women are operating in a popular culture that places significant weight on how women look. Beauty is a major part of the economy, no doubt because of the American preoccupation with youth: a $20-billion-a-year cosmetic industry ("We're selling hope in a jar," one executive said), a $33 billion diet industry, and a $300 million cosmetic surgery industry—all before a woman puts a stitch of clothes on her body. These expenditures are worthwhile, say some, if it helps women present an image that conveys an aura of authority. Even gray hair, well packaged, brings respect; at that point in life, most women have developed self-confidence that shines through, with or without the help of cosmetics and designer labels.

"This is a good-looking crowd," Betty Friedan commented, looking at the glittering assembly of women present at the 1991 International Women's Forum annual gala awards ceremony in Washington, D.C. She had read that day in the *New York Times* about the meetings the women attended with members of the U.S. Senate and several Bush administration domestic policy advisers. Elegantly dressed, articulate Forum members vocally challenged several U.S. senators to start paying attention to women's issues or lose money and support from previously loyal women. Their comments, delivered directly and forcefully two weeks after the Clarence Thomas–Anita Hill hearings, were more effective than protests outside the Capitol.

If our culture values women who convey self-confidence, then women need to know that they must pay attention to their personal style. They'll catch more flies with honey than with vinegar, and in this case, honey may be how a woman projects herself. Furthermore, we suspect the opposite may also be true: Women will be ignored unless their demeanor commands positive respect.

There are numerous outrageous examples of bias by men against women they consider unattractive or unworthy of attention and respect. For example, U.S. district judge E. B. Haltom made it clear that he did not believe a woman who claimed she lost her job after spurning her boss. Noting that the woman "wore little or no makeup and her hair was not colored in any way," and therefore she was "not attractive" to the boss, he concluded that she did not merit sexual attention.

Ann B. Hopkins, an accountant at Price Waterhouse, was denied elevation to partnership despite having brought in more business than any other partner candidate. Hopkins won at least $34 million in major consulting contracts in a matter of a few years—the best record of all eighty-eight partner candidates. She also billed more hours than any of the others in the fiscal year prior to the partnership nominations, clearly acting as a rainmaker even prior to being a partner. But after a lengthy evaluation process, Price Waterhouse put her candidacy on hold, and then decided not to repropose her.

When Hopkins asked her supervisor what she might do to improve her chances of partnership, she was advised to "walk more femininely, talk more femininely, dress more femininely, wear makeup, have her hair styled and wear jewelry." In that case, the U.S. Supreme Court decided that this advice constituted negative sexual stereotyping and ruled in her favor.

We deplore such examples, but they prove we live in a world of sexual stereotyping. But instead of pandering to these stereotypes, women can make them work to enhance their effectiveness. The right answer, of course, is to say that the culture which allows sexual stereotyping must change so that merit and not personal style is rewarded. But we are also practical. For change to happen, women must be in positions of power to lead by example. We do not hesitate to generalize about men and women and conclude that if there were more women federal judges we would have fewer instances of such blatant prejudice as shown by Judge Haltom, and if there were more women than men on the managing committee of Price Waterhouse, Ann Hopkins would have been accepted as a partner or rejected for good and valid business reasons.

FEMALE AUTHORITY: AN OXYMORON OR A ONE-TWO PUNCH?

Some executive women told us they often found themselves square up against the old conundrum: How can a woman preserve her feminine qualities and be seen as authoritative at the same time?

Professor Linda L. Carli of the College of the Holy Cross conducted a study on gender patterns in speech behavior. She concluded that it is difficult for men to perceive women as competent. No matter how smart or well prepared women are, social stereotypes are powerful barriers to acceptance. "For men, it appears that it's more important that a woman be accessible and likable than competent in order to be influenced by them," she said, reporting on her findings.

But some women aren't taking the time to bridge the gap between friendship and authority. Because they are smart and have an opinion, they think they should be listened to, and are frustrated when they are not. Executive women across the country told us countless stories of the difficulty they had in asserting their opinions and projecting authority in the workplace, angry that they weren't "being taken seriously." Sally Hughes-Whitman,* a financial executive and striking blond, went so far as to pull her hair back in a demure bun and to wear only gray suits and white blouses. "I discovered a long time ago if I didn't neutralize my appearance it was distracting and we couldn't get down to work," she told us.

Hers may be an extreme example, erring on the side of authority rather than approachability. We don't think that a pretty dress is the cause of inattention on the part of predominantly male audiences. The problem goes deeper than women's superficial coverings.

Tackling the female-authority dichotomy requires that we understand its origins—not just culturally, but its role in women's upbringing and formative adult years. As women's awareness is sharpened, they can then develop a more effective strategy for behavior in primarily male business environments. Outward appearance is only the first part of the equation to achieve the personal accessibility that Professor Carli concluded was crucial for women. Speech patterns, body language, and learned skills of communication that convey self-confidence and project authority are as important as dress and style in positioning women as leaders among their business peers.

Marilyn Swartz Lloyd, president of Beacon Management Company in Boston, calls this quality of persuasive authority the most important skill for executive women to develop. "When I was director of the city's Economic Development and Industrial Corporation, we waged a battle in support of a new light-manufacturing zone. The stakes were high: hundreds of jobs for city residents. But the opposition from property owners was fierce.

When we first proposed the idea, we were trounced at the zoning commission," she said.

"Eight months later, we won with a unanimous vote. The difference was a full-scale campaign of persuasion to every possible group we could address. I discovered my title and institution didn't mean much unless I could personally energize and excite my troops and, as a team, develop a strong, useful, and winning program.

"The basic point is that women must develop constituencies. Whether those constituencies elect a woman to office, applaud her work in the private sector, or offer support as she works her way up the corporate ladder, that support is her strength. And to earn that support, she must be able to persuade others of her goals. This is the best way to achieve our objectives, whether they are to save the world or a piece of it, make a million dollars, support a family, change the way civilization looks at culture, or ensure that someone reads our poems."

Swartz Lloyd graduated from an all-women's college, as did many of her peers who rank high on the personal-currency scale. The connection between the two is obvious, many researchers believe. Graduates of women's colleges may have an advantage over their sisters at coed schools in asserting and communicating their views since their educational experience was conducted in an atmosphere that rewarded risk-taking, leadership, and communication by women. Their professors aggressively encouraged these women to excel and believe that no horizon was too high for them. The research and data on women's colleges bears this out: Their graduates are twice as likely as graduates of coeducational colleges to earn doctoral degrees and their alumnae comprised 50 percent of the women members of the 1990 Congress despite the fact that only 4.5 percent of women who have bachelor's degrees graduated from women's colleges.

In coeducational schools, women may face such a chilly climate that researcher Catherine G. Krupnick suggested college catalogs feature a warning label: "The value you receive will depend on your sex." Male students are called on more often by professors and contribute impulsively, while women tend to hesitate and then enlarge on the ideas of a previous speaker. Women are taught early that assertive, angry, challenging tones are strident and unfeminine, whereas men assume that such tones of voice will compel attention. Women may perform better than men in written assignments, but Krupnick warned correctly that the ability to use language in public settings and hold an audience is a more valuable skill in advancement than the quality of work done in private. Perhaps for that reason, executive women graduates of Harvard Business School told us 50 percent of their grade was based on class participation.

If executive women did not learn these skills in college, they start their careers at a disadvantage. Educational experiences for women are key in determining their later success, but in general, institutions of higher learning are not serving women well. As Margaret McKenna, a lawyer, corporate director, and president of Lesley College, stated, "the college degree is an avenue to economic power, but women's entry into these channels toward economic power has been restricted by the way institutions of higher learning think about women students."

Thus, many women enter the business and professional world less well prepared than their male peers. Diminished self-esteem and inadequate communication skills that fester in early adulthood can be hard to overcome. The business world shouldn't be surprised, then, that men surpass many women in professional achievement in adulthood.

Women executives, however, are encouraging each other to learn an authoritative communication style that contributes to powerful personal currency. Although graduates of women's colleges may have an initial advantage, other women can catch up. Many women are returning to the classroom for advanced training, sent by their companies, as part of government-funded retraining programs, or simply for personal career and skill advancement. Margaret McKenna noted that women comprise 57 percent of students twenty-five years of age and older on campuses. Universities that understand women's learning styles, involve students in leadership positions while they are there, make programs of learning accessible to students, and reinforce a woman's strengths, self-esteem, and skills will be the road to power for women, according to McKenna.

Even outside the classroom, women can overcome early socialization and learn to communicate forcefully and project authority. Eleanor Morgan suggests that women be alert to rules of the workplace culture that may disadvantage them. For example, many women learn from others through dialogue. In some cases, they must resist the temptation to dialogue too much, to talk in incomplete sentences that sound like patter.

What Morgan described is the art of personal small talk, which many women do effortlessly. But because small talk tends to be intimate, often concerning the details of individuals' lives, it works against an image of authority. Women may be better advised to limit their small talk in business settings to such topics as politics, news, and sports (assuming that conversation about these topics comes effortlessly)—subjects about which opinions can be expressed forthrightly. This is not to say that one style of talking is necessarily better than another, but as linguist Deborah Tannen pointed out, both sexes would do well to learn the communication strategies typically used by the other group. Since women are striving to project authority in a male-dominated business culture, they must understand how to be successful at it. "Read the *Wall Street Journal*," one woman suggested. We may not like the fact that men perceive women who try to be friends as dependent and insecure, but if that is the case, women must stick to conversation that preserves the independence of men and enhances the equal status of women.

Some women do this effortlessly. Sally Hughes-Whitman is one. "I had three brothers and learned to talk 'man-talk' from an early age. Sports, business, and politics were standard fare in our house. But I also know that talking man-talk does not mean you're not feminine."

Savvy women executives are also sensitive to men's feelings of uneasiness in making conversation with them. One newspaper publisher in a large Southern city recalled the frank admission of a new male department head. "He was a talented guy, and was transferred to my newspaper from another paper in our chain. I didn't know at the time that he had never worked for a woman, and was uncomfortable about it. But our paper was in a good growing market, and it was a smart career move for him.

"Our first few meetings were fine," she recalled. "One day he said to me, 'You know, I was worried about what I would talk to you about. I assumed I didn't have to bone up on sports scores, but I had no idea what you were interested in. Then I discovered I didn't have to do anything; you didn't waste a lot of time with extraneous talk at our meetings. You just got right down to business. I like that.'

"I just laughed," she said. "It never occurred to me that men would worry about how to make small talk with women!"

Once women have progressed from the small talk prior to the business meeting to the actual meeting itself, women must again be alert to how their communication style supports or undermines their authority.

Radcliffe president Linda Wilson described what she calls multichanneling, the ability of women to think and act on several levels at once. "Many women see connections among ideas. They don't have tunnel vision. They can talk, think, and listen at the same time. They say things several times, and gain insight with each telling. It is part of our excitement. But men get impatient with what they see as a lack of focus and a lack of discipline at meetings. To some men, multichanneling is a distraction, not creative thinking."

What is positive behavior for many women may be regarded as negative by men, although each style has its own benefits. The problem for women arises when one style is dominant and therefore acceptable in the business culture.

"It is too bad that women bear the double standard," said one female bank executive. "We all know that men are 'forceful,' and women are 'arrogant.' Men are 'logical and direct,' and women are 'unfriendly.' Men are 'authoritative,' and women are 'too macho.' We can't win."

The double standard she described is a tough balancing act, but successful women have demonstrated how to communicate effectively. Some women have learned simply to be aware of how their regional or cultural speaking style conveys stereotypical assumptions. A Southern accent comes across as slow, soft, and laid back; a Bronx or Brooklyn, New York speech pattern conveys aggressiveness, considered more negative in women than men.

Risk-taking is a critical element in speaking as well as in behavior, but for many women, it is a learned skill. Some women feel more comfortable in raising points tentatively, both to deflect criticism and preserve relationships with those around the table who may disagree with her. She will say, "Should we think about . . . ?," rather than "I think we are missing the point unless we . . . " Her comment will be brief, quiet, and questioning, rather than commanding and certain.

Women are now beginning to understand why this pattern is so prevalent. Women use language to make connections and interact; men use it to challenge, command attention, and debate. Many women have experienced business meetings in which men challenge presenters on various matters, asking "tough" questions or hammering home an opposite view until the presenter acknowledges his point has validity. The questioner may not even care deeply about his own view; he may just pursue it to see how long it will take for the speaker to back down. It's a public intellectual sport that few women play. Women prefer to use gentle persuasion to bring the consensus around to their point of view.

"Women are tentative even with other women," said one female bank president. "A woman I wanted to hire came in to see me and asked, in a little voice, if she could work for ninety percent pay, but work full-time hours, so she could feel free to leave work at a regular time to take care of her kid. She was so apologetic and deferential, but it was unnecessary. She apparently thought that if she were paid the full salary we'd require her to be around all the time, even nights. I told her that her issue was speaking up for how she intended to work!"

Many women not only have a tendency to make statements sound like questions, but they are also afraid to ask direct questions at business meetings. Unfortunately, some women have a habit of prefacing their questions with self-deprecating remarks such as "This may be obvious to everyone else, but . . . ," or "Perhaps we covered this in the past, but I need a refresher on . . . " A woman who asks such questions should be aware that she is reinforcing a hierarchical ladder of informational power. Those who know the answer or have the information are superior to her by virtue of being knowledgeable. Even men who do not know the answer (and many women recalled instances in which men told them, after the meeting, that they were glad she asked) prefer to remain silent, finding their own way, independently, and preserving the appearance of equality with the other men at the table.

Even when women speak out with confidence, many report anecdotes of offering their opinion and having no one respond positively. Then, when a man offers the same opinion some time later, his colleagues agree and credit him with the idea. One woman, upon hearing that story from a peer, exclaimed, "I thought I was the only one with that experience!"

Psychology professor Florence Geis heard the story so often she conducted a study to find its causes. Not surprisingly, social stereotypes reared their ugly head again. White men are expected to be competent, rational, and in charge. So when a white male takes the floor at a meeting to put forth his views, he is greeted with approval.

"But females," Geis explained in an interview, "are expected to be less intelligent, less competent, and they are not expected to take the initiative. So when they speak out, they are violating social expectations and we disapprove of them." Often others remain silent or change the subject after she speaks. It is only when a man makes the point that others respond.

Sometimes negative stereotypes occur even when women are silent. One corporate director recalled a board meeting at which the chairman announced to the directors, "The next presentation is a bit complicated. Some of you may have trouble following the figures and analyses behind the numbers. Susan, why don't we use you as the litmus test. If you don't understand any part of what is being said, please just speak out and stop us at any time."

"I don't think he honestly knew how insulting he was," Susan said. "But I stopped him in his tracks. I simply said, 'John, I think you'd better use someone else. I did my doctoral dissertation on this subject and I'm pretty familiar with it.' Lucky for me it was the truth!" Susan had turned the tables on the chairman, politely, by telling the others that she already understood the subject, at the same time raising her status in the eyes of the board.

Susan communicated her authority effectively. But when such communications are perceived as boasting, women have encountered a catch-22 situation. Women are reluctant to boast, but they must find the right moments to project their own achievements and information, in order to project authority. Men do it all the time, often to acclaim. But women are judged by women's societal standards, which expect women to be gracious, self-effacing, and modest. Therefore, communication that comes across as boasting from women creates a negative reaction or even backfires.

Most women have found that speaking out more often at meetings does not necessarily help to project competence. "Bright women are more likely to challenge authority and tell others outright what they think," said a female bank executive vice president. "But the bright men are often quiet at first, almost deferential. They play the political game. There is male bonding that takes care of the person who talked. In a meeting there may be one guy who is a jerk. They all know it, but they deal with it in another way. Women sometimes have a compulsion to talk up, to challenge, that is untimely and not subtle. My boss asked me once whether I was contributing to the discussion or challenging someone's authority. I thought I was contributing, but obviously it didn't come across that way."

Geis noted the same dilemma. "For women, it appears that simply offering a substantive contribution is enough to elicit others' displeasure."

This can't-win scenario is discouraging to many women who have experienced it time and time again. If women are not perceived as bold and authoritative, they will not be influential in male-dominated circles. Yet many men are less comfortable with assertive women, and some are even threatened by them. Some men prefer women to be likable and nonthreatening—and meek.

Sally Hughes-Whitman discovered that, in those instances, women must project authority with their feet, by leaving for greener pastures. The thirty-seven-year-old mother of three recounted her experience at one large insurance company: "I had a terrific job as regional director of the company's investment real estate. I was responsible for the purchase, operation, and disposition of the company's real estate portfolio, and also for the resolution of problem loans, foreclosures, and bankruptcies. I was directing our entire corporate real estate strategy.

"I was doing very well, and my boss's boss, the senior vice president, took me to lunch one day. He said I had great potential for the company; my only downside was that I was 'a little aggressive.' He said the company wanted to send me to the Center for Creative Leadership in North Carolina, for an intensive one-week course. I was pleased to have been chosen, so of course I went.

"At the end of the week, I was evaluated. The trainers told me not to change a thing; that my assertive style was most appropriate if I wanted to be a corporate leader. Well, at that point I had no choice but to reevaluate how far I would go in that insurance culture. I found another job with a better company. Now I have even more responsibilities, and I serve as a director of the company.

"I told my boss the truth about why I was leaving. I felt badly about it, but I also told him that companies will lose talented women who have confidence and the professional leverage not to keep hitting their head against a wall. They will just go find another place to grow."

Sally Hughes-Whitman epitomizes a confident woman who is liked, respected, and projects leadership in a culture that welcomes her talents. She demonstrates the powerful combination of female-authority, the one-two punch that senior-level women believe is the magic ingredient in bridging the double standard for women and helping them gain influence in The Club.

But an effective communication style that commands attention is not enough to develop personal currency. The challenge, top executive women repeated frequently, is to catapult women into the visibility loop. Once their names start appearing in the business media read and watched by The Club, they cannot be ignored.

WHAT'S WRONG WITH THIS PICTURE?

Despite being 52 percent of the population, women are almost invisible as authorities or figures of interest in the popular press. While women stop short of calling the news media biased, it is clear that most mass communication organizations are oblivious to the single gender picture they present. Executive women have to work harder, therefore, to develop the public visibility in these media outlets that is so critical to enhancing their professional stature.

Part of the problem may lie with the nature of a reporter's job. Most reporters are under pressure to produce a complete story by a fixed deadline. It is easier and faster for a reporter to reach out to a familiar name on a Rolodex who can be counted on to return the phone call than to seek out an unknown female source. Habit becomes routine (a reporter's "comfort zone"), and the frequency in which certain business leaders are quoted in the press becomes another catch-22 situation. Are they quoted and covered often because they are leaders in The Club, or are they leaders in The Club because of the frequency with which their names appear in the business pages of the paper and in the electronic media?

Reporters' sources must be reliable, honest, and quotable. If male executives can be counted on to provide helpful information and are willing to be quoted by name, the reporter will continue to use those males as sources—particularly if the editor, male or female, never complains about the lack of diversity in the stories.

Access to the popular press simply does not happen as easily for an executive woman as for a man. To make visibility work for her, she must first understand what she is up against.

Television, the most pervasive medium for communicating news and shaping opinion, reaches virtually every American household. The fifty-or-more specialized cable channels, including business and financial services, public affairs channels such as C-Span and all-news networks, will reach 70 percent of American homes by the end of 1993, industry experts predict. For over 40 percent of Americans, television provides their sole source of news. The majority of Americans feel that television news is more believable than newspapers; not surprising, since the information is more immediate, easier to receive, and more intimate with the benefit of attractive, persuasive messengers.

But female opinion leaders are rarely seen on television. On PBS's "MacNeil/Lehrer," 87 percent of its American guest experts were men; on ABC's "Nightline," the percentage was 89 percent. Perhaps the producers of these shows just don't know many accomplished women in business, government, politics, or academia.

News shows aren't the only offenders; fewer than half of all characters on entertainment television are women, and the single most common female job portrayed on television is clerical. The reason may be as simple as the fact that women constitute just 15 percent of all producers, 25 percent of all writers, and 9 percent of all directors on prime-time entertainment series.

Women realize it is tough to break into the world of national television and be invited onto the most respected programs as newsmakers or experts, but perhaps the world of over 12,000 different magazines offers a more hospitable environment. Targeting the audience of professional/managerial adults who admit to reading 13.3 separate magazine issues each month is undoubtedly more effective than taking a chance on the diverse mass audience of television. Moreover, women know that the readership of the "trades," or specialized business publications, is vast—the combined circulation exceeds 72 million a year—but the readers are exactly those members of The Club that executive women must reach.

A review of some of the most popular and influential magazines, however, is discouraging. A 1991 study showed that references to women in major newsmagazines averaged 13 percent. Women were invisible, in stories from reproductive rights (eight male references, no females) to food (twenty-three male references, no females) and Democratic presidential nominees (thirty-six males, no females).

Occasionally, executive women are featured in stories, particularly in popular magazines that attract a wide business readership. But they are rarely used as experts or sources of news or opinion in their professional field. More often, the story is about them as women, and the story is negative.

"Why Women Still Don't Hit the Top," blared a headline in a *Fortune* magazine cover story on the nation's top executive women. When will women finally make it into the highest ranks of corporate America? "Not in this millennium," the female author asserted. Is it the fault of corporate America? Not by a long shot. Women are not rising to the top because "they quit or deliberately leap off the fast track. They miss their children. They miss not having had children. A better opportunity comes along. Or they just get tired and want out of the rat race."

Is it surprising that any captain of industry, after reading those generalizations in the *Fortune* story, might decide not to hire or promote a woman executive?

Phyllis Swersky, former executive vice president of A.I. Corp., was among the women featured in the article, shown standing at a polished boardroom table in a crisp red and white summer dress. The quote underneath the full-color picture was "I don't cook. I don't take my children to malls and museums. And I don't have any close friends."

Phyllis's close friends got a laugh out of the picture and quote, showering her with notes and calls, pledging friendship and take-out meals. But Phyllis, the mother of three children under the age of seven, was not amused by the negative stereotype presented by the article, particularly since she felt she had taken great pains to explain to the reporter that she and her family were doing just fine, and she had made a special effort to convey her enthusiasm about business issues to the reporter. But the reporter had her own point of view—and that was that Phyllis couldn't have it all. Someone must be suffering from the achievements of a top executive mother, and it must be her children and her personal life. Phyllis disagreed.

"You don't have to be childless to be most energized by a career," Phyllis said. "The most important thing is the influence and impact I have on the children. I can build a good solid relationship with them and still have a career. Fathers have been doing it for a long time with the full approval of society."

Phyllis may not have realized how one or two informal comments would be used as the focus of her profile in the article, but negative stereotyping of women executives in magazines is prevalent. *Life* profiled an AT&T executive with an eight-page spread of photographs and commentary. The quotes the magazine chose to enlarge?

"I thought I could do it all. I was so naive."

"There isn't enough of me to go around."

"I have no energy for romance."

"By the time the old guard retires, I may just be too old."

Business Week is not much better. For example, while the reporter who profiled Merck's Judy Lewent may have thought he was complimentary in a full spread about her career, other executive women who read the article may have been understandably discouraged. Lewent was "intense, aggressive, and definitely hard-charging," who puts in "70-hour workweeks." "Excruciatingly well organized," Lewent and her husband "have opted not to have children because of their busy careers." This is a role model for executive women?

Perhaps the daily newspaper industry may offer women executives the best opportunities for exposure in front of a readership of opinion leaders, with its elite audience of older, educated, and married readers—in short, likely members of The Club.

Women focus on the business pages of newspapers because business news and analysis is avidly read by Club members. The power of the business press is great by its choice of news stories for the business pages and its choice of sources or subjects. Business reporters and editors are the gatekeepers between potential news stories and the business and professional world that acts and reacts to such stories. Fortunes are made, careers are broken, stock prices rise and fall on the stories that come across the wire. The success of the *Wall Street Journal*, other financial publications, segmented newsletters, and syndicated columns on personal finance and financial reports has shown that a wide audience of opinion leaders follows news from the business world.

But women are just as likely to be invisible in newspaper coverage. One study indicated that only 11 to 12 percent of page-one references are to women.

Women have emerged in the business world in great numbers in the last decade; over 41 percent of all managers are women, a striking increase in just ten years. The number of feature stories on these women-as-women-in-a-man's-world shows that they are newsworthy, even if the slant is negative. But women are simply not as present as men in hard news stories, according to Bernice Buresh, director of the Women, Press and Politics Project.

"There is a double standard operating in news," said Buresh. "We learn more about women as people, but it is harder to find out what they do for a living. We know that she is attractive and the mother of two boys, but few reporters explain how she became an expert in international currency transactions, or how she built her company. Women will be quoted if they are thought of as authorities, but there are fewer of them. Women are generally absent as sources of information in the press."

We conducted an informal survey of our own, to test our belief that executive women are missing from the business pages of newspapers. Business and economic news receive a great deal of attention in the press, particularly in times when the average reader is more knowledgeable and concerned about economic issues, from the national recession to trade policies with Japan. Articles about the economy, stock market, individual companies, and personal finance frequently appear on the front page of the newspaper as well as in the business section. Stories about the local economy, companies, or business leaders appear in news sections, and features about workers, families, or money matters appear in life-style, "insight," or editorial pages, and even in Sunday supplements. Even the smallest general circulation newspaper provides regular coverage of news from its community's business leaders.

We chose to analyze the content of business and economic articles from three newspapers: the *Wall Street Journal*, indisputably the nation's most influential business newspaper; the *New York Times*, regarded by some to be the nation's best newspaper and read by most national business opinion leaders; and the Fort Myers, Florida, *News-Press*, a daily paper in the Gannett chain, that services a growing and active market in southwest Florida.

The articles analyzed spanned seven general categories: individual industries, workplace issues, international business and economics, the stock market (including bonds, mutual funds, and currency), individual companies, the economy and personal money issues, and legislation and politics affecting business. In general, stories that focused on a single individual or which quoted only one individual were not included.

While women business reporters covered a significant number of the stories, business women did not appear in print as often as women reporters. Of all the sources and subjects mentioned in all the stories, women accounted for just 12.3 percent of the references.

We were not surprised by the results of our survey. Women executives are silent in the hard-news sections of the business pages. Women appeared most often in stories about workplace issues (child-care choices and human resource issues) and personal finance (but often as the object of the story, not an authority). There may be some rationale to an argument that suggests female experts are difficult to find in stories that concern the automobile industry, for example, or a particular company such as Shawmut National, IBM, Digital, or General Cinema (although female analysts abound in all fields). But it is harder to justify the virtual absence of women as sources in articles about the advertising, retailing, publishing, or mutual fund industries.

Furthermore, it is harder to justify the absence of women in large "sampling of opinion" articles, where clearly the reporter has wide latitude to reach out to a wide variety of executives or professionals. In sampling executives about what was needed to help the nation's economy, a *Times* reporter chose twelve men and one woman.

The *Journal* was no better, asking for comments about President Bush's trade mission to Japan (twelve men), President Bush's 1992 State of the Union address (fifteen men), President-elect Clinton's Little Rock economic conference (thirteen men, despite the good example set by Clinton by including many female economists and business leaders in his two-day economic forum), NBC's fairness regarding its General Motors truck fire story (nine men), and President Clinton's economic plan (nine men).

Executive women are as invisible in the business press as they are in senior executive suites. Some women have suggested there is a vicious circle at work there, and to break out of it requires a deliberate strategy by women to increase their personal currency.

PERSONAL CURRENCY: MAKING IT HAPPEN

Developing positive personal currency and visibility go hand in hand. Personal currency is important because it is a powerful form of leadership that stimulates others to act. Many individuals have experienced the impact of a person who makes them want to do better, and achieve more, so they can earn praise and acknowledgment. This powerful person may have been a parent or a teacher, but recognition from him or her meant a lot.

The positive personal power that moves others is more forceful than negative power, the threat of punishment or withholding praise.

An individual can develop this quality without achieving any public visibility, but often the reverse is not true. A substantial degree of personal currency is usually required before a woman can begin to earn the visibility that is so essential to achieve leadership in The Club. It develops in five stages:

First, a woman must have a basic level of stature or achievement. This may consist of action she has taken, a position she holds, or an idea she puts forth. She might have given a talk, chaired a committee, or been appointed to a particular post. Cuban-born Micho Spring, as a thirty-year-old female deputy mayor in the predominantly Irish male world of Boston politics, was newsworthy.

Second, a woman must convey warmth; the first punch in her one-two punch of authority. She need not look like Cybil Shepard; rather, a winning smile, a degree of wit, a habit of returning phone calls immediately, or an open-door policy in her office may be enough to convey a personality that can win others over. Without saying a word, it is obvious that she likes people and they respond positively to her.

Micho Spring's "smile is as broad as her face and shoulders are narrow," the *Boston Magazine* reporter gushed. "She moves quickly but gracefully, appears unrattled in almost any situation, and makes decisions in the course of conversation."

Third, she must convey authority, the second punch in her one-two arsenal. She has a high degree of self-esteem and confidence that comes through to others. "Whenever I'm particularly concerned about something, I know [Micho] will be responsive," said a Boston city councilor in the magazine story. "She *is* aggressive; she is the kind of person who would aspire to power in any job she held. I identify with that."

Fourth, she must have an opportunity. She is ready to talk about a subject, let herself be interviewed, take credit for an accomplishment, or put forth an idea. She may even initiate the opportunity herself, although in many cases, if she has developed to the third stage, the press may come knocking on her door, as Micho Spring found out.

Finally, she is at the highest level of personal currency, where her private and public life are integrated. She is for real, not scripted. Her public image conveys what she is like all the time, whether she is calm and poised like former Vermont governor Madeleine Kunin, passionate and sharp like former congresswoman Geraldine Ferraro, pious and focused like Mother Teresa, or authoritative and unafraid like Margaret Thatcher. At this level she is totally at ease with publicity, visibility, and interrogation. Her message is consistent. She responds in the same way to presidents or school-children.

It is at this last level that executive women are the most successful at using press visibility to enhance their public power, as Micho Spring has done by her frequent appearance on a popular public affairs television program, and in her many speeches to community and civic groups.

One technique to enhance visibility is to focus on publishing opportunities in the professional world, suggests Sally Berger of Chicago. "Publishing leads to recognition and recognition leads to acceptance. Women can become better known by having their ideas well known," said Berger, a prolific author of health industry articles and producer and host of her own television program. "There is a whole world of industry publications out there—a great opportunity. But many women are so busy doing their job they are anonymous. They have tremendous expertise but it is not well known. The day where business comes in by word of mouth exclusively is over. You must market yourself. Women should seek out publishing opportunities and they'll become better known. Women who have a higher profile have more self-confidence and women with self-confidence feel less vulnerable."

Becoming better known by expressing her personal ideas fosters an intimacy with audience that enhances not only a woman's visibility but her receptivity, Berger believes. "Why do people return Barbara Walters's phone calls? Because they feel they know her. Her name precedes her call. The same thing happens to a businesswoman. More people are aware of her existence and feel they know her."

As businesswomen become better known, they may make their way into the business press where other members of The Club are covered and profiled. But ease and accessibility in dealing with the press does not just happen. Top women executives stressed that long before their names ever appeared in print, they had researched the business pages of their key publications as thoroughly as if they were researching a potential takeover target. They shared these observations about preparing for press coverage:

1. Women should monitor the placement of news about women in influential publications in their community or industry. Is the placement

determined by subject matter or by sex? Are women always featured on the "life-style" pages and men on the front page of the business section? The goal is to be covered on the business pages, not as the subject of a life-style feature.

Businesswomen must cultivate coverage by reporters assigned to the business and financial pages, and resist most coverage elsewhere in the paper. If a news organization only covers women in the sections geared primarily to a female readership, women may want to bypass that publication or coordinate an effective approach to its editors to sensitize them to the placement of their stories. Stories about women-who-make-it-in-a-man's-world may sell papers, but they do little to enhance the professional reputation of women with their own male peers. For example, a major daily newspaper would have provided a greater service had it placed an article entitled "Beyond Corporations' Glass Ceiling" where it belonged—on the business pages instead of on the Living Pages—complained an irate reader in a letter to the editor. "The placement of the story was insulting, but perhaps not surprising for a newspaper that lists twenty top executive spots on its masthead, with only two of those positions being held by women," the reader concluded.

2. Individual women or women's professional organizations should conduct their own informal survey of how often women are quoted as sources or subjects in straight business news stories in the publications read by The Club. Then they should quietly share the survey with reporters they know and trust, using it as an opportunity to introduce local business reporters to prominent businesswomen in diverse fields, and expand the press Rolodex of business contacts.

3. Women in business must make it their job to get to know business reporters, particularly those who cover their industry. Women must read their pieces and send them notes or call if the pieces are particularly good. These points of contact give women a chance to explain their own professional position, background, and experience. This is also a good opportunity to offer to be helpful where and when they can, even on deep background, to check facts or the reporter's understanding of how a particular business operates. In particular, women should pay particular attention to female reporters, who may appreciate the extra effort on their behalf.

Maryanne Kane, business editor for WHDH-TV in Boston, noted a reluctance on the part of women to seize opportunities for visibility. "I have male analysts and businessmen call me all the time, suggesting stories, sharing information, agreeing to be interviewed on air. Naturally, I turn to them when I need an expert or commentator on a particular story on television. They become part of my Rolodex of experienced businesspeople I've worked with, who will return my calls and appear on air when I need them. I've never been called by a woman yet, although I would welcome that. But I just don't hear from them."

4. Women should monitor the use of titles and other references with regard to men and women. In a straight news story, is it relevant that the firefighter, air traffic controller, real estate developer, or letter carrier was a woman? If there is undue emphasis on the fact that a judge, board member, or other newsworthy individual is a woman, the emphasis may give rise to the implication that her presence or prominence was due to factors other than merit. *Broadcasting's* lengthy interview with Lucie Salhany, chairman of Twentieth Century Television, was notable for never deviating from straight business questions about costs, television partnerships, financing, distributing, and pending legislation, despite the cover headline touting the interview with "Fox's First Lady" rather than "Fox's Chairman."

5. Women should monitor the treatment of news articles and the coverage of news as it affects women. For example, will a mandatory reduction in credit card interest rates make it more difficult for women (who are more likely to work part-time or have checkered job histories) to obtain credit? If tax credits for the cost of health insurance premiums are proposed, how does that impact women's ability to obtain health insurance if they are primarily employed in service jobs where employers do not offer it? These are issues (and omissions) that require commentary by prominent women in the economic community; the goal is for the reporter to call women for their opinions before such stories run. Similarly, women must monitor the slant of stories, particularly the use of headlines to convey the essence of the information. Irene Natividad, chair of the National Commission for Working Women, recalled that when the National Women's Political Caucus surveyed voters' attitudes toward a woman as a presidential candidate, 57 percent of American voters believed a woman could do a well as, if not better than, a man as president. But many headlines distorted the story, proclaiming "Nearly a Third Oppose a Woman President" and "Many Voters Oppose Women in Oval Office."

6. Women should also monitor the inclusion of personal details about women in a news story. If her age, marital status, physical appearance, dress, or residence are mentioned, are they included in stories about men as well? Who are the reporters who are the most offensive? Women clearly want to avoid those reporters. In Boston, women were outraged at one snide and superficial newspaper profile of Susan Weld, the governor's wife, that appeared in the *Boston Globe*. ("Kitty She Ain't," screamed the tabloidlike headline.) The intelligence and accomplishments of this Harvard lawyer and Ph.D. scholar in Chinese law was trivialized ("no makeup, no hair dye, no spike-heeled shoes") as she was portrayed chasing a pet rabbit around her stereotyped spacious Cambridge "Ameri-British" home.

After a woman has become a sophisticated reader of the local and national business pages, and has established contacts with the trade or general circulation business reporters, she should expect that she will be called for comments or opinions and she should be prepared.

Micho Spring remembers her early hesitation and shyness in dealing with the press. "I was so naive at first, I thought it was beneath me to talk to the press. I was just concentrating on getting my job done. That is why someone like John Sasso, former governor Michael Dukakis's chief of staff, was so brilliant. He understood that you don't make policy first without the press person understanding it and communicating it well. It's the same in the private sector. No company can be isolated from the real world of press coverage, and if you can't explain what you are doing, you should rethink it."

Micho Spring and others shared what they had learned over the years in dealing with the press. "Always return phone calls" is one rule that generally applies.

"Most businesspeople define success as avoiding the media," Micho observed. "It isn't. But you do have to know who to avoid. You have to know which reporters are intelligent and honest and won't burn you, and you have to know how to deal with ones who are biased.

"You can be both offensive and defensive," she said. "You should use the media where you can; reporters are always looking for stories, and businesspeople are far too shy about being sources. That is power."

Women must be clear and prepared when speaking with a reporter. Is the conversation for full attribution, deep background, or on the record but not identified by name ("an industry executive said")? Be willing to trade information. Assume the worst questions a reporter can ask, and have an answer prepared for them. "I'll have to get back to you on that" is better than "no comment."

A top executive who is sophisticated in dealing with the press is an asset, and not just in times of crisis. "Some companies are unbelievably naive in dealing with the press," stated one business editor. "They have in-house public relations executives who don't even return phone calls. I remember once we were working on a story on the region's fastest-growing companies, and we were under deadline pressures. One of the companies we had chosen to feature was in the health care business, and I called their p.r. person to set up an interview with one of their top executives. She actually turned me down, saying she was too busy with a photo shoot that day for a marketing brochure. Can you imagine what might have happened to that company's stock if we had run the story, featuring them?"

How do women executives get visibility if all press calls are routed through their public relations gatekeepers? "Set yourself up," suggested the business editor. "When I call a company, I want the best. I want an expert. I don't ask for a woman.

"But," she continued, "an expert is the person who talks like one. An expert is the person the company gave me to interview. So get to know your public relations person. Tell him or her that you'd like to begin speaking out on topics x, y, and z, and when press calls come in, you'd be happy to be interviewed. Or better yet, give them a story about a client you have just landed or a project you are working on. Ask them if they think it is newsworthy for the local business press.

"I love company public relations executives who call me with stories. The smart ones give me options; 'it's a long feature,' 'it's a thirty-second read.' I may not use it this week, or even next week, but I just might need it one day when another story falls apart. I tell them to keep being a pest. It is not a personal affront if I tell them I am busy right now on something else. Our business is to be bothered. We would bother them if we were after a story, so they should bother us."

Being prepared includes thinking about the press when something is about to happen, reporters suggested. "The best executives to work with are those who'll flag us in advance," one said. "I'll never burn them in return. After all, they are the ones who know an announcement about a merger or new business partnership is going to happen this afternoon, or they expect that the Supreme Court will rule shortly on an important case they argued in court three months ago.

"Let's take the court case. A local law firm that represented a major software company lost a chance to get publicity in an important case on copyright of computer programs. The partner in charge knew that the decision would be announced soon, but neither the law firm nor the company had a communications plan in place. The smart move would have been to coordinate in advance a spokesperson from the company and the law firm, ready to talk when the case came down, explaining the issues and the decision.

"But instead, the decision came down, and we didn't know whether to cover it or to what degree. We called a source at the bar association, and ended up with a lawyer from another firm who agreed to be interviewed on the record, in a hurry. As it happened, the decision was favorable to the company, and the law firm that handled the case was angry that another law firm received publicity for talking about it. But that's the way it goes!"

One executive woman whose skill in dealing with the business press helped advance her career is Trudy Sullivan, a retailer who rose through the executive ranks at Federated Department Stores and then left to start her own chain of specialty stores. Trudy's example is more striking because she endured months of potentially negative press, recounting the detailed story of the spectacular success and then bankruptcy of her company, T. Deane. But through it all she gained the respect and admiration of her peers in The Club.

Trudy Sullivan epitomizes female-authority. After working for many years as a department store buyer and manager, she saw that few retailers were catering to the niche market of larger women who liked better clothes. In 1985 she started her own retailing company, T. Deane, with four stores in high-income areas. Before long she had twenty-one stores across the country, and sales had zoomed from zero to $18 million in three years.

The reason for her success was Trudy herself. Her advertising research showed that women needed to relate to someone, the woman who was running the company, the woman who wore their size. Trudy became the best spokesperson for her company and her customers. She spoke with authority and confidence about their needs. Her company's advertising featured Trudy, while newspapers across the country featured news stories about her retailing success. She made frequent appearances on television talk shows and at special events.

A business writer described Trudy's style: "On the screen, just as in her stores, her hair and face were beautiful. She spoke well, explaining without resentment that she led an active life and didn't need to be thin to do it. This was believable. You could look at Trudy Sullivan hard and still not see the slightest trace of a thin person wanting to get out. Her wrists were bracketed in gold, a scarf encircled her neck. But as her voice and smile and anecdotes differentiated her from the stiff mannequins who often represent the fashion industry, the audience listened."

Trudy's retailing concept and stores were a success, but when the third round of venture capital financing unexpectedly pulled out in 1989, Sullivan was stuck. She frantically worked to find alternative financing, even a new owner, to raise the capital necessary to stock the stores. On the day before her final deal was to be signed, the prospective owner pulled out. Sullivan filed for Chapter 11.

"When that happened, we got as much publicity as if U.S. Steel had gone into bankruptcy," Sullivan recalled. "Our bankruptcy was front-page news despite the number of other companies going under at the same time. So I'd say visibility is a double-edged sword. I wouldn't want anyone to have to live through what we did, even though much of the press coverage was sympathetic."

The experience, however, didn't cause Sullivan to lose her sense of humor, class, or style. One of her senior executives caller her "the consummate CEO," who "never lost her cool." When Harvard Business School called asking to make a case study of what happened to her company, she laughed. She said it would be a better mini-series.

She also admits the visibility she gained in the business community, even with the stories of her bankruptcy, had a positive effect on her business career. She is well known as an authority on specialty fashion retailing.

"After the story in the paper about T. Deane going Chapter 11, the son of the chairman of a local private retail company, Decelle, called me. I didn't know him, but he had read about me. He said they needed a consultant from the outside to help them analyze some merchandising issues.

"I didn't know there was a hidden agenda. When his father asked me to be president of the company, I warned him that people would think he lost his mind because of the publicity about T. Deane's bankruptcy. There were a lot of unemployed but experienced retail executives for him to choose from, and plenty who hadn't gone Chapter 11!

"He said he wanted someone who knows what it's like to be there by yourself. He thought I was that much wiser coming to him, having gotten an $11 million education in my own company." Sullivan's final visibility, which she regarded as negative, actually helped project her authority and business acumen.

Trudy Sullivan is now president of Decelle, running a $50 million profitable private company "with no debt," as she notes. "It's refreshing now to just run a business without worrying about the public relations angle," Sullivan said. "I push the business out front, not any one executive. But certainly I'd say that visibility is an important part of a woman's career strategy, particularly because women are still more novel, more newsworthy. If you can stand the challenging publicity, do it."

Trudy Deane Sullivan had the advantage of running a business that featured her in advertisements as a strategic marketing technique. She paid for her initial visibility, although she found out that the paid advertisements generated much more unpaid publicity, as she herself became the newsmaker. But it was Sullivan's calm, approachable demeanor, even in the face of adversity, that reinforced her reputation as a competent executive, as well as her willingness to respond to the press in an honest and forthright manner.

THE RISKS—AND THE REWARDS

Visibility has its downside, of course. Dealing with the press is risky and riding out the inevitable negative story requires a tough skin. Sometimes there is nothing that can be done about such stories, particularly in cities where individuals are caught in a newspaper war between competing dailies. Other times, sensitivity to how a reporter might play a story can prevent a possible disaster.

Micho Spring finds herself always checking how the press might react to an account of a particular event, thinking it through before it occurs. "I know this makes us paranoid, but it is important for women to understand. I was a trustee of a public community college, and one day I received a call from their personnel department. A relative of mine had applied on her own for a job at the college and had put me down as a reference. This is a perfectly nice lady and I wanted to help her; certainly she had done nothing wrong. But I honestly didn't know how to answer the question, because I could see the headlines now: 'Ex-Deputy Mayor in Patronage Scam at State College.' That's how the story would come out if it were ever known that I had acted on her behalf."

Micho's instincts were probably correct. She trusts in her own ability to understand the power of press visibility and measure its public impact. Women who have studied the press, become accustomed to dealing with it, and benefited by it should always follow a pattern that has worked for them.

Mary Gordon,* scientist, academician, consultant, author, and high government official, should have trusted her instincts, too. Mary started her professional career with an exceptional academic record and a string of fellowships and awards. Early in her career, she became interested in the scientific side of space exploration and developed a dual-track career as a research scientist and a consultant to companies interested in exploring space—an unusual role for a woman. Her expertise was timely, as attention to using space vehicles and missions for private research became a national issue. Mary began to write and speak on private space science ("invented the term," one admirer said), and soon consulted with major institutions, companies, and the federal government.

Mary Gordon had always appreciated and used publicity well. It was as critical a tool of the trade for her as word of mouth from her distinguished national client list. She used publicity often, giving interviews about space exploration for newspapers, magazines, and television, and creating news for placement. Her tortoiseshelled glasses, red hair, and trademark navy blazer made her a familiar face accompanying the articles and her refreshing enthusiasm about space careers even generated several adolescent fan clubs.

There were few women at Mary's level, and one of Mary's missions was to encourage women to be quoted as experts, particularly in the thousands of popular articles written about space and science. She consistently talked to many senior-level women about being available for media quotes. She believed that visibility was a critical asset for women in their personal marketing plan, and showed them how to use it.

Mary's reputation and visibility led to an appointment to head up a new federal office overseeing the transition from the use of space for defense purposes to civilian use. But now the problems started. Her years of success in science had not really prepared her for what happened. The culture at the federal level was unique. Most of the officials and elected representatives she dealt with had been prominent elsewhere; their own egos and reputations had grown as their public careers and visibility increased. They did not welcome Mary's appointment or her ideas.

Mary's first few weeks as a public official were difficult. Her style, so well received at private companies, did not work in the jealous world of the public sector. One sympathetic senator explained to her that this was not uncommon for those who came in from the outside, and shared with her the story of a well-known Fortune 500 CEO whose first year as a cabinet secretary had been similarly difficult. But Mary had little patience for the endless parrying and politics, including that of her subordinates in the agency. She had a job to do.

The month her federal appointment was official, the leading California daily newspaper called her for a news story. She granted a phone interview, which was her custom; it never occurred to her to check policy on press relations. After all, the president himself had announced her initial appointment at the White House with a major press event.

The story received extensive coverage; the combination of an attractive, nationally known female scientist, a new federal agency, and the general subject of space exploration made her appointment a compelling front-page story for the business section. She was hailed as the commanding general of a new agency that would soon rival all others in influence and revenues, and embark the nation on a new course.

Little did Mary realize that this article would make her life miserable. When it appeared, both her scientific and public sector peers were shocked and outraged. Mary had unknowingly violated an unwritten rule of public service: publicity about a nonelected official is considered inappropriate self-aggrandizement at the expense of those who run for office.

The following year was stressful, as Mary endured the snipes and stares of those in government and her colleagues in the scientific community. A year later the newspaper called again, looking for another story about the agency. Contrary to her practice, Mary ducked the press. This time, the story was devastating, because the reporter was forced to quote from whatever source he could find—and he found her enemies, gleeful for the chance to stab her. Her photograph was again large, but the context was ripping. She had forced resignations, stirred up old resentments, ruined the mission of space exploration, kept changing direction, and worse. Buried deep in the story was a statement of great support from an influential senator, but the overall effect was negative. Mary was stunned at her first bad press, and concerned that her former clients and scientific peers would undoubtedly see it. How had this happened?

Mary didn't realize that learning the rules about visibility in a new culture is important for professional success. In retrospect, she realized she should have talked to the reporter, arranging this time for others to share credit and be quoted. She should have understood that since she already was newsworthy, the story would not go away, and dealing with the press is always preferable to ignoring it. But she missed a chance to turn it to her advantage, and use the occasion to smooth egos and solidify relationships with members of The Club who could determine her future success.

Mary survived the one negative story because her reputation was intact among those who knew and respected her. She received calls and letters from friends in the scientific community, administration officials, and many clients, urging her not to be worried about the story. Mary had experienced the circular nature of visibility: media coverage provides entrance to a network of opinion leaders, which becomes the base of her power currency. Visibility is the insurance policy that builds professional equity in the community, but in those moments when insurance is needed because of negative press, membership in The Club takes over.

Despite the occasional tough story, Mary and Micho firmly believe that public exposure is worth the risk. The real benefit of visibility, they say, is to advance public consideration of issues women care about. Visibility is a necessary precondition to earning the credibility to speak about issues, and a tool to creating awareness about these subjects. "The new world women seek will come about when women articulate it," Mary said.

The sophisticated use of personal presence is where women's real power currency flexes its muscles. Women who have tried this strategy successfully show that the development of personal power comes in stages. A woman is recognized and respected as an outstanding professional. Through a combination of her stature and visibility, she achieves membership in The Club. There she is respected and admired by her peers and the larger community of opinion leaders. It is at that moment, speaking out on issues of concern to her, advancing the economic status of women, that she is most effective.

Men have used this model effectively. Lee Iacocca has an admirable track record as one of the nation's top chief executives in the automobile industry, in part due to his own autobiography and willingness to talk to the media. Therefore, when he becomes one of the first to speak in favor of a national health insurance system, arguing that his cars cost hundreds of dollars more than those of foreign competitors because of the health insurance premiums his company must pay, policymakers listen. When David Kearns resigned as head of Xerox Corporation to continue his personal crusade to improve the nation's educational system, linking improvement in education to economic productivity, educators paid attention.

We are beginning to see examples of women using their hard-won positions of prestige and influence to advance broader concerns across the country. In California, Dr. Frances K. Conley, a neurosurgery professor, briefly resigned in public protest over gender insensitivity ("I don't like the word *harassment*") at Stanford Medical School. While sexism was commonplace at Stanford—a steady stream of inappropriate attitudes and offenses, according to some—it took Dr. Conley's resignation and protest to catch the attention of the dean and faculty. The precipitating action was the dean's intention to appoint Dr. Gerald Silverberg as chairman of her department. Silverberg, who was reputed to be insulting to women, would only perpetuate the acceptability of sexist behavior toward women, Conley thought. Believing that institutions must value leadership sufficiently to examine closely the behavior and ethics of those at the top, Conley could no longer stand by and be silent as a "bad apple" moved into position of executive power.

Breaking the barrier of silence was extraordinarily difficult, Conley found. "As women, we are socialized to respond disproportionately to disapproval. We teach our daughters to cooperate with men and not compete against them," she said. "Therefore, in a traditional white male environment, it becomes very difficult to change certain microinequities because they have become part of the culture of that environment which is defined as 'normal' for that particular environment."

Part of the accepted behavior of the culture is to be quiet and go along with the actions of others. But Conley could no longer be silent, despite the enormous cost. "The horizontal hostility and resentment directed at women who blow the game by proving that you do not have to fold to get by, that you can hold out for the integrity of your work and survive, is unrelenting and unforgiving," Conley said. "All this takes a huge intellectual, spiritual, and physical toll. What we are up against here is nothing less than women's survival in a world that wants us dead. Silence equals death."

Conley's resignation and public discussion of the reasons made her national news. She received hundreds of letters from women across the country, while the dean agreed to reconsider his decision to appoint Silverberg. Faculty and students discussed women's concerns, planning programs to raise the consciousness of men and remind women of their rights. Female students felt empowered to speak out against insulting behavior, a risky proposition in a male-dominated culture where success depends upon acclimation. But Conley had led the way.

Going public certainly has risks, but women such as Dr. Conley who are at the top of their profession feel they have little to lose. Making a difference for the younger women coming along is often a prime motivation for breaking silence, overcoming any qualms about embarrassment. A professional reputation that has been developed over decades can't be diminished by speaking out on behalf of women.

Thirty years after becoming the first female partner in the international law firm of Baker & McKenzie, lawyer Ingrid Beall sued the firm for its discriminatory treatment of her, resulting in her dramatic loss of income. After a change in management at the firm, Beall, a tax partner, began to be excluded from important firm committees, and was not given the quality and quantity of assignments from others in the firm that would generate income. The treatment she received was demeaning, but Beall was not afraid to go public with her complaints after settlement negotiations broke down.

The public read and heard about Beall's lawsuit in interviews she gave to the *Washington Post*, CNN, and WNYC-FM and in publications that picked up on the story, such as the *New York Times*, the *Wall Street Journal*, and the *Los Angeles Times*. Dean Geoffrey R. Stone of the University of Chicago Law School commented on her bold action, noting, "You're talking about a very distinguished lawyer here. This isn't a crackpot."

"I've never been much of a feminist," Beall said. She may have been too busy, graduating second in her class at Chicago Law School and serving as editor of the Law Review. Beall worked in the firm's Brussels and Paris offices, helped to build Baker & McKenzie's far-flung international practice, and handled complex international tax issues for some of the world's largest companies. An active participant in bar association activities and alumni activities, she served as national president of the University of Chicago Law School Alumni Association. Beall taught law courses, participated as a panelist at many seminars, and served on many firm committees, chairing its Financial Committee. The result? "In recent years I was just systematically denied work so that my compensation would go down drastically," Beall said.

Instead of quietly retiring as the firm had hoped, Beall sued. "I don't have thirty years practicing law ahead of me," she said. "The young [women lawyers] cannot do it, because then they are troublemakers. And if you are a troublemaker it's hard to move to a new job. On the street it gets around and there is very little sympathy for young ladies who cause trouble." Beall may not think of herself as a feminist, but in standing up for better economic treatment of female professionals, she certainly acts like one.

Beall's willingness to speak to the media about her lawsuit will have an immediate impact on the way firms treat women, whatever the outcome of her own proceedings. Other women are also finding ways to use their understanding of the media to impact the treatment of women. Using their personal power currency in Hollywood, senior-level women in the entertainment and production industries are banding together to strategize how to raise women's concerns in television and movie scripts. "These efforts will literally affect what you see on the screen," said Nancy Alspaugh of Group W Productions. "This is not about advancing any of us in the group; it's about the way women are depicted."

Some women have discovered that they need not be prominent executives or professionals to harness the power of visibility and make a difference in their community. All it takes is an event, issue, or opportunity and the willingness to step into the spotlight. Lois Gibbs was a homemaker who started asking questions, spoke up, discovered Love Canal, and paved the way for corporate responsibility for toxic cleanup. Candy Lightner was a mother who started asking questions, spoke up, got mad at lawyers, judges, and legislators, and founded Mothers Against Drunk Driving. She discovered men and women across the country who felt the same way she did, and gradually, state by state, they changed attitudes and laws about drinking and driving.

Our current heroine in the change-the-culture category is Teresa Fischette, a thirty-eight-year-old part-time ticket agent for Continental Airlines. Continental announced that female employees must wear foundation makeup and lipstick or be fired. Fischette did not wear makeup, but had company records that showed her to be a model employee, including monthly report cards on personal appearance. She wrote six letters asking Continental to reconsider. On May 3, 1991, Fischette was fired.

Fischette went public, to news organizations from radio to afternoon television talk shows. She could have noted, as did others, that with such Neanderthal management practices, it was no wonder that Continental went bankrupt. But attractive and poised, Fischette's message was conciliatory and consistent. "I didn't just want my job back," she said. "I wanted to make a difference in my own company."

And make a difference she did. Continental changed the rule to a guideline, and reinstated Fischette. But despite her victory, Fischette did not gloat over Continental's surrender.

"Surrender—I don't like that word," Fischette said to a *Boston Globe* reporter. "I see this as win-win situation. I didn't take on Continental. I took on outdated attitudes." Then Fischette took a month of unpaid leave to work on women's issues, using her newly established personal currency to make a difference for other working women.

Fischette has mastered the lessons of visibility: project a personal style that commands respect and admiration, use a well-developed aura of authority to step into the limelight when opportunity presents itself, understand how to deal successfully with media representatives, and deliver a message that improves the economic status of all women. Businesswomen across the country are learning that this formula works. As they move into the ranks of The Club, they are using their visibility and professional status to form effective personal relationships with their male peers.

CHAPTER FIVE

FORGING FRIENDSHIPS

A Business Reality

I can still feel the embarrassment and rage that I experienced when the front door of a private club in one of our major industrial cities was slammed in my face a few years back. I did find the correct 'ladies door' and I did go to the luncheon we were sponsoring. But the hurt, the shock to my confidence returns whenever I think of that city.

—Alice Hennessey, senior vice president for human resources
and corporate relations, Boise Cascade Corporation

Barbara Martin* had reached senior executive ranks as chief financial officer at one of New York's major investment banking institutions following a short career as a computer programmer. After earning her M.B.A. she progressed on a fast track from financial analyst to the position she now holds. Two of her company's directors had invited her to serve on the board of directors of their corporations, where she was the only female. Barbara was well known in the small world of New York chief financial officers, even though she seldom attended civic or charitable events.

When Carol answered an urgent call from Barbara to join her for breakfast, Barbara did not look like a confident and successful executive. Rather, she seemed to be under stress as she unfolded the story of what had happened a few days earlier.

"I've hit the glass ceiling," Barbara told Carol. She was the highest-

---

*An asterisk denotes that we have changed the name of the person quoted, and in some cases the name of that person's company and its location as well.

ranking woman in her company even though she had never been responsible for a division, product, or line operation. Her relationship with the
presidents of the outside operating divisions was excellent and they often
communicated closely with her to keep the lines of information open with
corporate headquarters. There was no doubt that Barbara was supportive
and well respected in the field. Many of the division heads used her as a
sounding board for their budget deliberations and shared their proposals
with her prior to formal review.

Three years earlier, John Robertson* had been brought into the company as a potential successor to Norman Bains,* the chief executive officer
and Barbara's boss. The two men had first met at a charity golf event, and
now were golfing partners. Robertson, a career banker, was given the position of chief operating officer.

Barbara had been reporting to Norman, with whom she enjoyed a
good but professional relationship. She was now being asked to report to
John, to "show him the ropes," as Barbara phrased it. Barbara dedicated
herself to helping John, and was stunned when her record of continuous
stellar performance reviews came to an abrupt end. After one year, John's
evaluation of her was unexpected. As Barbara put it, "It was tough, and I
disagreed with it. I didn't think I could be brilliant for all those years and
then suddenly become so stupid." Barbara considered leaving the company, because she had decided that she respected neither John's ability nor
his managerial style. But she was also unwilling to give up her career with
the company just because a new boss turned out to be difficult. She felt
isolated. She saw no immediate solution except to try and persuade Norman Bains to allow her to report again directly to him. After discussion, he
agreed.

Life returned to normal for Barbara. The company had a banner year,
and she felt she had contributed to its financial success. She politely refused John's half-hearted invitation to golf, not wanting to give up a weekend day for him. That was not her style. She thought the past tensions
between them would go away if she just remained civil but distant. But last
year Norman announced to Barbara that John would likely be named his
successor in the coming year.

Barbara felt she could no longer be silent. Confident in her long and
open relationship with Norman, she told him of her opposition and concerns about John. After two years of closely observing John, Barbara now

felt she had ample reasons to tell Norman why his choice of John for CEO was a poor one. She was concerned that the relationship within the entire senior executive team was being affected by John's style, and she was convinced that Norman was listening to her. After all, hadn't he respected her opinions on past business matters?

Recently, Norman and John had invited Barbara to meet with them. The meeting was to be part of her annual review regarding her accomplishments during the past year and they asked her to tell them how she saw her future with the company.

Barbara was not prepared for what unfolded at the meeting. Norman started by saying that he and John knew of her reservations about John's position as the next chief executive officer.

Barbara was shocked. How could Norman have betrayed her confidence so openly? The revelation that Norman had told John of their private conversation stunned her into silence. She sat mute as Norman and John told her that they were troubled by her attitude, an issue that became the sole focus of the meeting. She was asked to tell them within a month what her plans were. Not sure if they were hoping and suggesting she would resign on the spot, she asked for time to think before making a response.

"So here I am," Barbara told Carol. "In retrospect, I mishandled the whole thing. What do I do now?"

After a successful career in which she made few missteps, Barbara had hit a major career obstacle and there were few people with whom she could confide. Certainly there was no one inside the company. At home, Barbara's husband was no more consoling. He could not comprehend how she had stumbled into this situation. She now turned to Carol, whose reputation as a successful female executive suggested she might be helpful in the ways of organizational maneuvering.

Carol reassured Barbara that her problems were not unique, knowing the experiences of other senior-level women who had encountered similar fates. Carol dissected the clues to Barbara's situation:

• She did not understand that her previous excellent performance in the financial area did not necessarily give her the clout to criticize John, who, as a career banker, had demonstrated an ability to produce profits. Not all vice presidents are equal; power goes to the rainmakers, not to expense and support executives.

- She had not recognized and used communication styles that would help bridge the gender gap in talking to Norman. Her issues about John's style, while obviously important to her, did not impress Norman, who had a good relationship with him. Straight business issues regarding John might have been more convincing.

- She had not developed the personal currency within the broader community, which often comes from being visible in civic and business organizations. Reputation and respect from her business peers in the community would have strengthened her stature with Norman, but more importantly, they would have accorded her immediate respect and status from John.

- She neglected the importance of techniques for building personal friendships with those in the inner executive circles. If she had established a friendship as well as a working relationship with Norman, he would have strategically helped her manage the situation with John right from the beginning. He would never have surprised her with the meeting with John. Similarly, she ignored the importance of establishing a personal connection with John. Alliances are often forged outside the office, and whether or not Barbara played golf, she should have found a way to meet John halfway. Her distance from him only worked to weaken her position.

- She neglected to collaborate with other senior women for support and problem solving. At any stage in her experience with John and Norman, objective, seasoned businesswomen could have provided careful analysis and frank feedback about the unfolding events, helping Barbara develop a winning strategy to handle John and Norman and move her own objectives forward.

Barbara's story was not unique, as women who share similar experiences and problems have discovered. Bridging the relationship gap to men is a tricky exercise, but one that is essential if women are to become influential in The Club.

Sheryl Murphy,* a Los Angeles career banker, explains how close relationships can make the difference between being inside and outside her own bank's Club. "It's an issue of socialization. I never felt like I was part of what was happening when the previous management was here. Now, I'm 'one of the guys.' I worked with them before at another bank, I shared their values, and now I'm one of the guys running this zoo, now that our gang is at the top. When I moved to this bank, I said, 'I want my guys with me' and they came. Now I'm the one, the guy at the top."

How do women achieve ease "with the guys," as Sheryl did, and why is it so important?

In Chapter 1, Sally Berger showed how personal relationships and friendships help solidify personal power, bring in business, and achieve goals. In Chapter 2, women of diverse professions stressed that developing relationships with those who give business is a key strategy for rainmaking success.

But even if an executive woman is not a rainmaker, the other professional success she seeks is often dependent upon forging positive relationships with men in power. There is a difference between having members of The Club know *of* you, and *know* you, as Micho Spring found out in the face of negative press, when her male peers came to her defense. Visibility in business and professional circles for women is a good start, but it is visibility strengthened by friendship, the link to the qualities of "fit" and "trust," that will bring women full membership in The Club.

Sheryl Murphy explained: "When there are changes at a corporation, all the guys have a support network. They leave together. A woman is often stuck there. What does she do? Should she stay and try to make her way in with the next group, or should she go? Who will take her? The guys are all off following one of the other men to a new company. Men hire their business school buddies, or their friends from the old job, and form a whole new company. Watch a company change, and you'll see a few go, and then they all go together. They follow each other out. It's harder for women to do that if they are not part of the group—the old issue of isolation."

Building relationships with men is not just another instance of women trying to fit into men's social culture, standing like debutantes at a ball, seeking approval and a little attention. Relationships go two ways, and there are many sincere men who are bewildered as they try hard to understand the best way to solidify friendships with women in an era of sexual sensitivity, particularly at the workplace.

Traditionally, executive women erred on the side of acting professional and tough. A cool, schoolmarm demeanor was a good defense mechanism; many women thought it was required behavior. They were never to slip up, to show any sign of femininity or warmth. Such displays were considered unprofessional.

But now, women with power don't run the risk of being perceived as unprofessional if they develop friendships with men inside and outside their company. Their motives are not suspect; they are just acting the same as the other men in The Club. They have nothing to lose and much to gain.

Sheryl Murphy told how her prior personal relationship with her bank's new chairman increased her power immediately. "One hour after Peter Bird* came to the bank to take over as the new chairman, my phone flashed. Our phones spell out the name of the caller, and it was BIRD. That word was all over the bank in a second, because two senior executives were in my office at the time and saw it. My power increased overnight, as well as my ability to get things done, only because I knew Peter from when we worked together at another bank, and he called me the first thing when he came here. I was his best buddy here. It's a little thing, but important. Men don't want to work for women because they are perceived as having no power, so we have to show them we have power in every way we can. Close relationships with other powerful people are part of that."

Sheryl Murphy understood that her ability to get things done with her peers at the top level depends on her personal power, but some women, like Barbara Martin, still think that hard work is enough. They overestimate the value of excellent performance and underestimate the importance of human traits and personality. Women who have concentrated on their credentials and careers may not have been socialized to value the art of being charming or open with others, but it is a behavioral trait that is valued in the workplace. Developing close relationships with others is not the same as being well liked. A woman can be well liked from afar, and still not have anyone in The Club know her well. She is the woman who rarely goes out to lunch or travels with her male peers, and never wants to.

"Women talk about competence all the time," said Sheryl. "They miss the dynamics of relationships. Some men have more personality than brains, but those are usually the ones who 'get it.'"

Sheryl didn't know Barbara Martin, but she had anticipated Barbara's problem. Barbara had missed the importance of the personal factor.

Cathy E. Minehan, chief operating officer of the Federal Reserve Bank of Boston, agrees that the combination of being known by decision makers and a reputation for good work is important for women. She was the first woman in the Federal Reserve Bank of New York's management training program in 1968, and steadily worked her way up through the Federal Reserve system. "My work style is no different than men's. I expect others to do a good job, and to be competent and confident. But relationships are important. I was always known as being on a 'particular team' for most of my career in New York. You have to build relationships along with demonstrating competence."

Nancy Alspaugh, a Hollywood television producer, warns that in some businesses, relationships can be more important than competence. "Being well known is important in the entertainment business. You need a proven track record, of course, but you have to be well known by the powerful men in the industry. That is why mentors are so important for both men and women in Hollywood. Then if you are well thought of, the agents will take your call. You're really considered talent once you have an agent. And once you have an agent, your superiors will respect you more."

Men have often had mentors to guide them through the behavioral minefield of the workplace, but for women, mentors are sometimes hard to find. The reluctance of some men to spend time mentoring women is a gender difference that impacts their advancement in The Club as much as any other factor. The reasons are understandable: men prefer the company of other men; the two executives may not see each other often; the woman may not know what to ask; the mentor may rarely see her in work situations enough to give good feedback; and some mentors simply do not take young women seriously. Worse, "you then face the 'sex thing,'" one physician observed. "Many men are just uncomfortable with a social or friendly relationship with women."

Perhaps for those reasons, senior women who described the role that individual men played in their careers rarely used the word *mentor*. Instead, they talked about a "great guy," an "extraordinary individual," a "male feminist," a "real supporter," a "father of daughters." In many cases, their influential male supporter did not work with them, but was a member of The Club. These men laid out the informal guideposts in The Club that were less obvious to women, and made sure that women were included in the right places at the right times.

One chairman of a medical department at a prestigious teaching hospital recalled how she made it into the "information loop" of advancement in the competitive medical world. "I had a mentor who told me, 'You're going to get a fellowship.' And he made it happen. At that point I figured out there was a Medical Club. Then I said, 'I'm interested in the next promotion. What do I have to do to get it?' His response was, 'I didn't know you were interested,' but he told me how it worked. I did what he said, and I got the promotion."

Cheryl Wills, president of Erie Coast Communications and the first woman president of United Way in Cleveland, believes the need for partnership with male Club members never stops: "It is important to say something positive about those men who have reached down and found us. We didn't get there solely by our merit or by accident. These men need positive reinforcement. We can't let them think we don't need them anymore, just when we *do*.

"The key for black women," Cheryl said, "is being mentored by white males. Wives of these men may be threatened; others who meet you and find out you know the man think it is odd you don't know the wife, and assume something from that fact about your relationship. But we need white males to mentor us because there are few black males in The Club who can.

"Let me give you an example. In 1980, I was the first female president of the United Way, and also the first black. Being president is expensive; the president has to take people to lunch, come up with a staff, and pay his own way to meetings. Dick Baker, managing partner of Ernst and Ernst, knew that as the head of a black funeral home, I didn't have the corporate resources that major CEOs did, so he established the first President's Fund. It wasn't just for me, but from now on, whoever was president of United Way could have enough money to travel, hire his own person as staff, and carry out responsibilities in the same way his predecessors did. He created a level playing field, and opened the door for women, minorities, and others in the community to assume leadership roles in the United Way, and ultimately in The Club.

"In Cleveland, a lot of business activity goes on at private organizations that are both racist and closed to women. With the President's Fund, you didn't need access to corporate memberships at those places. You could hold your dinner meetings, thank-you receptions, or kick-off breakfasts any place you wanted. Dick Baker had a wonderful idea with that Fund; he removed a very subtle barrier to membership in The Club, and helped me be successful."

In every community, top executive women can name extraordinary men who recognized their talent and potential, asked them to serve on important task forces or committees, invited them to private dinners and functions with other members of The Club, and acknowledged their contributions publicly, enhancing women's visibility and prestige in the eyes of others.

Developing relationships with members of The Club is not just important for personal success. If women ever hope to move into key positions on company boards of directors, on legislative policy committees of business trade associations, or onto key public policy task forces or other seats of power in the economic community, they must be well known to those doing the choosing.

"You simply do not put a stranger on a board or in an important job," one woman said, and we agree. We would use the same criteria. Generally, a member of The Club must be personally acquainted with the individual being considered, or must find someone else who is. Personal testimonials by those who know a candidate well are critical in evaluating issues of fit and trust.

But being chosen for these important positions is only half the story. Women will be much more influential if they are also known by those they are trying to influence. While public visibility will help give a woman the immediate credibility she needs until others get to know her well, it is her personal power that will be most convincing as she begins to express her views to her audience of peers.

We believe that the combination of public visibility and solid personal relationships is a strong one. It is relatively easy for women to develop a measure of public recognition. Breaking into circles of friendship with male members of The Club can be a little more difficult.

Few women have run into outright barriers such as they encountered twenty years ago, when women first began to protest their exclusion in public places. Scenes like the one in New York on the birthday of the Great Emancipator in 1969, when Betty Friedan and others tried to be seated in the Oak Room of the Plaza Hotel to eat lunch, were common in cities across the country. The Oak Room did not serve women from twelve to three o'clock, the key hours just before the stock exchange closed for the day.

In Boston, Deborah Sinay, vice president of sales and marketing for WCVB-TV, recalled her days working in advertising for the Jordan Marsh department store. Jordan's "had a table" at Locke Ober's, the popular downtown restaurant in the days when the first-floor dining room was reserved for men. Deborah accompanied her boss and a client to lunch, and was stopped by the maître d' as she entered the restaurant. "Why don't you go shopping?" he said to her. "Not even, 'Why don't I seat you all upstairs?'" Debby remembered.

Such stories are rarer in the 1990s, although not entirely. We admit we were shocked to hear of an experience an Oregon physician encountered recently: "I was with a good-sized medical group, with sixteen physicians; we specialized in internal medicine and pulmonary diseases," she told us. "Some of my partner physicians wanted to merge with another, smaller group, and they suggested I go meet the most senior physician there and see what I thought of him. So I called him up, and suggested we get together for breakfast or lunch.

"He told me, 'I won't have lunch alone with a woman.' At first, I didn't understand him. I thought he was kidding. But he was perfectly serious, saying he was a Mormon, and would not have lunch with me.

"I was outraged. I said, 'I may be your future colleague and you're not going to have lunch with me?' I protested back to the other physicians, but none of them would back me up. I said, 'What if he had said he wouldn't have lunch with me because I'm black, or a Jew? Would you still want him as one of our group?'

"They didn't get it. This guy had a large patient base, but as far as I could see, the numbers in his group were pretty shaky, with high receivables and not something we wanted. But they made excuses for him, and decided to merge. I decided to leave. I was so disgusted I didn't want any part of it. Sure enough, it turned out to be a disaster for the group."

This incident is the exception, as few senior women have reported outrageous snubs by male peers. But many women described personal experiences of what they called benign neglect.

A female executive vice president of a large banking institution remembered one recent incident: "There were six of us on the management committee: the chairman, president, me, and three senior vice presidents. One Sunday in March the chairman invited everyone but me to his home to watch the NCAA basketball playoffs. When one of the senior vice presidents walked in his family room, he looked around and said, 'Where's Anne?' Evidently there was an embarrassed silence and everyone let it pass, but I heard about it the next day at work. I made light of it, but underneath, I was really hurt. The truth is, I know those afternoons are not about *basketball* at all. It's about bonding, information, and friendship."

The fact that she shared the story with a group of her female professional peers was the first step in acknowledging that these incidents happen to many. Although the others had similar stories to tell, they were not discouraged. Excluding women from peer groups has become unacceptable, as demonstrated by her colleague's instant recognition of her absence and the fact that he brought it to the group's attention. She knows the chairman will never exclude her again.

A California executive recruiter said women should just ignore the men who won't change: "It will be too frustrating and it's not worth our time," she said. "There still are men who are macho, who have no comfort zone with women. But then there are others who are real supportive. You have to find those. There is an enlightened group of CEOs coming along, men with daughters. We should concentrate on them."

Many of the women we talked with agreed with her and shared ideas about building relationships with men in The Club: "I think you have to first try to understand men," one corporate director said. "Many of them are just as uneasy as women are. I remember one asked my advice about a younger woman who worked in his company. He was very proud of the fact that she had just landed a big new job with another company. On her last day in the old job, he really wanted to tell her to go spend some money on a new wardrobe for her next job, so she'd look more like a top senior executive, but he was afraid that it would be the wrong thing to say. I just told him that if I were the woman, I'd really appreciate his suggestion!

"You really have to like men and be like men at times," she continued. "You have to share their stories but never act on any of them. That is off limits. Stories are a learning activity, not something to take advantage of later on. It's the equivalent of the locker room, only one on one. I know some women who chase men out of their office when they come in to gossip and just talk, but I think that's valuable time. Of course women shouldn't confide anything important to them!"

Another corporate director suggested that women take the lead, and just invite men out for breakfast or lunch: "I particularly like breakfast; it doesn't take much time, and power breakfasts are common. You don't even need an agenda; just tell him you thought it was time to catch up, or you want to ask his advice about a couple of things."

These women said that if women are serious about adding more women to The Club, it is the women who will have to make the extra effort at building relationships with men. Many men simply do not care if they know women or not, and don't bother to make the effort. They feel there is not much benefit in it for them, and there may be some risk.

But we think the culture may be changing, as it becomes less and less acceptable to exclude women from business and social gatherings where economic leaders converge. The steady collapse of all-male social clubs illustrates the point.

GENTLEMEN OF THE CLUB

It's not surprising that we think about men's clubs when we begin to talk about issues of exclusion and relationships. The presence of these grand old institutions gives them more cachet than they deserve, perhaps, but the decline of their importance in many cities is analogous to the changing climate for men and women in the rest of the business world.

Many of the men who joined these clubs and who have remained as members were socialized at any early age to associate only with other males. From all-male preparatory schools to all-male colleges and universities, upper-class, educated white men made a natural transition from school to the world of all-male social/business clubs at work. Even at coed universities, the tradition of all-male social clubs endured.

It was not until 1991 that Princeton University's oldest eating club, the Ivy Club, admitted women. This "breathlessly aristocratic" haven includes such alumni as Supreme Court Justice John Harlan and former secretary of state James A. Baker 3d, as well as scions of well-known business families: Wanamaker, Auchincloss, Scribner, and Rockefeller—surely a gathering of future Club members.

The Ivy Club welcomed women members enthusiastically, but the welcome at Yale's Skull and Bones was anything but warm. When its student members voted to accept seven women into the secret society in 1991, its alumni board of directors declared the election void. Skull and Bones was "drastically out of step with Yale and, what's worse, flagrantly discriminatory and bigoted," its seniors warned the alumni. A bare major-

ity of the alumni agreed, voting 368 to 320 to admit women. But unde-
terred, old-guard alumni, led by conservative columnist William F. Buckley, Jr., went to court to block the admission of women.

Why the big fuss in this day and age over admitting women to a secret
society? Should women want to join any club that doesn't want them as
members?

Young women at Yale have undoubtedly realized that economic
power will be the leverage for change in their adult lives. Just as they have
been prepared academically to work alongside their male peers in the business world, so must they also build the personal relationships that influence activities and decisions at the top executive level. Their 1991 classmates will be counted among the members of The National Club many
years later, if the past roster of Skull and Bones alumni is any guide.

In the public policy world, President George Bush is a member, as are
Senators John Kerry, David Borin, and John Chafee. In addition to Buckley, McGeorge Bundy and William Sloan Coffin are alumni. In the business world, its roster includes the president of the Blackstone Group, the
former chairmen of U.S. Trust and Bankers Trust, the chief executive of
Baxter Travenol, and the founders of Donaldson Lufkin & Jenrette, the
brokerage firm. Bonesmen attend an annual reunion, and as one member
said, "There's a natural tendency to do business together. There's a certain
trust, a certain comfort level, they develop in the club."

While alumni such as George Bush and William Buckley may not feel
any urgency about admitting women to their sacred enclave, contemporary Yale students are aware that the world has changed, and even in the
most private of clubs, exclusion of women who may be their peers in every
other arena is hard to justify. As one student explained, "We're not getting
good people because they don't want to be part of an organization that
would discriminate against women—particularly if you have any future in
politics. You never know when you're going to have to explain it away."

This view of the political landscape also applies to the business world
where, in most circles, executives who seek the best talent are sensitive to
projecting an image of a corporation that is exclusionary.

From the Skull and Bones and Ivy Club to the world of city social
clubs, some male executives just traded one cozy reading room for another.
But as more women entered the business world in the seventies and eighties, attacks escalated on the membership criteria of these all-male institu-

tions. To some women, the continued existence of all-male clubs is an irritating reminder that women are continually accorded second-class status in the business world. The presence of a few all-women's clubs is little consolation, as many of these were started, and remain, as social enclaves primarily for professional volunteer women.

The importance of these clubs varies by city. In some communities, every gathering and decision of importance occurs in the one or two most prestigious clubs. In other cities, the clubs are relics of a bygone era, and matter little to men and women. Even those that have admitted women have not necessarily changed the climate of hospitality toward new members. A female member might bring a guest to lunch, but it takes a very brave woman to sit down at the "members table," joining other unaccompanied members if she is not personally acquainted with any of the diners.

A chilly reception is often not worth the emotional time or effort. One Virginia executive told us how she unwittingly became embroiled in a controversy regarding a local yacht club in the early eighties: "I had just been transferred by my company to its division in a growing Virginia market, and I was the top executive there. Our company was a major advertiser in the local daily paper, and the publisher and advertising manager took me to lunch at a local yacht club not long after I arrived. While we were eating there, they introduced me to a number of members of the chamber of commerce, elected officials, and others who were eating there—all men, but I didn't think that was strange. I was used to that.

"My company pays for one club membership for its top executives, and I decided that this yacht club was convenient, and I might as well choose it. I'd rather sail than golf, so it made sense. The publisher agreed to sponsor my application, and I didn't think any more about it, until the membership committee called my office, looking for a photograph.

"I was the first woman to apply, and that started a furor. One anonymous member wrote a letter to the chairman of our company, saying he wasn't sure if 'management knew what its local manager was up to.' The chairman called to tell me not to worry.

"I wasn't sure I wanted to get into a big fight about admitting women, but since the publisher was behind me, I kept my application in. His newspaper did a big story on the issue, quoting members of the yacht club who said things like, 'We don't want any single attractive women hanging around,' and 'What did she think she'd find there?' All I said was 'no comment.'

"The night of the vote at the yacht club, the members who were opposed to me kept a filibuster going until they lost the quorum. So then they needed a special meeting. The publisher was ready to sue the yacht club and the city if we lost the vote, because the city had deeded the piers and slips to the club, but it wasn't a totally clear-cut legal issue. He needed my permission to sue, of course, and at that point I decided I had enough. I didn't want my introduction to the community to start on such a contentious note, so I withdrew my application.

"But the controversy was not over, because when I withdrew, a number of women in the community were just furious with me. They wanted to press the issue. Finally the yacht club heard I was getting married and invited me to join under my husband's name. I said no, since my company was paying for *me*, not my spouse.

"Several years later, of course, the yacht club began admitting women, and now the local executive women's group meets there regularly for dinner meetings."

Most top executive women we spoke with are now members of such clubs, or have been invited to join. However, few thought that this was an issue worth fighting about. The symbol of such clubs, particularly those that still decline to admit women, is more important than what goes on inside.

It is the symbolism and anticipated practices of these clubs that disturb many women who are invited there, and there is not unanimity on how to respond. The requirement of entering such clubs by a "ladies" or side entrance is still prevalent in many communities and prompted a heated debate among three women.

"We long ago stopped requiring blacks to use separate facilities and entrances—women are no different and I absolutely refuse to use a 'ladies entrance,' no matter what the occasion," said an executive from Los Angeles. "It's positively abhorrent."

"It depends on the occasion," said a Baltimore bank president. "If I were invited to dinner or an event I didn't particularly care about, I'd refuse to attend if I had to use the side entrance. But I can see where I might make an exception—if I were the only woman being honored at a major gathering of executives in my profession or community, and it was important to me to stand up and be recognized in front of that predominantly male audience, I'd do it. The visibility and acclaim would be worth it. So I'd use a balancing test."

"I don't think it's worth getting upset about," said a consultant from Chicago. "I always view my role as making others feel as comfortable as possible, particularly clients. It diminishes my stature to make a fuss about such a trivial matter. I wouldn't even call attention to it. While I obviously wouldn't host any events at such clubs, if someone wanted to meet me at one, I'd adhere to the club rules. If that's where my client or business peer feels at home, I'll act accordingly."

There is no one right answer, of course. In our opinion, all-male clubs have a right to exist as long as they own up to what they are all about and don't claim any special treatment from taxpayers. We don't believe any club that discriminates against a class of individuals should receive preferential tax treatment (as some country clubs do, claiming open space status) or liquor licenses. We do not think that such clubs should use public property, as another yacht club did for years while denying female boat owners the right to moor their boats near the club facilities. We agree that public employees should not be allowed to entertain or attend or hold meetings at any clubs that discriminate or that tax laws should permit deductions for "business expenses" at such clubs. We agree with those who would prohibit public contracts to companies that pay for memberships in discriminatory clubs and we use such paid memberships as a litmus test in evaluating the moral code of companies, politicians, and institutions.

But if a group of men clearly wants to associate with just other men and not include women (or other minorities), that's okay with us. We will accept their statement at face value and judge them on it. We know that many clubs are secluded retreats for members whose tastes and idiosyncracies are less than modern. It will be left to the clubs and their members who seek the stimulation of talented new people and ideas to win the acceptance of prominent men and women and the paid memberships and sponsorships of corporations and institutions. We are confident that contemporary values will win the day, and nondiscriminatory clubs will be the survivors in a competitive social and business marketplace.

NOW YOU SEE IT . . . NOW YOU DON'T

The fact that many all-male clubs have opened their doors to women does not mean that the old-boy network is dead. In many cities it has just moved to other locations. The challenge for women, therefore, is to build relationships with its members that are so strong that the men will insist the women also participate in the network no matter where it finds itself.

If the old boys are not at the private clubs, where are they? Depending on the community, there are several places that they gather: hotels, athletic clubs, or private charity dinners.

Carol remembers her introduction to Boston's long-standing Commercial Club, a social institution of the city's economic leaders that meets quarterly for a black tie dinner and speech. The Club had never admitted women, and held its dinners at a private club that was also closed to women. Most of the chief executive officers and senior executives in the city were members, as was the president of the Federal Reserve Bank of Boston, whose board Carol had joined in 1978.

"Frank Morris had arranged for William Miller, the secretary of the treasury, to come to Boston and be the speaker at the next Commercial Club dinner, and he wanted to invite his entire board. When he informed the club officers about it, they reminded him that no women were allowed, but Frank showed them what he was all about. He told them if I were not invited, no one else was coming either. I think I was the first woman to attend a Commercial Club dinner." In 1992 the Commercial Club counted 8 women among its 208 members.

From black tie dinners like the Commercial Club to breakfasts at diners, the integration of the old-boy network moved slowly. One top-level woman newspaper executive explained where The Club in her city met each day. "A friend told me that when it was announced that I was the new publisher, the good old boys weren't happy," one Southern woman recalled with amusement. "They were used to gathering each morning at the local diner with my predecessor. They'd all discuss the news of the day, local politics, real estate deals or what not, and then go off to city hall, the paper, or their companies. Finally, when one good old boy was complaining loudly, my friend said to him, 'Well, don't you think she eats breakfast, too?'

"Gradually I worked my way into the morning breakfast ritual, and we became fast friends. They figured out that I eat breakfast, too. A number of years and two jobs later, when I had sold my printing company and was looking for another opportunity, a number of the boys were very good to me, making calls and contacts. When I thanked one for a particularly helpful call, he drawled, 'Why honey, you're *family*, now.'"

Sometimes the way to integrate is with money. Club members gather where there is money to be made or given away, and if a woman can put money on the table, too, she is included. Charity dinners, sometimes honoring a male member of The Club, are a common gathering place for Club members, and a woman who sits on the dais at one of these dinners as a sponsor instead of a spouse sends a megamessage to her dais peers and the hundreds of ticketholders in the audience: She has arrived at the level of other sponsors.

At the same time, the list of committee members, honorary chairmen, and event sponsors sends another message to those who glance through the program as the tributes pour out for a particular captain of industry. At one such black tie dinner for the Boy Scouts honoring a bank chairman, the four male chairmen of the dinner were the chairmen of two manufacturing companies, a consumer products company, and an international engineering firm. There were eighty-eight individuals listed in the program as members of the dinner committee, only one of whom was a woman. There were fifty-two vice chairmen, of whom two were women. There were fourteen members of the "advisory council" for the Boy Scouts, all male. The three-tiered dais on the stage of the hotel ballroom was a sea of sixty-four black ties, with one woman in a glittery red dress.

The audience of several thousand Boy Scout supporters, many of whom were employees of the corporate chairmen who bought tables at the dinner, received an unmistakable message as they looked to the dais. The business community in that city was male, and few women had arrived at that level. Not only was The Club male, but corporate contributions were given to male causes. The Boy Scout dinner was one of the biggest events of the charity dinner season.

We are not quarreling with honoring male executives or missing the point that it is his peers who will write the corporate checks and show up at the event, raising money for a worthy charity. We are suggesting that women who have the resources to write a check should figure out which charities The Club supports, and if it is important for her to be part of The Club, the charity circuit usually welcomes contributors of both sexes equally.

Civic and charitable dinners are held in communities across the country, and often present an all-male picture. But some male business leaders are now sensitive about the image these events project to the business audience, the press, and public policymakers.

In one large West Coast city, a former manufacturing executive became president of his state's industrial trade association and found himself presiding at its annual black tie dinner two months later. Much to his chagrin, his board of directors on the dais were all white males, surrounding the association's two honored guests, the House and Senate chairs of the Legislative Committee on Commerce and Labor, both female legislators. He wondered how his legislative package would fare in the coming session and vowed to find several female manufacturing executives for his board and legislative committee within the year.

In the same city, one of the first acts of the new male executive director of the chamber of commerce was to appoint a task force of directors to restructure its unwieldly, predominantly male, ninety-member board of directors and eliminate the five tiered dais at its annual meeting.

Charity committees and civic association events are accessible to women, but when the old-boy network moves to weekend sporting retreats, women have a hard time breaking in unless they are superbly skilled fly fishermen or skiers. We are not sure how the Skull and Bones will handle its annual gathering at Deer Island, a resort on the St. Lawrence River, when the Bones becomes coed. But many corporations have run retreats at sports resorts for its senior executive ranks with no problems of discomfort among the attendees or jealous spouses left at home. Admittedly, ostensibly social retreats of those who are acquaintances in the business world and not co-workers is a different story. Here, women are outsiders and are likely to remain so. Most women have little desire to go on such trips, where hours spent in the wilderness is the main activity, but they are not unmindful of the value of long stretches of time with their business peers in a totally different and relaxed setting.

Helene Wilson,* the only female member of the board of directors of a failed commercial bank in Texas, explained how she became aware of the "club within the club" of bank directors. "It really is a boys' club from which we are excluded. When one of the boys was chairman, the board meetings were very quick. There was an agenda and we all moved through it rapidly. The goal seemed to be to get out of the boardroom by two o'clock. When his vice chairman suddenly resigned, he didn't tell the board, and no one asked about it at the next meeting. I assumed that all of the other outside directors knew the story, and I knew the cardinal rule about not bringing up new matters at the board meeting itself. So I let it

go, but I was used to the nonprofit world, where there would be great discussion at the board level if a key executive left.

"We had a board dinner one night, and I overheard all the men talking about the hunting lodge where they had all just gone salmon fishing
together. That's when I began to put it together: the chairmen kept them
all in line, all informed, at these salmon outings. I was just the token.

"After the regulators came in, and disaster hit, the feds told the directors they were going to have to run the bank. Some of the outside directors, including me, protested. I like being on the board, but I wasn't a
banker. We had around-the-clock meetings; I remember one night lying
on my kitchen floor at one o'clock in the morning while I was on the
phone with one director. Another director, a veteran of these salmon fishing trips, finally broke ranks with the chairman and got mad at a meeting.
This was very unusual. You never show emotion at a meeting. He pounded
the table and said he'd been lied to about the real estate loans. That broke
the ice, and from then on, the outside directors acted as a team, and I was
on the team. We ousted the chairman and tried to save the bank.

"You know, men play at games," Helene said. "That's how they work.
The games are an extension of work. The new chairman of the bank told
me that he learned a lot about other men by how they play racquetball.
Maybe there is merit to these games outings, but women are left out. I
decided it was important for me to get to know the new chairman outside
of the bank and its board meetings, and for him to get to know me. So I
invited him to a charity function that I was helping to run. He brought his
wife, and I brought my husband, and we sat together and had a lovely time.
He got to know me and many of my professional peers better. Now he calls
me outside of board meetings for advice on various subjects."

Helene had found a strategy to build relationships with men that
seemed to work. Other women told us that they had only figured out the
intricacies of relationship building by trial and error, and that women have
to teach each other the techniques that work. "I get subtly excluded," said
one senior-level financial executive in New York. "I've never been anywhere where I've felt completely part of The Club. A small element of
that is my own personality, but not all of it."

"As I look back," said this executive, who had been treasurer of an
international manufacturing company and executive vice president of a
major financial institution, "I think women are too worried about the

quality of their work. Men are worried about getting ahead and figuring out the right people to know. The next big improvement in the lives of senior executive women will be engineered by women. It will be the forty-five-year-old woman telling the thirty-five-year-old woman who will tell the twenty-five-year-old women what's important—like relationships. We have a half life of memory on these subjects and we forget to pass it on. At the same time, men's greater awareness will come about by women raising these issues of exclusion."

In New York, she sees a particular problem, "the backyard enclave," as she calls it. "You never hear men say, 'My neighbor in New Canaan is Susan, with Lazard. Let's get her view on whether to do that public offering or not.' This back door approach is open to men who have other powerful men as their neighbors or golf partners in the exclusive suburbs. This doesn't work for women, because usually we don't live there. Exclusive suburbs is where wives live, not where senior businesswomen live. Most of us live in the city. Even if we did live out there, we are not called on; few men will call the wife of a male neighbor to discuss a business issue.

"These neighborhoods are not going to change in a hurry. High-end suburbs will be high-end suburbs. The men in power have wives who have quit. This niche of highly compensated men lives in these enclaves."

One strategy executive women have used to overcome the high-end neighborhood problem is to develop relationships in the city near the workplace, by opening their city home to a wide range of guests. One woman who has done this successfully is a member of The Club in San Francisco. A partner in a leading real estate firm, a director of several business associations, and a Democratic party activist, she chose her city town house specifically for its location and room layout.

"When you walk into her home you enter directly into a Great Room, with fireplace and skylights," said an admiring Club member. "It's the kind of room that can hold 150 people for a political event, sixty people for a charity buffet and concert, or twenty people around a table for a serious breakfast meeting. The point is that Suzanne* has an open-door policy and everyone in the business community is used to going there—for seven-thirty A.M. bagels and an off-the-record session with city officials or for five P.M. cocktails to meet an important out-of-town visitor. Her house has become the hub of the wheel, an old-fashioned salon where all the opinion leaders of the city gather. When Suzanne hosts an event, you know everyone else will be there and probably just the person you've wanted to get to know better. As a consequence, everyone in town knows her, and her circle of relationships gets larger and larger, because she never knows who will show up, brought along by someone else. This wouldn't have happened if she lived in the suburbs or anyplace other than five minutes from downtown.

"Everyone has been there so often that some Club members just ask her if they can use her Great Room to host a meeting or event *they* are having, particularly if they want the privacy of a home and not a restaurant or office conference room. She never says no."

Informal social/business events, whether planned around a particular cause or person, can be the setting for women to get to know men better, but some women initially feel uncomfortable in going to such events alone. It is easy to fall prey to the notion that "no one will miss me if I don't show up." "I'm not good at those kinds of things," or "I have too much work to do back at the office (or at home)." That's just the time that women should make the extra effort to go and speak to three more men they don't know well.

The only tenured black professor in one college of a prestigious university described a scene that executive women in any male-dominated profession could relate to. "Every month I was invited to the college tea, where I was the only black person," she said. "All the whites would politely ask me about the only black person they knew, assuming I knew him or her, too. I felt out of place. I thought it was a waste of time, so I stopped going." She laughed at the recollection.

"I was so naive I didn't know that was where information was exchanged. No one *told* me that was where I was sized up, where judgments are made, relationships formed. Now I don't miss a tea. I've become trustworthy and my personal currency has increased—because, of course, those monthly gatherings weren't about *tea* at all."

Sometimes, forging friendships with men involves attending events that women might just as soon skip. But one woman, a Wall Street executive, suggested that women's own activities need not change if women are willing to invite men to participate in them. That way men will have a better chance to get to know them as friends.

"I have a weekend home in horse country," she said, "and at first I just went there by myself every weekend, to unwind and ride. Then I started inviting my personal friends to spend a day or a weekend.

"As I became more accustomed to entertaining and letting guests just do what they wanted to do, I decided to invite our senior executives and their spouses for a day. Some came, some didn't, but it was very informal and relaxing. They enjoyed it.

"Not long after that, I joined a skeet shooting club in the area, as much as a way for me to meet local people as anything. But when the club ran events, I started inviting men from the company who wanted to try their hand at it. Some of them really enjoyed it and they've become regular guests at my house. They've obviously come to know me a lot better than they did before, but I think the real trick was matching them up with skeet. I've provided an activity for them as well as company and a place to come to. That's the key, I've discovered—most men socialize around an activity, while women socialize around talk. That's why we have breakfast or lunch together, but men prefer something to *do*. So women who want to build relationships with men have to find something to do with them."

Many executive women have found that the level playing field they seek in the corporate world actually begins with a level "playing" field. Recreational sports have become the activity that men and women can use to build personal relationships and often the sport of choice is golf.

THE LINK THAT COUNTS

In the course of our study of issues confronting top executive women, we would ask women what, if anything, they saw as a barrier to further advancement in senior management, in rainmaking success, in gaining membership in The Club. Over and over again, we heard variations on the same theme: *golf*.

From one senior vice president of a national insurance company: "The president of our company invited a male employee who reports to me to play golf with him, but he didn't invite me. Since I don't play golf anyway, I don't know whether to be upset or not, but I have to admit I didn't like it."

From a partner in a national accounting firm: "I finally learned how to play. Golf's not so hard, but the problem is the country clubs. They are the most sexist, and don't allow women to play at the times the men are playing. One day I had three male clients from Detroit flying in to play golf with me. They arrived at ten A.M. and we had to sit around until we were allowed to tee off at one-thirty."

From an executive vice president of a bank: "I happened to wander into the chairman's office as he was approving an expenditure of ten thousand dollars for a golf charity tournament, just as he was also preparing a letter and press release announcing massive layoffs and closings of branch banks. I spoke up and stopped it right there, but he honestly did not understand the connection, how it would look to employees, for the senior executives to be off golfing while the employees were standing in unemployment lines."

From the senior vice president of a consumer product company: "In these very tough times, we are all working extra long hours, doing the work of those who have been restructured out. I don't mind that. What I do mind is that it is perfectly acceptable—even an honor—for the top guys to take off a few days and fly away to play in some big golf event. Meanwhile, if there were a major quilt show that I was interested in attending, I'd be laughed at if I took a day off to travel to see it."

From a senior television executive: "I'm on the board of a local disease foundation, and we were planning a fund-raising event at which we were going to honor a local executive. At the lunch meeting at which we were going to choose our honoree, all the men discussed the candidates in terms of their golf games. It is so silly, but it is absolutely true that men get their work done on the golf course. Golf is a part of their job; for women, it is hours away from the office that we have to make up."

From a partner in a major law firm: "Golf! I lost one of my biggest clients to a lawyer from another firm who had a chance to golf with him. I still burn when I think about it."

We heard so many stories about golf that we began to pay more attention to the intersection between golf and business. We realized the importance of golf had been right in front of our eyes all the time, but because neither of us played golf, we had missed it as an issue for executive women. But golf is central to many business circles and members of The Club.

As the takeover of RJR Nabisco was played out in the business pages and subsequent best-selling books, the nation's business readers became acquainted with perhaps the most notorious executive golfer, Ross Johnson, the former chairman of RJR Nabisco. "A ten-handicap player, he did business over golf, he relaxed over golf, he spent his spare time watching golf. He had played every major golf course in the country—and belonged to most. . . . Johnson, who earned more than $2.7 million in 1987, had trouble remembering what was his and what was the company's. . . . Most of Johnson's golf memberships were paid by the company, and the corporate hangar was equipped with golf club racks and carriers, since the chairman couldn't be expected to tote his own."

To a lesser degree, this same picture is painted in many executive suites. Some executives, like Harold Poling, the chairman of Ford Motor Company (eight-handicap) see a direct connection between executive skills and a golf game: strategic play, striving for balance, dependability, accurate timing, and consistency. Corporate sponsorships of golf tournaments are an important form of targeted advertising that is becoming more important, according to former professional golfer Jane Blalock, who now consults with companies on golf issues as president of her own sports marketing firm.

"An LPGA event may cost five to six million; a PGA event twice that," Blalock said. "This is just for the name, not the expenses. A local event may cost half a million. But the costs are worth it. A company buys an image and name recognition, with the company's name in headlines on the sports pages for a week or more. It's a good way to entertain clients in hospitality suites, and usually a charity benefits from the proceeds. It's a legitimate sport, straightforward and clean. Golf is becoming a real phenomenon in business; even I was surprised, after moving from 'inside the ropes' to the business world."

Jan Thompson, vice president of marketing for the Mazda Motor Division, explains why her company sponsors executive golf clinics for women. "If you don't play golf, you'll wind up in charge of lunch."

The more we investigated the world of golf, the more we began to realize that the appeal of the game made sense. There are few activities that men and women can do together, outside of the office, that lend themselves to developing a personal relationship in real quality time. Even traveling on a corporate plane, recommended by one executive woman as her best strategy to get to know Club members well, presents participants with alternative choices of sleeping or reading.

Unlike tennis, golfers can talk while they play, and the players are not playing against each other, which can be little fun for opponents of unequal ability. While swimming, skiing, and sailing are not win-or-lose competitive sports, there is not much opportunity for quality conversation in those activities. So it is not by chance that a glowing business story on the "best companies for women" began with an anecdote of a female vice president playing a round of golf with the chief operating officer. This quality time is the chance to "build trust and build the comfort level" and is "very critical in terms of who will get promoted," the story related.

There is no doubt that women across the country are catching on to the importance of golf, a lesson that we learned late in our careers and have not yet acted on. Although only 22 percent of all U.S. golfers are women, the LPGA reports they accounted for a record 40 percent of the 2 million Americans who took up the game in 1989. From 1985 to 1990 the number of women golfers has increased 35 percent to 5.4 million, and the National Golf Foundation predicts there will be 8 million women golfers by the end of 1993. Two thirds of these women are employed, a group one advertising research study called "young actives." Advertisers have noticed this group. For example, the New York Times Magazine Group decided to sponsor a women's golf tournament in Vermont. Its *McCall's* and *Golf Digest* magazines will sell premiere sponsorships to major corporations for $90,000 each, giving them ad pages in the magazines and tournament program, as well as cable television spots and booths and banners at the event.

Although the number of women golfers is rising, Blalock warns that executive women may be missing the boat if they don't get outside their offices and on the golf courses soon. "Most of my clients are companies that are very concerned that their otherwise bright female M.B.A.s are missing something," she said. "I go in to talk to their executive groups and tell them about the value of golf in business; it is really an international language today, and an important part of doing business. Companies are anxious that their women get out there and play."

And why don't more women play? Blalock has observed several handicaps.

"First, men aren't afraid to play if they don't play well; women think that they have to be good to get out and play. That's simply not true. The score is not the point. Golf is just a comfortable business environment. It is easy to develop a relationship with a fellow chief executive officer, client, or peer on the course; much easier than just walking into his office. You can tell a person's emotions, their temperaments, their personality. It is easy to become friends on the golf course.

"Another problem is what I call the guilt factor," Blalock explained. "Women don't yet think of golf as part of their work. Not many companies give women time off during the week to play. But those women who do take time off have noticed an increase in their business. There is a definite cause and effect. Even on a sales call, golf is a common conversational ground for a woman to speak to a man about and most men who golf are enthusiasts and react positively to someone who plays. That gives women an immediate leg up.

"More and more companies are now urging their women to get rid of the guilt factor and play, particularly those that sponsor tournaments. For example, the Newport Cup is a big seniors event, sponsored by companies like Xerox and New England Telephone. They pay nine thousand dollars for each player to enter and the companies are looking for women in the senior executive ranks who play. If women executives would only learn to play golf and go out there, they will find they are at a big advantage, even within their own company. The companies I know *want* their women to play.

"I know for senior-level women it may be hard to start," Blalock said. "They didn't grow up playing sports, like the men did, in Little League or Pop Warner. It is better for younger women coming along, who at least played some sport, but I know many older women did not. But that shouldn't stop them. There are many intensive golf training weeks they can join, and then just start playing."

Or can they?

Blalock is well aware of the final reason many women have not yet caught the golf fever: the discriminatory attitude of many country clubs toward women players. The most famous is Burning Tree Club, outside Washington, D.C., where Dan Quayle plays but which bars women as members and guests. Sandra Day O'Connor, an avid golfer, wanted to join, but Burning Tree wouldn't hear of it.

Burning Tree is in the minority in barring women; only about 20 of the nation's 5,000 private clubs still restrict women totally. More often, however, women face restrictions so severe that they might as well be banned from the premises. One lawyer described a visit with two female and one male companions to a privately owned but publicly accessible golf course. While the male paid the greens fees for the foursome, the women carried their clubs to the tee. The owner, seeing the women, grabbed some bills out of the cash register and slammed them on the counter, yelling "This isn't a playground! Get out!"

But Blalock believes the landscape is changing. The old rules restricting women from playing on weekends and Wednesdays are disappearing. In 1989, interior designer Jan Bradshaw filed suit against the Yorba Linda Country Club in Orange County, California. Even though she had purchased a full-price membership at the club, she was not allowed to tee off before 11:00 A.M. on Saturdays and 1:00 P.M. on Sundays, and was barred from voting for officers. The club agreed to change its policies.

The wake-up call to the golf industry about discrimination, however, was delivered at the 1990 PGA Championship, scheduled to be played at Shoal Creek Country Club near Birmingham, Alabama, a segregated club. When corporate sponsors, including IBM, America Honda, Toyota, Anheuser Busch, Lincoln Mercury, and Spalding, threatened to withdraw their $2 million in advertising, the club agreed to admit a black and the PGA Tour stated its tournaments would only be played at clubs that were nondiscriminatory.

The following year, golfing professional Tom Watson resigned from the Kansas City Country Club, where he learned to play golf, in protest over the club's refusal to admit Jewish businessman Henry Block. "Let's discriminate right now, each one of us, privately, between what is right and what is wrong," Watson said. "At work, at the country club, at home with the children (especially at home with the children), let's make our own personal choices that help, rather than hurt."

We might say the same thing to corporate executives who play at country clubs that impose gender-based restrictions on players. Those barriers that are based on sex and not ability to play, congestion on the course, or any other neutral factor are as discriminatory as those practiced by Shoal Creek or Kansas City. Golf is a good way for women to develop important personal relationships with their business peers, and corporate executives can help women succeed in business by making sure the course is open for them.

While golf may not be the activity of choice for all women, it is clear that men and women who want to build personal relationships and work in partnership in The Club must continue to spend the time necessary to get to know each other. This quality time is necessary if men and women are going to stop fearing or ignoring each other, and begin to act as peers who like and respect each other and value each other's ideas. This is the basis of sincere adult friendship. When that occurs, positive things will begin to happen in the business and professional world.

CHAPTER SIX

THE COSTLY WAR
OVER SEX DISCRIMINATION

My Natural Science 5 section man said to me,
'Women can't be doctors.' When I asked another
professor if he'd take me as a tutee, he said, 'I
don't take girls.' When I complimented another
professor on a lecture, he stared at me for several
moments, then said: 'Would you like to come and
see my etchings?' When I tried to get birth control from a doctor, he said, 'Educated women
make wonderful mothers.'

—Holly Worthen, Radcliffe College, Class of 1965

If men and women could just be friends in the workplace, life would be
easier. Unfortunately, relationships between the sexes are complicated,
and executive women have experienced everything at work from sly flirta-
tions to offensive harassment and blatant discrimination. While we would
like to report that all work situations are positive for women, and that
some women have risen to senior levels without a hitch, such is not the
case. Many women who have made it into The Club have confronted significant gender bias in their relationships with male peers and superiors.

OPPOSITES ATTRACT

Let's first address the issue of "romance." No woman we spoke with had
ever conducted a serious and successful romantic relationship with a co-
worker and none recommended it. Several women insisted that such a

relationship would be the kiss of death to a woman's career (no pun intended). A few went further, warning that single business and professional women should never bring dates to company events, lest they then become the subject of office speculation and gossip.

We think such a warning may overstate the case, but we also realize the backlash of a romance depends on a woman's status and the culture of the company in which she works. One unmarried bank executive vice president was emphatic about social situations. "I never ever mix my business and personal life. I am quite comfortable attending company events by myself; I have a chance to talk to my male peers and pay attention to their wives. I don't have to worry about whether a date is having a good time or what the senior officers think of him—because I know right away they will size him up. Is he someone on their level, or not? Are we having a sexual relationship? How did I meet him? The questions would go on and on, and I don't need that. And then their wives would get into the gossip mill, too. I'd rather their wives see me as a spinster than a social being. I'm less threatening that way."

But another woman, a director of two Fortune 500 companies, did not think that being unmarried and bringing a date to an event was a problem. She was sensitive to the culture in which she operated, and had assessed the acceptance of dates of other unmarried individuals at previous company events. "One corporation has an annual retreat for directors at a lovely resort, and spouses are invited. I have brought a date to the last few, and my fellow directors have been most hospitable to him. He had a good time, I felt perfectly comfortable, and it worked out just fine."

Even the unmarried women who introduced their dates to business peers, however, would hesitate to date an individual at the office, a customer, or competitor. Most of the time the risk is not worth it, and most women believe their careers would inevitably suffer.

"This is a bigger issue than the usual Mary Cunningham–William Agee speculation," one woman said, recalling the intense media coverage during the early eighties of the young blonde executive who enjoyed a rapid career rise and eventually married the former chairman of Bendix Corporation. "Mary Cunningham made basic mistakes, like dropping Agee's name in conversation too many times, spending all her time with him, holding hands with him in public, and taking credit for work others had done, thus setting up her enemies.

"Agee was Cunningham's boss, but unfortunately, the dynamics are the same even if the woman is as powerful as the man," she added. "Invariably, the gossip will affect her more negatively. She will lose respect and power, and possibly her job. But 'boys will be boys,' and the men will survive."

The business and professional world is the most obvious place for men and women to meet, become friends, and develop more intense relationships. The fact that "power breakfasts," civic task forces, and lengthy golf outings might lead to romance is not unexpected. But executive women agreed that certain rules of common sense apply.

- It is certainly bad business judgment to develop a romantic relationship with a married man.
- If the man is a customer, competitor, or co-worker, women must analyze the conflict of interest situation early in the relationship and decide which has priority, the career or the relationship. One or the other must change.
- It is bad business judgment to date a subordinate or a superior in the same reporting structure in the company unless the woman is prepared to change companies.
- By their conduct, women must set the example for others in the company.

Women who advocated tough standards for office romances are not just concerned about the career effect on the woman involved, but also about the total productivity of the office. Their experiences and observations concur with reports that have shown productivity and morale decrease in working environments where romances are well known.

A COMPLIMENT OR AN INSULT?

A romantic relationship implies a union of equals, in which both parties welcome the companionship, attention, and love that develops. More often, however, women have dealt with *unwelcome* attention from male business acquaintances, superiors, and co-workers. In some industries the problem is particularly widespread. The $7 billion music business, for example, is called "a sanctuary for sexual assault."

"Sexual harassment is so widespread in our industry," one television executive said, "that I don't know any women who *haven't* experienced it at one point or another in their careers. That's why we were all so upset over the Clarence Thomas–Anita Hill hearings. It brought it all out again. We were more angry about what was accepted as common practice all along. Our outrage is all about the denial and silence that we've endured for years."

Many women who have spent decades in the business world have not forgotten their earlier experiences. A fifty-year-old Houston venture capital executive could recall the precise details of incidents twenty-five years earlier. "My boss harassed and harassed me, and I didn't know how to handle it. I came home and cried my eyes out to my fiancé, but he didn't know what to do either. It was two weeks before our wedding, and I didn't have the stamina to confront it. Also, I needed the job. So I tried to forget about it, and eventually changed jobs. Then I never did anything, because I was so busy being 'focused' on my career. That's what all my male mentors told me was important: to be focused, like the men were. Well, the hell with it. I'm sick of being focused. I'm mad that I ever had to put up with it and mad that I didn't do something then."

The Hollywood and Houston women sounded like many of their peers who also experienced some type of sexual harassment early in their careers, when it was a part of normal behavior between the sexes and before it became actionable. In many cases, blatant sexual harassment was considered part of standard social interaction—even a compliment. It was a private matter, evidencing the status of a relationship, not a matter of law and certainly not a concern of an employer. The experiences of these women confirm extensive polling data and studies which show that a majority of women all over the world have experienced incidents of sexual harassment.

But poll results are not particularly meaningful in determining how many women who have now reached senior executive status have suffered from harassment at the hands of men and have succeeded in spite of it. We suspect that a woman's actual experience as a victim does not predict whether or not she will label herself a victim. With the hindsight of age and the benefit of success, some women may resist the self-designation of "victim" and may continue to rationalize and dismiss past negative experiences as they go forward.

Whether a woman thinks that she has been harassed depends on who does it (her boss, a co-worker, a client), the type of behavior, the context in which it was done, and her own state of mind and career level. In talking to many executive women across the country, we found a wide variance in what was considered sexual harassment. Most had experienced some form of it, but usually early in their career. These women all realize now that sexual harassment has little to do with sex and a lot to do with power. Now that they are older, more mature, self-confident, and powerful, they would not tolerate what they tolerated when younger, and would not allow others to be harassed. Of course, many of them are finally in a position to stop it.

Age gives women an advantage, said Elaine Victor, a television producer in Paris, who warned that senior executive women must now stand up for younger women. "As older women, we are fine. We can fight, argue, push. We have social standing and clout. But I worry about the lower-level women. They are not okay. Their problem is that they have to put up with fascists," she said.

Most women who have reached middle and senior levels of the business and professional world have matured and developed self-confidence. But one study suggests that these women may also be more autonomous and independent than their male peers, acting as mavericks in the organization. Instead of being assimilated into the male environment and accepting the prevailing culture, these women are not hesitant to challenge behavior that is offensive to them and to others. They consciously decide not to be victims, and know ways to fight back. This style often disturbs men who are their professional peers, resulting in descriptions like "too aggressive" or "troublemaker" being applied to strong-willed women. Unlike younger women who often just leave lower-level jobs in the face of harassment, older women tend to be highly invested in their careers or positions and choose to stand and fight.

Many senior-level women who are now working to eradicate sexual harassment in the workplace may be more sensitive to such incidents not only because they experienced it themselves, but because when they endured it, they did not have female mentors, superiors, or role models to stop the behavior nor any legal or corporate remedies to guide them in dealing with it.

Despite the fact that Title VII of the Civil Rights Act of 1964 opened many doors for women in the business world and eliminated blatant forms of sex discrimination and legal barriers to professional employment opportunities, it was not until 1977 that a court ruled that a woman who was forced to submit to sex to keep her job was a victim of sex discrimination. The courts were finally beginning to understand that in the context of a working environment, sexual harassment was not an issue of social compliments; it was nothing more than unfavorable treatment women received but their male co-workers didn't. *But for* their gender, women wouldn't be subjected to it.

But defining sexual harassment that was actionable under the law was more difficult. In 1980 the Equal Employment Opportunity Commission finally issued guidelines to help employees and employers understand what was prohibited. The "quid pro quo" (no sex; no job) was clearly illegal and advances had to be "unwelcome" (to eliminate the problem of the office romance). More difficult, however, was the concept of a prohibited "hostile environment" that female employees were forced to tolerate.

How hostile was hostile?

The courts took their time in defining prohibited conduct and outlining what women had to prove to make their case. It was not until 1986 that the U.S. Supreme Court allowed women to prevail even if they couldn't show economic harm. Bank employee Mechelle Vinson's supervisor fondled her in front of other employees, followed her into the ladies' room, and exposed himself to her. Yet her employer, a bank, argued that she had not suffered any tangible loss because she had not quit her job. The court said that psychological harm resulting from a hostile environment like Vinson's was enough to sustain a claim for sex discrimination and harassment.

Millions of women who had entered the work force in the 1960s and 1970s could relate to the experiences of Mechelle Vinson. They, too, had endured unwelcome abuse, tolerating it because they believed that preserving relationships with superiors who hold the key to present employment and future advancement was preferable to quitting. They found the problems were often worse as they advanced as the only women into male-dominated professions. Women often fared better in female-dominated professions, where a critical mass of women made discrimination less likely. But harassment flourished in environments where men were more numerous, and the women who were the pioneers in male professions such as finance or manufacturing were often grateful for having been accepted into formerly closed environments, and were not anxious to rock the boat. Furthermore, before 1986, they had no legal remedy.

By 1991 the courts had expanded the notion of hostile environment. No longer were outrageous facts like those in the Vinson case necessary to support a charge of sex discrimination because of harassment. Nude pinups on the wall could be considered illegal, and even in predominantly male workplaces, it was the "reasonable woman" who set the standard of what *she* considered offensive, not what "the good old boys" thought.

Some executive women find themselves in a dilemma as they attempt to balance the weight of outrageous conduct endured by some women in the workplace and the degree to which employers should be liable for in-cidents of sexual harassment that management *should* have known about. As senior executive officers of corporations and business institutions, women know how difficult it is for corporate executives to police the pri-vate behavior of all its employees, and to define precisely what constitutes a hostile working environment.

As incidents of sexual harassment and publicity about harassers in-crease, senior executive women now have a key role to play in the contin-uing volatile debate between the sexes in the workplace. They are the confidantes, role models, and mentors for younger women who have been subjected to harassment and also advise their male peers and the corporate community at large about how to handle allegations of harassment.

As corporate executives, women are also concerned about the bottom line impact of sexual harassment. Large corporations lose about $6.7 mil-lion a year each because of issues related to sexual harassment, such as low morale and absenteeism. Defending and settling cases is expensive; Kmart paid $3.2 million to settle one case. The United States Merit Systems Pro-tection Board reports that absenteeism, job turnover, and lost productivity due to sexual harassment costs the government an estimated minimum of $189 million a year. Extensive surveys of major corporations show that as employees experience multiple incidents of sexual harassment, their opin-ion of their company and managers declines, along with their job satisfac-tion and organizational commitment. They are more likely to look ac-tively for new employment. Costs for lost productivity are bad enough if caused by legitimate issues of competitiveness or social policy, such as mandatory health care coverage or unfair international trade policies. To lose this much annual productivity because of unnecessary and indefensible actions against one gender of American workers is inexcusable.

"This isn't just an issue of sex," said a Cincinnati retail executive. "This is a question of management style. A lot of management is still done by intimidation, man against man. When it becomes man against woman, the intimidation is coupled with the specter of sexual aggressiveness and power. In an intimidating, fearful management style, there is always the implied threat of reward and punishment. The threats just change if the object is a woman."

To no one's surprise, many men are struggling with understanding the proper behavior toward female co-workers and subordinates. They may have learned an intimidating management style early in their careers, never worrying that male subordinates would complain about it. But language, threats, and the male culture of a free-wheeling work environment now may fall under the scrutiny of a "reasonable woman"; and if she doesn't like or is intimidated by it, a man may suddenly find himself the victim of a lawsuit. Who's running the place, anyway, men ask? Hasn't this gone too far?

Senior executive women who have worked beside these men for decades are well aware that despite changing legal standards, social behavior between the sexes hasn't caught up as far as the workplace is concerned. There is still a wide gap between how men and women regard offensive or hostile conduct. One survey found that 67 percent of men polled said they would be flattered if a colleague of the opposite sex propositioned them, while 63 percent of the women would be offended. Understandably, many men are confused and nervous at the very time that women are trying to forge friendships with them, anxious that their male peers not retreat into the safe confines of the old boys club.

"It must be nerve-racking for men today," said a female partner in a New York City law firm who often defends corporations accused of ignoring sexual harassment by its workers. "When a former employee can come forth and accuse a man of sexual harassment perpetrated years earlier, sometimes at a critical career moment, like Clarence Thomas; when an apparently romantic interlude can turn ugly the next morning, as we saw with William Kennedy Smith; or when "normal" behavior of a popular single male, pursued by willing females, can cut short a career and perhaps a life, as we saw with Magic Johnson—is it any wonder that men are wary?"

Many executive women who are asked for advice about the new rules of behavior in the workplace conclude that it is important to distinguish between the "hostile environment" (pinups, jokes, and sexist conduct) and the "quid pro quo" (sex in exchange for reward).

"I'm worried that we are pushing men back into the safety of all-male enclaves just at the moment when we want to reach out to them as friends," the New York lawyer said. "I think we have to be careful not to appear to be so humorless, so rigid, that we make them uncomfortable. After all, women are not so fragile that we're going to be harmed by pictures on the wall or words. Sure, it's crass, in bad taste, and low class, but in my opinion it's wrong to expand the definition of sex discrimination to the point of silliness."

Many senior-level women said they decided early in their careers to take a decidedly relaxed attitude about hostile environment issues, ignoring terms of endearment, absorbing compliments on appearance or dress with a simple "thank you," and, as a last resort, "playing deaf and dumb" in the face of off-color jokes. They refuse to become rattled or upset, but just remember who behaved boorishly, knowing they could one day use the information. In general, they felt that the importance of preserving working relationships with male co-workers and business peers outweighed the importance of the uncomfortable moment.

"What do you do when a man calls you by your first name, or calls you 'dear' in front of male business peers?" a female business school student asked a female guest panelist one afternoon.

"They can call me whatever they want to," the investment banker replied. "I've got the money."

A hospital president and chief executive officer heard her answer, and agreed. "Everyone at the hospital calls me Susan—from the maintenance staff to the chairmen of the medical departments. The doctors, of course, are all called Dr. So and So. But that doesn't bother me. I'm the one who's running this place."

A woman's executive status and her professional field are major factors in deciding how to handle inappropriate remarks. "When someone asks my advice about a situation, I first have to understand the context," an advertising executive said. "In the advertising and retailing world, small groups of men and women work together informally, with a great deal of creative spirit, tossing out ideas, making connections, in a free-wheeling attempt to generate sparks. When does kidding become harass-ment? Do we want to stifle communication? That's a very different envi-ronment than a staid insurance company or law firm."

Many women who have successfully negotiated the path through pre-dominantly male organizations suggest that calm rejoinders are more ef-fective than accepting harassment or reacting too defensively. They don't create wars with men, but manage the little battles by engaging others verbally. "You can't let the chauvinism continue," said one. "We should use words and even a little humor to educate the offenders instead. It's a conversational game that requires self-confidence, but it must be done."

Holly Worthen recalled some of the discriminatory lines she had en-dured for her Radcliffe College class reunion; other women suggested lines that might have put offending males in their place at the time. "Women can't be doctors?" "Oh, you'd rather just have all women be patients?" "Professors don't take girls as tutees?" "Well, how about 'women'?"

One smiling, round-faced, demurely dressed veteran of many corpo-rate battles recalled how she dealt with personal remarks. "They'd tell me I had a nice ass. I said, great, you just concentrate on my ass while I use my brains to beat you."

Some women will tolerate inappropriate comments silently, up to a point. While they may not have let an offender know that unpleasant comments bothered them, some women were moved to stop harassment that bothered others. They used their common sense and awareness of the impact of their actions in deciding when and how to take action.

"I was working in the advertising department of a major national re-tailer," recalled a woman who is now senior vice president of a large adver-tising agency. "I had worked my way up and had put up with the jibes of the advertising manager over the years, teasing all the young women about their skirts, their dates the night before, their sexual desires and pushing them to go out to lunch with him. I thought he was annoying but harm-less, and gave it back to him as good as I got it. But I finally drew the line when I saw one of the younger girls crying in the ladies' room. It was her first job out of college, and she didn't know how to deal with him. She thought that all working environments were like this, and she'd have to face a lifetime of this kind of stuff. So I went to the vice president of human resources and told him what was going on. He stopped it fast, for everybody. I learned a good lesson. I should have done it sooner."

Women at senior-level positions agreed that they often set an example for the standard of their own companies, insisting that younger women be identified to clients by their full names and professional backgrounds, stopping off-color humor or social events that give rise to harassment incidents, and emphasizing that executives monitor the many ways in which the company communicates how it values women. The behavior of guests or customers, however, is a much more difficult issue.

"Every year we invite a distinguished panel of business school professors to judge our company's most talented finalists in our Entrepreneurial Team of the Year award," said a manufacturing vice president. "One year, two women on my staff told me they had real problems with one particular judge at our award banquet. His behavior toward them was very offensive and coercive. I just tucked it away and remembered to omit his name from the list. But the next year, two members of our board specifically asked for him. When I told them my reasons for not including him, they laughed it off. They didn't believe it. So he was reinvited, but I really prepared my staff, role-playing how to handle him. We watched his every move, and were ready to document every word he said and publicize it if he did it again. I convinced my staff that they were empowered to bring him down if he misbehaved. Fortunately for everyone, he was all right, but there is a fine line between being courteous to a guest and chastising someone."

Determining when to be polite and tolerant and when to file a complaint is not always easy. "These are tough calls. The more subtle the behavior, the more frequently it has to occur to justify a complaint," suggested a university president.

The least harmful harassment, most agreed, was the generalized sexist remarks, office humor, inappropriate behavior, and boorish conduct, often addressed to many women rather than one individual. There is strength in numbers in confronting and eradicating it, executive women advised. "There are usually one or two guys who do it to a lot of people," the New York attorney noted. "If word gets around about him, and women share stories and information rather than enduring it silently, this will empower women as a group to make a fool of him. Few companies or institutions want a real 'jerk' to advance to senior levels, and women can derail someone like that somewhat easily—unless he owns the company, of course!"

The next level of harassment is seductive behavior, often directed at one woman. The conduct is inappropriate, offensive, and unwelcome, but usually not accompanied with threats. In these instances, women must take care to scrutinize their own personal style of behavior, paying attention to not giving off subtle signals that will be misinterpreted by others. This self-analysis is often the first layer of protection against harassment. It is a fine line between being charming and acting seductive. Some men prefer to read the latter behavior, when women think they are projecting the former.

"This is where women absolutely must discuss the situation with other women," said a Los Angeles banker who had counseled many women who were upset about unwelcome conduct directed to them. "And not just any women. You need someone who understands the dynamics of the environment, someone who understands the law and the likelihood of success, and someone objective, who can help a woman assess the harm to her career if she goes public. If a woman is attractive, it will be seen as her fault. If she is unattractive, she won't be believed. If she makes a public complaint, the issue will be the woman's character, not the man's behavior. And the stakes are different. A man's career will be seen as his life. A woman's career will be seen as just a job.

"Other women can provide a reality check on the facts," she continued. "When a woman is the subject of this kind of behavior, it is easy for her to lose perspective. Is she overreacting because her pain is so acute and her work situation so stressful? Or is she overcompensating, enduring a lot of nonsense in an attempt to continue a cordial relationship, when she should just stiffen her spine, raise her voice, and say, 'Knock it off!'"

Sometimes what begins as seductive behavior escalates into sexual bribery. A woman can still refuse, but when the harasser is a customer or client, the situation becomes more complex. Even precise attention to language is necessary. Did the client or customer ask to continue working on the deal over dinner, or did he suggest dinner after work was finished? The difference is not minor, and sometimes, women should not even trust their own judgment to assess the reality of the situation.

"This is when a woman really needs to brainstorm with other women to strategize the best approach," one retailing executive said. "What is legitimate business behavior and what constitutes a road to trouble? I remember when the general counsel of a New York cosmetics company called our chairman. I was called into the office to help him formulate our response to the information that one of our senior buyers was harassing a female representative of the cosmetics company. She was just trying to do her job, obtaining large cosmetics orders for her company with our national chain. But our buyer insisted that business had to be done over drinks and dinner, and then kept bribing her with our business if she'd agree to sex with him. She finally complained to her own company, and said she wanted to be reassigned to another account. We were glad her company called us!"

Sexual coercion with the threat of punishment is a frequent manifestation of sexual harassment, and sometimes a woman even experiences outright sexual assault at the hands of those she works with. One reason such cases are underreported may be that women still confuse the manifestations of friendship or a sexual relationship with issues of power. If they understand that the harassment dynamic is one in which men attempt to wield power over women, they will be better prepared to deal with its consequences. For this reason, in all instances executive women urged women to document the experiences in minute detail. Exactly what day and time did it happen? Where? What were the exact words or actions? What was she wearing? What was she doing? What did she say? Did she clearly communicate that the action was unwelcome? Whom did she tell, and when?

This type of log is critical both to help women and their advisers analyze the situation objectively, and also for the moment that a woman decides she will take some action to stop the conduct. This evidence gives a woman leverage and a tool for the proactive use of power on her part. Without it, her unclear recollections may give rise to the implication that she wasn't that bothered by the conduct, or thought it was harmless at the time.

A woman's remedies at this point are varied. Some corporations have instituted confidential procedures by which a woman can bring information about a harasser to a designated executive or committee, promising that her identity will not be revealed without her permission. The advantage of this approach is that the company receives critical information about a person; the woman may not know whether she is the only one to complain, or whether her recitation of events is helping to confirm a pattern and practice of illegal behavior. At the same time, she may not know how the matter is resolved. Nothing may happen to the harasser, and his actions may continue.

In some instances, such procedures are irrelevant, useless, or more dangerous for the woman. "I had an important job with a large and grow-ing computer company," recalled a high-technology executive in Dallas. "I was project director of a big account, but I was being continually har-assed by the number two executive in the company, the chief operating officer. The sexual harassment committee, which was based in the human resources division, reported to him. He owned considerable stock in the company. I'd be crazy to go through the process. I transferred to another area of the company, so I wouldn't have to work in the same building with him. I'm sure he forgot about me and just picked on someone else, but my career was stalled for several years. It was definitely a backwards move. But what was I going to do, tape his conversations and threaten him? Even if I moved to another company, the high-tech world in Texas is small. I couldn't survive with a negative reference from him.

"Harassment is rampant," she said. "You put up with it, work around it, and do what you can. I've seen careers derailed, diverted, and ambitions lessened. Women simply stop trying as hard. It's as powerful a glass ceiling as anything else I know."

But now that sexual harassment has become unacceptable, women have more power to stop it, executive women believe. They cite numerous instances of men, from U.S. senators to small-town executives, whose own careers were stalled, derailed, or ruined when allegations of sexual harass-ment became public.

"That's why logs and the collective power of other women is so impor-tant," a Washington, D.C., public relations executive stated. "Women have the power to threaten men with exposure now, if they don't stop it. I know one case in which a small group of us brainstormed with one of our friends. We collected detailed evidence about a harasser who was a well-known public figure in Washington. We contacted a mutual friend at the *New York Times*, provided confirmation from others who had also been victim of his actions, obtained legal opinions from female lawyers who were experts in this field, and compiled it in an impressive package. Then our friend took the package to the harasser privately. She laid it all out for him, and said simply, 'I've already called the *New York Times* and they have this information for a story as soon as I give the word. You have a choice. The story on the front page of the *New York Times* or this stops. Which do you want?' It stopped. He knew she had the power to do it."

As women gain more power in the workplace and become stronger economically and psychologically, and as there is more public awareness of the legal remedies for sexual harassment, many women believe that incidents of sexual harassment will diminish. Perpetrators will become more fearful for their own economic future, and less able to hurt women who refuse to become their victims.

What is tougher to combat, women warn, is the more subtle form of sex discrimination that often occurs only when women have reached middle and senior levels in their business or profession. Entry-level salaries, opportunities, and career paths are often equal for both men and women, but clearly, the playing field does not always remain equal as women move up the career ladder. This may be the classic problem of the pyramid; if there are fewer spots at the top, where the rewards are greater and therefore the competition fiercer, the battles become more intense and the weapons nastier. As the criteria for advancement becomes more subtle and subjective, so do the means by which some men try to eliminate female competition. Recognizing those key moments when the women understand that the deck is stacked against them is critical in obtaining membership in The Club.

DISCRIMINATION THAT MATTERS

Dr. Frances Conley, the neurosurgeon at Stanford University who resigned to protest widespread sexual harassment of women, received a standing ovation from the mixed audience at the American Medical Student Association meeting in Washington, D.C., in 1992. One student tossed her a tough question: "If someone is being blatantly sexist, I can deal with it. But what do I do when they ignore me?"

The question was a good one. This young medical student had already recognized a clear pattern that signals the type of sex discrimination and bias that confronts women as they move into middle and senior ranks in business and the professions— discrimination so insidious and complex that some women put up with it for years, not knowing how to fight back. In many of these cases, the men who perpetuated the unfair treatment were unaware of the effect of their actions; they were just behaving as they had seen other men, often their superiors, behave.

We chose four stories of women who have fought sex discrimination to illustrate the problems of bias against women, although we could fill another book with many more. However striking and tragic these examples are, it is important to note that they are not unique. Other women who have faced "the water drop torture treatment" or "the plaque buildup of microinequities" of discrimination have chosen to leave their employer and go elsewhere, start their own business, or change careers. They didn't fight. Other women fought quietly, hiring tough lawyers to negotiate the best severance package possible in exchange for promises not to sue and accepting a gag order. We spoke with many of them, but their stories can't be shared.

Nancy Ezold, Teresa Contardo, Dr. Maureen Polsby, and Dr. Margaret Jensvold shared their personal histories and their advice to other women. Nancy Ezold, a lawyer in Philadelphia, fell into the "too" trap (too assertive, too demanding, too smart) of criteria for advancement. She discovered that standards set for her were different than standards set for her male peers. Nancy Ezold shows other women that self-confidence and belief in her own abilities must be at the core of a woman's value system if women are to prevail against discrimination and prevent it from happening to others.

Teresa Contardo, a Boston stockbroker, was such a superperformer she was invited to advance into the management ranks of her firm, but she still suffered pervasive economic discrimination at the hands of her superiors. Teresa Contardo's story shows that business institutions which allow sex discrimination to fester might see women work for and do business with their competitors as a result.

In Washington, D.C., Dr. Maureen Polsby endured sexual harassment and retaliation, and then uncovered corruption and research fraud by her harassers, while Dr. Margaret Jensvold, the only female physician working on research about premenstrual syndrome, was forced out of her job by superiors at her research institute. Drs. Polsby and Jensvold show the impact of sex discrimination in public policy matters that concern all women, their employers, and taxpayers.

These are four professional women with impeccable credentials and track records of success. The discrimination they endured was subtle and ongoing. They all fought back, not only for themselves, but for other professional women.

FIGHTING TO THE SUPREME COURT

Nancy O'Mara Ezold was thirty-five and the mother of one son when she began law school at Villanova in 1977. She had her second son while she was in law school but still graduated with her class while also working part-time and winning the school's prestigious Reimel Moot Court Competition. After working at two law firms after graduation, she was hired in 1983 by the well-known Philadelphia law firm of Wolf Block Schorr & Solis-Cohen as a litigator. She was warned when she was hired that it would not be easy for her at Wolf Block, since she was a woman, had not attended an Ivy League law school, and had not been on Law Review. Nancy wasn't particularly worried; she was confident about her abilities.

But she did not expect to be treated differently than other associates, and when she was given only minor matters to work on, she raised the issue with partners and requested more complex cases. The partners promised to pay more attention to her assignments. When some of the virtually all female staff of paralegals complained about not being paid for working long hours of overtime, Nancy spoke up on their behalf. The partners didn't like that, and began to brand her as someone too concerned about "women's issues."

Nancy's evaluations were good, however, and getting better year by year. "Exceptionally good," "unafraid," a "valuable asset," a "hardworker," and "effective," the partners wrote.

She was surprised, then, when, in November 1988, she learned she would not be recommended as a partner. She was told she could stay with the firm's litigation department as an associate at a fraction of partner compensation, or relinquish the commercial litigation and white-collar criminal practice she had built over eight years to work on domestic relations matters, a stereotypically female area of law, and become a partner a year later.

By contrast, several male associates were recommended for partner despite having evaluations with such comments as "not real smart," "not responsible," "very lazy," "less than tactful," "sloppy," "immature," "phlegmatic," "offended clients," and demonstrated "shoddiness in thinking." Nancy had been forced into the "trap of shifting criteria" where standards applied to her were not applied to her male peers. She was criticized for being too assertive, while male associates were criticized for not being assertive enough. Nancy was labeled "demanding"; obviously what the firm partners expected was a woman who would be nonassertive and acquiescent.

Nancy left the firm in June 1989 and sued Wolf Block for sex discrimination. The federal court agreed that she had been treated differently because she was a woman, warning Wolf Block that a law firm is not entitled to apply its standards in a more severe fashion to female associates than to males. It ordered the firm to pay back pay and make her a partner in litigation.

But the fight was not over. In 1993, Nancy was still waiting for the appeal process to take its course, discovering that her case had significant implications for all victims of discrimination. For much to the shock of experienced employment lawyers, a three-judge panel of the Court of Appeals threw out the findings of the trial judge and said that Wolf Block's subjective decision making was not discriminatory.

"Women are caught in a real catch-22 now," said one lawyer, commenting on the reversal in her case. "Law firms can assign women to less complex cases and then refuse to promote them, saying they lack necessary complex litigation experience. Any employer can subjectively determine criteria for advancement and then subjectively determine whether someone meets the criteria or not, without fearing review. Tenure cases, surgical cases, many executive cases are all up in the air now as we try to figure out how on earth these three judges, by merely reading a transcript, could conclude that a federal trial judge who listened to three weeks of complex testimony was clearly wrong in his findings of facts."

Now a litigator in another law firm, Nancy is philosophical and patient. Had she ever thought about not suing Wolf Block?

"Not for long," she replied, without hesitation. "I've worked hard throughout my life. I knew I was as qualified or more qualified than the men who were made partners. They just picked on the wrong person."

Nancy often speaks to groups about her case, and has had her story featured in newspapers all over the country, as well as on popular television shows. Whether or not it will be upheld, the trial court's opinion in her case has been widely copied and circulated to partners in law firms across the country, often accompanied with instructions from associate review committees or executive committees for partners to use more care in writing evaluations of young lawyers.

"I couldn't have predicted the publicity," Nancy said. "But it serves a purpose if it discourages other employers from discriminating and gives heart to women who fight."

Nancy has now talked to many women who have experienced discrimination and who ask her for personal and legal advice.

"I tell them to be aware of it, and to do something about it. Many people who have come to me have suffered it for a long time and they have done nothing, futilely hoping their job performance will ultimately be recognized. I understand their fears: loss of job, loss of livelihood, retaliation, stagnation, impact on their career, alienation from their fellow workers, and the great amount of money it takes to fight. On another level, there is the fear of embarrassment over a negative employment decision or condition of work. People who have glowing résumés of outstanding performance and high income forget all that when they are discriminated against. Their initial reaction is to believe that they are not competent. But the system won't change unless we all do something."

Discrimination is so economically irrational, Nancy says, that it is almost hard for some to comprehend. In a time when society at every level is becoming more diverse, and the economy so in need of the talent, energy, and productivity of all its educated citizens, there is no reason for anyone to justify jettisoning an individual with a good track record and the promise of excellence in the future.

"I was speaking before a mixed law school student group, and one male student asked me why, when I was so qualified and had such good reviews, didn't the firm make me a partner?" Nancy recalled. "I responded, 'Because of sex discrimination.' 'But,' he said, 'the firm put so much money into training you and keeping you for all those years. Why would they do it?' I responded a second, and then a third time, 'Sex discrimination.' He honestly couldn't understand the concept of discrimination. He knew that employers make decisions every day based on their best business judgment, and yet when an employer discriminates against an employee, they use no business judgment."

Nancy is appalled at the lack of business judgment she sees every day in her law practice, as she reviews cases against companies and institutions accused of white-collar employment discrimination.

"There is discrimination in every occupation and profession," she said. "The statistics and the stories bear it out. The glass ceiling is very real."

The prevalence of these cases has changed her own self-definition. "I guess I've been a feminist all along without ever labeling myself one. But now I have a new awareness about how bad the problem is."

Ezold experienced gender bias in a matter of promotion from associate to partnership status, the most critical moment in the career of lawyers in private practice. As former Boston Bar Association president Margaret Marshall has noted, the issue of "rainmaking" and a partner's future contributions to the economic well-being of a law firm weigh heavily in considering the relative merits of men and women for promotion. Decision makers may see achievement in men evidenced as ability, and achievement in women as effort. It is not uncommon for lower expectations of *future* performance for female professionals or managers to impact negatively on how they are rewarded, say researchers who have studied the issue. Bias against women in giving promotions and raises will only subside when effective past performance by a female is viewed as repeatable. Bias may be even less likely to subside when an assessment of a woman's future performance is speculative, and not necessarily based on past performance. In Nancy Ezold's case, intelligence, assertiveness, demonstrated ability, hard work, and effort were not enough to overcome gender bias on the part of male partners in her firm who were simply not going to confer on her the partnership awarded male associates and reward her with a status that conferred a lifetime position with the firm. They moved the hurdles higher and asked her to jump them again.

TOLERATING BIAS NO LONGER

Nancy would not jump for her superiors, but Teresa Contardo played the good girl for Merrill Lynch for years, enduring a wide range of biased treatment. When she first applied for the position of stockbroker in 1972, Merrill Lynch had never employed a woman above secretary or staff assistant in New England, and wasn't about to start. Teresa brought a complaint and won the job.

She prospered in the position despite the male pornographic pictures left at her desk by co-workers, the repeated sexual innuendos, and the unwanted, improper touchings at office gatherings. She ignored the lewd remarks, the birthday cakes in the shape of a phallus, and the presence of "exotic" female dancers. She never complained to management about this conduct, preferring just to work hard, six days a week.

Hard work paid off, and Teresa became of one of the top producers in the office, winning favorable office space, complimentary reviews, and recognition in the Win Smith Club, the second-highest category in Merrill Lynch's national organization. But that did not keep the male office managers from persistently stacking the deck against Teresa. She was excluded from various company outings to which male brokers were invited and at which important information was exchanged. She was not informed that the manager had tickets to sporting events that were available to male brokers for favored customers. She was denied opportunities to allow her clients to participate in the highly desirable private placement of tax-sheltered limited partnership shares in real estate. The best-producing accounts of departing brokers were reassigned to other male brokers in the office. But the final straw was when she discovered that she was given no compensation for serving as a product coordinator for the office, while a male broker received $258,000 for a similar assignment. In August 1984, Teresa joined Drexel Burnham Lambert, and sued Merrill Lynch.

Six years later, Judge Walter Jay Skinner of the U.S. District Court listened to her story and found that what Merrill Lynch did to Teresa was "covert, and habitual, even mindless, and illegal." She was the victim of Merrill Lynch's "undisciplined system of subjective decision making" that always favored the men over the women. This pervasive indifference on the part of Merrill Lynch to the right of female employees to earn a living and enjoy equal opportunities with their male colleagues was sex discrimination, the judge said. He awarded Teresa $250,000 in punitive damages, although only $1 in nominal damages, noting that she had continued to enjoy a rather successful career at other firms. He ignored her psychiatric and legal bills and how much more money Teresa could have made in the booming 1980s had she not been burdened with the attention her lawsuit required.

Mindful of the toll that such a lawsuit takes, Teresa now is helping others. "Ever since my story appeared in the *Wall Street Journal*, I've been hearing from women all over the country. One woman broker was out sick; she was fired while she was out and her accounts divided up. Another has been with her company almost thirty years, and is supporting her dying husband. Her job is being eliminated. Some are single parents. They can't do what I did, and sue, so I just try to help them however I can, being supportive."

Teresa knows that just filing the lawsuit changed behavior in Merrill Lynch, and that younger female stockbrokers are grateful to her. "Our firm is not the worst," said a female broker at another Merrill Lynch office. "I've seen those things elsewhere. But her award should have been higher. She deserved it. The publicity about her lawsuit brought a lot of changes to our office long before the judge's decision. That's the good part about the whole thing."

Talented women like Teresa Contardo should not have to leave their employer in a hail of publicity and legal entanglements to change the way businesses are run. Perhaps she could have improved the culture and management practices in the office by being a part of the Merrill Lynch management group herself.

"This case is filled with paradoxes," said one member of the Merrill Lynch defense team. "Teresa is a person of tremendous will and talent who was invited to break through the glass ceiling in the early 1980s and be a part of management. She declined, because she didn't want to give up what might be a larger income, generating sales. But Merrill Lynch really wanted her in management."

He didn't deny that the other male brokers excluded her from products and benefits that would have enhanced her rainmaking success even more. "But they skewed it against men *and* women," he said. "Brokers are brokers. Social policy isn't at the front lobe of their brain."

The judge ruled that the treatment of Teresa Contardo was sex discrimination. In the end, because of a lack of supervision, standards, procedures, and poor management, Merrill Lynch lost a highly productive senior executive woman to a competitor and received negative national publicity about its treatment of women.

Perhaps few people care about what Teresa Contardo went through at Merrill Lynch. In the larger scheme of things, it may not matter much that a female stockbroker couldn't make more money. Certainly the monetary award didn't make much difference to the bottom line of Merrill Lynch. But there are several reasons why businesses as large and prominent as Merrill Lynch should care about the essence of Teresa Contardo's legal decision.

First, it sends a loud-and-clear message to its female employees. Institutionally, Merrill Lynch did not value women if it allowed the inequities against Teresa Contardo to continue, and if it continued to fight her lawsuit. Reversing that message will take extraordinary communication skills on the part of management.

Second, equal and respectful treatment of women can provide Merrill Lynch with better utilization of a wasted resource—women. Merrill Lynch's management and board of directors should be concentrating on ensuring that the company has the talent base it needs to compete globally in the next decade. To shut out one half of the brains, managerial talent, and rainmaking skill available to them is not good business judgment. Teresa Contardo made money for Merrill Lynch in the years she worked there, and made money for herself. Now she is making more money for Smith Barney, which is benefiting from her years of experience, significant client base, and loyalty.

Third, like any business institution, Merrill Lynch should be focused on improving the quality of working conditions, productivity, morale, and energy of those who work for the company. A critical mass of women in positions of power and influence can make a positive difference in the way institutions are run, inspiring and empowering a diverse work force to achieve its goals. Publicity like that generated from Teresa's lawsuit did not help Merrill Lynch attract the female management talent it needs to develop that critical mass. Merrill Lynch may respond that it invited Teresa Contardo to be part of management. But in face of what she was subjected to, no one blamed her for refusing to participate as a willing member in the management culture that pervaded the organization. The larger question for Merrill Lynch is how it will attract and retain other senior executive women to its management ranks.

Fourth, the decision sends a message to Merrill Lynch's female client base. If all the female customers of Merrill Lynch expressed their displeasure at the treatment of Teresa Contardo by abandoning the firm, choosing competitors who provide equal or better service and products, then perhaps Merrill Lynch would pay attention. If Merrill Lynch does not value women, why should women bring Merrill Lynch their money and business?

Finally, eliminating discrimination is morally right. The management of business institutions should be role models for moral behavior, not the subjects of federal case law that labels their actions overtly insensitive, stereotyped, mindless, and illegal. We can only speculate whether the managers and fellow brokers who evidenced such behavior and were the cause of the unfavorable decision against Merrill Lynch were ever disciplined by the company, or whether the only measures of performance that continue to count in Merrill Lynch are sales and earnings. What is the moral compass other than profit that guides Merrill Lynch in the 1990s?

Merrill Lynch is not the only Wall Street firm to be sued for sex discrimination. Goldman Sachs, Kidder Peabody, Bear Stearns, and other competitors also face lawsuits brought by their senior executive women. It is doubtful whether Merrill Lynch or any other company faced with a legal decision and resulting publicity like Teresa Contardo's has quantified the economic harm from the event. We suspect that there are few national rankings evaluating firms on their treatment and respect for women, a 1990s "worst firm list," to use a strained analogy to Seventh Avenue's "worst dressed list." But it may come. Just as those who fought apartheid used the successful economic boycott of South Africa and companies that did business there to publicize their cause, women may begin to flex their economic power at home and boycott companies that treat sexism casually.

"I was on the search committee for the underwriters of our multibillion-dollar bond offering," said a female attorney for a public authority charged with a decade-long infrastructure and public works project. "Merrill Lynch and the others came in and made presentations to us, and I'd always ask about recent publicity regarding their sex discrimination suits. The folks who came to see us were always embarrassed, and blamed it on someone else, and didn't take responsibility. I noticed they'd usually send at least one woman on their team; whether it was to neutralize the effect of the sex discrimination publicity, I don't know. I can't say I had too much effect, except to let them know I was aware of it. One of the big firms ended up with the business anyway. Hopefully the woman on the team received the credit.

"I think we won't make a big impact in taking away business from them until there are more women on the selection committees," she said. "We must make a serious statement that we won't do business with firms that discriminate, just the way the board of our local United Way has said it won't admit an agency as an affiliate if it violates its policy on sex discrimination and harassment."

But some companies that solicit business from the public sector have found that diversity in their work force is a requirement, not a frill. A token woman in a municipal bond department or on a presentation team is not good enough to meet public requirements for diversity. Companies have lost large accounts because they had too few women or minorities to satisfy public agencies, pension funds, and others.

According to Klein Associates, a Cambridge, Massachusetts, consulting firm, this attention to diversity and discrimination is the "tip of the iceberg." Managers had better focus on how they are perceived and actually treat women, Freada Klein said. "Losing business because of discrimination is the wave of the future, not just isolated incidents."

Public agencies and governments should be the first to state as a matter of public policy that they will not do business with private companies that discriminate, but unfortunately, in some cases their public track record is no better. Citizens who are looking for another example of misuse of their hard-earned tax dollars need only look to the conduct of some government agencies and the money spent defending the behavior of government officials against charges of sex discrimination.

HARASSMENT IS A POWER GAME

Neurologist Maureen Polsby had impeccable academic credentials and was offered a prestigious National Institutes of Health (NIH) research fellowship. She left her residency at one of the nation's largest medical centers in order to begin what she had reason to hope would be a successful career diagnosing and researching nervous system diseases.

Dr. Polsby was, by her own description, a get-along type of team player. "I've always tried to fit in, to placate everyone," she said. Even when her boss, Dr. Thomas Chase, propositioned her for sex, she was more concerned with his feelings than her own.

"He was being unfair and manipulative," she explained. "I was flattered by his attention but very uncomfortable. In most kinds of interactions, men send signals, and if you are interested, you flirt back. It's not common for a man to make an overt pass without getting any indication that you're interested in him. It is such a crude thing. But when he's your boss, it's worse than just crude. You want him to like you. You need him to give you recommendations and good projects. So you have to be careful not to reject him harshly, and he knows it.

"I was in an awkward situation. I told him it had nothing to do with him personally, but I'd be working for him, and I didn't want to get in that situation, because it could potentially be a big mess. I thought I put him off nicely, and that he took it okay."

She thought that would be the end of it, but she was disheartened when his earlier promises of certain research opportunities turned out to be false. "My job description bore no resemblance to the job he had originally offered me. I got all the low-level assignments and I was expected to help the male staff fellows with their projects rather than have projects of my own. In many cases I was better qualified than they were. Once I didn't go to bed with Dr. Chase, it was as if I didn't exist.

"I kept trying to make the best of everything. I didn't even complain for about a year. I did everything I was told. It was a plum job, after all, and I was pretty lucky. Even if the men were getting the better things to do, it was still a plum job. But as time went on, there was no doubt I was being exploited more and more. When I was able to accomplish significant research despite my circumstances, Dr. Chase and others took it over."

Then Polsby was told that because of a shortage of fellowship salaries she could not have the crucial third year of research, thus preventing her from publishing the results of the previous two years. However, Dr. Chase managed to find salaries for any male fellow who wanted a third year. Finally, she filed an EEO complaint and, according to her, NIH retaliated.

"Suddenly I got a letter from the American Board of Psychiatry and Neurology saying there was a problem with my residency credit. I couldn't be considered eligible to take my board certification exam unless NIH said so. NIH thought they could force me to drop my complaint if they used the board against me. But that just made me more determined to do something. They are so arrogant they think they can treat people any way they want. And they can, usually. NIH has a budget of about nine billion dollars. My boss alone had controlled a seventy-million-dollar annual budget. My friends told me I should learn to play the game and not fight them. It was a David and Goliath situation. Everyone felt sorry for me."

Without board-eligibility, Polsby's career as a neurologist was destroyed. Then, one of her patients tipped her off to yet worse news. "This man is a retired college professor and puts out a newsletter for other patients with his disease; they all know each other since they are in the same patient organization, and share information. He went to the library and read the medical journal article resulting from the NIH research project in which he had participated, and he realized the data presented in the article was fabricated. Most of the tests had not been performed on the patients. This was a project I had initiated and had then been taken over by Dr. Chase and two of my other male colleagues."

Polsby filed a lawsuit in federal district court, and informed members of Congress investigating fraud in medical research. "It took quite a lot for me to fight back. Finally I said, 'I've had it. Enough.' At some point you have to fight. Once I decide that, I don't give up. I'll keep pursuing it, talk to reporters, talk to Congress, expose them. I'm not going to shut up. If someone doesn't stand up to them, they'll never stop mistreating people. It's not just me.

"I was alone with my lawsuit for years. I didn't even know there was a women's rights group at NIH. Most of the women who belong hear about it by word of mouth. Women don't want anyone to know they are a member; it might hurt them. It is an underground sort of thing."

Self Help for Equal Rights (SHER), the women's advocacy group within NIH, and the Federation of Organizations for Professional Women publicly supported Polsby when her case became known to them. "But the process was never easy," Polsby said. "If I'd known what I was up against, I'm not sure I would have done it. I thought I grew up in a free country. I didn't realize how much things were stacked against me. The discrimination was blatant, but NIH said there was none. The so-called EEO investigation was merely a cover-up. It is worse than if there were no process at all, because you *think* you have recourse.

"It's like getting raped. Will you report it and fight it? If you don't, it's like saying it's okay that it happened. But if you fight back, you get victimized all over again. What happened after I filed my complaint was worse than the circumstances which led me to file the complaint in the first place.

"The support of women's groups made an enormous difference. The first few years I was all alone. I didn't even have good legal advice. The lawyers just didn't understand the research world. I was so depressed and desolate, but I couldn't *not* do it. I couldn't stomach the idea that these guys would get away with it. I didn't have anyone to talk to or affirm what I was doing. But I just felt I had to pursue it. These guys aren't going to change just because it's the right thing to do. But if a couple of men lose their jobs because of my lawsuit, the rest will be forced to change. They will think twice before they harass women, steal research, and falsify data. They'll know they might be held accountable for it."

WOMEN'S JOBS: WOMEN'S HEALTH

Maureen Polsby might not ultimately prevail in her own lawsuit, but she was not the only female physician to have fought the immense power of the federal scientific community. Dr. Margaret Jensvold had done five years of research on premenstrual syndrome (PMS) and had been named by the Association for Academic Psychiatry as one of the six most promising psychiatry residents in the United States. She had no reason to expect that she'd be the victim of sexual harassment almost immediately after she was hired in 1987 as a medical staff fellow by Dr. David Rubinow at the National Institute of Mental Health Menstrually Related Mood Disorders Program, despite the fact that she was the only female physician studying premenstrual syndrome and no female physician has ever been tenured by means of advancement through the fellow system at NIMH. Nor did she know that a previous female physician conducting menstrual research, Dr. Jean Hamilton, had brought a sex discrimination complaint against Rubinow's mentor.

"Rubinow was taught institutionalized sexism and he perpetuated it," Dr. Jensvold said. "I'm at least the second generation of victims of discrimination at NIMH."

The microinequities started at once. She was falsely accused of creating problems with staff about a parking permit. She shared her research ideas with a second-year medical fellow who agreed to collaborate with her. Then he carried out the project with her boss and cut her out. She asked to attend an international conference on PMS and was refused, although the second-year medical fellow attended and later admitted he intentionally excluded her. She was never told funding was available for her to attend. When she complained, the harassment escalated. She was told she was excluded because she was "competent and attractive."

Dr. Jensvold was relegated to nonvalued research. She was not allowed to write review articles, collaborate on articles or conference presentations, work with summer students, follow patients, teach a course, or work with drug companies. Finally she was ordered into psychotherapy as a condition of her work, given three male psychiatrists to choose from (there were no good female psychiatrists, she was told). She terminated the sessions and then discovered her boss had decided to terminate her fellowship even before he directed her to go into psychotherapy.

Finally, a year and five months after she began work at NIMH, Dr. Jensvold initiated informal EEO counseling. Three months later, after experiencing retaliatory actions obstructing her future professional opportunities, she filed a formal EEO complaint.

"I thought about filing the EEO complaint for at least six months," Jensvold recalled. "I had tried every possible way of dealing with it. I couldn't get around the 'control and blame' style. First they controlled my activities and then they blamed me. At that point I really didn't have a choice. Another female doctor told me that she had had the same experiences with my supervisor, but her advice was to 'smile and pretend nothing is going on.' She warned me that if I did that, I would never be included, but they wouldn't attack me either. But she was wrong. She didn't have Rubinow as her supervisor. Her supervisor protected her. I had no way around Rubinow and no one protecting me from his actions."

Three years after bringing the complaint, her lawsuit was still pending in federal district court. Her career as an academic, biological psychiatrist was over and her legal bills were unmanageable. "My finances are totally ridiculous. I worked to put myself through college, and essentially put myself through medical school. I was paying off my education loans, and then just when my income should have gone up, this huge expense comes along."

But in spite of the tragic turn of events in what should have been a promising career, Jensvold retained a sense of the absurd. "The NIMH defense was one that only a psychiatrist could invent. They said that all my good interactions with people at NIMH were projections of positive feelings I had about my ex-husband, and all my negative interactions were projections of negative feelings I had about him. They seem to be able to understand women only in terms of their status as someone's wife or exwife."

The psychiatrist with whom Jensvold was forced into psychotherapy revealed his diagnosis of her in his deposition. His diagnosis of Dr. Jensvold was "personality disorder not otherwise specified, with selfdefeating personality traits and paranoid traits." According to Jensvold,

"This is *the* ultimate blaming-the-victim diagnosis. When they say I am paranoid, they are saying I am imagining it. When they say I am self-defeating, they are saying I am causing it. When they say it is my personality, they are saying the problem is intrinsic to me, not my environment or anything that is being done *to* me. They are making the typical harasser argument: She is imagining it *and* she caused it. Well, it recently occurred to me that if they can label me, then I can label me. I've decided that I, in fact, have a self-empowering personality."

Jensvold asserts this is the first time that self-defeating personality disorder is being used in a legal setting, making *Jensvold* v. *Sullivan* a precedent-setting case. Others say the diagnosis of self-defeating personality disorder is still unsettled. When the diagnosis was proposed in the mid-1980s, it was controversial and incurred protests, debates, letters, and articles. Some predicted that the diagnosis, if accepted, would sooner or later be used against individual women in a sexually discriminatory way and so female psychiatrists have been monitoring it carefully. But "to have the NIMH-employed psychiatrist introduce this sex discriminatory diagnosis into a sex discrimination lawsuit against the NIMH is mind-boggling. It is very revealing about how they view women," Jensvold said.

Jensvold is an advocate of patients and an advocate of women. She has written a paper about the ways in which psychiatry is used as a weapon against recipients of sexual harassment and how to prevent the misuse of psychiatry. "My lawsuit against NIMH is as significant a contribution to health and science as any biological study I could have conducted there," she said.

Jensvold has been heartened by the moral support of other women scientists, employees at NIHM, and even members of Congress. "The fight is exhausting but empowering. My advice for other women is to connect with other people who are going through it. Billie Mackey, president of SHER, the women's support group at NIMH, told me there would be retaliation and how it would happen. If she hadn't warned me, the viciousness and intensity of it would have taken me by surprise.

"It was important for me to talk with other women who were further along in their cases. For example, when I had the choice to drop the EEO process and go to court, I got on the phone and asked other women how they had weighed the options. It was a big help.

"The Federation of Organizations for Professional Women was also there for me, and started a Legal Defense Fund to help with my lawsuit and that of Dr. Polsby. When I called Viola Young-Horvath, the executive director of FOPW, she knew exactly what I was talking about, because she was a former NIH scientist. I feel no one can go through this alone and survive. Not having the support of others— women or men—would make this lawsuit impossible for me."

Jensvold is being helped by other professional women, but she also knows her case has helped others. "Several women at NIMH have called to thank me for the lawsuit. NIMH has now put together a fast-track list of women who might get tenure, and they are on it.

"Even the American Medical Association is aware of my case. One woman on the AMA's governing board asked me how many women have to fight the same suit against the same people before things change?"

Viola Young-Horvath describes the NIH as a "predominantly male enclave at the high levels, full of men who are intellectually unquestion-ing of their own behavior and decisions." Bruce Nussbaum, author of a book examining the federal development of drugs for AIDS, said that in the federal government medical establishment, "An old-boy network of powerful medical researchers dominates in every disease field, from AIDS to Alzheimers. They control the major committees, they run the most im-portant trials. They are accountable to no one."

Billie Mackey notes that the situation has not changed much at NIH in the twenty years since the women's organization was founded. "We were able to start a day-care center, but over the years, things have actu-ally become worse for women scientists at NIH. Most of the senior execu-tive positions are occupied by white males, and the harsh and unfair treat-ment of women has continued," she said.

"We work with women who have experienced problems, helping them assess their situation and brainstorm strategies to solve problems. We don't believe in being radical, but sometimes people view us as radical because we advise women to stick up for their rights. At the same time, not all women can take the stress of filing an EEO complaint, and we know in most cases the filing of a complaint destroys a woman's career. Even when women win their case, and a judge orders reinstatement, NIH stalls. A woman can win her lawsuit in court, but it's business as usual for the perpetrators back at NIH."

Women's professional organizations across the country, including members of the Congressional Caucus for Women's Issues and the Society for the Advancement of Women's Health Research, have been following situations like those of Dr. Jensvold and Dr. Polsby with alarm, not just because of the effect of sex discrimination on promising careers.

Dr. Jensvold explained: "NIH and NIMH have recently come under serious criticism for failing to include women as research subjects. Now it is clear that they are also excluding women as researchers. The effect of these two things on women's health is very destructive. You cannot improve women's health research if women researchers are systematically shut out of NIH and NIMH."

Dr. Estelle Ramey, past president of the Association of Women in Science and professor emeritus at Georgetown University Medical School, agreed. "In the past, differences between men and women were ascribed to biological differences. These differences were then cited to exclude women from positions of responsibility. Now we see a very interesting thing. Male scientists are typically in charge of laboratories and research, and they put only men in their studies. They now claim that it is acceptable to put only men in studies, and to have only men doing psychiatry because men and women are the same. *Vive la différence* is gone.

"The fact is, both responses are born out of ignorance. They hurt the quality of research performed and skew the results. There are differences between men and women. When you exclude women from research or practice or health care delivery, you exclude the possibility of bringing to bear on the problem differences which may lead to solutions. Ultimately, you hurt women. One need only consider Margaret Jensvold's situation— an all-male team of psychiatrists examining the biological psychiatry of premenstrual syndrome—to understand how flawed the work will be.

"For example, heart disease is studied more in males, and this is true in every species. In conducting research in this manner, scientists are in fact studying heart *failure* in men; and failing to study heart *success* in women. Studying heart success in women could help us to understand how to make men live longer. So nobody benefits when you exclude women from research protocols or decision making. Nobody benefits when you exclude women as research subjects or as researchers."

SHER has been working with Congress and other women's professional groups to urge passage of specific language in NIH's funding authorization that would direct the agency to pay attention to women scientists and women's health. "Women have more visits to physicians. They are listened to less. They have less health insurance coverage. There is less research on women's health and we have evidence that sex and age discrimination have impacted women's health research," Mackey said.

"Any time you have mostly males studying diseases, they don't look to see which disease needs the most study; they just look at what interests them. Some diseases get a lot more money but they are not the killer ones. They don't have the impact that others do. We know women would make a difference in what is studied and the working environment in which it is studied."

Examples abound, according to Mackey and others who track how money is spent. It is not just the hot button of fetal tissue transplantation research that for years precluded study of various diseases that impact on women patients or caregivers.

"One researcher developed a test that will identify women who carry a gene that guarantees they will contract cancer if they are exposed to Xrays," Mackey said. "With the emphasis on annual mammograms for all women to detect breast cancer, it would be much more efficient to first identify women who should not ever have mammograms. We need researchers to repeat her research and duplicate results so that this test can be verified and used widely. But this can only be achieved by others outside the research establishment, urging Congress to fund this research specifically, and ordering the Cancer Institute to contract it out. We're organizing to help make that happen."

NIH's history indicates that, left alone, it is incapable of making funding decisions that consider both sexes equitably. In 1987 the NIH spent $648 million researching heart disease, the leading cause of death for women. Yet major recent studies (including the use of aspirin to reduce the risk of heart attack) have been done on men. That's fine for 48 percent of the population, but what about the other 52 percent?

In 1989, NIH allocated only $8 million to applied contraceptive research development and only $3 million to contraceptive safety, despite the fact that 112 of every 1,000 American girls ages fifteen to nineteen (compared to 13 in the Netherlands) will get pregnant and 45 will have abortions (compared to 14.2 in Canada). The United States is the only developed country where teenage pregnancy is on the increase and teen mothers now make up 61 percent of all women receiving Aid to Families with Dependent Children. Every public dollar spent to provide contraceptive services saves an average of $4.40 in funds that would otherwise have to be spent to provide medical care, welfare, and social services to pregnant women.

Combating teenage pregnancy and reducing the burden on taxpayers is only one small element in a cost/benefit analysis of scientific research on women. Women are the fastest-growing group infected with the HIV virus, but the official definition of AIDS has been based on symptoms that appear in men. As a result, women are often incorrectly diagnosed, making them ineligible for AIDS drugs, clinical trials, Medicare, or social service benefits.

Major depression affects women twice as frequently as men. About 7 million American women suffer from its effects, leading to 30,000 suicides annually and costing society an estimated $16 billion a year. Approximately 70 percent of antidepressant prescriptions are given to women, but women have often been excluded from the early phases of new drug testing and from large-scale clinical trials. Breast cancer has increased 36 percent between 1982 and 1988, killing 44,000 women each year, but in 1988 the NIH halted a major study on breast cancer and low-fat diets because of cost considerations. Problems related to osteoporosis will kill as many women as breast cancer, and NIH estimates that one half of all postmenopausal women suffer from osteoporosis. Direct medical costs resulting from hip fractures alone come to $10 billion annually, yet the budget for osteoporosis research is just $25 million. Overall, in 1990, the NIH spent just 13.5 percent of its budget researching women's health and only six of the top sixty senior appointive positions in national science and technology policy were held by women.

Mackey has struggled for women's rights for twenty years in Washington, D.C., and does not expect the situation to improve rapidly. She knows that SHER must continue to act as a monitor and advocate in the debate about biomedical research and funding. The controversy requires women's voices, as congressmen are divided. Has NIH fallen prey to political intervention, undermined by ideology and fear, and has it persistently ignored women's health concerns? Or are attempts to mandate particular funding for research on women's health "micromanagement" and disruptive?

The bottom line is that sex discrimination against women in science is uneconomic and hurting America's productivity and competitive position. With a work force that is increasingly female, the business community should be concerned about keeping women healthy. With a national health care bill that is rising faster than businesses and taxpayers can pay for it, the business community should be concerned about funding those areas of medical research that will generate the highest return for the taxpayers' investment. Scientific breakthroughs in areas such as contraceptive research and breast cancer might well lower health care costs for businesses and their employees, as well as improve the quality of life for many of them. But these do not yet seem to be issues that concern national policymakers in either the private or public sector.

Women in the business world might suggest that women's role in science mirrors that of women in other areas of the economic power structure. Why should we single out discrimination against two female physicians when there are female retailers, architects, investment bankers, and construction workers who also experience discrimination? Institutional discrimination against women is prevalent in many fields.

But businesswomen of all fields and taxpayers should rail louder about discrimination against female scientists because our economy can least afford to lose their talent. Our national economy is increasingly dependent on technology, science, and research, and the fastest-growing occupations are mathematical and computer scientist jobs. Many other jobs require scientific and mathematical proficiencies. At a time when the United States is experiencing a shrinking pool of scientists, engineers, and mathematicians, our economy's ability to compete internationally may depend on how quickly the most prestigious corridors of power become inclusive rather than exclusive to 40 percent of its present medical students and over half the talent pool of its citizens.

It is shameful, says Billie Mackey and other women, that the federal government spends hundreds of thousands of dollars to defend its scientists who harass women instead of telling them to stop, or moving them from positions of managerial and budgetary responsibility. The country can no longer afford discrimination in a professional field such as biomedical research, which may be one of few economic engines of growth in the coming decade. The research NIH supports has brought an explosion of knowledge about disease, spawning powerful drugs and the growth of biotechnology companies and products. It was government grants and scientists that spawned these new inventions, perhaps inadvertently. But like Merrill Lynch and other private companies, the public sector must also demonstrate a policy of valuing its female employees. Adopting a policy for the personnel manual is not good enough.

The reason for this proactive stance toward women is not just because it is legal and morally right. It is also good economics. A federal industrial policy that only considers the benefits of raw resources, the tax advantages or credits for capital investment, or rebuilding infrastructures is missing the most important ingredient in the recipe for economic success: 52 percent of the country's intellectual capital, its women.

CHAPTER SEVEN

INTERNATIONAL REALITY

The barrier is more often an issue of women *getting* the jobs in foreign countries than their capability once they're in them.

—Cynthia Livingston, partner, Cambio International

Few U.S. companies utilize women effectively in international assignments. A survey in the mid-1980s of 686 U.S. and Canadian firms with at least one foreign subsidiary showed that less than 3 percent of international managers were women. Overall, there were over thirty-two times as many male as female expatriates being sent overseas. Yet this 3 percent figure was hailed as a significant improvement from the prior five years, when there were virtually no women. By 1989 the figure had risen to 5 percent, but 80 percent of companies surveyed said there were disadvantages to sending women overseas.

International executives like Sandy Lawrence and Tomye Tierney couldn't disagree more, arguing that companies that use women in international assignments have a strategic advantage over their competition. In the 1990s, the global economy offers women like them opportunities rather than barriers to advancement.

Sandra B. Lawrence, vice president of Worldwide Strategic Marketing, Family Imaging Products, at Polaroid Corporation, is one of many senior-level executive women who are bringing their talents to the corporate world and managing an active home life. Charged with developing and implementing strategic directions and marketing programs for Polaroid's consumer business on a worldwide basis, Lawrence's background and personality fit well with the model of the successful global manager for the 1990s.

"I lived in Turkey as a very young child and in Australia from age eleven to fifteen," Lawrence said. "My father was interested in world travel, and even took me to the Soviet Union in 1964. As a child, I was acutely aware of other countries; my Australian friends all preferred Japanese-made products over American brands. Those preferences made an impression on me even then."

Lawrence attributes her later success to an upbringing that allowed her to be free to set goals and achieve them. "Perhaps because my father was a corporate executive, or because my parents treated me the same as my sister and brother, I never experienced any cultural or gender bias or diminished expectations. No one tried to divert me from my interests, although as an undergraduate at the University of Maine I had to work hard to persuade the dean to change my major to business instead of math. When I got all A's, he agreed.

"But then when I was looking for work in 1971, all that employers wanted to know was my typing speed. I figured out I'd be better off with an M.B.A., so I got one," Lawrence recalled.

"Xerox was looking for women in 1972, so I signed on with them and worked in sales, but I was really interested in marketing. So finally, in 1975, I landed a job at Gillette as an associate product manager in the personal care division, and I was on my way!"

Lawrence has had a varied and dynamic career, but one that looks orderly in hindsight, with each experience building on the next one. She and her husband were able to coordinate a move to London in 1981. While he taught at the London Business School, she acted as marketing director for Gillette's $40 million European toiletries business. When they returned to Boston, she directed Gillette's new ventures for three years, and then became vice president for new products and business development, overseeing the personal care group in the United States, Canada, and Europe.

Lawrence was busy establishing a joint venture with Shiseido Cosmetics at a very busy time in her own life, but frequent travels to Japan were no problem, even when she was five months' pregnant. "I just properly informed our Japanese hosts that I would not be going out at night, and as the senior member of our team, that meant no one went out. It was fine with us," Lawrence said.

In 1990, Lawrence left Gillette and became president and chief exec-utive officer of her own company, which imported and retailed roses from Equador. But two years later she returned to the corporate world when Polaroid enticed her with a unique opportunity to manage worldwide mar-keting for its consumer products. "This is just exactly what I want to do now!" she said.

There are thousands of women operating successfully in the global marketplace, but Tomye Tierney, vice president of international market-ing and sales for Genzyme Corporation, is one of the most outspoken about the opportunities for women and the companies that hire them. She has traveled all over the world for Genzyme and her previous employer, Baxter Healthcare, dealing successfully in Europe, Africa, the Middle East, and "even playing golf in Japan with the Japanese!"

Tierney's own background matches the qualities often cited as neces-sary characteristics of a global manager. "As a teenager," Tierney recalled, "I was always mapping out places in the world to go. I decided to go to Europe instead of going to college, and landed in Brussels. I didn't speak French, but I learned it there."

When Tierney decided to return to the United States to go to college, she pursued a degree in economics at California State University and went on to get her M.B.A. in marketing at the University of Southern Califor-nia. In California she began working for Baxter Healthcare; "I kind of fell into international marketing," she said.

Tierney's natural curiosity and love of travel were advantages in her job for Baxter, "but so was being a woman," Tierney states. "I was highly visible. I'd go to meetings in Japan and be the only woman and they'd remember me. In Argentina and Brazil, or almost anywhere in the South-ern Hemisphere, men are extra charming to women. They make you feel very special. In Eastern European countries it's the same. The first physi-cian I met there kissed my hand; it turned out this was their custom. More importantly, they gave me great respect as a businessperson, too.

"I've found the easiest way to get along is to conform to the culture of the host country. In Italy, which is often conservative for businesspeople, I initially wore suits. Then on one trip I wore a dress, and the men I'd been dealing with for some months said, 'Oh, so you're a lady, too!' Their whole mood changed," said the attractive brunette.

"In Germany I discovered that men often hesitate to ask a woman a question in front of their peers. I learned that it was better to schedule private time with them, especially with those who were instrumental to the results I was seeking.

"Before I went to Japan, my company provided me with a tutor twice a week for two months. I learned a few basics of the language, the culture, economics, politics, and important courtesies. This approach can save companies embarrassment when sending new employees overseas with no cross-cultural training."

Because of Tierney's personal preparation for every new culture, she rarely encountered situations she could not handle, even as a single woman traveling alone. "You project and carry yourself to convey professionalism," Tierney said. "If I ever thought I was detecting a sticky situation, I'd often use the cover of communication difficulties. But such situations are extremely rare, and I've had many more wonderful experiences. Foreign hosts are so generous and accommodating to American businesswomen, particularly those who convey a genuine interest in their country. For this reason I recommend learning as much as possible about the country you are going to visit. I learn as much as I can about the culture, history, politics, and religion. It's so important to listen; I try to do this carefully before speaking, and try to tune into their style."

Tierney initially had no interest when a recruiter called her about the position at Genzyme. "I was perfectly happy in southern California. I didn't even know where Boston was," she joked. But Genzyme wanted an executive who could get results, and Tierney became intrigued with the idea of working for an entrepreneurial company. She discovered that Boston was closer to Europe. "Now I can go for just a few days or a week," she said. "When you think about how many women travel domestically for their companies on business, often for a week or more, the idea that women can't or won't travel internationally is simply not true. You can get business done in Europe just as easily as you can in California from an eastern city like Boston."

Tierney is building up Genzyme's international business at a whirlwind pace, as the company is growing dramatically. But she does not shortcut her successful international marketing and sales techniques.

"Women often have better interpersonal skills than men. They approach relationships on a win-win basis, while I've often seen men take a more confrontational approach. I've found that ongoing contact is important, even if I have nothing to say. It is like a friendship; you keep in touch just to keep up the relationship, if it is valuable to you. Many of my foreign contacts have told me that men come over to their country and make promises and then they never hear from them. I keep my promises and they hear from me. Follow-up is one of the most important keys to success."

Tierney is on the road most of the time and she loves it. "I get cabin fever if I'm in the office for three weeks or more," she laughs. "When I get out there, things happen. If I'm here, busy work finds me."

A GLOBAL GLASS CEILING?

Lawrence and Tierney are still the exception, as many companies have not yet realized the competitive advantage that a female talent pool can bring.

"I had not planned on starting my own business initially," said Kathleen Hagan of Hagan & Company, a thriving international consulting firm. Hagan had significant international business experience working for a public authority directing its overseas offices and developing opportunities for overseas trade before she opened her own firm. "Companies take me seriously as a consultant, but they would hesitate to hire someone like me at the vice presidential level. Too many companies just don't recognize the many talented women out there with international experience who could fit in very well in their company and contribute to its bottom line. One reason for this may be the fact that many U.S. firms are inexperienced in general in recognizing the skills set, experience, and abilities required for successful international business development."

Is there a global glass ceiling? Some executive women state that as the American economy grows increasingly international, and American companies seek to expand their revenue base in countries where personal relationships are often a critical factor in doing business, the status of executive women is of paramount concern. Will the international arena be closed to women and more subtle barriers to success be erected? Or will executive women have some distinct advantages in the global marketplace?

This is not an idle question. With a significant portion of the American work force comprised of women and the economic stakes so high, companies need seasoned executives who can operate internationally. If they do not look to women executives to fill that role, women will find their own opportunities in this new marketplace. Women are establishing their own companies in record numbers. Employment at women-owned firms now surpasses the Fortune 500's work force of 12.3 million employees, according to a study by the National Association of Women Business Owners. Female entrepreneurs are not waiting for corporate America to discover their talents and send them abroad.

There may not be a clear answer to the question of whether women will encounter corporate barriers or find great opportunities internationally. To a great degree managers of American companies, some of whom are understandably discouraged about America's competitive position in the world, will determine the outcome. They see a U.S. economy losing its position to nations that in the 1950s and 1960s could hardly sustain themselves. Few observers would have expected these industrialized nations to dominate world markets in the 1990s.

There are many reasons why other nations are outcompeting the United States. Some managers point to factors such as rising civilian research and defense spending in Japan and Europe, massive infrastructure investments in those countries and elsewhere, plant and equipment investment in Japan triple the U.S. rate, personal savings rates in Japan and Europe that are three to five times the U.S. savings rate, and American education lagging far behind that in other nations. The lack of savings and investment capital in the United States and the turmoil in American banking institutions have made these banks limited players on the world capital stage. A 1991 list of the fifty largest banks in the world revealed only two in the United States, with Citicorp ranking highest at only number twenty-two on the list.

Pessimists warn that other countries are buying the U.S. productive capacity. In 1977 no more than 3 to 5 percent of the manufacturing capacity in the United States, by value, was owned by non-Americans. By 1990, foreigners were exercising greater control over American manufacturing, employing more than 10 percent of American manufacturing workers, according to Labor Secretary Robert Reich. The litany of foreign-owned companies is a roll call of former American greats: RCA, CBS Records, Columbia Pictures, Doubleday, Mack Truck, Firestone, A & P, Pillsbury, National Steel.

Without a scorecard, it is hard to tell the international players apart.

The competition for customers in a world market does not resemble the Olympics, with each contestant carrying a country flag, hoping to bring home the gold. The international lines are blurred, as more than one fourth of all U.S. exports bears the name of a foreign-owned company. For example, Honda produces cars in Ohio and Sharp manufactures microwave ovens in Tennessee. In "American" companies such as IBM, McKinsey, or Baker & McKenzie, as many as 40 percent of its employees may be foreign, and foreign companies are establishing subsidiaries in the United States.

In a global marketplace, does the name or primary nationality of a company matter? Some executive women believe that it matters a great deal. While there may be little that managers can do to change external competitive factors such as exchange rates and investment capital, visionary and realistic executives realize that American business cannot utilize human capital in the same way it has in the past. Some would go even further and say that American business needs new leadership to recapture its once preeminent place in the world economy.

"The value that Americans bring to the world economy is our productivity," said Reich. "Fundamentally, our advantage is people."

The integration of the United States into a global economy will grow as international capital markets merge, trade restrictions ease, and new markets open. If American business is to regain its health, it must develop a cadre of international executives who can work effectively overseas. Therefore, in the competition for talented business employees, the globalization of the economy is a major window of opportunity for executive women.

WHAT'S WRONG WITH THESE REASONS?

Women with international experience often have a difficult time persuading companies that their experience is transferable to corporate needs, as Kathleen Hagan discovered. Women have to push for foreign assignments even inside their own companies. In a 1988 survey, 83 percent of women who won overseas assignments had to introduce the idea to their companies. They had to persevere and overcome such stereotypes as "women have no stamina," and a foreign country's culture would be "too tough" a place for women to work. In some cases, the women had to wait until their male peers had turned down the international assignment before they could convince the company to let them try.

Corporate managers give many excuses for the startling disparity among the numbers of men and women in international assignments, in some cases blaming females disproportionately. But the failure rate is high regardless of gender. It costs two to three times as much to send a manager overseas as to have him or her operate domestically, and understandably, it is human nature to want to take fewer risks when the costs of failure can be high. Researchers have concluded that 25 to 40 percent of all expatriates do not succeed overseas and personal problems cause up to one quarter of all expatriates to cut short their tours of duty.

If the goal of all managers is to minimize failure and maximize success, then companies must examine whether there are problems that women encounter that men do not.

Women are not interested in international assignments, cautious executives state. Hogwash, say executive women. The "not interested" stereotype is an old trap. How many times does a women have to be turned down for something before she finally gives up and takes her time and energy elsewhere? At that point, she is usually accused of "not being interested."

Women may be interested, but surely their families are not, companies retort. If a woman is married or has children, companies assume relocation will be very difficult. If she is single, companies assume she may be less effective professionally, or more restricted personally, than her male counterparts if there are cultural or social taboos limiting her activities.

The exact opposite may be true. Married male executives who are given international assignments may face severe problems with family life. Foreign assignments place great stress on a nonworking wife, who suffers a loss of self-identity, friends, and is often culturally isolated. With only the designation as "Mr. X's wife," she feels a loss of power and self-control. If the children are unhappy, the burden of dealing with their concerns usually falls on her. Working wives may have difficulties as well, as they are "asked to jump off their own career paths and abandon healthy salaries and trustworthy hairdressers just so they can watch their self-esteem vanish somewhere over the International Date Line," according to a wife who had been posted to Bangkok, Taipei, and Beijing.

Single women told us they had encountered few difficulties overseas and found international assignments personally rewarding. Married executive women stated that international assignments were a positive family adventure. Their husbands were accepted readily overseas, and were an asset to their careers. Two-career couples often have already established an arrangement that meets family needs; secure husbands of executive women are proud of their wives' achievements, respectful of their personal goals, and not threatened by either absences from their wives or the likelihood of changing their own career directions to accommodate an international assignment. These husbands are used to dealing with the dynamics of a successful wife, and like it. In many cases, it relieves pressure on them to know that an equal partner is moving ahead in her career; an international assignment may be a welcome sabbatical or change in direction for a husband. Increasingly, companies are trying hard to place the "trailing spouse" in an appropriate position, particularly if the spouse is male.

"My children come first," said a female international marketing manager in New York City. "But my career is important, and I make career decisions in partnership with my husband. We make decisions about what is best for the *family*." She was stating a personal philosophy also shared by increasing numbers of men.

"My company recently reorganized the international marketing division," she said, "and my boss asked me to spend two weeks a month in Europe. When I said no, because of the children, and asked him if he'd send the whole family for six months at a time, he was surprised. He said, 'Would you have given me that answer if you were a man?'

"I answered him right back that it didn't matter what gender I was; a man would have answered the same way. *Parents* have children, and families do best if they are kept intact. And besides, I knew he didn't need me there just two weeks out of a month. He finally decided to ask the same question of his wife, who had a full-time career. He came back and said that she had the same reaction that I did. I know because of my forthright stand he respected me more. I was willing to accommodate the company's needs to send me abroad, but I still placed my family first." She and her boss then worked out an arrangement that was not gender-based but showed basic common business sense.

Some executive women have discovered there are many countries where men are automatically accorded great respect and accommodating husbands bring women an advantage. Professor Heidi Vernon-Wortzel, professor of international business at Northeastern University, notes that when husbands and wives work together internationally, they are often treated quite differently. "The husband's opinion is more likely to be solicited and his conclusions given more weight. Particularly in Asia, he is likely to be invited to participate in male-centered social activities that exclude his partner wife," she said.

Rosanne Esposito, product manager for Danzas Corporation, a Switzerland-based international transportation company, relocated her family from New York City to Bellevue, Washington, with ease. "My husband worked for the city of New York," she said, "but he was very happy to be a house husband in Washington and try consulting for a while. When we moved, our children were nine, seven, and six, and we felt they would have more opportunities in Washington. Meanwhile, my job has become much bigger and the challenges greater. I belong in the American headquarters office in Washington now, rather than in New York."

Esposito began her career in international transportation services "by accident." With a master's degree in English literature, no foreign languages, and no passport, she did not fit the profile of an international executive. Yet her entire career has been spent in the customs brokerage business, beginning with part-time jobs while in college in 1970.

"I received on-the-job training," Esposito related, "which I suspect is happening less often now. Companies are looking for people who have management skills and a management background, promoting operations executives who come up through the ranks. Good financial skills and personal management skills are important, but there is also more of an opportunity for women now in international trade. It is one field in which you'll find women in positions that are revenue related, not just staff. Companies are looking at an individual's capabilities, not gender. The only criterion is whether or not you can perform. The evolution of moving women into management positions is gradual, but the standard is a simple one. They have to show they have profit-and-loss-center experience. I'm responsible for revenues and administration, and over the years I've shown I can deliver."

Esposito suggests that companies be flexible in considering candidates for international work. "Smaller companies are often more willing to move women into these positions. The lines of authority are more informal, there is a diversity of functions, and there is less concern about what an administrative position is and what constitutes an executive position. After all, with computerization of exporting and importing regulations, duties, currency, and all the other material of our trade, the whole concept of who *types* versus who *manages* is no longer relevant. Companies need people who can work independently, who are keyboard literate, who are smart and flexible. Often those individuals are women, not older men."

Large traditional companies that assess candidates for international assignments often ask the wrong questions. Instead of looking only at the professional and managerial skills of executives, companies should pay more attention to their personalities and psychological makeup. Does the executive enjoy challenges? What is the executive's life-style? Can he or she live without a health club, Lincoln Town Car, and ESPN? Is the person tolerant and flexible? Does the manager enjoy foreign travel and new experiences? Are there special considerations related to children's schooling, elderly parents, or a spouse's community activities that would make relocation difficult? According to international management professor Arthur Whitehill, the truth is that the traditional Yankee businessman would rather stay home. Companies may find out that their executive women are more suited for international assignment than their executive men.

Finally, companies think they are serving corporate interests when they assert that although they'd happily send women overseas, women would be ineffective because foreigners would not accept them. On its face, this seems to make sense. Executives are taught that the cardinal rule of international business is to accept the cultural mores of international business partners. When in Rome, do as the Italians do. In many cases women in other countries do not receive the same cultural acceptance of professional women, so companies conclude that American women will not be accepted as peers of foreign businessmen.

This rationale is also used to explain why women are not considered for managerial positions that are charged with supervising growing numbers of nationals and third-country nationals hired to work for American companies. Not only would foreign clients and customers not deal with a woman, but home office executives believe that the company's own non-American employees might resist supervision by a woman.

This assumption, however, is false. The truth is that American businesswomen are not only accepted overseas, in many cases they are more effective than American men. "Foreign women are a third sex," stated Professor Wortzel. "They are not automatically accorded the same inferior status as women in the country they are visiting."

Kathleen Hagan explained: "The stereotype of American women being aggressive allows them to work with us. We are more readily accepted, because they expect American women to be intelligent, serious, and capable. They have respect for a woman's drive and ambition that brought her to a position of prominence representing an American company. But they are also less threatened by American women. Frequently, foreign businessmen will tell you much more than they would tell male executives, because they feel more at ease with a woman. Being a woman can be a great advantage, because in many cases the foreign men treat women so well."

Bernice Cramer, president of Paos, an international strategic-design-planning company, agreed. "In Japan, I was actually a media star with my own TV show for two seasons and many, many TV and newspaper appearances. Obviously, much of this publicity was because I was a Japanese-speaking American woman, although I hope some of it was for professional reasons as well. In any case, it helped me in business!"

Rosanne Esposito had the same experience with Middle East customers. "I've never had any problems because of my gender," Esposito said. "Foreign clients just want to know if I can get the job done. I've even dealt for years with an all-male Saudi Arabian company which would have taken its business elsewhere if it wanted. But I know my business and give excellent service, which is what they want."

Women are also effective because they bring distinct skills to the international arena that many men do not. For example, many women have not had an easy path early in their careers, and have had to demonstrate initiative and resourcefulness just to reach the point of being chosen for international assignments. Resourcefulness is a quality that may determine their success overseas, as well.

In one of her first jobs, Kathleen Hagan worked for a U.S. senator and dealt with government officials all over the world in the name of her senator. "It is second nature to me now to call the minister of trade in foreign countries when I need something, because I learned early in my professional life not to be intimidated by anyone. I'm accustomed to working as an equal with high-powered men and getting to the person who can make things happen. Those skills are valuable in the international arena, and reflect a woman's view of herself. If she views herself as powerful and capable, she will handle herself in an authoritative manner and achieve her goals."

Many women are also skilled at building relationships, which is critical in developing international business ties. Patience, personal attention, a willingness to create harmony, and superb communication skills help build those relationships. "American companies have earned a stereotypical image of running in and out of foreign countries, just doing a quick deal," Hagan said. "But you have to look at the long term. Trust is important, and personal skills and a long-term view build trust more effectively than an aggressive manner. Deals have to be win-win. I've seen U.S. executives whose attitude is that the foreigners will have to learn how to do business the American way. Women usually ask what our foreign partners need to win. Women are perceived by foreign partners as being more able to understand the customer and client side of the table. That's why they receive high degrees of acceptance."

Some women believe that because they see themselves as a minority in many business settings, they bring a natural sensitivity to other minorities. As such, they are more apt to understand diversity and respect other cultural heritages. White male executives may not. "In one African country I was watching a group of Texas men doing oil work," one woman said. "They were disgusting, chainsmoking, loud, vile, and drunk, with bellies over their belts. The Africans dismissed them totally as ugly Americans and would have nothing to do with them. In my observation, there are many countries where sending an American male as a company representative would be suicide."

By contrast, most women are perceived as having a family orientation (or at least an interest) and a concern for broader community issues. This perception is often a distinct advantage in certain countries where ties to family, religion, and social concerns outweigh business interests. In the United States, executives often keep their family, religious, and social concerns separate from their business life. Overseas, however, forging these personal connections are sometimes a precondition to getting down to business. "I've made arrangements for the teenage children of my Italian client to come to summer camp in the States; I've gone to church with them on Sundays when I'm in Florence, and the purpose of our business dealings is to improve the computer literacy of his country," said a software sales manager. "I never talk about sales revenues or profits. Ours is a personal relationship."

Cynthia Livingston, a partner in the international management consulting firm of Cambio International, has studied the potential for women to succeed as global managers. "I've assumed that women have the same technical competence and functional experience," Livingston said. "What has become clear is that women do have a distinct advantage over men."

The reason for this disadvantage, according to Livingston, is that while women have acculturated to the male values and norms of the business world, in the international arena they can also leverage their female qualities. In many American business cultures, masculine qualities such as individual achievement, assertiveness, and material success are highly valued. These, however, are not qualities that are universally valued in other cultures.

Successful global managers have demonstrated innate or acquired characteristics that more often resemble female strengths: cultural sensitivity, tolerance for ambiguity and change, flexibility, cross-cultural communication skills, leadership at coalition-building, patience, and persistence. Traditional American management styles often do not work in foreign cultures. Men are perceived as direct, assertive, competing, and controlling, while women are more apt to be accommodating, receptive, and intuitive, bridging to a conclusion that benefits all parties. While gender generalizations do not apply to all men or all women, they occur often enough to become valid guidelines.

"Some international recruiters," Livingston said, "have recommended that their clients specifically look for women executives, rather than men, knowing that women will more likely possess the qualities needed in an international manager and be more successful. But it is not just a factor of the personal qualities women bring that will give companies that hire and promote women a big advantage. On all three economic fronts—North America, Japan, and Europe—the declining number of workers is also a real factor that favors women. There is an economic opportunity for Americans to gain on Japan and Europe, because companies in those places aren't particularly happy hiring what they consider to be 'immigrant' employees. In many cases they aren't smart enough to hire American women yet, but more American companies are now beginning to understand the potential for women to succeed as global managers."

THE AMERICAN ADVANTAGE
AND THE MYTH OF EUROPEAN EQUALITY

While American women may be welcomed abroad, the perception that European women are considered equals in European society is false. With rose-colored glasses, American women look overseas to some European countries and note with envy the great gains women have apparently made, particularly in the public sector. By 1988 women had comprised 38 percent of the Parliament in Sweden, 34 percent in Norway, 15.4 percent in West Germany, and 14 percent in Switzerland and Ireland. In comparison, by 1991, women had yet to attain 6 percent of U.S. congressional seats. Some women in Europe have achieved the top positions as well: Margaret Thatcher earned the respect of world leaders as prime minister of England, while women such as Ireland's president Mary Robinson are helping to chart a new social course for their respective countries.

The influence that these elected women have had, particularly in forwarding social programs affecting working families in many European countries, is well known. For example, France, Austria, Finland, Germany, and Italy offer generous family leave at 80 to 100 percent of normal pay. But this rosy picture may be misleading.

The truth is that many countries that purport to offer services such as child care and after-school care are not providing enough to move great numbers of women into executive positions that demand extra working hours. These services are primarily run by the public sector and in many countries there is a shortage of available slots for the children of working parents. This lack of child services and irregular school hours and days makes it difficult for women to hold down full-time professional employment in these countries.

For example, in the United States, 25 percent of women workers are part-time, versus 52 percent in Norway and 60 percent in Sweden. Sweden has the most sex-segregated work force in the Western world, with 40 percent of educated women in four categories (secretary, clerk, cleaner, and nurse). In this respect, the profile of working women resembles the United States in the 1950s.

"There are few women in business in Sweden because of the relatively low salaries for women, the high taxes on those salaries, and the amount women would have to pay for child and home care," explained a member of the Swedish chapter of the International Women's Forum. "The glass ceiling in Sweden is really thicker than in the United States. Sweden is a small country with a small business community, and the men choose their own kind to promote from among their friends."

In Britain, despite pledges by Prime Minister John Major to place more women in positions of power, Britain lags behind other European countries. In the United Kingdom, women constitute only 6.3 percent of Parliament, and few women are seen in industrial and professional roles; one survey found women represented only 9 percent of all managers. The gap between women's and men's pay in Britain is one of the widest in all Europe.

In France, women account for 42.5 percent of the labor force (in comparison to a European Community average of 39.4 percent), but one architect laughed at the notion that women in France have achieved parity with their American sisters: "France is operating at about a 1960 level for women. Women are still thought of as secretaries, teachers, and nurses. Women still suffer unequal pay for equal work, have to work for people less knowledgeable than they are, and have a hard time getting things done. There are still lots of 'archaic' qualities about the business world in France, none of which help women."

Martika Jonk, a partner in a Netherlands law firm, said that although on the surface her country looks like it is tolerant of women in top positions, many businesses and professions are still quite conservative. "It is only recently that women have begun to return to work after having children," she said.

There are few women in management positions in Germany; the estimated 1.5 percent are clustered in "female" staff areas despite the fact that 40 percent of German workers are female. These figures should not be a surprise even though many American business executives view European nations like Britain and Germany to be on a par with the United States.

As Professor Rosabeth Moss Kanter of Harvard Business School commented, "Globalization does not mean homogenization." Despite instant communication by fax and phone and common visual images (more often than not via CNN), Europe is not one culture, and countries within it will remain diverse. American management practices and culture will not immediately be transported overseas. It will take much longer for women in European countries to reach the level of acceptance that their American female counterparts have attained in business and the professions. For the foreseeable future, then, American business has done a much better job of developing numbers of well-educated, experienced women for middle- and senior-management positions. This is an executive talent pool that European countries cannot match, giving American companies a distinct competitive advantage.

NEW GLOBAL COMPETITORS

Despite the number of women who work, Eastern Europe is further behind its European counterparts in providing significant economic opportunities, although countries that were open to Western influences such as Hungary have more prominent working women. More women than men have studied languages, economics, and trade, and the Baltic countries have a few female political leaders such as Marju Lauristin, deputy speaker of the Parliament in Estonia, and Prime Minister Kazimiera Prunskierne of Lithuania, an economist.

However, more Eastern European women seem to be losing their jobs (and the corresponding social services tied to jobs) than are gaining new ones. For many women, the economic stability they seek would bring them the freedom to stay home with young children rather than the imperative to work. Despite the stereotype of professional women working side by side with male colleagues in Eastern Europe, the reality is far different.

The former Soviet Union provides an example of the vast difficulties facing women. Despite its great number of professional women, the daily reality facing them is quite different from the stereotypical perception. Education alone will not propel these women into positions of economic empowerment in their country.

"The Soviet state has manipulated women over our history," said Alevtina Fedulova of the former Soviet Women's Committee in Moscow.

"You can just look at the old posters. First they praised women as a mother and homemaker. Then when the state needed women workers, it sloganized women as tractor drivers and construction workers. Then when it needed scientists, it sloganized women with books in their hands. Now it wants women to go back home. Well, we can't.

"Women are absolutely at a loss," Fedulova said, explaining how the work of her committee has changed from fighting the threat of worldwide nuclear war to crisis intervention at home. "We understand there are women who should feel more confident because they have the skills to go into business, but there are psychological differences. Three generations of Soviet women have received guarantees from the state, but now they are faced with their own decisions about who they are, where they will work, and how they are going to keep their family fed. We are all trying to dress and act as if we are fine, but we are not. We have nothing to hide. This is the most critical time for women. We are laying the foundation for a new society in which women can no longer be left out. We'll never have a democracy if the doors are locked for women at decision-making levels."

But the doors of The Club remain locked for many women across the world. Despite the prominence of some individual women who have become public world leaders through family power (Indira Gandhi, Benazir Bhutto, Corazon Aquino, and Violeta Chamorro, for example), the utilization of female brainpower has not taken hold in the private sector of even the most economically powerful countries.

In Japan, for example, even in government only one percent of women are at management levels, and the average woman's income is only one half that of a man. Although four out of ten Japanese workers are women, many companies force their women to resign when they marry or have children. This is changing slowly.

The reasons are partly cultural, and these cultural expectations generate a catch-22 that proscribes corporate policy. Relatively few Japanese women want to work full time outside the home after they get married. They are taught that a wife's duties are to cater to the needs of the husband and family. Even if women want to work, the pressures of three-hour commutes and lack of child-care services make it difficult. Japanese women also hold the family purse strings and are responsible for major purchases. Despite the fact that Japanese women are marrying later and having fewer children, women at this point have little desire to put up with the sixteen-hour working days that are common for their husbands. Husbands, tired after long days of work, business socializing, and commuting, have little desire to pitch in and help at home, reinforcing the role division between the sexes. And because women have little political or economic power in Japanese society, they have little power to change the working environment in a way that would benefit both men and women. So the status quo remains, in part because few women who remain at home are dissatisfied.

Some working Japanese women, however, are dissatisfied, finding that conservative-minded employers and husbands are unwilling to accept their desire to work. Sexual harassment is accepted as part of a male working environment, and despite a new law prohibiting it, there are no penalties. Convention and the small number of women in executive positions discourage a Japanese senior executive from having a woman report directly to him, thereby limiting the opportunity for women to rise in management. It is no wonder that 85 percent of female workers feel discriminated against; surprisingly, Japanese firms seem not to have made the connection between their treatment of women and women's ambivalence about fighting the corporate and social culture. Japanese executives prefer to blame the victim, basing their refusal to promote women on the fact that women lack attachment to their jobs.

This bleak picture for Japanese women is a rosy one for American business. Japanese women are underutilized by Japanese businesses, and even in the face of a labor shortage in Japan, the situation is not likely to change soon. The answer for frustrated Japanese women may be to seek foreign employers, but those employers know that because of social mores, Japanese female executives can't be used effectively in positions that require customer contact in Japan. However, American women can be utilized effectively by both foreign and American companies. Perhaps American companies will wake up to this natural competitive advantage before their foreign competition does, hiring away American women who seek international assignments.

One woman who has developed a successful career working for a Japanese firm is Judith Barzilay, vice president of import-exports at Sony Corporation of America. A former teacher and librarian, Judith became an international trade lawyer in her thirties, and worked for the Justice Department, a private law firm, and Sony's law department before she was recruited to work for the operating side of the business.

"I had no idea I'd ever be doing this," Barzilay said. "But my Japanese boss encouraged me to leave the law and go into business. In American companies, it's not so easy to do that. The Japanese don't put people in pigeonholes as much as American companies seem to. The Japanese are willing to try talented people in sales, marketing, and logistics without regard to what they were doing before."

Barzilay, like other women in senior positions in international trade, believes that being a woman is an advantage, even in a Japanese company. "I'm very team-oriented. I take care of my team; I'm considered a good mother to them. I don't consider that a sexist comment; in Japan, it's important for the team leader to be a parent, man or woman."

Barzilay has traveled to Japan and the Far East on business. "I deal with Japanese suppliers, ocean carriers, air carriers, freight forwarders, and many company executives. I've been excluded more by Americans than by the Japanese. The Japanese really do their homework. They know who I am and the level of my authority. It's a contrast to some American company executives who assumed that my male subordinate would make the final decision.

"It's the same when Japanese executives come here to visit, and I am in the position of hosting them. They are fascinated by me, and spend time looking at all my awards, degrees, honors, and citations on the wall. There are not many executives with law degrees who are running departments, and credentials are important to the Japanese. I also have pictures of my husband and children in my office, which helps to make another positive statement. They know I am a serious, solid citizen with a family."

Women who deal with Japanese companies state it is important to distinguish between Japan and the rest of the Pacific Rim; even as Japan is becoming more hospitable toward American women, the traditional Asian barriers are falling much easier in Taiwan, Thailand, Singapore, the Philippines, and Hong Kong (which has the best attitude toward women in business).

Timothy Hough, chief executive officer of GJM Holdings, Ltd., an apparel manufacturer, believes that women have an advantage over many men in those countries. "In Hong Kong, women run the factories. The issue is competence, not gender. Women can do better. I wouldn't send a macho American male to some of those countries to do business."

Barzilay would look forward to an eventual posting in the Far East for Sony. "This company wouldn't block me from any assignment because I'm a woman. For instance, I'd love to go to Singapore, where Sony is setting up a logistics company. My family would be excited to go as well."

Just as the regions of the Far East differ from each other and differ for working women, the various countries of Latin America are diverse. Women are treated differently in Brazil, European Latin America, Indian Latin America, and the Caribbean Latin America; in Mexico, it may be as difficult for male business executives to conduct business dealings as for women because of a long-standing hostility on the part of Mexicans toward North Americans. In Africa, race may be more of a factor than gender, and the Middle East (with the exception of Israel) is by far the most difficult area for American businesswomen.

But in most countries, it's the effort that women make that counts, according to Patricia Smothers, the only woman on the Texas International Trade Commission.

"Obviously, knowing the language is important," Smothers said. "Executives in foreign countries will take you more seriously if you have made an effort to learn about their culture. There is a great deal of building relationships before doing business. Most initial trade missions do not come back with concrete results, but that's all right. The social interaction is what is required first. There are many women in Texas who own their own businesses, speak Spanish, and have been doing business in Latin America for years very successfully. However, they built their relationships over time, not overnight."

Going into meetings with the right attitude is important, suggests Smothers. Unfortunately, often the macho, ugly American attitude comes out in a meeting. An immediate shutdown of discussion can then occur. In one meeting held with top officials in Mexico, the president of a leading Texas chamber of commerce found himself totally ignored during the negotiations after starting the meeting with a confrontational remark. Most of the remainder of the discussion was directed to the black woman president of another Texas chamber of commerce who began by indicating a desire to work with Mexican officials on common concerns and then proceeded to discuss with them how best to accomplish the set goal. "Politeness is always important and appreciated," noted Smothers, a veteran of many trade missions.

Bernice Cramer suggests that utilizing women executives in the face of an increasing global marketplace is an effective business strategy at home as well as overseas. "The area most in need of understanding is the word *international*," she said. "It doesn't mean 'everywhere else outside the United States.' Rather, it means that we are part of an international whole and can no longer see our markets and our companies as isolated and protected entities. That's why international skills and perspective are so essential to all American companies today—not just to sell overseas, but to continue selling at home."

As in their historic reluctance to move women into international assignments, justifying their decisions on outdated assumptions, American executives are generally blinded by their belief that their way is the best (and even the only) way, Cramer states.

"'If we only say it again a little louder, surely they'll understand us,' is the Ugly American's refrain overseas," she said. "Corporations would rather not examine the basis of their own decision and management frameworks—it's easier to get other people to bend to your way of doing things. Many American companies have been blindsided in our own market by foreign competitors who were willing to take a fresh look at reframing their strategy, while we slumbered on in perfect confidence that we owned the American consumer.

"Do women have a unique contribution to make in this perspective?" Cramer asked. "Perhaps our willingness to tolerate uncertainty and plurality of decision inputs, our tendency to excel in language, and our patience will be virtues—in our head offices as well as in our overseas branches!"

THE NEW GIRLS' NETWORK

Many executive women in international trade reported meeting women of their level in professions and government ministries in other countries, although fewer in private companies abroad. But women like Tomye Tierney, Judith Barzilay, and Rosanne Esposito are encountering more women in the United States who are active in international trade, and they are benefiting by each other's experiences.

"There are many more women in our field," explained Rosanne Esposito, who, as the first female chairman of the board of the JFK Airport

Customs and Brokers Association, has attained membership in The Club of her profession. "I am meeting them at industry group meetings."

Esposito belongs to both her own professional trade association and a women's professional network and sees an important role for both. Organizations such as the National Customs, Brokers and Forwarders Association of America, to which companies belong, monitor legislation and negotiate trade issues affecting her industry. Organizations such as Women in International Trade meet the professional needs of individual women who belong.

"Women in International Trade does a very good job of providing a forum for women to get together and meet other women in the same field," Esposito said. "It has a good mix of entry-level women and us senior women, and while the programs generally concentrate on issues related to our field, there are also self-improvement programs that women would not receive in regular trade associations."

Judith Barzilay, another member, agreed. "My company belongs to the American Association of Exporters and Importers and the Council of Logistics Management, but I find a great benefit in the networking I do at Women in International Trade. One woman in our department was hired because I knew her from that group and recommended her to my predecessor."

Professional development groups for women in international business are springing up across the country, often under the umbrella of the national Organization of Women in International Trade. From city to city, these nonprofit groups are attracting new members with monthly speakers, newsletters, membership directories, consular corps receptions, and active trade missions. For women who seek international assignments, the experience, advice, and collegiality of other female members of such groups may help them devise effective strategies to land the positions they seek—if not in their own companies, in others. In this respect, these international groups are like thousands of other women's business and professional networking groups that are helping their members combat the barriers of the comfort zone and prepare them for ultimate leadership positions in The Club.

CHAPTER EIGHT

THE POWER
OF COLLABORATION

Knowing a meeting is coming up is like visiting a good friend. It puts me in a positive frame of mind, lifts my adrenaline to creative levels, and gives a broad and sensible frame of reference to otherwise hectic and intense days.

—Member of a women's professional organization

Despite the professional joys and opportunities of senior executive status, life at the top can be lonely at times. A major job change, even a long-desired promotion, often entails compromises along with rewards. Career setbacks or confrontations are draining. A few executive women, equating isolation with strength, feel they must "tough it out" alone. But success is hollow and failure harsh when it is not shared with friends. Even power, when exercised by one individual, can feel empty.

But none of this has to be. Thanks to support groups, business forums, and a variety of networking groups, executive women need never feel isolated. Nearly every major economic center in the world now boasts one or more organizations where businesswomen can share professional information and contacts and, together, exercise group power. These organizations are not a fringe benefit or occasional resource; they are central to the well-being and success of women executives. To ensure that support is always there, women are joining forces with other women, sometimes to the bewilderment of men.

Corporate director Anne Billups* related one such dinner conversa-

*An asterisk denotes that we have changed the name of the woman quoted, and in some cases the name of her company and its location as well.

228

tion with a fellow corporate director. He was a retired broadcasting executive whose views gave a clear picture of how some corporate executives perceive the activities of women's groups.

"I was attending our annual corporate directors' dinner in New York City and found myself seated next to a charming, older gentleman," Anne said. "I had never met him, since he had retired from the board before I joined, so I knew very little about him.

"Picture the scene," she went on. "A lovely private club, off Park Avenue, a quiet, seventh-floor dining room, oak-paneled walls, mammoth fireplace, Oriental carpets over polished wood floors. Full-sized oil portraits of past club presidents, all portly gentlemen with walrus mustaches, hung from the ceiling, illuminated with spotlights. Need I mention the club only recently admitted women as members?

"We were seated at tables of eight, and by the time the filet of beef and red wine arrived, my dinner companion had told me about all the bright women he had hired in his days as a corporate executive. But then he began to rail against women's biggest mistake: going off in groups of their own.

"'How can women—and blacks and Hispanics and Asians, for that matter—hope to be accepted in the corporate community if they keep reinforcing their differences?' he asked. 'This country is a melting pot! I was the son of immigrant parents, an outsider, and I worked my way up, understanding and accepting the culture I was in. What's so bad about that? Why do women need their own groups? Why does anyone?' He was quite worked up about the subject and obviously had strong views about it."

Anne tried to explain the benefits of some of the organizations she belonged to, while stressing that women can also contribute to the general business community as well. He remained unconvinced. Somehow, the men's club environment reinforced the validity of the position for him and made him comfortable enough to have the frank conversation with Anne. He saw the existence of separate organizations as sinister and divisive, contrary to his melting-pot image that perpetuated the existing culture he knew so well.

"What he couldn't imagine," Anne said, "was that the setting is parallel for women in their professional organizations. Just as he felt comfortable to express his views in the men's club and corporate boardroom, surrounded by male corporate executives, women also feel freer to express what's on their minds when they are feeling most comfortable. For some women, that is with other men. But others are guarded in primarily male environments and I don't think he could relate to that."

Anne's dinner companion is not the only corporate executive who sees diversity as splintering, rather than strengthening, the business environment. That is not surprising, given his attachment to the melting-pot concept that blurs distinctions. A more graphic image for accommodating diversity is the salad bowl, in which a variety of colors, tastes, and textures creates a dynamic whole.

Forging the connection between women's professional organizations and the community-at-large of business executives is a challenge for leaders in both arenas. But the connection can be made, without either group changing its fundamental values. The goal should be to discover their commonality, with partnership as the final objective.

The first step is for both groups to understand each other. In Boston, several executive women shared the story of how group support and group power became an essential part of their perspective and helped them come of age in their respective professions.

A BOSTON STORY

In May 1985 in Boston, Carol, then president of The Stop & Shop Companies, Inc., and Sheryl Marshall, then vice president of Drexel Burnham Lambert, organized a breakfast meeting with a select group of other senior-level businesswomen. Their objective was to plan a major fund-raising event for Evelyn Murphy, then the state's secretary of economic affairs and a candidate for lieutenant governor. The support and enthusiasm of women's groups across the state would be an essential component of Murphy's financial base. The event was a cocktail party held at the Copley Plaza in Boston that launched Murphy's campaign with a war chest of over $100,000 raised solely from women.

Buoyed both by the success of the fund-raiser and Murphy's election, this ad hoc coalition of Boston businesswomen took a closer look at its role in the community. "Perhaps we wielded more political and economic power than we had realized," one said, describing the group. "We were company presidents and vice presidents, bank executives, stockbrokers, real estate managers, law partners, real estate developers, heads of major organizations, and college presidents. Three of us had been senior appointees in Boston's city government and four were directors of the Greater Boston Chamber of Commerce."

Women in the group served as directors on more than thirty corporate boards, including the Norton Company, the Dennison Manufacturing Company, Ames Department Stores, Lotus Development Corporation, John Hancock Insurance Company, and Time, Inc. They sat on a wide range of nonprofit boards, from colleges and hospitals, to human service agencies and arts organizations. Many of the women had founded or served as officers in other women's professional organizations, such as the Women's Bar Association, New England Women in Real Estate, or the Boston Club for Business and Professional Women. Appointed to various state commissions, they were active nationally as well; one served as the first female president of the National Council for Urban Economic Development, and another as president of the National Council of Savings Institutions. Of the twenty-four women, three were African American. The majority was between forty and fifty years of age.

Four months after Murphy's fund-raiser, the group coalesced at a member's Beacon Hill home and established a name and identity. They decided to call themselves the Women's Economic Forum, and their mission would be to advance the economic empowerment of women at all levels of the community. Knowing that public policy choices are often the greatest barriers to economic advancement, the first objective of the group was to continue active involvement in the political process, and encourage and support female candidates and governmental appointments.

Second, the group decided to act as a center for information on public policy issues. Armed with information, it would decide how pressure could be brought to bear on the many critical issues affecting women. Third, the women targeted the largest female representation possible in the city's powerful business and civic organizations, which had a history of strong influence on public policy and economic issues. Finally, the women worked to coordinate with other women's organizations, enhancing their individual strengths through the power of group collaboration.

Because a high degree of trust and candor was essential, membership in the Women's Economic Forum was limited to businesswomen having personal relationships with other members. They shared breakfast expenses twice a month, but in no other way formalized their existence.

They wanted no officers and no added responsibilities in their busy lives. The women wanted only a safe haven to strategize and brainstorm. Neither seeking nor requiring publicity, they decided to keep their existence relatively quiet.

During the rest of the 1980s the Forum had a major effect on women at the highest levels of business and government. They supported dozens of female candidates to the state legislature, Boston school committee, and city council, helping to elect and reelect many of them. They monitored appointments made by Boston's mayor, by the governor, and other elected officials, noting each appointee's positions on key issues affecting women. They suggested and campaigned for potential appointees.

They campaigned for welfare initiatives, reproductive rights, day-care programs, and other issues affecting the economic advancement of women. They developed strategies to influence key officials, such as lobbying for a proposal to establish school-based health clinics that could dispense birth control information. They focused city-wide attention on the courage and effectiveness of an inner-city elementary school principal, ensuring that she receive a major award honoring outstanding city employees. When Lieutenant Governor Evelyn Murphy became a gubernatorial candidate in 1990, they worked hard for her election.

Forum members took advantage of every appointive office and corporate opening to suggest Forum members and other prominent women for nomination. One Forum member advised that if prominent women would "just show up" regularly as active participants on business boards, they would rise to leadership positions. As a formula, it seemed to work.

For example, shortly after the Forum was established, Jane Vogel,* a manufacturing company president, reported that she had been asked by the chief executive officer of a commercial bank to serve on the nominating committee for one of the state's major business organizations. The organization was notorious for its poor representation of women. Although a high percentage of the work force of its members was female, only four of its fifty-two directors were women.

"I need an action plan, here," said Jane. "Our first meeting is next week. There are eight slots open, but there's no limitation on the number of directors. The nominating committee could recommend to increase the number, if they wanted to."

The Forum quickly formulated a plan for Jane. Every woman would make sure that her company was a dues-paying member of the business organization. Eight Forum members volunteered their résumés and Jane agreed to suggest all eight names to the nominating committee.

"This will test if they are serious," Jane said. "In the face of these eight quality names and the companies they represent, the committee has to consider them. If they take any less than four, we may have to really reconsider our relationship with that organization. Doubling the number of female directors when the base number is so low is not a stretch at all."

Four of the women were selected; a small inroad, the group admitted, but progress nonetheless.

Forum members were often asked to recommend women for board positions, and often suggested one another for both corporate and nonprofit boards. The Forum gave this effort a great deal of attention, although they knew progress in placing women on corporate boards is slow. A 1990 survey of top sales firms in Massachusetts conducted by the Boston Club, a fifteen-year-old organization of over 200 business women, showed that in 1987, 55 percent of the Boston-area firms had no women on their boards; by 1989 that figure had decreased by only 9 percent. The women knew that boardrooms are the site of Boston's power structure and that corporate executives and directors are key actors in shaping the policies of public-private partnerships and allocating corporate resources to the community.

Forum members underscored their economic commitments with generous financial contributions. Individually they contributed thousands of dollars to nonprofit causes each year. In addition, most of them were in positions to bring corporate charitable resources to the table. They realized that targeting charitable activities to support those causes that helped women become independent, and refusing to lend their names or money to those that did not include women as full participants or recipients, was collaborative power that worked.

For example, they investigated how the local United Way allocated the almost $50 million it raised each year, sensing that if they didn't pay attention to how the United Way responded to women, no one would. Once the Forum pursued United Way board membership, change was rapid. After a popular local magazine criticized the United Way for its lack of diversity and published a picture of its all-male campaign cabinet, the following year the cabinet included a woman who was also a Forum member. Soon other women appeared on the United Way's cabinet, board, and various committees. By 1989 one Forum member was the first female chairman of the board and had appointed the first female chairman of the important allocations committee. In 1990, when the United Way's male executive director announced his retirement after seventeen years, the search committee for his successor included two Forum members. The new executive director of United Way, Marion Heard, was the first woman and the first African American to lead the United Way in Boston.

This list of accomplishments does not diminish in importance another function that evolved within the Forum. It became a support group. For all members, the personal connection among them gradually became the group's most important asset. Although influential and self-confident on her own, each member felt that by collaborating and sharing experiences, she enhanced her individual effectiveness. To this end, the group was flexible according to individual needs. Sometimes, the agenda for a meeting was scrapped and a critical issue addressed. For example, when Susan Tennyson* casually mentioned a shift on a nominating committee, the group quickly responded.

"I was on the ladder of succession to become chairman of a leading nonprofit organization," said Susan. "I had served as a director for many years, chaired committees, and served as an officer. Suddenly, the nominating committee moved a fairly new CEO into the officer lineup. I liked him, and thought no more about it. But when I mentioned it casually at a meeting one morning, my friends were alarmed, and clued me in on what was happening. After much discussion, they suggested an approach which I never would have considered!

"'Go right to him,' they said. 'Tell him you're planning to be chairman next year, and you hope he'll want to do it after your term is up.' Well, that's exactly what I did. What could he say but 'yes'? And the nominating committee went along with it, since we had co-opted them by deciding it between the two of us."

When another member's company was suddenly involved in a takeover fight, the group deliberated over possible strategies to help her. When one member's company was the subject of a negative profile in the *Boston Globe*, the group collectively helped thrash out a response. Often, the group's perspective was clearer on the nuances of a given problem than that of the woman who brought the issue to the table. As one Forum member said, "All of us had achieved success in a male system, whose reality is not quite our own. Each of us derives support by moving back into a female system, where connections, sharing, and process are paramount, and where each of us can openly question and challenge our view of the events surrounding us."

One Forum member described the meetings "as a place to recharge my psychic battery." Another called the Forum "a source of wise, dependable counsel, where ideas can be tested and implemented, where integrity and mutual respect abound. It is an interdependent force of extraordinary talent and knowhow."

FROM COAST TO COAST, CONTINENT TO CONTINENT

Among women's professional organizations, the Women's Economic Forum is one of the most successful, having encouraged its members to grow as leaders in the business community and as feminists. But it is hardly the only one of its kind in the country. Between 1975 and 1990, as increasing numbers of professional women moved into executive positions, women's networking organizations have proliferated. Today, groups like the Women's Economic Forum (or its statewide successor organization, the Massachusetts Women's Forum, founded in 1990) can be found wherever there are substantial numbers of women with stature in their business communities. Some groups are relatively small and, like the Women's Economic Forum, limited to women with senior status in their professions. Some are open to a broad membership and welcome a cross section of occupations, from printers to dentists.

Other women's organizations meet the needs of women in particular professions. Female band directors, helicopter pilots, and bowling writers have their own associations, as do women artists belonging to Roman Catholic religious congregations and American women married to Europeans living permanently in Paris, France. Women no longer have to figure out the subtleties of a career in mineral resources, soil science, plastics, cosmetics, or cell biology by themselves; they just have to join their respective women's professional organization. There are also associations just for minority women, such as black women lawyers or publishing executives.

And these organizations are proving their worth. Although many women have joined mainstream professional organizations with their male peers, women's networks have also grown in size. The for-profit National Association for Female Executives, Inc., has attracted 248,000 women, up from 145,000 in 1987, while the Society of Women Engineers, founded in 1950, saw its membership grow dramatically to over 16,000 as more women entered the profession in the years between 1975 and 1990. Some women's professional groups are offshoots of the mainstream group. For example, the Boston Society of Architects has been very supportive of its Women in Architecture Committee, according to Elizabeth S. Ericson, principal in the firm of Shepley Bulfinch Richardson and Abbott. Ericson, who served as secretary of the Boston Society of Architects, described the Committee's work as "consciousness-raising about the competency and imagination of women," which "builds credibility in the community."

A broad-based support group may begin quite simply, with an impromptu brainstorming session. That is what happened in Margaret Potter's* kitchen in Danvers, Massachusetts, in 1984. She and her friends, some in their twenties, some in their thirties, some older, were discussing what they wanted for themselves, their children, and other women and children in the remaining years of the twentieth century. They talked about encouraging women to run for office and about women who sometimes need moral or monetary support. They talked about the different meanings of power to women and men, and they talked about depictions of women in the media. Wanting to do something more than talk, they took action together. In 1985 they became the North Shore Women's Coalition, determined "to pursue a greater understanding of the issues that affect all women; to provide mutual support to one another; and to influence the decisions that impact our lives." Within five years the Coalition had over 300 members and an impressive list of accomplishments, including an annual "starting over" scholarship for women over age twenty-five, candidate questionnaires, events and endorsements, monthly programs for members, and a generous contribution to a new shelter for abused women and children.

While the Coalition's issues are primarily community-based, many of its members are also active in North Shore Women in Business, an independent women's business organization of over 250 members who gather regularly to discuss business and make referrals. Its former executive director, Georgina Keefe-Feldman, one of the founding members of the North Shore Women's Coalition, is not surprised that organizations of community women are now focusing on economic issues. Describing the membership of North Shore Women in Business, she says, "Many of our members are supporting their families. The group's activities are focused on helping these women be successful in whatever job or profession they are in. Members give each other marketing, financial and referral ideas, as well as introductions to other potential sources of business in the community."

Other women have discovered the benefits of collaboration. Women Business Owners of North Florida decided that its 150 business members could best learn from and do business with corporate women, and that corporate women could also benefit from the association with female entrepreneurs. By inviting several corporate women to join, Women Business Owners may be leading the trend for many such women-owned business associations.

Some of the first networking support groups were the inspiration of individuals defining a need. Diane K. Winokur, a San Francisco management consultant and president of Winokur Associates, remembers her reasons for beginning a group in the San Francisco Bay area. "In the mid-seventies, I was working for a management consulting firm to train minorities for senior management positions in major companies across the country. As I visited these companies, often for a week at a time, the same thing happened over and over again. I would get to the company, and I'd receive a note or a message from a woman in management—and at that time she was most often in middle management—wanting to meet me while I was there. They were so proud of the fact that a *woman* was coming to their company to consult with senior management that they wanted to connect with me. Sometimes I'd hear from two or three women, and I'd always try to have dinner with them, preferably together. Much to my surprise, I'd find that the women usually didn't know each other. How isolated they were!

"Returning home to San Francisco, I thought it would be a good idea to get together some of the women I knew there. I made a list, and invited them all to a lunch. Well, we ran out of space. Everyone wanted to come. I'll never forget the feeling we all had after that first lunch—it was so wonderful just to be together, to meet each other. One woman would say to another, 'Oh, I heard there was a woman at the bank—so now I've finally met you!"

Diane Winokur's group continued to meet, becoming the Bay Area Executive Women's Forum, later merging with two successor groups to become the Women's Forum West. Like every other networking group, Women's Forum West has its own personality, which Winokur describes as "mature, diverse, and dynamic." It generally meets for dinner, with a speaker selected from the membership. One popular format is the "round-table," when members meet in small groups to discuss a topic during dinner, and then report their thoughts to the entire group. An annual two-day retreat provides an extended opportunity to share information.

"I remember one retreat with great warmth," says Winokur. "We had a discussion about friendship. We shared the fact that all of us feel very lonely and isolated, and miss friendship more than anything else, due to the constraints of our busy lives. For all of us, the Forum represents a bank of friends that is irreplaceable."

"Our friendships often overlap into business, as I'm sure happens in other groups. Members make a special point of choosing their accountants, bankers, and lawyers from Forum members. I changed all my banking relationships to the Bank of San Francisco because Fran Streets is senior vice president there. I'm an investor in Ruth Owades's ten-million-dollar floral mail order company, Calyx and Corolla, as are other Forum members. The list can go on and on about ways in which we have supported each other over the years."

Founders of networking groups for women in particular professions often sought to develop industry recognition for the few women in male-dominated fields. Such was the case in 1977 in Washington, D.C., when forty women involved in the transportation field established Women's Transportation Seminar (WTS). WTS is now a national organization of transportation professionals with more than 2,300 individual members of both genders, and twenty-four chapters. Its 1992 annual conference featured such mainstream topics as the Clean Air Act and privatization, as well as a workshop on managing diversity and a luncheon address on career success.

"WTS gives women in transportation positions, still very much a minority group, a peer group to support and assist them with advice, strategies, and news of job opportunities," explained its national president, Ann M. Hershfang. "Positions on local chapter boards and conference-planning committees provide training, confidence, and visibility with their employers. Programs provide a chance to meet and mingle with top public and private leaders.

"WTS gets members to talk across modes," noted Hershfang. "That's what makes it different from other women's transportation organizations, such as Women in Transportation, an affiliate of the American Public Transit Association, or Women in Aviation."

Another broad-based national association, the International Alliance, celebrated its tenth anniversary in 1990. The leaders of fifteen prominent networking organizations blossoming across the country first met in Washington, D.C., in 1979, and Mandy Goetze of Baltimore recalls the discussion. "We knew there would be value in sharing ideas, programs, information, successes, and problems," she said. "And it has worked!"

Deane Laycock of Boston was the first Alliance president. Ten years later, Alliance members represented twenty-two separate women's business and professional organizations from around the world, serving as an umbrella organization that unites, supports, and promotes professional and executive women. Emphasizing mentoring, communication, and promotion of women's interests, Alliance members are often newsmakers, appearing frequently as "Women Leaders of the Year" in *Savvy Woman* or quoted on the front pages of leading newspapers. As the growth of international business and communication technology increases sharing among Alliance members, American women are learning that their Dutch, Swiss, and other network sisters are dealing with many of the same concerns about male-dominated workplaces.

These groups have not been static. As the founders of the first networking organizations moved into senior positions, their own needs changed and, in some cases, new groups formed. The challenge for these women was no longer how to move into senior management positions, or how to balance the pressures of work with the demands of a young family. Now, bringing in new business, finding capital, and marketing globally were the challenges.

The International Women's Forum, founded in 1980 and probably the most elite group of its kind, brought together women of significant and diverse achievements and encouraged them to exert a collective influence on issues of worldwide concern to women. With forty-nine chapters in North America (thirty-six in the United States), Europe, Eastern Europe, Asia, Latin America, and the Middle East, the International Women's

Forum provides a link through which members like Cathleen Black, Marian Wright Edelman, Polly Bergen, Ellen Gordon, Donna Shalala, Barbara Hackman Franklin, Muriel Siebert, Sandra Day O'Connor, Alice Rivlin, Josephine Natori, Franca Fendi Formilli, Claudine Escoffier-Lambiotte, and Margaret Thatcher can reach their far-flung professional colleagues.

Still another international organization of leading businesswomen is the Committee of 200. Representing more than seventy industries, its members own businesses with annual revenues of over $10 million, or manage corporate divisions with more than $50 million in annual revenues.

Wherever women's networking groups are found, they are effecting change. In San Diego, where *Time* magazine has dubbed women "the power base" of the community, women influence much of the city's policy. Not only are the mayor, the deputy mayor, the leading newspaper publisher, and the foremost philanthropist all women, but in 1990 four of the nine city councilors, the heads of the school board, the chamber of commerce, the Centre City Development Corporation, and the Republican and Democratic county committees were also women. In Oklahoma the Women's Concerns Forum, a networking organization and center for social service information, spurred the creation of the Hillcrest Center for Women's Health, the Women's Resource Center, a rape hotline, and the Mayor's Commission on the Status of Women. Founded in 1980, the Women's Concerns Forum has today evolved into the Tulsa Women's Foundation. Recognizing the growing importance of women in business, in 1990, Tulsa's mayor and chamber of commerce sponsored the first special Conference for Tulsa Business Women, focusing on the economic, social, and legislative issues affecting women.

The Missouri Women's Forum tackled the issue of women and political power at a conference entitled "A New Decade of Leadership: Women State Legislators" after the 1990 elections. Moderated by International Women's Forum member and former lieutenant governor Harriett Woods, the conference gave women legislators the opportunity to address the needs and future of their region. In New York, the New York Women's Forum targeted women as board members at a special session held in November 1990. Prominent board members of the International Women's Forum addressed the special challenges women face as board members, how women can rise to leadership positions on boards, and how the number of women on boards can be increased. In the same month, business-women in Maryland echoed the same theme at the Entrepreneurs Trade Show, jointly sponsored by the Executive Women's Network in Baltimore and the *Baltimore Business Journal*. The Executive Women's Network, already thinking about the next generation of business leaders, has established a unique mentoring program that matches promising high school seniors with executive women. The Boston Club has initiated the dynamic Enterprise Council program, designed to review and advise the business plans of members who want to start their own companies. All these accomplishments are especially striking, given the relatively short time that most of these organizations have been in existence.

Women's networking groups have gained valuable visibility through a variety of publications. "Connections," a monthly newsletter for Massachusetts North Shore Women in Business, publicizes women who own or are executives in local area businesses. In Tulsa, Oklahoma, the Tulsa Women's Foundation publishes *Tulsa Woman*, a quarterly newspaper that highlights and celebrates women of achievement, including an honor roll of Tulsa businesswomen. Across the country, many other women's organizations have published similar directories or newsletters.

In 1990 the *New England Journal of Public Policy*, a biannual publication of the University of Massachusetts at Boston, devoted a special issue to the concerns of women. Entitled "Women and Economic Empowerment," the journal contained twenty-six articles, fifteen written by members of the Boston Women's Economic Forum. In addition to sounding the theme of change in public policy initiatives for women, the articles called for changes in the private sector, for the empowerment of women, and for increased collective action. They argued a need for more adult literacy programs, affordable child-care and after-school programs, maternity benefits, universal health care, reproductive freedom, and equitable pay. They did not hesitate to describe the barriers that must fall in the business world, calling for greater sensitivity to family issues—such as parental leave and flexible work schedules—and more creative career paths. They discussed the unfounded gender assumptions that guide too many corporate decisions. The articles expressed interests and concerns that run deep within the Forum and that continue to be explored.

Readership response to "Women and Economic Empowerment" was intense and enthusiastic, suggesting that the time had come for more women's groups across the country to "go public" in a concerted and strategic manner, putting their thoughts for the future in print and on the airwaves.

"With all the talking, analysis, and planning going on in support groups, more of it should be heard by a broader audience of other working women, consumers, families, community leaders, media, and policymakers," said one woman in Pennsylvania. "Business and professional women have an opportunity to speak out as one powerful voice on such issues as health insurance, employment training programs, access to capital, and financial education for young women. Communicating what we believe to others is the natural next step."

MAKING THE MAGIC HAPPEN

Regardless of the many successful and productive collaborative activities started by executive women, thoughtless stereotypes continue to pervade our culture. Women who have made it are "queen bees"—rivals pitted against one another, more aggressive and competitive than their male colleagues.

"Intense and often unsavory competition among women may be one of our best kept secrets . . . so elusive that is isn't often recognized by men, so graceless that it is almost never acknowledged openly by women," proclaimed Kathleen Hirsch, in "Women vs. Women," a May 1990 Sunday *Boston Globe Magazine* feature with two-inch headlines. Presumably, this reasoning goes, if there are few slots at the top reserved for women, the only way to get them is to claw away at competitors.

The reality is just the opposite, say many executive women. Successful senior-level support groups are remarkably free of competition, jealousy, and ego posturing. Although some executive women at times act and sound like their male peers, those who gravitate toward support groups often share positive feminist values. They help one another achieve specific goals and delight in one another's successes. They speak warmly of the candor of group discussions and of the powerful dynamic created when the group zeroes in on an individual problem. "Everyone has your best interests at heart," says one support group member. "They're thinking about what's best for you. Generally, after we've chewed over a problem we come up with a solution. The dilemmas we discuss are often not the kinds of things you'd go home and tell your husband about. He wouldn't be able to offer the range of perspective that the group can, because many of the women in the room have been there, too."

The candor, trust, and focused, productive discussions do not, however, happen automatically, as any woman in a dysfunctional group can bitterly attest. They are the product of deliberate choices, the coming together of essential values. To the extent that women embrace those choices and values, they can make the empowering magic of a support group work for them.

Determining a sense of purpose takes first importance in making a group work. From the beginning, the goal of the Women's Economic Forum was clear: to empower women at all social levels for lives of economic independence. This focus continues to guide nearly all its activities and discussions. For many of the members at first, placing women's economic interests foremost required discipline. It was hard to stay clear of extraneous activities such as monitoring legislation that could have sidetracked their efforts or duplicated the work of other groups. Today this economic focus has become a fundamental way for these women to look at the world around them.

Second, the group must agree on strategies for attaining its goals. The most realistic strategies are those that work within the current economic, political, and social system. Many of these executive women see no virtue in rejecting capitalism, despite some of its flaws. They do not avoid traditional business and philanthropic organizations, whether or not they are bastions of male authority or stumble and lose sight of their mission. They prefer to add female talent, visions, and voices to existing institutions. Instead of skirting around the current political system, they believe it is far more productive to support female candidates and others who share their objectives. Yet even as women work within the system, they are exploring other avenues to achieve political and economic equality, such as forging alliances with outside advocacy groups or certain members of the media.

Third, to reach their objectives, support groups are comfortable with power and know how to use it. They recognize that while power often masquerades as money or status, true power is the ability to bring about change and to attain goals. Their members are committed to a strategy of collective power based on relationships, placing the agenda of the group first. In an ideal group, members are self-confident, successful individuals, at ease with themselves. Having already achieved considerable stature in their professions, they can set aside their personal career needs and focus on others. "What do you need?" they ask each other. Familiar with exercising power on their own, they are eager to explore and practice ways of using the power of the group to help individual members. To a large extent, successful support groups of senior executive women are models of female power-building.

Nancy Korman, a partner in a public relations and graphics firm, explains the strength of groups such as the Women's Lunch Group, which she founded in 1973.

"Years ago, women gave dinner parties and behaved like demure hostesses while the men around the table cut deals and advanced their careers. Today, when I entertain, women benefit as well. The word *power* is no longer frightening to most women. If there is one accomplishment in my life I look at with pride, it is the strength and continuity of the Women's Lunch Group. During a particularly heavy snow storm, the Harvard Club answered its phone by saying, 'All events are canceled except for the Women's Lunch Group.' To me, that emphasizes the fact that we are a sturdy bunch and willing to stick with it over the long haul."

The sturdy bunch is action-oriented. One member hired another member, a landscape architect, to design her new garden. A tip about an opening on the State Board of Higher Education led to another member's appointment. Another member first heard about her new job as CEO of a private educational company through the group.

"We barter information, trade stock tips, and discuss job openings," said Korman. "Members are not allowed to talk about their kids, husbands, or emotional crises."

Which is not to say that many groups don't place a high value on the personal relationships that develop as members share stories with one another. Many groups find that feminism as a shared core value helps them to achieve a high standard of interaction, providing them with a vision of what human relations might be. The group is a safe testing ground for that vision. Successful groups seem to have decided that if they are serious about changing society at large, they must begin by making their particular group different, by nourishing inside their small circle the ideals and values that they hope to see outside it.

Senator Barbara Mikulski sees a parallel between women's organizations and the old-boy network. "The boys just laugh at each other's jokes and listen to their stories endlessly. This fellowship and friendship leads to mutual support. So let's imitate the old-boy network. Not every get-together of women has to be utilitarian and functional. Just being together for mutual support is enough. It's like the sewing circles and great book discussion groups of old; those weren't about sewing or books. They were about support, just being together, just taking the time to listen to each other."

Will senior executive women outgrow their support groups? Not if the networks grow and change along with them, suggests Diane Winokur.

"It's interesting to look back and see how we all have progressed, along with our networks, and to look at where we are now," says the San Francisco consultant. "Many of us are in our fifties, and the issues are quite different for us now than when we started."

Many senior-level executive women have decided to communicate informally with each other on issues of particular interest, while remaining active in their own women's professional organizations, helping younger women advance in the profession.

Karen Hastie Williams, a partner in the Washington, D.C., firm of Crowell & Moring, participates in one such group of women law partners.

"We intentionally decided we did not want another formal organization, but we meet periodically in one law firm or another. Most of us went to college in the 1960s. Now, thirty years later, we are the senior women partners in our firms. We share information about such things as how firm management committees work, billing issues, and of course we refer business to one another. We work with associate evaluation committees and recruitment committees to assist younger women in our firms, and we help each other brainstorm problems. Collectively we know we can be a force for change, even though there are only a few of us in the firms."

As senior-level women shift from corporate and professional positions to new opportunities or careers, many keep strong ties to the women's organizations that supported them earlier in their career.

"One thing that strikes me," Diane Winokur observed, "is that many women we know across the country are reaching a certain level and are now leaving companies as a result of their own personal choices or because of economic restructuring. These women have been accustomed to being surrounded by large corporate resources, and their identities are established by their business cards. Now they are out on their own. But they are still active, contributing members of their professional groups."

It is not surprising that these executive women have continued to find the support, information, and friendship they need in their forums and other groups. Their professional network is a place for them to hold on to the identity they used to have, while moving to a new place. A great number of these women will start their own businesses, or run for public office, or take some other path that requires leadership and maturity. The future agenda for these groups will be to help these women in the challenging next stage of their professional lives.

JOINING FORCES

Women are discovering that a coalition of women's organizations can be a powerful force for change. Elinor Greenberg described the origins of the Colorado Women's Leadership Coalition (CWLC), established in 1988 by the Women's Forum of Colorado, the Alliance of Professional Women, the Junior League of Denver, and the Colorado Women's Economic Development Council: "In the mid-1980s, I had conducted some research on leadership issues, and realized that we had extraordinarily talented women in leadership positions in Colorado. In 1986, when I was president of the Women's Forum of Colorado, I began to meet with leaders of other women's organizations to see how we could collaborate effectively," Greenberg said. "We wanted to focus on the economic contributions of women to Colorado, and work with newly elected governor Roy Romer to remove economic barriers for women. We first had to decide whether we were issue-oriented.

"We concentrated on two ideas: communication among the various women's organizations and leadership development of individuals and organizations. We thought that if we could improve our communication, we might come up with more effective leadership strategies. We also wanted to have an intergenerational impact, with experienced women relating to younger women, teaching them what we had learned so they don't stumble over some of the same territory that we did.

"We wanted to focus on how women today pass on knowledge to each other," Greenberg explained. "Women are organization addicts. We form organizations the way our mothers had coffee klatches. But we've not been very good, yet, at bringing private knowledge into the public arena."

The CWLC is now comprised of twenty-eight women's organizations, from the League of Women Voters to the Black Women for Political Action and the Council of Jewish Women and represents over 22,000 Colorado women. Each organization pays $100 annually to the Coalition and sends three delegates to the CWLC board, which meets monthly.

"Our committees are cross-organizational," Greenberg said. "We've decided to limit ourselves to four issues: health and human services, education and training, business development, and appointments to boards and commissions."

With such a diversity of organizations and professions, is it difficult for the CWLC to agree on issues?

"Obviously, some issues are more critical to certain groups than others," Greenberg replied. "For example, when the National Women's Business Council decided to hold a hearing in Denver on women and telecommunications, six of the Coalition's member groups were most interested in cosponsoring the hearing and the reception for the Council and participating actively.

"Often we can't say that the Coalition stands for X or Y. That doesn't bother me because it's not the point. The challenge in developing partnerships is coalescing the diversity of purposes and thought of the potential partners. Our individual organizations and their members can take stands and influence policy. On some issues, all twenty-eight groups may agree. On others, one or two groups may take the lead and the rest may just act as an information-sharing vehicle. But this is a time of great opportunity for women's organizations. If we act more wisely, we'll see new ways of functioning together emerge. This is what I call the emergence of new 'network organizations' that rely on the potential power and creativity of collaborative diversity."

Mary Giddens, chair of the Florida Women's Consortium, believes that a wide variety of women's groups working together is an effective strategy, and that the collaboration of traditional business and professional organizations with more activist groups, such as the National Organization for Women (NOW), works well. She and others see an important role for organizations like NOW, pushing from the outside and refusing to compromise, acting as an "edge to the wedge."

"Those groups can grab the headlines and keep external pressure on an issue while other organizations such as Business and Professional

Women or the American Association of University Women, which are perceived as more moderate, can negotiate effectively behind the scenes," Giddens said. "In that way, such organizations complement each other."

The Florida Women's Consortium generally achieves consensus among its more than thirty member organizations, according to Giddens, who was also past state president of Business and Professional Women.

"Our mission is the empowerment of women and the exchange of information among groups," Giddens said. "The Consortium takes positions but individual groups take the lead in implementing the strategy."

"It's important for women, with as many things as we have to do, to focus an organization tightly on its main objective," said Kate Gooderham, state president of the Florida Women's Political Caucus. "Let some organizations do what they do best and let the other groups come to them to assist."

Many political observers believe that the Consortium, whose establishment was originally encouraged by a staff member of former Florida governor Bob Martinez, was responsible for blocking passage of restrictive abortion legislation advocated by Martinez at a special legislative session in 1989.

THE NEW TRAINING GROUND FOR THE CLUB

Coalitions of women's organizations are emerging in state after state as women rediscover strength in numbers. They also know that as men and women prepare themselves to be more effective managers in the nineties, hierarchical power will be less and less a determinant of success, and will be replaced by personal power and skill in interpersonal relationships.

The new managerial work of this decade, according to Harvard Business School professor Rosabeth Moss Kanter, will depend on more personal relationships that involve joint planning and joint decision making. "Internal competitors and adversaries will become allies on whom managers will depend for their own success," explained Kanter. "At the same time, more managers at more levels will be active in the kind of external diplomacy that only the CEO or their selected staffs used to conduct." Author Sally Helgesen agrees, calling this nonhierarchical style of leadership the "strategy of the web."

Because of these changes, a new role has evolved, perhaps unwittingly, for women's networking groups. Women have the opportunity to get considerable practice developing interpersonal skills and management strategies. As management becomes more horizontal and companies more closely resemble webs or interdependent networks, the skills and strategies of these women will be called upon often. As for leadership abilities, what better place for women to refine the leadership skills so often needed for membership in The Club than in these professional organizations and support groups?

If leadership is the art of getting things done through people and the cultivation of an organizational climate in which individuals grow as they contribute to common goals, these groups provide fertile testing grounds. In the midst of their peers, women can experiment safely with new ideas, test strategies, and receive knowledgeable, honest feedback. From this base, leadership and power in mainstream business associations or corporate roles become easier. To an important extent, coalitions, consortia, organizations, and support groups are the training ground for a new kind of leadership, at a time when the nation's complex social and economic problems demand change.

"We trumpet that," said Denver-based Jill Baylor of Stone & Webster, 1991–92 president of the Society of Women Engineers (SWE). "This is one reason we urge women in the engineering profession to join SWE. With women comprising only about five percent of the engineering profession, we need every avenue for women to show they can excel. In our organization, women can be in local, regional, and national leadership positions through officerships and committee chair positions—a great opportunity for many to develop their individual leadership skills."

Why should women strive to assume leadership positions in such organizations? Baylor thinks the opportunities are too good to pass up.

"Leadership brings visibility," said Baylor, explaining one of the priorities of her presidency. "Visibility is very important for women in the engineering profession and we must step up every possible form of visibility available to us to showcase talented women."

Most senior executive women who are members of prestigious networking groups like the International Women's Forum exhibit essential elements of leadership. First, they are not afraid to articulate a vision of the future and lay out specific strategies that can achieve that vision. (For example, "We will have women in line to be president in every major business organization in the next five years, and here's how we'll do it.")

Second, they inspire others, communicating the new direction and creating an enthusiastic constituency committed to achieving the vision. Finally, they know how to motivate, keeping others moving in the right direction, even in the face of major obstacles.

Professor John P. Kotter of the Harvard Business School confirms what women have already learned on their own, that "individuals who are effective in large leadership roles usually have had a chance, before they get into important jobs, to grow beyond the narrow base that characterizes most managerial careers." For substantial numbers of women, networking support groups provide that chance for growth.

Leadership skills can be learned, said Elinor Greenberg. "There is a difference between what an effective board does and what an effective leader does," she explained. "Boards first facilitate. But I see women making a major error—they facilitate forever. They don't move on to focus and, after that, to an integration of new ideas into an ongoing organization. We must now concentrate on developing female leaders who will be task-oriented and respect process but not be consumed by it. Many women's organizations are now moving effectively into positions of public leadership. They are no longer just concentrating on moving women into positions of power; they are also using their intelligence in public roles to influence decisions and affect societal change."

Greenberg and others see that there is still a dearth of leadership at many companies and civic and business organizations, resulting in cultures that are not sufficiently adaptive to handle rapidly changing economic and social environments. The best managers are, by their nature, necessarily short-term focused. What is needed now is a new cadre of visionary leaders, with bold ideas and the confidence to inspire others. As such women emerge from their professional organizations and networking groups, they are ready to lead others in The Club.

As women move into mainstream business and civic organizations, however, they still need the support and feedback of their own networking groups to increase their effectiveness.

"It's locking in your base," explained one business owner in Minneapolis. "You really need a protected safe zone of individuals who know you well and support you so when women move out in the business community, they will be known to represent a wider constituency, even as they build on it.

"I was the chairman of our local chamber of commerce," she said, "but I also had been president of our local chapter of Women Business Owners. When a chamber member would undercut me on an issue, or try out a negative slant on me with the press, we caught him doing it right away. Every woman who heard about it told him that I had her unqualified support and she knew me well. If I hadn't taken the time to know those women business owners and be part of their network for years, they might have said they didn't really know me. At the same time, I had a greater standing in the community by being chairman of the chamber than just the Women Business Owners, so you need to move out and do both."

LEADING THE CLUB

Executive women who are determined to affect change in the broader economic community realize the real challenge of their leadership skills occurs when they assume influential positions in mainstream organizations and associations. Statewide coalitions of women's organizations, no matter how inclusive, are still seen by some to be contrarian or radical. For the National Organization for Women or the American Association of University Women to advocate child support legislation or gender-balance requirements for state boards or commissions is expected; when the chamber of commerce advocates such positions, policymakers pay attention.

Clearly, women must move themselves and issues they care about into the purview of the mainstream business and civic organizations. But Kate Gooderham of Florida suggests one reason for the difficulty in moving women into The Club: "We have to take the fear factor away—the fear of feminism. Some business and professional women are reluctant to advocate issues that benefit women in mainstream groups; some men fear women whom they perceive as feminists, possibly because of the lesbian overtones to feminism. Actually, most people, men and women, are feminists but don't know it. A lot of concepts they support, like equal pay and respectful treatment of women, are so mainstream already that they don't know these are feminist goals."

Gooderham suggested one technique to overcome the fear factor and allow women's views to surface. She insisted that every woman who serves as president of her local Women's Political Caucus chapter be given funding to participate in a community leadership program sponsored by the chamber of commerce. Limited to thirty-five up-and-coming community leaders, Leadership Florida involves its participants in a twelve-week program of meeting community and business leaders and studying regional issues.

"This is a good way for women to ask some questions that need to be asked," said Gooderham, who was given the funding to attend by an admiring client of her consulting firm. "When we talked to the county sheriff, for example, I could ask him why there was no minimum security facility for women. At the same time, male community and business leaders could get to know me, and the Caucus, and understand what we were all about." After the Leadership Florida program ended, Gooderham and other participants joined an alumni group to continue the important relationship-building and networking with other promising community leaders.

There are many women's professional networks in southwest Florida where Gooderham lives, from the Women's Network of Cape Coral to the American Association of University Women and the Fort Myers Women's Forum. But of fourteen mainstream business development groups in the area, in 1992 there were only 64 women out of 332 board members, ranging from less than .5 percent on one board (the Business Development Corporation of Southwest Florida) to just over 50 percent on another (the Lehigh Acres Chamber of Commerce, with a woman president). Nine of the groups had 25 percent or fewer women on their board of directors.

Slowly, as more women are becoming known by business leaders, the picture is changing, according to Gooderham. "They'll look at boards with no women and say, 'Well, we do need one or two.' It doesn't qualify them for sainthood, but at least they're thinking about the involvement of women." Furthermore, as Gooderham is well aware, women cannot just wait to be discovered and nominated for board membership. Most of the mainstream business organizations are membership associations, open to those who pay dues, show up at meetings, and participate. Women who have demonstrated a serious interest in the mission and objectives of such organizations and who actively volunteer on committees or projects are more likely to be selected for leadership positions.

Other women insist that change in mainstream business organizations is happening too slowly. "They laughed when we started the Women's

Chamber of Commerce," said a businesswoman from San Antonio, Texas. "But one or two women on the board of the regular chamber was not good enough. Women could never get to the top of that organization. Now we have our own organization of over five hundred members and we have forced others to treat us on an equal basis with the other local chambers of commerce. Whether it's a trade mission or a legislative hearing, the SAWCC is included with an equal seat at the table."

Women's business groups sometimes agree with mainstream groups on issues affecting the business community, but at other times, women can and do point up the folly of legislative positions taken by traditional business groups. In that regard, women who have formed their own organizations and speak their own mind about business matters may be more effective than the token women who have tried unsuccessfully to influence the positions of mainstream groups.

For example, at a 1992 Boston legislative hearing on a bill that would require employers to educate their employees about sexual harassment, traditional business groups such as Associated Industries of Massachusetts opposed the bill, arguing that sexual harassment was already illegal, and that requiring education on the issue constituted overregulation. Noting that the bill contained no penalties for violations, a representative of the 250-member North Shore Women in Business group said, "We're talking about putting up a poster and putting a piece of paper in an employee's paycheck once a year. This is not a radical bill." Her own delegation of prominent businesswomen effectively pointed up the weakness of AIM's opposition.

Another strategy to move issues women care about is to work for their adoption by mainstream groups. What may start as a radical proposal offered by a "radical group" may gain currency when adopted by a traditional professional organization. While this strategy takes time and usually requires at least several women to have first assumed leadership roles in the mainstream group, the outcome is worth the effort, say women who have made it happen.

Attacking gender bias in the judicial system is a case in point, said Phyllis Segal, national president of the NOW Legal Defense and Education Fund. The idea to resocialize sitting judges began with discussions at the Fund in the early 1970s, but only came to fruition when the Fund was able to energize women's professional networks and then mainstream groups. "That professional connection and then the connection to women in the bar across the country was important," Segal explained.

Female litigators and women who were participants in the court system had observed judges' gender-based stereotypes and biases for years, but during the 1970s, they were joined by social scientists, legal researchers, and advocates of women's rights who began to take more serious note of such problem areas as the treatment of rape victims and battered women, and the economic disparity between divorcing parties. Because of the seriousness of the problem, as early as 1970 the Fund considered establishing a judicial education program, but because judicial education itself was such a new field, taught primarily by other judges, the idea languished.

It was not until 1979 that the Fund's National Judicial Education Program was launched, in part because of the formation of a new professional women's network, the National Association of Women Judges. These experienced female judges brought professional credibility to the objectives of the project, and helped the Fund obtain the endorsement of such other mainstream groups as the national Center for State Courts, the National Judicial College, the California Center for Judicial Education and Research, and the American Academy of Judicial Education. At the seminars and conferences sponsored by these groups, judges began to look at gender bias in the courtroom for the first time. Even the most reluctant judges became impressed with the content of the program, and asked for it to be given in their own states.

In 1983, New Jersey established the first statewide task force on gender bias to look at the problem of sexism in the state court system; ten years later, almost thirty states had active task forces examining and eliminating gender bias in the judicial branches, and many have gone beyond their original mission to become vehicles for broad institutional reform. The long process ("water on a stone," said Sylvia Roberts of Louisiana, who initially proposed the idea to the Fund) has accomplished a great deal, but is not finished. The next goal is to incorporate training on gender bias issues into substantive areas of the law and judicial decisions, rather than have the subject of gender bias be a stand-alone program. For example, medical negligence education programs might include material documenting the medical profession's disparate response to male and female complaints and its differing treatment habits based on sex; civil damages seminars might focus on the economic consequences of psychological damage from rape, battering, and custody battles and the contribution of homemaking; employment litigation material might include sociological and psychological theories of why women respond differently than men to sexual harassment in the workplace.

Despite a continuing agenda on the issue of judicial education, however, the success of the program to date shows that the process of moving ownership of an idea from a women's rights organization to a women's professional organization and then to mainstream professional organizations works well. Both male and female members of The Judicial Club now speak as eloquently on the importance of eradicating gender bias as did the original activists. But simply introducing ideas to organizations is not enough. Key women must move themselves or others into the organizations to persuade, even manipulate, those groups to carry forth the desired agenda.

Sociology professor Norma Wikler was involved with the judicial education reform movement from the late seventies, and it was her research skills, scholarly knowledge, personal energy, and the resources of the Fund that combined to make the careful strategy of social change within the judiciary happen. She and Lynn Hecht Schafran, who succeeded her as the director of the National Judicial Education Program, both serve as advisers to many of the state gender bias task forces, and are members of the national Gender Bias Task Force of the Association of Women Judges.

"There must be change-agents who have the vision, skills, energy, and time to drive the reform engine," Wikler explained. "Organizations can endorse an idea or agenda, but in most cases, it is individuals who educate, persuade, advise, and move the issue along. This change-agent role is important and in some cases is hidden because of the nature of the organization. Sometimes the institution is hidden from public view by design, as are the workings of the judiciary or a private gathering of business community opinion leaders. Success in those realms requires a combination of triggering internal acceptance and advocacy, while still maintaining sufficient control to chart the direction and course of the issue. This can be done by women who are themselves respected and influential members of the mainstream organization, or, as in the case of judicial education, the change-agents can be outside advisers or staff to the members."

Change does not only occur when women's groups have allied with mainstream organizations. Some professional mainstream groups are beginning to understand that joining forces with women's organizations to achieve certain objectives advances their own self-interest as well.

"For example, the Society of Women Engineers is a member of the American Association of Engineering Societies, the umbrella group of various engineering organizations," explained Jill Baylor. "As president, I have a seat on that board. On any group like that, one or two women out of twenty-five or thirty is not enough of a critical mass to push ideas forward.

"But AAES has specifically discussed the need to encourage women and minorities in the engineering profession and the continuing challenge of interesting young women in studying math and science," Baylor said. "This is becoming a universal goal. Other engineering organizations that are members of AAES also have their own specific committees addressing the needs of women and minorities, and many women who are SWE members also serve on those committees."

Baylor described an example of how the presence of women in mainstream professional organizations adds talent, expertise, and energy to advancing the objectives of the group. The cross-fertilization of female leaders from one group to another is a powerful dynamic that not only keeps issues women care about in the forefront but enhances their own development, Baylor believes. Women need to be active in their professional specialty, but they can also benefit by the visibility and leadership skills that a women's organization provides.

"There are many fields of engineering, but the challenges women face in the profession are so common that a diverse group of women are attracted to SWE," Baylor said. "I am a senior member of the Institute of Electrical and Electronics Engineers. The two organizations are different, but each is valuable. I see a definite movement of the views and opinions of women who are SWE members into the other associations that they are active in."

There is a place for both types of groups, because when women assume leadership positions in mainstream professional groups, they are aware that they must represent the entire membership and advance the mission of the organization.

"My constituency in the Denver Bar Association was different than the Colorado Women's Bar Association," said Jane Michaels, the third female president of the Denver Bar. "There were some issues such as abortion that were just too controversial, although I did urge the Women's Bar Association to take a position on it. But other issues, such as the need for more women and minorities on the bench, met with general agreement. It's a balancing act. Women officers risk being seen as too one-sided if they push for certain things in a mainstream group."

However, Michaels and other women who have led mainstream groups agree that women often bring distinct advantages: "The notion of a role model is still important," Michaels said. "Just being there shows other women what is possible. Leading a professional organization or business group is a tremendous opportunity. It is important that both men and women observe women as leaders, and achieve a level of comfort with that vision. It was really comfortable for me, leading the bar association, and I felt particularly rewarded when others told me that I had raised their level of enthusiasm about participating in bar association activities."

Michaels was describing a leadership style that reinforces good works by others and demonstrates commitment to the organization and its members, a positive style for a president of either gender. In mainstream groups as well as The Club, although the very fact that a woman has made it to the top sends a powerful message about inclusion, actual performance counts more, according to Rosanne Esposito, former chairman of the JFK Airport Custom Brokers Association.

"I think the fact I was a woman was never really an issue," Esposito said, relating her prior service as treasurer and vice president. "You do have to demonstrate that while you are leading the organization you are very good at dealing with the issues of the association. How did it fare under your term? There was a lot going on in the time I was chair, and I did a lot of public speaking. In that sense, because I became more well known in the profession, it may not take as long for the next woman to become chairman."

Slowly, more executive women are adding the "first woman chairman" description to their professional association credentials, even as the mainstream groups and the professions they represent remain primarily male-dominated. Some will be able to influence the mission, agenda, or priorities of the organization; others may just break down gender barriers by the excellence of their leadership skills and their own commitment to hiring and nominating other talented women.

Women who have reached such positions say that the personal benefit of these mainstream leadership opportunities is their increased personal power in The Club. As they moved from positions in women's professional organizations to broad-based groups, their self-confidence and stature grew as well, increasing their personal currency and forging stronger relationships with their peers. As they became better known, trusted and respected, new doors opened for them.

Micho Spring's professional history provides an example. A member of the Massachusetts Women's Forum, she was acquainted with many women in Boston, but in her role as chairman of the board of United Way, she developed a close working relationship with many male chief executive officers and community leaders. These men came to know her well; she was no longer just one of many company presidents in the city, or a face on a Sunday public affairs television program. One retailing chairman nominated her to serve on his board of directors; other Club members asked her communications strategy firm to represent their companies.

But Micho's personal power did not end after her term on several community organizations expired. Like many women across the country who have become powerful members of The Club, their effectiveness is often greater after they step down from important positions. The visibility and influence they have gained while holding these posts gives them the freedom to speak forcefully as individuals to an audience of their business peers, corporate employees, the media, and political and community leaders about issues of concern.

It is at this stage that the imprint of executive women will be the greatest.

CHAPTER NINE

THE IMPRINT OF WOMEN

The Public Club

There are few state boundaries that matter any-more. Women in the United States Senate or House will be Everywoman's elected official and it's up to businesswomen to help get them elected.

—Sally Berger, Ernst & Young, Chicago

Women's experiences in professional networking groups and mainstream business and trade associations have forced them to confront the political world, whether or not they had any prior interest in it. This exposure to the public sector has had a singular effect on many executive women, who have then become energized, actively pursuing issues of concern to them and helping elect more women to office. With their considerable personal resources, the power of their professional positions, their leadership abilities, the collaborative power of women's professional organizations, and their clout in The Club, executive women are making a real impact on the public sector.

It is no accident, some women believe, that among the front-burner issues in 1993 were family and medical leave, child immunization, universal health insurance, welfare reform, and lifting the reproductive counseling ban. The timing coincided with a dramatic increase in the political activism of many executive and professional women. Influential in the business world, they have also achieved status as "players" in the political world and for many there is no turning back. They believe women holding public office make a difference, and they have shown that their support can make a difference in electing them. From raising campaign funds to advising on economic issues, executive women are getting involved.

Some women were not always comfortable in the public sector, preferring to focus their attention on such details as return on equity and gross margin rather than legislative strategy or task force agendas.

Carol's first initiation into the public sphere occurred in the mid-1970s, when the retailing industry became involved in proposed legislation mandating returnable bottles and cans.

"I knew all the retailing and business leaders," Carol said. "But we had a senior vice president who handled our external and legislative issues; the public world was *his* domain. When the 'Bottle Bill' issue heated up, I was invited to a meeting at the State House, and I called him in for a briefing."

Carol, now a seasoned veteran of many political campaigns and an avid participant in public policy debates, laughed at her early naivete.

"I always skipped over the political pages of the newspapers and didn't even know the names of the senate president or speaker of the house. Our company vice president was clearly nervous about sending me up there. 'Why don't you let me go in your place,' he said. 'But they invited presidents of Massachusetts retailing companies and I'm going to go,' I told him. 'Now what did you say the senate president's name was?' His eyes rolled up in his head. I'm sure he thought that in one half hour visit I would undo all the careful relationships that he had tried to bridge over the years in behalf of our company and our industry.

"That visit really opened my eyes. In all my years in Boston, I had never set foot in the State House, Once I did, I was hooked. Most of the legislators were men and none understood our business. Legislative decisions were rarely made on economic merits—like, for example, on increased sales tax revenue that would accrue to the state by allowing stores to open longer hours. Religious leaders had more influence than business leaders. I began to understand that this was a world I had to learn, just to protect our retailing interests! I had not even focused on women's concerns at that point."

In most states, the seat of state government lies far from the center of economic activity. Thus company executives in big cities do not easily mingle with legislative leaders at power breakfasts or in private clubs, and the city's leading newspaper is often the only guide to political events and personalities. Because of geography and the disdain felt for the political process, many executives leave lobbying to one person in their corporation or to an industry trade group.

However, when executives rise to senior status in their companies or to leadership roles in their trade associations, they find they must understand and supervise those who handle the day-to-day legislative issues for their industry. When the time comes for business leaders to show up, women must be as ready as their male peers. Whether the debate is over telecommunications policy or custom import duties, women in The Club often find themselves negotiating head-to-head with policymakers and public officials.

As Carol discovered, the legislative process is like making sausage; you should never watch how it is done. Women invariably experience what a telephone company executive from Seattle called the "wake up" factor: "One day you wake up and realize that these same legislators who are making decisions about your industry are also making decisions about issues of more personal concern to you: domestic violence, child care, reproductive rights, education, aid to families with dependent children, and public appointments. Many of us didn't need the Thomas-Hill hearings to paint a picture of who the decision-makers were. We had already met them up close."

The inevitable question that executive women asked was, "Why aren't there more women in public office?"

PASSION AND PURPOSE

In the 1970s and 1980s many businesswomen concentrated on advancing their own careers. There was little impetus for vast numbers of working women to become involved with the political world. Despite the death of the proposed federal Equal Rights Amendment, most statutes that denied women equal opportunity or treatment had changed and the 1973 Roe v. Wade decision guaranteed women a minimum right to reproductive choice. These developments meant that many early activist women were free to redirect their energies to their professions.

But by 1992 the picture had changed. Women were worried and began a dramatic shift in their extracurricular interests. While few of them were ready to give up their careers for the uncertainty of a new one in the public arena, they were ready to lend their time, energy, and money to help the many talented and serious women who aspired to public life and to focus public attention on issues affecting the economic status of women.

Jean West, president of West Companies of St. Paul, Minnesota, and a member of the Committee of 200, noticed a great difference in the attention executive women were paying to The Public Club in the space of just one year. "The Committee of Two Hundred has never been political. It was never the purpose of the group, and politics was never discussed. I always assumed most of the members were Republican, as businesswomen who led companies of substantial size. But at our 1992 conference, I was astounded to find that at every table, there was a vigorous political discussion going on. Furthermore, after our business meeting, we made time for anyone wishing to share information. Several women got up to describe their involvement with women's political organizations. Our next newsletter listed the addresses for those groups. It was a totally different atmosphere than had existed for the previous ten years."

VIVE LA DIFFÉRENCE?

The reason for the increased level of political activity on the part of executive women was not just because women have moved *themselves* to positions in which they are able influence the political process. Women were also beginning to understand that there were vast gaps between the opinions and actions of male and female legislators over issues that concern them, such as fear of crime, presence of toxic waste dumps, and insecurity about continuing health insurance coverage. While some men thought and voted the way women hoped they would, no longer would many women trust their fate to a benevolent male elected official. "It's not good enough," stated one business leader in New Mexico. "From now on, I'm only voting for women."

Margaret Hagen, professor of psychology at Boston University, perhaps expressed it best: "I try to believe that the gender of the people in power has no effect on their values or priorities or the decisions they make," she said. "I try to believe that the gender of the scientists and fund givers at the National Institutes of Health has no effect on the type of research funded, on the type of disease or patient studied. I try to believe that the gender of scholars and educators has no effect on selection of subjects of scholarship or on the achievement of young men and women or the tenor of education.

"I try to believe that the gender of corporate executives and managers in no way affects their attitudes toward parental and hardship leave, flexible working hours and day care.

"I try to believe that the gender of elected and appointed political officials in no way affects the passage or enforcement of laws regulating reproductive rights and responsibilities. I try to believe that the gender of priests, ministers, counselors, therapists, and physicians in no way affects the counsel or care given to different clients and patients. I even try to believe that voluntary membership in organizations that institutionalize gender-based social inequities will in no way predict differentiation in the attitudes, beliefs, policies, or practices of those members toward men and women. I really try.

"I know there are misogynistic women and humanitarian, egalitarian, androgynous men, yet if I know nothing of two candidates but their genders, I will vote for the woman. The odds suggest that she has had to face the possibility of pregnancy from her girlhood to the present; that she has been the primary caretaker of her children and her aging parents; that she has suffered from numerous social and financial gender inequities; that she has an understanding of the priorities and problems of women; and that she has an interest in increasing possibilities for the fulfillment of women's varied potential."

Hagen thinks women have even further to go than the euphoria over the 1992 "Year of the Woman" elections might indicate. "Looked at one way, only six percent of the Senate is female," Hagen said. "Looked at another way, the increase from yesterday is three hundred percent. I do not know how many breakthrough women comprise a critical mass beyond which there is no more wall, but I welcome every one."

Working women want to see more females in The Public Club, but for most of them, the reality of contemporary issues is the motivating force behind their involvement and their belief that women candidates will impact results. International Women's Forum member Sheryl Marshall cites the status of children as a prime example. "About one in five children is growing up in poverty, compared to one in ten elderly citizens," she said, "but the federal government spends about ten times as much for each person over sixty-five as it does for each person under eighteen. In the nine years from 1978 to 1987, expenditures on children fell by four percent, while spending on the elderly rose by fifty-two percent. I want an elected official who advocates for children and stands up to vocal, affluent seniors."

This concern about children may be expected from executive women like Sheryl, the mother of a twelve-year-old daughter, but as Investment Services Group vice president of Donaldson Lufkin & Jenrette, she also understands economics. "The future of children is a bread-and-butter issue," Sheryl said. "Children will be the work force of the future, and will contribute to the social security system that's going to support huge numbers of working women in their elderly years. I happen to think the country's future economic well-being may depend on what public policy makers do to assist children today."

Until the 1990s many executive women were content to communicate with their own legislators and let it go at that. But even businesswomen who had little connection with the political process have been suddenly jarred into noticing the absence of women when a crisis hits and are aware of imbalance in political establishments across the country. For example, Kentucky was notable for having the least number of women in the state legislature at 4.3 percent in 1993 (in contrast to a national average of 20 percent or Washington, the highest, with 38 percent). Low percentages of women might not have mattered much in the past, but women started to notice in 1990 in states like Louisiana, whose legislature (with only 2.1 percent of women legislators that year) passed an extremely restrictive abortion law.

The events in Louisiana provide a striking example, but there is no doubt that women in public office make a difference. Gro Harlem Brundtland, the Harvard-trained physician who served as Norway's prime minister, argues that women in public office in her country resulted in a stronger emphasis on issues like child care, education, and family life. The same scenario could be true in the United States. A 1991 study of female officials done by the Center for the American Woman and Politics at Rutgers University documented huge gaps between male and female legislators over women's rights, health care, and children's issues. The study suggested that female public officials are more likely to involve more private citizens in government, pay more attention to the poor, and conduct public business in the open.

Surprisingly, a study in Connecticut revealed that more men than women believed that the presence of women in public office has had an influence on leaders considering the impact of policies on women, and that the presence of women has changed the way managers conduct themselves in meetings. Both men and women agree that women leaders have reshaped the public policy agenda, although the low numbers of women in office has meant that issues such as gay rights, reproductive freedom, and family leave legislation have not been uniformly successful.

Clearly, women bring their personal experiences and perspectives to issues that arise in legislative bodies. For example, Congresswoman Patricia Schroeder of Colorado has introduced legislation addressing the special concerns of families in the military; Senator Barbara Mikulski has pushed the National Institutes of Health to pay more attention to the study of women's health concerns. Virginia's attorney general Mary Sue Terry is leading the fight to open the Virginia Military Institute to women students. California treasurer Kathleen Brown tells potential investment managers that to qualify for consideration in bidding for the state's $67 billion public employees' retirement fund, they must include women on their team.

Like women in senior executive ranks, women in public office are also visible role models as they demonstrate that a career in public life is accessible to women. Many women believe that it is no accident that half the Connecticut congressional delegation is comprised of women. They ran for office in a state that enthusiastically supported Ella Grasso as governor from 1975 to 1980.

MEMBERS OF THE PUBLIC CLUB

Executive women are supporting other women, not only because they want the woman to hold public office. They are beginning to realize that this may be the shortest route to seeing more women in the key *appointed* positions that affect how public policy issues are decided. They know that female officeholders generally appoint more women chiefs of staff, commissioners, judges, and cabinet members. But the utilization of women's leadership skills varies widely across the states, according to a 1992 survey by the National Women's Political Caucus. Massachusetts governor William Weld, a Republican who was elected in 1990 in a close race largely on the support of women who crossed party lines to vote for him, appointed women to 45 percent of his cabinet positions. In addition, his policy adviser is female, as well as half his judicial appointments. Women in other states, however, fared less well, with cabinet appointments ranging from 26.3 percent in New York, 20 percent in California, 17.6 percent in Arkansas, and 13.6 percent in Colorado to 6.7 percent in Delaware, a startling underutilization of female talent.

"We are not just watching our elected officials," said Elinor Greenberg, a member of the Women's Forum of Colorado. "We discovered that there are hundreds of boards, commissions, and task forces that influence public policy, and many are operating without the participation of women. For example, the governor of Colorado appointed a Commission on Math, Science, and Technology to try to determine how we can encourage more students to study those fields. Despite all the studies that have shown that girls are sidetracked from those disciplines at an early age, only one of twenty-two members on the Commission was female. And yet there are many women in Colorado who have exactly the appropriate expertise that is needed on this issue. The Colorado Women's Leadership Coalition jumped right in with candidates and now nine women serve on the Commission, and I serve as cochair."

The Coalition was able to help the work of the Commission because it had already developed a relationship with the governor of Colorado. For many women's groups, relationship building and education is the first step in the long process of influencing The Public Club.

"We started with the female legislators," said an investment banker from Illinois. "Because so few of them had come into public life from the business world, they didn't know many of us. We established an informal arrangement so they could access any of us for background on issues they confronted. We became their kitchen cabinet, in many respects.

"Then we moved on to getting to know the women cabinet members, commissioners, and department heads. As we progressed, we dealt more and more with the other appointed and elected officials of both genders, and I think many of them were happy to have businesswomen they could call on for advice or feedback in addition to the chamber of commerce lobbyist. They knew we would give them the straight answer, or if we didn't know, we'd find out. They also knew we'd give them our own perspective on how a particular issue or piece of legislation would affect the economic status of women.

"At the same time, we kept our eye on public appointments. We sat down with our membership lists and our lists of women's professional groups throughout the state. Did they need a trustee for a public college in the southern part of the state? We had several candidates. Did they need an engineer or investment banker on a public authority board? A pension expert for a task force on restructuring the state's retirement system? A Republican? A Democrat? We had them."

RAINMAKING:
THE PUBLIC/PRIVATE CONNECTION

The public equivalent of rainmaking is bringing in campaign donations, one of the most solid barriers to women excelling in public life. Candidates need to be skilled at fund-raising in order to be successful, particularly if they are challenging incumbents or have little name recognition. Yet women in the public world often face the same handicaps that executive and professional women do in trying to bring in business: Men give political donations to other men, and men raise money through their network of male friends and business acquaintances. Only recently have women been able to tap into money donated by other women, and even at that, in most cases women candidates raise less than men.

"It is hard enough at the school committee and state legislative level," said Sheryl Marshall, who has raised campaign contributions for female candidates all over the United States. "But when you are looking at a gubernatorial seat, a congressional race, or a statewide United States Senate race, women must raise millions of dollars. That's an imposing challenge."

In local races, female candidates had always relied upon the contributions of some women in the business community or women with disposable assets who were as inclined to write a check to their local candidates as to the local dress boutique. But a sea change began to take place in the 1990s, as business and professional women mobilized nationally to help elect women candidates across the country.

"Change takes place through the political process," said Sally Berger of Chicago. "There are so few women in the United States House and Senate that no one is minding the store. Businesswomen, no matter where they live, must support women who are running for office. The world is getting smaller. A California woman senator will be on a subcommittee on health research or other issues that benefit all women nationally or even internationally. We can't afford to turn our backs on women who are running outside of our own states. We all volunteer for tasks in the business world, but there is nothing more important for any of us, as businesswomen, than making sure we have responsible women in Congress."

For the executive woman in Cincinnati or Atlanta who doesn't know how to access the campaign committee for a female senate candidate from Pennsylvania, for example, or who wants to make sure that those women with the best chance of winning are given a good financial foundation, prominent national political organizations make it easy for her. Operating much like a mutual fund, which pools investors' money and relies on professional managers, these political organizations pool contributions, study races, candidates, and the dynamics of particular campaigns, and then fund those candidates with the best chance of success. Like many women's professional organizations, these groups leverage the power and resources of their members to bring about dramatic change in the status quo.

Emily's List, which stands for "Early Money Is Like Yeast" (it makes the dough rise), is a donor network and political resource founded in 1985 for pro-choice Democratic women candidates. Members pay $100 to join and pledge to donate $100 or more to two or three recommended Democratic women candidates. Majority Council members contribute $1,000 or more to Emily's List each year. Emily's List scrutinizes races, analyzes past campaigns, and helps candidates plan successful races. It contributed $1.5 million to fourteen candidates in 1990 but raised more than $6 million in 1992, as more executive women discovered Emily's List, swelling its membership roles to over 24,000.

"I would not be the governor of Texas today if it were not for Emily's List," repeats Ann Richards at many fund-raising parties for the powerful organization. Businesswomen across the country responded, organizing gatherings of their friends and associates to hear more about the track record of Emily's List and, in some cities and states, formed their own Emily's List clones. Perhaps due to the success of Emily's List, in 1992 pro-choice Republican women founded Wish List (for "Women in the Senate and House") to raise money for female Republican candidates.

"Emily's List started 1991 with no members," said founder Ellen Malcolm, "and we hoped to renew our previous level of thirty-five hundred contributors. By July 1992 we had fifteen thousand members and were adding hundreds of new ones every day. The business and professional women who can commit three hundred dollars or more are contributing enthusiastically, because they know this is a way to exercise their economic power and really make a difference in the public world."

Executive women have not stopped at supporting Emily's List (whose candidates won twenty-five out of fifty-five congressional races in 1992). The Fund for the Feminist Majority (the Washington-based think tank), NOW, the Women's Campaign Fund, and the National Women's Political Caucus have all seen increased support from business and professional women. For example, there are more than 300 multiparty, grass-roots political caucus chapters across the country, many having achieved impressive results. The Texas Women's Political Caucus was founded in 1971 to pass the Equal Rights Amendment and support women candidates. Barbara Jordan had been elected to the state senate in 1966, but other women followed, as Sarah Weddington and Wilhelmina Delco ran for the Texas House of Representatives and Sissy Farenthold ran for governor. These campaigns produced a crop of women political activists statewide. Armed with the assistance of executives and professionals like International Women's Forum member Linda Wertheimer Hart of Dallas who raised campaign money from prominent businesswomen across the state, Texas women elected Ann Richards governor of Texas in 1991, defeating an opponent who personally contributed $8 million to his own campaign.

In Minnesota, activist women joined forces to mobilize for the 1994 U.S. Senate race and formed Minnesota $$ Million (M$$M), now one of 170 separate women's organizations affiliated in the Minnesota Women's Consortium. The goal of M$$M, according to Barbara Stuhler, cochair of the effort and also a Forum member, was to raise at least a million dollars in campaign pledges from women across the state, even before they identified a particular pro-choice woman as the Democratic candidate for the Senate seat. That way, the money would be there for her when she decides to run.

"We're making an effort to get the bulk of the money from people who will write a check for a thousand or get a hundred from ten friends," Stuhler explained. "It's easier to raise money from a few people but also important to raise money from a broad base."

The steering committee is targeting business and professional women with means and a reputation for being generous, and the strategy is working. Jean West, cochair of the development committee, announced that 22 percent of the goal was met even before the kickoff breakfast to launch Minnesota $$ Million was held. "I hope we'll soon be changing the name to Minnesota $$ *Millions,*" West said.

Whatever the ultimate name of the effort, it is a model that concerned businesswomen in other states may consider copying, particularly if a successful coalition of women's organizations is already in place.

Women such as these are demonstrating that women can "make rain" for the political campaigns of other women, but there is a difference. Men long ago figured out the connections between proximity to political power and the size of campaign contributions. Some generously funded all candidates, ensuring that they had access to the eventual winner. Many businessmen protected their self-interest by supporting the Republican party's laissez-faire approach to capitalism (raising $2.2 million for the party in just one 1992 lunch) while some Democratic candidates found a few major donors on Wall street, such as Bruce Wasserstein, Arthur Liman, and Warren Buffet. Some question whether wealthy industry executives care about public policy issues or just want the ability to reach an elected official with a personal phone call. Often directed by trade association lobbyists, they fund candidates heavily, even if they have little enthusiasm for the individuals.

Many women executives, however, are approaching the rainmaking side of the campaign trail with passion for issues and with little thought to a personal or business agenda. "Working as a stockbroker is my profession," said Sheryl Marshall, "but raising money for women candidates is the most important thing I do, next to raising my daughter. I'm trying to make sure that she will be an adult woman living in a world with more opportunities and fewer barriers."

Enthusiasm is catching. As executive women raise more money for women candidates, they are also encouraging more women to consider running for public office. As the barriers to political success start to fall, women are becoming more successful; in 1992 in Cook County, Illinois, for example, women judges won twenty of twenty-six races. Female candidates are discovering that they are benefiting from women who no longer hold them to impossible standards; they are receiving votes just because they are women. "When we get 51 women in the United States Senate and 218 in the House of Representatives, then we can start weeding out the worst ones," said one female real estate developer.

But in many communities, the rainmaking clout of powerful women was not just restricted to women candidates. According to Harvard Business School professor Rosabeth Moss Kanter, an organizer of Business Leaders for Clinton-Gore, the role of women in the 1992 elections represented a shift of political paradigm; in just one city, Women Leaders for Clinton-Gore, a group of business executives, lawyers, bankers, and other professionals, raised $1.2 million in two months for the Democratic party. Male candidates up for reelection are noticing that groups of powerful women can mobilize other check-writing women they have never met, and they are acting deferential.

PARTY PRESSURE

It is true that women were once less interested in running for public office. A 1990 survey by the George H. Gallup International Institute reported that only one third as many women as men had ever thought about running for political office, but of those women who had, more women than men had considered the state legislature or Congress. The prospects for the future look slightly better, as almost half as many women as men thought they might run in the future. More women than men reported being motivated to run for office by concern for the community, particularly issues affecting children and education.

Harriett Woods, two-time candidate for U.S. Senate from Missouri, says getting women interested in running for office and overcoming the institutional and cultural barriers that women candidates face is just part of the problem. Lack of time is another. Although most women work, many are still burdened with family responsibilities, making an all-consuming run for political office even more difficult.

But executive women are determined to help change the picture. "Women have always progressed faster when they have the support of other women, whether it is in the corporate world, in academia, or in family life," said Sheryl Marshall. "The time is absolutely right for women candidates now. They have the support of women as well as men; they will have more funding, and women are now more apt to cross party lines and vote for a woman candidate, no matter what her affiliation."

Women are also finding there are many men joining them as partners in their goal to elect more women to office. Former advertising executive George Dean has founded 50/50 by 2000, an advocacy organization to elect women to public office. He often speaks to groups of businesswomen, believing the challenge can be approached like any other business problem. Dean has little tolerance for those who say it will be decades before a large number of women move into elected positions.

"That sounds to me like the people who said in 1969 you can't sell hosiery to women in a supermarket at the time we and Hanes launched L'eggs hosiery," said Dean. "It sounds like the people who said you can't sell those little cars to Americans when Toyota, Datsun, and Honda were first introduced in this country. What all these products had in common were the quality of the product, the need, the timing, and, of course, the value. I would add that they were also marketed and advertised superbly.

"Do we have the 'product' in the form of good, qualified candidates, who happen to be women? The answer is *yes, yes, yes*, and more are being developed all the time in our towns, cities, and state legislatures. Are they usually lawyers like the majority of men in Congress? No, but some are. They come from a variety of backgrounds such as education, social work, local and state government, health care, and political party work as well as women's organizations and congressional staffs. The female candidates tend to be seven to nine years older than the male candidates, sometimes because of childbearing or caring and sometimes because of the perception that 'they have to prove themselves' longer than do men."

George Dean believes influential women executives can also help women candidates by advocating support for such election reforms as spending caps calibrated to the population of districts, free media time, and limits on "soft money" contributions. "And if we can't get meaningful reform for fair and open elections that are truly competitive, then term limitations are the best, perhaps only, solution," Dean said.

Some executive women who are committed to working inside existing institutions have decided to focus their energies and resources on their own political parties, believing this is where they can be most influential. Prominent businesswomen like Sheryl Marshall have taken the time to run for and win spots as delegates to their political party conventions and caucuses. "I can't run for public office myself, but I certainly can take the time to run as a party delegate and make sure the party supports women,"

Marshall said. "I'm taking a week's vacation from the office to make my voice heard at our national party convention." Businesswomen who are adopting this insider strategy have learned about the success of pressure on political parties in countries such as Norway, where not only the prime minister but half her cabinet, the leaders of the two political parties, the candidates for mayor of Oslo, and 59 of 165 members of Parliament are women. This picture is not by accident; political parties in Norway have a rule requiring that no fewer than 40 percent and no more than 60 percent of its nominees must be women. This is a model that many executive women believe has great merit.

"Gender balance" is therefore becoming the watchword across the United States, as women scrutinize and demand equality in political appointments. They have begun to hold the political parties themselves responsible for the support and funding of female candidates. As a start, George Dean suggests that each party promise to have at least one third of its cabinet made up of women and field at least one hundred female congressional candidates.

If political parties and their leaders do not respond to the urging of women to be included equally, momentum may gain for the establishment of a third political party as advocated by Eleanor Smeal, former president of NOW and head of the Fund for a Feminist Majority. Modeled after Alice Paul's 1920 National Women's Party or the present Green Party in Germany, the women's party would focus the agenda on issues given high priority by women, push traditional parties into supporting more female candidates of their own, and become a powerful voice that must be reckoned with by other groups. In a time marked by widespread dissatisfaction with existing political parties, the emergence of Ross Perot as a credible presidential candidate and the continued advocacy of his supporters, the idea of a third party founded by women has become less and less a radical notion.

In October 1991, not long after the Thomas-Hill hearings, an elegantly dressed Republican businesswoman from California stood up at a White House briefing given by Roger Porter, President Bush's domestic adviser.

"I've been a Republican woman all my life," she said, "and have raised hundreds of thousands of dollars for Republican candidates. Let me tell you, if the Republican party doesn't find a way to address the issues women are concerned about, you will find us deserting you. I am now a *woman* first and a Republican second, and you'd better start paying attention."

Porter responded with a platitude, but the point was made emphatically by a woman who may not have so vocally challenged her party's leaders in the past. After the briefing, several Democratic businesswomen in the audience told her that they shared exactly the same sentiments toward many leaders of their party as well. Economic clout had given these women political clout, and as they converge with women who have been active in advocating women's issues from outside the traditional system, the potential synergy is intriguing. Whether or not businesswomen join the ranks of those women advocating a third party, the combination of the energy and money of America's executive and professional women with the political savvy of America's female candidates and political activists may dramatically change the profile of the two political parties.

KITCHEN CABINET . . . AND CANDIDATE

"Women in politics face the same glass ceiling as executive women do," said Ellen Malcolm, president of Emily's List. Businesswomen who have overcome barriers in striving for the top positions believe they can help female candidates overcome them, too, and they are joining forces in communities across the country, acting as advisers and think tanks for their public sisters.

In many cases, they are flagging the same obstacles they have faced in the executive suite. Just as executive women are sometimes judged by a double standard, the "too" factor again rears its ugly head when applied to women in public life. (Women are judged by a double standard when going for the top spots—"she's too tough, too strident, too focused.") Female candidates also had to overcome the perception problem that they can't be strong, effective leaders, as George Dean explains:

"Over the years, we at the advertising agency would test male and female announcers making identical claims for gender neutral products and have men and women viewers rate the statements and claims made for believability and importance. Generally speaking, female respondents would rate the statements or claims equally, whether delivered by a male or female spokesperson. About two thirds to three quarters of the male respondents would also rate them equally, but 25 to 30 percent of the men would rate the same claim or statement significantly lower when made by a female announcer. They apparently couldn't accept a woman in an authoritative role (or leadership position, by inference). These weren't your traditional Archie Bunkers and their sexism could well have been subconscious or otherwise unintended."

A legislative candidate in Nevada recalled the problem Dean described. "I fell into the 'too' trap early in my campaign," she said. "But my female business supporters suggested I change my navy suit to a dress and speak slower and more softly. They cautioned me that to be effective, I had to develop a receptive audience first, and then impress them with the strength of my argument."

Because they have lived with the same scrutiny, executive women understand that women in public life have to work harder and be more perfect. Every flaw is magnified, even on child-care issues, as Zoë Baird discovered in her quest to be appointed attorney general. But worse, every accomplishment is rationalized or viewed as an exception, a process familiar to executive women ("She may have done well on one project, but she can't repeat it"). They advise their public sisters to look for occasions to remind the public of their accomplishments, and find compatriots to do so as well. It's not boasting; it's establishing credibility.

In many communities, the political world is still perceived as a male domain, despite the increasing numbers of women who *work* in the public arena. Thus, as in male-dominated professions everywhere, some women find it difficult to establish native credibility in the hallowed halls of legislative hearing rooms or chambers. They are seen as unusual, outsiders, alien, making it more difficult for women's opinions to count. (Women can speak with authority in the home-school association, but their credibility on complex issues such as taxes or defense spending still requires a leap of faith from many male audiences.)

Furthermore, women in public life have been stereotyped by issues, just as women in professional life have been ghettoized. Women are expected to advocate for child care, just as professional women have been routed into human resources in corporations, wills and estates in law, and pediatrics in medicine. But can she oversee foreign policy or the space program? Can she advocate industrial policy? (Can a female executive build a plant or market a pickup truck?) Slowly, women such as Congresswoman Patricia Schroeder and Deputy Budget Director Alice Rivlin have begun to change this perception, but they are still seen as the exception and not the rule. Executive women know that issue stereotyping hurts, because female elected officials will not achieve full membership in The Public Club unless they are seen as credible and effective on *any* issue or crisis that is thrown their way.

In many cases, this handicap can be lessened by coaching women to speak with confidence and a mastery of the facts. After listening to one congressional candidate debate her opponent about job growth in a district facing defense spending cutbacks, several executive women quickly caucused. "She needs our help," said a bank economist to the group. "He's painting her as a peacenik and she's losing credibility. We'll develop ten talking points and coach her all day on Sunday." The candidate's performance in the next debate was a dramatic turnaround.

Finally, executive women are moving from the kitchen cabinet to centerstage, and running for office themselves. Congressional offices are already populated by women who have been radio station owners, travel agency owners, management consultants, private school founders, farmers, and lawyers.

Jill Long was a college business professor and comanager of her family's farm in Indiana in 1989 when she defied conventional wisdom by winning a special election to fill the congressional seat vacated by Dan Quayle. Long, who holds a Ph.D. in business, began her political career only six years earlier, when she won a seat on the Valparaiso City Council. Now, as chair of the Congressional Rural Caucus, Long is championing the economic interests of farmers, but she has also assumed a leadership role in reformulating welfare services to ensure greater self-sufficiency and is an advocate for comprehensive health care services for women in the military. With her business background, she is scrutinizing the bottom line of federal programs; her Task Force on Government Waste made recommendations that could save $60 to $85 billion if implemented.

Talented businesswomen like Jill Long are out there, says Theresa Coleman Bolling, head of the Kentucky Women's Political Caucus. "Our goal is to identify all the women's organizations we can find in Kentucky and coordinate with them, to exchange information and identify women who might run for office. We will train them and help them," she said. "I am a member of the National Association of Female Executives, and I know there are distinguished women in the Business and Professional

Women's groups, the realtors, the insurance women and other organizations. Most women can't belong to a lot of groups; we know that not every woman who belongs to one of those business groups will also join the Caucus. But if she's thinking about running for office, we are here for her."

Bolling believes that many businesswomen make good candidates. "In some races, your stand on controversial social issues like reproductive freedom is not important. Sometimes we have to go beyond those basic issues and look to what is relevant to the position that is being sought. Women bring attention to fiscal concerns, administrative ability, and integrity to public office."

And with the help of their sisters in the private sector, these new candidates are impacting the public agenda, refocusing the debate to domestic priorities.

CHAPTER TEN

THE IMPRINT OF WOMEN

Work and Family

Companies should not dismiss solutions simply
because they aren't within their own resources.
—Fran Sussner Rodgers, Work/Family Directions, Inc.

Executive women are helping move other women into public office,
believing they can make a difference on public policy issues. At the same
time, many women are impacting and shaping policy issues in the private
sector, particularly those affecting the family.

The public and private sectors are closely related. Historically, women
have accepted the total obligation of raising children and maintaining a
home, but their labors are neither compensated nor counted in standard
measures of economic output or product. Yet women who are overburdened by the total family responsibilities must often forgo not only economic opportunities but political and civic activities as well. If they cannot participate equally in those arenas, they will never achieve full
membership in The Club.

Many women who have successfully negotiated the path to The Club
have done so by balancing the demands of work and family. But their personal accounts are not the entire picture. The work/family dynamic is
really two stories, one personal and one institutional. Even executive
women who are single and childless want to bring their professional power
to bear on increasing private sector responsibility for American families.
Just because a well-paid working woman usually can solve her own family
issues does not mean that working families in general are well served by
the current structures and benefits of the workplace. The real imprint of

women in The Club will be felt when companies and families can both prosper, rather than suffer, in a community in which parents work.

A PERSONAL MATTER

Striking differences between men and women at the top of the corporate or professional ladder should not be minimized. The higher a woman's education, the more likely she is to be employed and the less likely she is to have children. Two thirds of women under the age of forty who have reached the upper echelons in companies and institutions are childless. This fact alone suggests that they are quite different than their male peers, virtually all of whom are fathers, many whose wives do not work outside the home.

Some of these childless, highly accomplished women are childless by choice, having made their careers their priority. Others concentrated on their careers because they could not have children. They took the same route to the top ranks in their professions as men, earning their credentials and devoting a lot of time to work.

Many other executive women, often older than these childless women or their male professional counterparts, no longer have family responsibilities. They have concentrated on their careers only after their children were well situated in school and did not need as much attention. Some worked part-time while their children were young, or did not work at all, beginning demanding corporate careers at a later age. Like CBS journalist Meredith Vieira who gave up a time-consuming job at "60 Minutes" to care for her young child, they simply left a corporate structure that couldn't accommodate them. They accepted this hiatus as a fact of life. Today, some younger women who have also had the choice to stay home have followed the example of women who took time out to raise a family.

"After my second child was born, I just decided I could not take the stress of my former job," said one former Fidelity Mutual Fund executive. "But that's all right. I'll be back to it in a few years, and I'll be working for a long time after that."

Not all executive women with families have reduced their previous work commitment, however. An increasing number of women has managed to handle both a demanding career and an active home life. They claim that the key to equanimity comes not from organization, but from attitude.

Phyllis Swersky, former executive vice president of A.I. Corp. and now president of Work/Family Directions, a $35 million private consulting firm, is the mother of three young children. Phyllis has always worked at a demanding job, often traveling to Europe and handling complicated financial negotiations and initial public offerings for her former software employers.

"I have three priorities," Phyllis said. "My family, my career, and me. Everything else falls far behind. For a while, I thought the only way to put my family first was to dramatically reduce the hours I worked, something I was unwilling to do."

But Phyllis, like many of her peers, found that the amount of time spent with the family was not the right answer. "What I changed was my attitude," Phyllis said. "When I was home, I gave my family my undivided attention. I didn't bring work home. If I needed to do work, I stayed late at the office and explained to them why I had to do that. Family time was their time only. I also increased my communication with them. For example, my children understood what an initial public offering was and were just as excited as I was. They brought the prospectus to school to show their classmates. They appreciate the fact that I set limits for any other intrusions on my time with them, including my friends and civic activities. When I'm with them, they are the center of my attention."

Phyllis was also blessed with a husband who put his family first, and who was an equal partner in parenting. More important, he was proud of Phyllis and her accomplishments.

Conversations with executive women across the country revealed a familiar theme. Women with children who also held significant executive positions were generally uncritical of their spouses, children, and family caregivers. They accepted diversity in family roles and did not try to think or manage every detail. They willingly gave up control in many family areas and were able to relax and enjoy family times without second-guessing the support system around them.

"My husband decided to stay at home once I received my promotion as vice president of engineering," said a television station executive. "He was a cameraman and took some grief from his union buddies, but we didn't care. After we had our second child, it really made more sense because I earned more money and was more interested in my career with the TV station. And he's a terrific father and a great home organizer. Our life has never run as smoothly!"

Obviously, not all women have husbands who are talented around the home. Those executive women report that having other caregivers at home was just as important as their office staff, and made their life as an executive run smoothly.

"I was determined that our house would run as well with me at work as it would if I were home all the time," said a bank executive vice president. "My husband never has to do more than he would have done if I hadn't worked and I arranged everything around that principle. It involved a lot of housekeepers, baby-sitters, and full-time help, but it was worth it to both of us and the kids. We are really like two fathers and one mother in the house."

One reason these women have been so successful in making their way into The Club is that they have refused to accept second-class status in their personal lives.

Scholar Susan Moller Okin has pointed out that the roots of social injustice start in the home. If a woman is working a second career at home, accepting unequal status by trying to assume responsibility for children and family matters as well as her job, she will most likely become second class at work. She cannot do both well.

We have seen the scenario too often. Two professionals marry, each holding an important job. Their income is approximately equal. After children arrive, the wife takes time out to care for them, and the husband's career and income surpass hers. It becomes economically sensible for him to progress while she accommodates his career. By age thirty or so, she is in an unequal position, economically and sometimes personally. Unless he is one of those few men who decide to go off track themselves, or to change directions when his spouse is ready to resume a career, the inequality continues.

"Men rationalize that they don't treat women differently, but they do," said a female Philadelphia technology company president who is an astute observer of corporate executives. "Men in high positions have a support system that is largely female—their wife, their secretary, their executive assistant. All these women take orders from the man. I'm not making a value judgment here, it's just an observation. People bring him paper, decisions, phone calls all day long. 'Do you want to say yes or no to this request?' 'What should I do about this and how should I answer that?' It's an easy behavior to fall into, delegating, giving orders, making decisions. I found myself doing it, giving orders to my husband like he was my subordinate. I had to catch myself as soon as I was aware that I fell into the same behavior trap."

Most women in The Club did not let the inequality scenario happen. They have rejected the traditional home role for themselves, that of primary family caretaker. They are willing to let someone else remember the dentist appointments and soccer matches and provide clean clothes. Perhaps instinctively they knew that if they did not demand equal status as "a father" they would slip behind. After all, fathers have held important professional and corporate positions and functioned at home as an important participant in family life for decades. Few of them worried about the content of next week's grocery list. Instead, fathers were present to interact, listen, and play with children.

Spouses interacting with family members as equal partners, not performing the chores of family life, binds the family unit. Cathy Minehan, chief operating officer of the Federal Reserve Bank of Boston, explained how she and her husband work to make family life a priority: "Our children are nine and eleven. We just never do anything without them, even on Saturday night. We all go out to dinner together. My husband coaches sports, and I participate in our home-school association, where I take a turn being responsible for a theme week at school. Our activity as a couple is to socialize with the parents of our children's friends, and we all participate in their activities.

"It's a lot of work to make a relationship work and make the family unit work, but it is worth it. We both do whatever it takes to make all of us happy. I've also found that by being as active as I am in the kids' activities, I've made friends with other women who are often willing to trade favors like carpooling on weekdays for transportation or playdates on weekends. I'm not denying there are hard times, but when these have occurred, that network of friends has been invaluable. Fortunately, those days are few and far between," Minehan said.

One of the highest-ranking women in the Federal Reserve system, Minehan was initially tentative about returning to work after the birth of her first child: "The worst day of my life was deciding to go back after my daughter was born. I had been out five months and I had experienced a level of freedom I never had. I thought I had died and gone to heaven. But the bank needed me, so I went 'just to help them out.' I was going to see how it worked, but I knew if I quit I could never go back to my former role. I figured if I went back, I could always quit," she recalled.

"I'm so glad I went back. And after my second child, I was very happy to go back to work!" said Minehan, now a twenty-five-year bank veteran.

Despite the fact that the women in The Club have figured out their own personal family arrangements, the status quo is shifting rapidly. The women at the top are not behaving just like many of the men who preceded them, assuming that because their own family matters were separate from their work life, this model works for everyone. Executive women are worried about other working women who do not have the luxury of choices.

"The key to all of our arrangements," said Kaye Ferriter, a partner at Coopers & Lybrand, the national accounting firm, "is to have full-time live-in help who becomes part of a team with me and my husband. This requires having a home which can comfortably accommodate another adult. It is critical to me that I am confident that my children are well cared for while I am working. Having someone at home who can also help run the house frees me up to spend more time with my children. But women at lower levels and incomes do not have that kind of housing. Managing family and work is much more stressful for them. That's the real issue. What will we do for the rest of the working women who can't afford what we can, but who must work?"

Ferriter had identified the critical issue for many women: economic slippage. Women in their twenties earn about the same as their male counterparts. Yet at age thirty-five, with two children, working full time, the average woman earns less than half the male wage. This isn't true in other countries, where maternity leave, preschool and other programs for children allow women greater economic equality with their male peers. Many executive women believe if the economic status of American women and their families is ever to improve, the remedy will begin with a support system of comprehensive family benefits.

FAMILY: NOT JUST A PRIVATE CONCERN

There are three reasons why women in The Club are focusing on the private sector's ability to resolve many work/family issues. First, women professionals who are coming along behind them are not going to tolerate the same rigidity that their predecessors endured in many corporate structures.

While some of today's executive women made it to the senior ranks by emulating William H. Whyte's profile of the "organization man" whose loyalty was to the company, they are a dying breed. Most of the baby-boom women who will dominate the corporate suites by the year 2010 resemble professional ballplayers who will play for any team that pays them and who know that they might be out of the game tomorrow. They are not necessarily disloyal to their employers. Rather, they are realistic about the chances that their employers will not be there in the long term. These "new individualists" are just as inclined to put themselves and their family needs first and find a job that fits, rather than fit their life-style to the demands of one particular job.

But these women (and many men as well) are exactly the executive and professionals that corporate America needs. Senior executive women believe that family-friendly benefits will be the distinguishing feature in the companies that can attract and retain these workers. Even those women who do not yet have children or dependent parents will be more likely to favor a company that shows a real commitment to an employee's needs and a flexibility to meet those needs. A corporate culture that puts a family or the individual first sends a powerful message to all its employees. A corporate culture whose criterion for senior management is a clear willingness to sacrifice family life for the sake of the company sends a negative message to many women, even those who have worked the extra weekends and nights.

"I've been the good girl for years," said an executive vice president of a financial services firm. At age forty-six she is unmarried and has few interests outside of a very demanding worklife. "I never minded the extra hours, the demanding projects, the crises I handled well. I kept being promoted and the work became more and more interesting. But now I'm looking around at my peers, men in this company and others who are hitting age fifty, going to their children's graduations, enjoying the golf course, assuming the public spotlight in civic associations. I've done none of that. Part of it is my own fault. I could have learned to play golf. I could have developed outside interests. I could have bought a weekend home. But I never insisted on taking the time. If I had a family, I might have. Without one, it was easier just to keep on working. There was always more and more work to do."

As senior ranking woman in her company, she had finally figured out the connection between a corporate culture that encourages employees to take time for their own interests and a corporate culture that is ever demanding, right from the top down. "No more," she said. "I'm putting my life first from now on. No work is that important, week after week, month after month, year after year. I'm taking some time for me now."

Today she would probably admit that she was part of the problem. She behaved like the men at the top of the company and had only a minimal understanding of the pressure her personal work style created in others. But she is the exception. Most women who have reached senior levels of businesses and the professions have great empathy for all working women and the conflicts they face. They will now be in the forefront of changing conditions for the women and families that come along behind them.

The second reason that work/family issues are critical is that the vast number of working women at all levels in the American economy desperately need relief. The United States ranks number three in dependence on women in the work force, behind only Scandinavia and Canada. If productivity is to increase, these workers must be accommodated.

"Wouldn't it be wonderful if on one day all across the country, every woman who works called in to the office and said her baby-sitter was sick or her elderly parent broke a hip?" asked one mischievous female accountant. "Every single woman, from stockbrokers and comptrollers to secretaries, bus drivers, waitresses, and schoolteachers would go on strike. Then The Club would figure out the economic impact of working women pretty quickly."

Even without experiencing a national strike of working women, companies and institutions can't afford to lose female workers. More important, American families can't afford to lose the income of working women, particularly since one fourth of all American children live primarily in female single parent homes. But most public and private employers are not family-friendly. More than 99 percent of American private employers do not offer child care, and the federal government still has no child-care or universal health-care policies.

Third, in addition to being concerned about "other working women," executive women are concerned about "other people's children" as a resource for the future. They know the long-term economic future of American citizens—particularly the needy and the elderly—demands attention to today's children and their families. They understand that in many cases the impetus to have children is not just because offspring give their parents great pleasure at ages two, eleven, or fifteen. Many parents would truthfully say that they just hope their children will be there for them when they grow older, bringing friendship and economic security.

This concept of children as future caregivers for all citizens is not universally understood by corporate executives. But many executive women who do not have children of their own are well aware that other people's children will be the resource for supporting tomorrow's elderly citizens—themselves included. These children are America's human infrastructure for the future, a real form of economic capital just as (or even more) important than steel or dollars. These children will be the workers and taxpayers that will pay the social benefits for all the baby boomers who will reach age sixty-five and older by the year 2020. Most likely these workers will be the minority children of today who suffer the highest rates of poverty and illiteracy and are more apt to come from single-parent homes. Although some male corporate executives are now talking about corporate responsibility for children and families as a national economic issue on a par with reduced capital gains taxes or investment in research and development, many more executive women do.

Extending corporate support and concern for children is not an exercise in family values but is a calculated understanding of the economic impact of their future earnings. Many executive women believe the answer to how to provide for future senior citizens is to make sure that companies that hire parents also provide for their children. This is not a radical concept. Well over a hundred countries compensate parents with money or time off when they have a baby. They also give them child-care and preschool services, rewarding parents for having and caring for children rather than punishing them. Although in many countries these benefits are the result of government social policy, executive women know that if they wait for official government-sanctioned social policy and increased benefits, America will have lost another generation of children. Transferring resources to families with children can be done more quickly by the private sector, and it is in companies' best interests to do so.

That's a tall order, but many women who are making their way into The Club (along with a small but growing number of male CEOs) see work/family issues as a priority and are attacking them one by one.

"If women were CEOs of 90 percent of our major companies and institutions and president of every major business trade association, here's what I'd predict," said the executive vice president of a national high-technology firm. "We'd provide child care and Head Start for every eligible child and after-school care in every community. We'd eliminate the notion of a Mommy Track. We'd have elder care services, enforced child support, and flextime. We'd have a universal system of basic and preventive health care coverage for all citizens, and American business would provide the moral leadership for such national family concerns as nutrition programs, housing, education, literacy, and employment training."

Her crystal ball may be predicting a vision of the twenty-first century, but some executive women are already moving in that direction. As more women move into senior management positions, they are helping companies understand the needs of a changing work force, demonstrating that family-friendly benefits improve bottom-line results. As executive women move into positions of leadership in industry trade associations and civic organizations, they are using their professional prestige to focus attention on workplace issues and to share models of effective solutions.

These women are developing their political skills to mobilize coalitions of women's organizations and form partnerships with mainstream associations. Through those, they are supporting public policy initiatives relating to family assistance programs. In some cases, individual women are even abandoning their original careers to work full time advocating policy changes that will improve the economic status of women and families.

Improving the plight of America's children is the first priority for many women.

CHILD CARE

Hard work and effective parenting are not necessarily incompatible, executive women state emphatically.

"We have to get rid of this notion that pops up everywhere from family court to the executive suite that a serious professional cannot be a serious parent, that the only good parent is one who stays home," said a female internist. "It is not only wrong, it is harmful to the growth of our economy. We need to figure out what services and support children need to thrive and develop and then provide them."

Good-quality, dependable, and affordable child care is the first line of defense against family stress and parental burnout and, in many cases, child abuse. While a few corporate and government policymakers may still believe that providing child care is still a personal issue, one which each family should work out for itself, many executive women know differently.

Child care is a private sector productivity issue affecting millions of workers. By 1995, 90 percent of all working women will have children under age seventeen and two thirds of all preschool children will have mothers in the work force. For them, child care is an economic necessity; fully two thirds of all women in the work force are either sole providers or are married to men who earn less than $15,000 a year. Staying at home with children is not an option for these women. Their family values are economic values: the value of putting food on the table and paying for shelter.

Unfortunately, child care is expensive. After food, housing, and taxes, child care represents the single largest expense for working parents of all incomes: 23 percent of the family income of low-income parents, according to one report, the amount that many financial planners suggest should be allocated to housing expense. Yet even for women who have the financial resources that would allow them to stay home, child-care expenses are viewed as an insurance policy to ensure that their careers are there when their children are older.

Even for families with older children, after-school care is a major cause of worry. America's working parents are monitoring anywhere from 2 million to 10 million "latch key" children.

"At three o'clock I can see my secretary tense up," one company president reported. "I know she is waiting for the call from her daughter, to see if she came home all right after school. If the call doesn't come, even I get worried."

Many large companies now offer a range of child-care services, including on-site programs, which help until children are of school age. It is harder for small businesses to do much more than offer resource and referral services (a "help" line for parents to identify child-care providers that meet their geographical and financial needs) or flexible benefit plans (allowing pre-tax contributions to meet child-care expenses). Unfortunately, neither of these benefits addresses the issues of child-care availability, quality, and cost. In the end, a comprehensive community-based system of affordable child-care services, after-school programs, and flexibility in corporate cultures is the only answer for frustrated parents who lurch from one baby-sitter crisis to another.

Improving the demeanor of parents is not the only goal. A comprehensive system of family services will increase the productivity of America's workers by reducing absenteeism and stress and improving morale. U.S. employers lose $3 billion every year because of employee child-care problems alone and yet many employers have found that investments in child care produce a high rate of return, actually saving the companies money in the long run.

As women move up the corporate ladder, they are inevitably influencing the corporate benefits related to child care, and also helping the corporate culture become more understanding of family issues. They know that when men as well as women are bold enough to demonstrate a commitment to family, the notion of a Mommy Track as a secondary career track for women whose primary interests center around family will finally leave our lexicon. The popular press coined the phrase *Mommy Track* and it stuck, enraging many executive women who saw accurately that the distinction in career paths made children exclusively a woman's issue rather than a family or corporate issue.

Felice Schwartz, who advocated a two-tiered career-track system for women, suggested that some women cost companies more because of maternity benefits and leaves, but that the long-term benefit of keeping them in the career pipeline was worth the expense. She may have been right about the latter notion but not about the former; in fact, pregnancy is predictable and does not result in more lost time for a corporation. Overall, the number of work days lost per year for men and women are about the same. Only because there are still relatively few women in executive suites are their absences more noticeable. Being few in number, it is harder for women to make waves and suggest the culture accommodate their family needs.

But the picture is changing, with women who have made real contributions to their employers no longer willing to be relegated to second-class citizenship. They are now insisting that corporations, institutions, and governments change their views and attitudes toward working parents. They want to modify the American fixation on short-term profits and results that relentlessly pushes the work ethic above all other priorities.

Many men agree with them, arguing that the perpetuation of the Mommy Track treats men as if they have no less right to a family life.

Women are also attacking the Mommy Track throughout the business community as well as in their own companies. As they achieve membership in The Club, their professional stature helps raise the issue of responsibility for parenting as they single out firms or institutions that are leaders and suggest new approaches for those who are not yet converts. They are also finding willing partners in other Club members, often men whose daughters are beginning careers in the business or professional world.

Women who chair professional organizations have found their visibility gives them a particularly effective platform to speak out about work/family concerns. Attorney Margaret H. Marshall, 1991 president of the Boston Bar Association, helped ensure the organized bar focused its attention on children and families by issuing a comprehensive report, "Parenting and the Legal Profession, a Model for the Nineties." Some lawyers might argue that parenting issues are personal and should not be a concern of a bar association, but Marshall saw it differently. Parenting issues relate to the increasing dissatisfaction felt by many young lawyers with their chosen career and directly relate to the status of women in the profession, particularly in private firms. While many law firms believe they are family-friendly and point to maternity and paternity leaves, day-care options, part-time work, and flextime arrangements, lawyers who try to cut down on work in order to spend more time as parents are inevitably penalized in a culture that measures job commitment and success by the number of hours spent and billed.

"Law firms are infant friendly," said Marshall. "Everybody can deal with the first year. What law firms have not thought about is family responsibility over the long term. It's as if children drop off the face of the earth when they turn four years old."

Parents of teenagers can relate to Marshall's insights. The front-page publicity surrounding the release of the bar association report gave New England lawyers a powerful vehicle to leverage change in their law firms and forced the management of firms to confront their own working environment and culture more honestly.

Executive women who have been in the forefront of the fight for child care and related benefits suggest there are many incentives that have proven effective in making change. They have shown how alliances among women's professional networks, mainstream business groups, human service advocates, and sympathetic legislators are producing mechanisms for firms to provide additional child-care support.

For example, Massachusetts is one of the few states that require any company or employer with fifty employees or more to sponsor child-care assistance programs as a condition to receiving contracts for goods or services from the state or any of its public authorities. In a political climate in which an increasing number of public services are being privatized, this bidding requirement is astonishing in its scope and creative use of the incentive of public dollars to reward private initiatives. What is even more astonishing, however, is that the legislation was conceived and advocated by an old-line traditional business trade association, the Building Owners and Managers Association (BOMA) of the Greater Boston Real Estate Board.

Marjorie Saltiel, a child-care advocate who worked for BOMA for several years to secure passage of the legislation, explained the "strange bedfellows" that led to its passage: "This legislation arose from the Private/Public Initiative for Child Care that BOMA undertook in the years when the concept of 'linkage' was popular, a requirement that commercial developers offer child-care sites in new projects or contribute to a child-care fund as a condition to receiving permits to build. Real estate professionals decided to ask a wide range of experts to help them study the whole concept of community child care and to try to remove zoning and other regulatory barriers to the development of more child-care facilities. The result was a twelve-point child-care legislative package covering everything from changed property tax rates for child-care space to zoning amendments to make it easier to site child-care centers. The state contract requirement was just one aspect," Saltiel said.

"The child-care package initially raised a lot of eyebrows at the State House, as legislators and human service advocates were not accustomed to seeing the real estate community come in and support something as positive as child care. Usually our lobbyists were roaming the halls only to oppose legislation that affected our industry. Now *we* were initiating legislation, and groups such as the nonprofit child-care industry (which preferred linkage) and municipalities were opposed to our package.

"Other business trade associations, including those representing small business, supported it; some opposed all of it except one or two pieces. In the end, the state contract provision survived, in part because we just let it take its course. We didn't call a lot of attention to it or try to claim a lot of credit for it until it was safely signed by the governor. I don't think even the real estate community realized how broad it would be until the regulations were enacted. BOMA received several awards from BOMA International for its work on child care. Now this law is a model for other states."

FAMILY LEAVE: NOT FOR CHILDREN ONLY

The care of young children is a social and business issue that even most corporate executives understand, even if they disagree about the solutions. But demographics suggest that the care of elderly parents may be an even more serious issue, one that does not lend itself to easy solutions. Studies at such major employers as Travelers Insurance, IBM, and the federal government show that from 20 to 50 percent of employees have some responsibility for the care of an adult dependent. Just as the seventeen-year average time period of child responsibility is ending, women may face an average of eighteen years caring for an elderly parent: the "daughter track." As with inadequate child-care assistance, productivity suffers and stress rises when employees try to balance the demands of the workplace and the obligations of family care.

"My parents are both elderly," said a New York banker. "They live in southern California and my brother lives in Maine and he's of little help. I'm flying on company business at least two weeks a month. If one or both of my parents fails I'm going to have to take time off and deal with it. I just don't see any choice."

In many ways, the issue of elder care is more difficult than child care. Elderly parents are often situated far from the child's home and workplace. In many environments it is less acceptable to raise parental care as an issue at work and few companies have policies or programs available to help employees deal with it (just 200 of 6 million employers, by one estimate). Some employers may have conceded that offering child-care assistance is an appropriate benefit for employees, but other than dependent care allowance programs, few have addressed the fundamental recognition of elder-care problems, despite the vast numbers of working women who are caring for parents.

Family responsibilities for children, infirm parents, siblings, or spouses have a major impact on an executive's professional life. Yet few companies have "time off" policies that make it easier. Executives with senior status rarely agonize over taking leave, of course. They just do it and check in with their subordinates and executive assistants from time to time. They know that their position confers the privilege of managing their own time, and even a member of the company's board of directors would hardly criticize a senior-level executive about taking time off to handle a family emergency. But at lower levels, employees cannot simply take an indefinite amount of time off without adverse consequences.

It is at this level that tension arises between conflicting philosophies. Should all employees be held to the same standard of attention and attendance and pay the consequences if they do not perform as expected, or should employers provide flexibility and understanding about life's unexpected family crises, just as they provide paid leave when an employee becomes ill or disabled? At some companies, the question is now moot. In February 1993, federal family and medical leave legislation was signed into law by President Clinton, guaranteeing workers at many firms up to twelve weeks of unpaid leave for medical emergencies.

The problem remains that few women can afford unpaid leaves. Fewer than 40 percent of working women have benefits, insurance, or other income protection that would allow them to take unpaid leave without severe financial hardship. Some states are considering a state temporary disability insurance plan, financed by employee and employer contributions, but those plans are difficult to initiate in depressed economic times.

Yet companies do not have to just follow the law regarding unpaid leave to keep valuable employees. Some employers have adopted innovative approaches to retain employees for the future.

In England, career break or reentry programs for women with young children provide career continuity. Women stay in touch with the company by working a few weeks a year, receiving monthly information packets, and attending employer-paid retraining programs. Some women work one day a week for as long as five years; others work two weeks the first year, ten weeks the second year, four months the third year, and six months the fourth year before returning full time in the fifth year. Many women feel there is little reason why American companies can't try this approach for both men and women.

TIME: HOW MUCH IS ENOUGH?

The necessity for some type of leave is unquestioned when family emergencies arise. But many executive women seldom require a lengthy periodic absence from work. The bigger issue is simply "time."

"A family or personal leave, while important, doesn't address the fundamental problem of most workplaces," said a real estate manager from Oregon. "Day in and day out, I need flexibility in personal time management. I don't want or need better caretakers or household help. I want better time with my children and spouse at the moments they need me. I do not have two lives, one at work and one at home. My family, civic, and professional lives are integrated into the person that I am. I do not punch a time clock. I work at home and I handle home problems at work. I don't subscribe to the notion that because I show a commitment to my family I am less committed to my employer."

She expressed a point of view shared by many executive women, as the issue of time is not one that just impacts younger women with growing families. Many senior-level women reflected on the continuing pulls of family conflicts, even with children long out of the house.

"I think the frustrations are more difficult now than earlier in my career," said a fifty-six-year-old cosmetics executive in New York, "because I have the sense I am running out of time. During the earlier stages of my professional life I juggled the children's issues, never letting them interfere with my job. But it really hit me when my only daughter was getting married and I very much wanted to take six weeks off to do all the mother-of-the-bride things, like looking for a reception hall, shopping for dresses, and planning the food. I felt that this was very much a once-in-a-lifetime event and yet I couldn't do it the way I wanted to because the company was launching a new product and making some complicated internal changes that needed my full attention.

"As it was, the wedding was fine, but I hired someone to take care of all the details that I would have enjoyed doing and I still feel bad about it," she said. "I can see that the same kind of issues are still going to come up. I have no elderly parents, but my husband just retired, and time with him is precious. Now that I'm at the peak of my career and have by all measures really 'made it,' I wonder why I am putting in all this time. I have a feeling that when grandchildren come along, that will be the issue that will force me to really confront my time priorities. I know already I will feel the pull to be with them more than I did with my own children when they were small. The bottom line is that at all stages of a woman's life, relationships are important, probably more than for most men. The fact that our children are grown and older does not change that. I see men from my industry who have retired and are having a hard time because their job and career was the all-important thing for them. I won't have a hard time in retirement at all!"

She was describing an inherent conflict between how employers value professional commitment to work and what employees value. Many workplaces have not yet accommodated the changing nature of work and the priorities of employees, even though improved technology has made telecommuting and flextime real options, especially for those in entrepreneurial, senior-level professional, or managerial positions. Some workplaces that would like to be flexible have been penalized by Labor Department policies.

Unfortunately, there are also employers who still do not believe that employees are working hard unless they can see them. But studies have shown that flexible family benefits build trust and loyalty from employees and create a positive impact on employee morale, tardiness, and absenteeism rates.

Flextime is not just an issue for women. Although few men take advantage of family leave benefits, more men are interested in flexible work options on an ongoing basis, especially as more men share responsibility for home and child care. In one study, more than half the men polled said they'd be willing to cut their salaries as much as 25 percent to have more family time and about 45 percent said they'd turn down a promotion if it meant spending less time with their families. But they are fighting a culture that still looks askance at men who choose family as an equal priority with work, despite the growing numbers of single fathers in the work force. Women may have to lead the way in changing the culture so that balancing work and family is acceptable. They will take the risks with their careers, and when employers find that they need these female executives and do not penalize them, men will notice and begin to follow suit.

Women are not advocating a reexamination of "time spent" because they would rather be at home or on the golf course. They recognize that the flight to part-time or flextime work could provide greater opportunity for improved labor productivity as well as greater community, social, and economic health. The downsizing of many businesses has not come about just because of economic softness, but an unspoken reluctant recognition that diminishing productivity has been an issue of concern to American business for decades. Fast growth and ample supply of capital and credit in the 1980s hid growing inefficiencies in the workplace. Added to that, many organizations believed that "full-time" work represented high status and "part-time" represented lower status with less-committed workers. In many environments, the most committed employees were those who worked *more* than full time—that is, worked extra hours, late into the night, and on weekends ("face time" as it is derisively known in some cultures). This perception of time as an indicator of performance is a fallacy, according to Lotte Bailyn, a professor of economics at MIT. She advocates that salaries should be based on skill and level of commitment, not on longevity or status.

But how do employers judge commitment? The distinction about the quality of commitment as it relates to full- or part-time work has masked an understanding of real performance and what qualifies an employee for advancement. The problem of time/commitment/performance is becoming worse as Americans spend more hours at work than at any time since World War II. Much of the reason for the increased work time is economic—families need more income (generally from both partners) just to keep up the standard of living that supported a family twenty to thirty years ago. But the work-until-you-drop spiral must stop if families are to remain intact and prosper.

Women initially accepted the old-line hierarchical bureaucracy of the corporate and professional workplace and the values that went with it, grateful to be included and grateful for part-time opportunities when they needed them. Now that they are at senior executive levels, helping to refocus the culture of the workplace, they are insisting on new values. They are inventing new outlets for employees' talents and abilities, helped by enabling technology and the economic necessities of many companies to downsize. Many executive women are at the intersection of two roads: They will change the old corporate model or they will abandon it and start a new one.

Kathy Hanson, manager of compensation and human resource systems for Staples, the growing office-supply company, notes that even in the most progressive companies, advocacy is needed at times.

"Staples is a young company in a new segment of retailing, with an employee base whose average age is under thirty," she said. "We determined we had to look for proactive ways to support families. For example, although we have standard health benefits, we didn't know enough about our range of needs to put new support policies in place, so first we conducted an employee survey.

"When the family leave bill was passed, we accepted its terms quickly because we had already been making these unpaid leave decisions on an individual basis. But when a woman in a senior staff position reporting to the CEO had a second child and was looking for part-time work, it was initially perceived as unreasonable. Senior management thought the company needed her all the time," Hanson said.

Kathy, a single parent, helped her senior management look at the reality of the life of their valued employee, whose husband also held a time-consuming executive position. The objective way she presented the facts and the solution won the day and part-time status was accepted. "My boss is young, with a four-year-old and elderly parents," she said. "He now clearly understands that these flexible policies make sense, for both the company and the employee."

FAMILY VALUES

In either case, whether women help to change the culture of existing business institutions or start their own companies, a value revolution is taking place. Family and community interests are starting to replace only material success as the status symbol of the 1990s, as fathers and mothers help rebuild the community playground instead of spending another weekend by the shore. This is occurring in part because families are searching for new ways to cope with an economic reality that does not allow for material excesses. The pattern may have begun in the 1960s when many of today's senior executives and managers participated in a popular revolution that rejected the stereotypical work ethic and material acquisitions culture of their parents. While this movement was halted temporarily in the 1970s and 1980s, even those who have full-time jobs are now questioning how they are spending their time and are seeking a return to a family-oriented way of life. Living to work may be replaced by working to live.

Women know the value of variable life careers with overlapping and interdependent talents and skills rather than a single career with résumé credentials and promotions accumulated like notches on a belt. Men have been slower to take their place in the family unit because the social culture devalued diaper changing, carriage pushing, and homework monitoring as women's concerns. Now, family activities are becoming highly valued again as the status accorded European luxury cars, designer clothing, and ostentatious second homes lessens. A new militancy is surfacing in the work force as more workers, usually highly valued ones, demand a balance in their families and their work. They are insisting that results substitute for time spent and they allow themselves the time to spend on community, school, and family activities. They are setting the stage for a new business environment.

A PRESCRIPTION FOR THE FUTURE

Activist members of women's professional organizations have identified the balance of work and family as a priority for working women and have adopted a two-pronged approach to affect change. On the public side, they have supported legislation that would establish national and local policies to assist families and they have supported candidates who favor such measures. But they have also worked hard to influence the private sector, applauding those large employers who have led the way to provide a family-friendly benefit structure. AT&T's offerings could serve as a checklist for a model program:

- nationwide child-care resource and referral service for children under age thirteen, covering 300,000 employees in all fifty states and over 6,000 work sites
- nationwide elder-care consultation and referral service for relatives sixty years of age and older
- dependent care reimbursement account that allows employees to set aside up to $5,000 a year, tax free, for qualified child care or elder care
- care of newborn or adopted child leave of up to one year, with guaranteed job reinstatement and six months of medical, vision, and dental coverage at company expense
- family-care leave for up to twelve months over a twenty-four-month period, with company-paid coverage for death benefits and life insur-

ance, plus medical, vision, and dental coverage for six months at company expense
- flexible time off to handle emergencies without supervisory approval
- an adoption assistance program of $2,000 for expenses associated with the adoption of a minor child
- $10 million AT&T family-care development fund, separate from the AT&T Foundation

Why did AT&T initiate such a comprehensive benefit program for its employees? "These are not just personal problems; they are part of a chain of events that ultimately become customer problems. There is a life both before and after office hours," said Charles Brumfield, director of labor relations.

John Hancock has received national awards for its far-reaching benefits program, which includes an on-site child-care facility for up to 200 children. Designed around the concept of "small home bases" of open spaces surrounded by classrooms, the center opened in November 1990 and is unique for its attention to such details as the texture of materials used in toys, changing colors, lights and music for infants, and a focus on books and reading time for children.

"We are helping parents to be more effective on their jobs by lessening the worry that goes along with raising a family and balancing a career," said Joan Burke, the company's executive resource officer. "It's a tremendous benefit for parents to have a world-class day-care center on-site, and to have the opportunity to drop in on their lunch hour and spend some time with their child during the workday. They feel better about both their roles as employee and parent."

John Hancock executives have thought carefully about services that busy parents need, and in addition to flextime, family-care days, emergency time, an elder-care access program, and flexible spending accounts, the company provides:

- a kids-to-go program for school-age children who need activities on school holidays
- a summer care fair
- family care consultants
- employee-assistance programs

- psychological service programs
- a fitness center
- corporate health services
- a dental clinic
- commuter services
- on-site stores
- "Choices" takeout dinner service five days a week

"At Hancock, we believe that everyone comes to work to do a good job and the company needs to be flexible enough to help make that happen," said Diane Capstaff, who has helped to put in place many of Hancock's policies. "We need to respect our employees' personal lives and support them as best we can with child care, elder care, tuition awards, wellness programs, and others."

It is easier for large companies to address the dependent-care needs of their employees, but coalitions of companies and organizations are also pooling resources to deliver services. The Collaboration for Quality Dependent Care, a $25.4 million initiative of 137 businesses, finances 300 local programs in 44 cities. But despite such corporate examples which demonstrate that employers can effectively address the needs of working parents, most employers and business associations have not followed their example. Many women feel they have barely made a dent in bringing about private-sector programs of comprehensive family assistance or changing the traditional business community resistance to uniform policies.

One reason, suggests Dr. Mary Jane England, a physician and president of the Washington Business Group on Health, is that although big companies tend to offer reasonably comprehensive benefit programs, they have not been comfortable supporting government mandates that tell small companies (often their suppliers) what to do. "They don't like to fight small business and small business tends to be more bottom line—oriented. That is why we have to demonstrate models that can be replicated and communicate with companies about what other companies have done. They will all ask, 'Why should I be the first?' We tell them they are not the first and that these are productivity issues."

England travels across the country in her position of helping companies address health care issues, working with such progressive leaders as

Governor Lawton Chiles of Florida and the chairmen of AT&T, Honeywell, Cigna, and Bell South. She believes that executive women are making a significant difference in the attitude of many companies as they move into senior management positions, often in the human resources area. "That job is no longer just a staff position in many companies," England said. "It is an important job with severe bottom-line implications and the individual who holds it is a key member of the senior management team. There are many senior-level women across the country who are at the forefront of thinking about and implementing these programs and advocating them at the Conference Board or in other business organizations. I don't see many women running small business trade groups yet, where they could help small companies solve the cost issue of family benefits."

One such senior-level woman is Monica Albano, director of human resources for HTM International in New Jersey. "My role as a member of our senior management committee is as a strategic business partner rather than performing an administrative backroom function," she said. "We believe there is no more complex an issue confronting management today than that of managing our human resources.

"As human resource executives, we must be able to manage change and ambiguity, largely because we must provide an added value to the corporation. In the last several years our companies have been downsized, upsized, and resized with the impact of global competition, new technology, deregulation, and slow economic growth.

"Now we must understand our 'community,' welcome diversity, manage soaring health care costs, enthusiastically support the change in demographics of the work force—all within an environment of more legislation and lawsuits than the nation has ever seen. These are complex issues which require complex strategies."

To assist executives like Albano, England's national health policy organization is helping to demystify the issue of family-friendly health care coverage and is working with over one hundred business health care coalitions across the country to study state and regional models of health delivery and financing systems.

Child health issues are significant social and economic concerns for companies, England believes. Not only does the United States rank among the highest of industrialized countries for infant mortality, but American companies and their employees pay about $5.6 billion a year to care for babies born with problems to mothers covered by insurance plans. Companies pay an additional $4 billion in hospital fees to make up for services provided to poor patients without insurance. One of the problems that England's group uncovered is that insurance coverage alone doesn't guarantee women access to prenatal care and other preventive strategies to reduce premature births. This is in spite of wide agreement that preventive care is more cost effective than medical care at a later stage.

"The United States is spending $800 billion on health care and we're not getting our money's worth," England said, citing the need to promote alternative health care delivery systems and public health care policies such as Oregon's, which provide preventive care at little or no direct cost to the consumer.

"Businesses are pragmatic. We have to keep showing them that their costs will be lower, their employees more productive, and their products more competitive in the global economy if we begin to tackle the financing and delivery of health care in a way that makes sense."

"If anyone had told me ten years ago I'd be working with corporate America in Washington I wouldn't have believed it!" laughs England, a former state mental health and social service commissioner, Harvard Kennedy School appointee, and insurance company executive. But she has found an arena in which she is clearly making a difference, as a respected member of The Club and a leading opinion maker on the front lines of national health care issues.

CHAPTER ELEVEN

THE IMPRINT OF WOMEN

Members of the Board

Women lose power on a board when they just represent the interests of women, not of share-holders.

—Dr. Matina S. Horner, director of the Neiman Marcus Group and Eastman Kodak

W omen have joined The Club in corporations and the professions and in civic and business associations. Now they are also taking seats in the nation's corporate boardrooms in ever-increasing numbers.

The image of a corporate board of directors as The Ultimate Club is supported by fact and anecdotes. Those who argue the existence of a glass ceiling for women or insist that the business community is a male-dominated closed shop offer as proof the small number of women who serve on corporate boards.

The push for more women on boards has been a long one. As early as the 1950s women had organized to increase the number of women directors; the Federation of Women Shareholders even drafted a proxy statement concerning women directors (subsequently rejected by the Securities and Exchange Commission). From then on, surveys have tracked the number of women board members. In 1969 in a survey of 1,300 boards, there were only forty-six women. Often these women were related to company principals.

By 1992 there were probably too many individual women to count, with 60 percent of all companies having at least one woman director, many of whom had business backgrounds. By the 1980s many of these women were recognized as "damn fine men" on the board, as director Jean Head Sisco was once called. In 1990 the statistics were even better: 58 percent of all companies had at least one female director and 133 of the top 1,000 employers had more than one.

"More than one?" A California director was not impressed with these figures. "Of course they should have more than one," she said, "particularly if they are large employers. The important fact is that 481 of those 1,000 large employers have no women directors and 386 haven't recognized that tokenism went out two decades ago."

Regional surveys have pointed to similar results, with still less than a third of companies having more than one woman director, and most manufacturing firms having none at all. Of 1,315 board members at America's hundred largest companies in 1992, only 7.5 percent were women.

Some might conclude that such statistics prove the notion of boards of directors as an old-boy network. Unfortunately, this stereotype is reinforced by true stories of how directors have been selected. Even directors who were chosen by the old method now wince at the recollection.

"The previous chairman of this company bought a subsidiary in New York and needed a director with a New York address," a male director related to his female colleague on the board. "I had done some investment work for one of the directors who told the chairman I was a nice fellow. Meanwhile, he told me I only had to attend three lunches a year and pick up a check and that would be that. No heavy lifting."

He became a diligent and attentive director, but such informal selection does not always produce favorable results. Joseph Mollicone, Jr., who set off Rhode Island's two-year bank crisis in 1990, forcing the private fund that insured one third of the state's depositors into insolvency, had no trouble raiding his Heritage Loan and Investment Company, in part because he filled the bank's board of directors with golfing partners. Mollicone is believed to have stolen over $13 million and his bank collapsed shortly after he fled the state. One golfer director recalled that he and another golfer were asked by Mollicone to be on the board, but in ten years he attended only two board meetings, explaining that the board didn't do anything.

Golf courses have been a good source for finding directors; one high-technology chief executive officer admitted being impressed with meeting hockey star Bobby Orr at a golf sporting event and invited him to sit on his company's board. Some of his other directors were also selected from prominent individuals he met in his social/charity circuit. But not all celebrities are interested in board service; even the "Today" show's weatherman, Willard Scott, declined to seek reelection to the board of a Virginia bank, citing the demands of a director's job.

Willard Scott had awoken to a new fact of life for many boards. Directors are no longer just the "parsley on the fish" at luncheon meetings, as directors were characterized by the former chairman of U.S. Steel. Corporate executives are beginning to realize the changing responsibilities of their directors as well, which is why they are looking to executive women to help enlarge their talent pool of smart, capable candidates.

Many executive women are not upset about the relatively small number of women serving on corporate boards. They know that turnover generally occurs slowly on corporate boards and therefore vacancies are limited. Women have moved beyond the numbers game, counting to see if every board has at least one woman. They know that tokenism no longer has a place in the corporate world and a woman, by her gender alone, does not necessarily make a difference on a corporate board. Simply arguing that every board should include a woman is too simplistic and misses the larger story of dynamic change at the board level. Women, like many men, will make their imprint on the agenda of corporate boards precisely because American business is in an era of great change when the talents and perspectives of dedicated board members are most needed.

The first change that is needed to help American companies and to increase the participation of capable women on boards is to reexamine the nominating process. In most companies and institutions, the informal selection process has been replaced by at least a serious attempt to reach out for talent.

The pool of director candidates will include more women because the greater risk and responsibility placed on directors means that qualified and interested directors are now harder to find. Headhunters report that searches for prospective board members are taking twice as long as in past years. Some executives are too busy running their own companies; others are limiting the number of boards on which they serve. Some executives don't want the increased responsibility or legal liability. Nominating committees are also getting choosier, no longer satisfied with the chairman's friend or neighbor. Boards of banks and thrift institutions are particularly hard to fill, since well-publicized lawsuits against directors and new laws governing their responsibilities have discouraged many potential directors from serving.

Outside directors should be able to demonstrate their independence by walking away from a board, and yet the "who needs this grief" attitude means that many business leaders will decline to serve when asked. The pay is rarely an incentive for former CEOs, as the average board compensation is $32,352 and presumably the days of private jets, generous consulting contracts, multimillion-dollar charitable contributions and lump-sum payouts are over.

The answer to this perceived bottleneck in identifying qualified director candidates will be a cadre of professional directors, men and women who have accumulated impressive personal and professional credentials in their working lives, who have served on many boards and understand the "board process" and who are ready to act as director of several companies or institutions.

A NEW PROFILE FOR DIRECTORS

"A corporate director is a bit like royalty," one female director in New York said. "They emerge from time to time in the throne room, nod sagely to their ministers, listen to their reports, wave to the royal subjects, and then disappear until the next public appearance. You never know if the monarch really is running the kingdom, getting good information, and supervising ministers without micromanaging, or if they are just figureheads, surrounded by yes-men, content to receive the adulation of the populace without understanding what they are doing or thinking. From the outside, it's hard to tell."

This may have once been accurate, when directors were just names listed in the back of annual reports. But in a rapidly changing economic climate, it is becoming easier to tell which directors are doing their jobs and which ones are still acting like "parsley."

Little has changed in the legal responsibility of directors. They always had ultimate responsibility to the shareholders for the economic health of the company and the use of shareholder money. What has changed is that directors are becoming public figures, under intense scrutiny from a wide variety of constituencies. With that degree of attention, golfing buddies may no longer pass muster and women may be a valuable addition to the board of directors.

This political attention, with its accompanying charges, counter-charges, debates, media coverage, back-room negotiations, demonstrations, confrontations, and alliances may seem strange to some corporate executives and directors who would rather just slam the door on their deliberations and post a sign: "Keep out." But the private sector is no longer really private. Their funds come from the public, they employ the public, their actions affect the social welfare of the public, and in many cases they are regulated by the public. Thanks to this political attention, the public now understands the effect of private business on the economic health of families and communities, from the taxpayers' bill for the collapse of savings and loans to the loss of manufacturing jobs to foreign countries. Even the promise of new jobs in a community is met with a certain skepticism from public officials and civic leaders who have been disappointed by previous corporate promises.

Because of this new scrutiny, the job of a corporate director is taking on distinct characteristics as the position begins to resemble a profession all its own. Directorships now entail job descriptions, responsibilities, and candidate qualifications. Just as women were gradually admitted to other male-dominated professions and excelled as judges, physicians, and elected officials, women who are entering the field of directorship are demonstrating their outstanding abilities.

There is no particular route to becoming a corporate director, although certain generalizations are valid. According to Dr. Marilyn M. Machlowitz, former executive director of the Corporate Board Resource for Catalyst, a New York consulting institution, about 85 percent of directors on corporate boards are recommended by internal sources. That means that women must be known to the CEO or other directors, even if a nominating committee of outside directors is the formal source for identifying candidates.

The requirement of a relationship with the CEO raises the old quandary about how women will become well known if they are outside the business community or are not already familiar with other board members. Catalyst helped solve that problem in 1977 by establishing the Corporate Board Resource, making available its national data base of women qualified to sit on corporate boards. Women's professional organizations across the country have provided similar services. For example, the Boston Club for Business and Professional Women published a book in 1984 called the *Corporate Board Resource*. Adopted from a similar publication of the Financial Women's Association of New York, the book contained profiles of twenty-five women qualified to sit on corporate boards, and was distributed widely to local chief executive officers and others who requested it. The resource book proved popular; the 1990 edition contained over a hundred profiles, and more than a thousand were distributed. Finding this model effective, other groups across the country have begun to publish similar compilations.

Even without such resource books to remind CEOs of the women they already know, the claim that "I don't know any women" does not ring true. In every community, women have reached senior levels in business and the professions, and serve in great numbers on major nonprofit boards such as hospitals, colleges, and business associations. Women have attained senior positions in government service; are partners in law, accounting and consulting firms; and run major nonprofit organizations. Furthermore, the notion that only other CEOs are suited for board service is no longer relevant in this changing climate. Companies with only CEOs on the board are as prone to mistakes as those with diverse boards, particularly when the crises they face may involve such wide-ranging issues as government investigations for product safety, political bribery, chemical leaks, oil spills, trading scandals, labor unrest, plant closings, and social responsibility—problems as familiar to board members in the 1980s and 1990s as the routine responsibility of dealing with management succession, executive compensation, and dividends per share.

Activist pension fund managers are becoming particularly attentive to the character, rather than career, of those nominated for corporate director spots. They seek candidates who demonstrate independence from management and personal assertiveness. In many cases, a fellow CEO does not fit the bill. Few funds want to seat directors themselves, but many support the election of new directors as the best vehicle for winning a voice in corporate affairs. They know that just because the candidate is not a CEO does not mean he or she is afraid to take risks, ask tough questions, or form alliances with the other independent directors.

In this new era of professional directorship, corporate executives, activist shareholders, and existing board members must come to an agreement about the qualifications of new board members. Clearly, a proven track record in the business or professional world is a starting point. Yet the candidate need not have been a chairman or president; significant experience at a large company should suffice.

As one woman director said, "The question of titles is really meaningless. A woman can be president of her own small company and some CEOs will be more impressed with that than a vice president at Ford Motor Company. For a while, the only women CEOs companies could find were presidents of women's colleges, so they invited them to serve. Those women were fine, but companies were also missing many other talented businesswomen."

For others, significant level of achievement in the professional world might be an equivalent qualification: a partner with corporate experience in a major law firm, a cabinet post in government, a business school professor. In all cases, these candidates should be mature, understand business and the environment in which a particular business operates, and have experience as a board member elsewhere. The candidate should be a leader in the economic community in which she operates, respected and known by other leaders, with a reputation that has endured. She should have demonstrated that she takes assignments seriously, performs gracefully, and evidences a personal chemistry that fits well with the group. While some of these qualities cannot be tested prior to board service, they can be asked about. Others who know the candidate can attest to her diligence, working style, and professionalism.

"I remember my first interview with the chairman of the nominating committee for the bank board," recalled a professional director from Chicago. "I think he was most impressed with my past service on the executive committee, finance committee, audit committee, and investment committee of several major nonprofit boards in the city. Clearly, I understood the role of a director and had been given important assignments.

"That particular chairman understood the skills that a director develops by serving on nonprofit boards. Not all do," she said. "But in many cases, the issues are similar. How do you evaluate a major capital expenditure? How can a board help the company understand and approach complex environmental questions? What are the cash flow needs of the organization? How is the budget set? And perhaps the most important intangible factor is the network of other board members and what an individual director can learn from the others on the board, watching how they approach and solve problems. Extensive board experience helps women develop a wide range of skills that are immediately transferable to a corporate board."

Boards may find the best candidates among women with nontraditional résumés, those who have had varied careers, developing their own credentials, critical skills, and personal currency rather than those who simply climbed the corporate ladder in one organization. Ruth R. McMullin of the Harvard Business School Publishing Group explains why.

"Directors must have active, probing minds, a problem-solving orientation, independence, and tough-mindedness. They must have an ability to set priorities and separate material items from trivial ones. Superior listening ability is important, as well as interpersonal skills that reflect an ability to understand and respond to the views and feelings of others. They must have highly developed communication skills and be experienced in democratic debate. They should be sensitive to consumer and shareholder activist issues. They must have high personal standards of ethics and morals," she said. "Women, with somewhat unconventional work histories, often have a diverse and unconventional way of understanding how to fulfill duties of care and loyalty."

She was describing many executive women.

McMullin did not mention CEO status or CEO-equivalency. She knows that boardsmanship is really a process, one that knits together the dynamics of the other board members into a cohesive whole that results not in group-think but in an independent and constructive unit. Asking the right question is sometimes the best skill a board member can bring to the group, and courage is one of the most important character traits.

Board members need courage in the face of increased public pressure on outside directors, much of it initiated by large public pension funds such as the California Public Employees Retirement System (Calpers). With its $58 billion in assets, Calpers could not easily vote with its feet and simply sell shares of companies it felt were poorly supervised. Its chief executive, Dale M. Hanson, began an informal process of targeting certain companies for conversations and, if necessary, exerting pressure by withholding proxy votes. For example, Calpers forced General Motors to agree to a corporate bylaw calling for a majority of its board to consist of independent directors, arguing that the presence of more truly independent directors would help prevent entrenched management (and prevent another $7 billion loss on its North American operations). Other companies under fire from pension funds and mutual funds followed suit; Sears trimmed its board by one third, eliminating five insider directors and agreeing to name several more outside directors. Bethlehem Steel, Johnson & Johnson, TRW, Sara Lee, Lockheed Corporation decided to add more outside directors, joining other companies that have increased the ratio of outside directors from three to one. And should corporations miss the message that an outside director does not mean a candidate suggested by the chairman, Calpers, the New York State Common Retirement Fund, and the Connecticut State Treasurer wrote to 300 companies suggesting future directors be nominated by a nominating committee comprised of outside board members.

Large institutional investors are not the only ones looking to corporate directors for oversight of corporate activities. Individual investors notice everything from the diversity of the directors to how many shares directors should be required to own and the size of executive salaries. In 1991, private investors used over 600 proxy resolutions to push for corporate changes, a 20 percent increase over 1990, and the SEC has proposed rule changes to make it easier for investors to communicate with companies by the use of proxy resolutions.

Shareholder and consumer activism is on the increase, with companies assessing their compliance with the Sullivan Principles, the MacBride Principles, the Valdez Principles, and the Maquiladora Standards, as well as equal opportunity, animal testing, consumerism, product quality and safety, and political activities. And if all these concerns weren't enough, directors are also under public fire for approving exorbitant executive pay packages.

In boom economic times, few shareholders, employees, or elected officials begrudged generous executive salaries and perks. But in a national recession, the media recognized a good story when it revealed that Michael Eisner, the CEO of Disney, earned more in one day than the average Disney employee earns in a year; that CEO pay doubled and tripled while earnings per share remained flat or declined; and that the 1990 median CEO annual compensation totaled almost a million dollars and many CEOs received annual compensation of many millions. These stories, read by laid-off employees, disappointed shareholders, and elected officials turned the spotlight on boards of directors.

In turn, outside directors are beginning to flex their muscles and pressure CEOs to announce their retirements, resignations, and corporate restructurings. Slowly, the balance of power within the corporation is shifting back in favor of the board, particularly when it is comprised of serious, intelligent, and independent directors. These new boards understand that the old ways of doing business no longer work in a rapidly changing corporate world. A company must build personal currency with its stakeholders so that when the public glare comes, it will be ready to deal with whatever issue is at hand, with political capital as insurance. This requires openness, information, good performance, accountability, and inclusiveness. A company does not necessarily acquire those attributes with a closed circle of board members.

VIVE LA DIFFÉRENCE?

Companies and nominating committees are casting a wider net and inviting more women to serve as directors amid a changing political climate for corporate boards. But does the presence of more women on corporate boards make a difference?

We did not know the answer to that question when we first started asking it. We had no preconceived point of view and were reluctant to state that boards should have more women on them "just because" they were women. But to shut out one half of the candidates for board membership for no reason other than gender or comfort does not seem particularly intelligent.

We really looked for an answer. On paper, all directors have the same responsibility. All should pay attention to the bottom line and performance measures, worry about their legal liability, the flow of information from the CEO, executive compensation, organizational development, audits, proxies, social responsibility, management succession, legal and ethical standards, long-term strategy, capital expenditures, and future directors. Independent directors do not fill specific needs, despite the fact that on some boards shareholders see a minority and a woman and assume they represent a race or gender. Men *and* women, whites *and* minorities, have responsibilities for the work force and a concern for social issues.

Not all women represent all women's views, of course, just as not all minorities represent the view of all minorities. Many men understand gender issues as well as women do and often represent them well. But because many women have had unique experiences in the business and professional world because of their gender, they can be valuable contributors to a CEO's roster of close advisers. These women will be what economist Juanita Kreps described as a new supply of problem solvers—pleasant company and a source of good ideas with a broadened perspective.

Most of the senior executive women we spoke with across the country had served as directors of corporations. Many were selected by fellow Club members who knew them personally, had served on nonprofit or other community boards with them, and had developed a personal relationship with them.

"Search firms and corporate resources data banks are helpful," said one woman in Los Angeles. "But no one will ask you to serve on a board if they don't know you and [haven't] worked with you—or if they don't know someone else who has. The searches and data banks are helpful in reminding them of women they knew but had forgotten, or perhaps even surfacing the name of a woman they can easily check out through other Club members. But I can't stress enough the importance of relationships, particularly among the outside directors. They have to work well together."

Many board members, however, are still chosen by the chairman or president of the company, and a director's relationship with the chief executive officer may be more important than how she gets along with the other directors. Many women described a particular dynamic at work between them and the CEO, an added value they bring to many boards.

"I bring my own expertise to the board, in much the same manner as any male director does," said a director in California. "But when a CEO asks me, I feel free to give him advice about women and work/family issues, as well as community, consumer, and social concerns. We sometimes have breakfast, just the two of us, to catch up on outside events. Just by being a woman, I am his window into a world he does not inhabit."

Sometimes the very independence that women (and some men) bring to the board allows them to play a role that other directors cannot. One director related the difficulty faced by independent board members in dealing with an inappropriate role taken by a fellow director who had been a senior-level insider in the company. "We had appointed his successor and held his going-away party. But he continued to maintain an office at the company and soon we heard that others were seeking him out instead of the CEO or other senior executives.

"The problem was complicated by the fact that he sat as a director on the boards of at least three other directors—the usual interlocking directorate/conflict of interest issue. None of those men were anxious to be the one to confront him about this problem, so I had to do it. I didn't mind, because my independence as a director was the absence of overlapping directorates, which allowed me to handle the issue more objectively. The others were grateful I was on the board to take over that assignment!"

A woman in Wisconsin described a similar experience on a large public utility board. "For a long time, I was the only woman on the board. My fellow directors were polite but I could sense they felt that one woman was plenty. But their attitude changed when another woman joined the board, an outspoken representative of an activist consumer group. She did not have the faintest idea about how to be a director, or her fiduciary relationship to the issues in front of us. She continued to do inappropriate actions, from bringing tape recorders to executive sessions, to encouraging her organization to bring frivolous lawsuits against the utility. I was outraged, and became the most vocal one who took her on at board meetings. I'm sure if I hadn't been on the board and other directors had done it, this woman would have screamed sex discrimination and hit them with that charge as well. But because I was the point person, she couldn't. I neutralized her, both on the board and in the community. One director said to me after a particularly tough meeting, 'Boy, are we glad you're on the board!'"

Some company executives use their directors well. A director in New York described her dealing with the company chairman. "If the CEO needs an enormous amount of control, it doesn't matter whether you are male or female. Conversation will be limited to what he wants to sell to the board. But our chairman takes advantage of the background and experience of all of us. For example, he talked to each director one-on-one about his successor, asking advice, getting feedback. Every director gave him a different prism. He spent as much time with the directors he didn't know well and who were relatively new to the board, like me. I know I suggested approaches to him that others did not and he listened intently."

We heard this theme repeatedly. "I find that some boards have rooted, rutted patterns of behavior," said a director in Houston. "The women I observe approach the board process from a fresh perspective because they haven't been trained in the tribal rights of the boys. For example, when I first joined the board, I asked the company to set up an orientation program for me. They had never considered it before. But when the next new director joined the board, a man, he was grateful I had led the way! He took me aside during the first coffee break and said, 'Do you know what all this jargon means?' I said, 'Well, Bob, I do now, but I didn't until I had the orientation program for new directors. You mean the chairman didn't tell you about it?'"

Boardsmanship does not just involve reacting to numbers and agenda items presented for approval in the boardroom. Ideally, the communication goes two ways, as each director brings skills, experiences, and ideas that complement other directors and company executives. In the rest of the nineties, business success may well depend on how clearly executives understand the changing society they are operating in and particularly on how skillfully they anticipate signs of trouble with their employee base, the regulators, the media, activists, and the changing nature of consumer tastes and standards.

Few companies can legally ignore the arenas of consumerism, politics, equal opportunity, environment, or social responsibility. Women have often gained prominence in those areas, so their presence on a board can symbolize a company's sensitivity to her areas of expertise. Women in the company look at the board and view the total absence of women as a negative factor and the presence of just one woman often as tokenism. But the inclusion of several women is viewed as evidence that the company values their contributions at all levels and in many disciplines. Many corporate executives also use their female board members as sounding boards about developing their own women executives and many women directors are happy to listen and give advice, even if human resource development is not their specialty.

In addition to their unique perspective, Phyllis Sewell, a director of Huffy Corporation, suggests that women's presence also sends a positive signal to the employees of an organization that it is open-minded. The visual presence of women on a board extends beyond the corporation's own work force. A woman's face on the annual report sends a positive message about the values of the company to investors and customers who notice such things, indicating that management is receptive to many points of view. Furthermore, other CEOs and directors on the board who have had a positive experience with a woman director return to their own business environments with perhaps an amended notion about the participation of women.

"I'm not sure I've changed the outcome of any particular agenda item at the board," said a utility director who has considered whether women on the board make a difference. "But I know I've changed the dynamic. The other directors are not as quick to let things go by, because they know I won't hesitate to stop and ask a question about something. They know I have done my homework and will catch anything that is not well explained or where the underlying assumptions may be weak. They know I will never embarrass the CEO, particularly if other insiders are present at the board meeting, but I will raise issues outside of the boardroom. Since I joined the board, the outside directors have lunch together periodically, just to brainstorm and make sure we are all on the same wavelength. I know I've been a valuable addition, and one of the other directors asked me to join his board. He didn't want me because I'm a woman, but because I'm a good director."

Dr. Matina S. Horner, a director of Time, Inc., for over nineteen years, recalled the attempted hostile takeover of Time by Paramount. Her long history on the board, her background in academics (where freedom of expression is an important value), and her deep understanding of the core mission of the company and the value this had for shareholders were useful in Time's takeover battle. "My experience, including that as a member on the Council on Competitiveness, my proven track record, and a record for integrity and independence of mind served the company well at that critical moment in its history and lent credence to my deposition," Horner said. "I was a serious director with a sincere and serious view about the events confronting the company. I was a different voice than those who argued that our only concern was the price per share."

Her experience is not unique. Today, women are not clamoring to join corporate boards just because they have been excluded in great numbers in the past. They are, like Caroline Marsh,* approaching the position with a high level of professionalism.

"There's something going on at the bank," confided Marsh, a bank director and former prominent city official, to a group of twenty-four executive women gathered around a law firm conference table in Texas. It was the bimonthly informal meeting of their business forum, a loosely structured support group of senior executive and professional women.

---

*An asterisk denotes that we have changed the name of the woman quoted, and in some cases the name of her company and its location as well.

"At the last two bank directors' meetings, I've noticed that one of my fellow directors has several large loans from the bank, and yet his name and loan haven't been presented to the board. We're to be advised if anyone on the board has a loan of over $250,000 and take a specific vote on it. He has three that total almost a million dollars, and no one has mentioned it."

"So what did you do?" asked a real estate developer in the group.

"I raised the question at our meeting last month. He was right there. There was a lot of throat clearing and statements like, 'Oh yes, that must have been an oversight,' but I might as well have been a skunk at the garden party. Then at yesterday's meeting, I noticed his loans are past due. And now there are even more. The rest of the guys just act like the bank is their money spigot, but I thought we had a fiduciary duty to the shareholders. I need to know if I'm crazy or overreacting or what. Is this just courtesy to a fellow director, or am I right that the bank should be following procedures?"

The women gathered around the table—law partners, retail and bank executives, stockbrokers, financial officers, economists, professors— quickly reassured Caroline that her alarm was justified, particularly when she outlined a history of loose adherence to board procedures on other bank matters, her exclusion from the audit committee, and the reaction of the bank president to her past concerns. They set about to form a strategy for her: Caroline would quietly resign from her position as the only woman director at her bank. She would leave a paper trail to the bank counsel, the board chairman, and the president. She would be firm but polite—strong enough to make her point, but not so inflammatory as to attract the attention of regulatory agencies or burn bridges with her fellow directors.

Several weeks later, Caroline reported back to the group. "I did it. I finally resigned. I liked being a director, but not at the expense of my reputation and potential liability. I was muddled at first, but your feedback clarified the situation. I'm not sure I could have done it so quickly and confidently without your support."

Few outside of Caroline's small circle of friends and colleagues ever learned of her resignation. But the wisdom of her decision was affirmed a year later when she encountered one of the fellow directors at a concert. He, too, had just resigned. "By the way," he said, "I took the liberty of passing your name along to the CEO of Universal Life. I told him you were a good director."

Caroline Marsh had reached the highest rung of the corporate ladder. She had gained membership in the ultimate Club of top executives who direct policy and influence events from the corporate boardrooms of economic communities across the country. But she resigned from the board, as other executive women have also decided to do in similar circumstances. Today, being visible as the only woman on a board is not worth lowering one's personal standards, as one of Caroline's colleagues had pointed out.

That women are being elected to corporate boards in greater numbers is no longer news. What is news is that these women are no longer tokens. They are making important contributions in partnership with other directors on corporate boards precisely at a time when the balance of power is shifting to outside directors. They are valuable members of The Directorship Club.

CHAPTER TWELVE

A VISION OF THE FUTURE

Thoughts for Corporate America

Corporate America must get over its fears of women in authority.

—John P. Mascotte, CEO, Continental Insurance Co.

Corporate executives are gradually realizing that energy and accomplishment have little relationship to gender and that women are an important pool of talent. At the same time, talented women have long ago understood that the right corporate environment is a major factor in determining their ultimate success. Senior-level executive women who emphasized skills such as rainmaking, personal currency, and networking also concluded that in the wrong corporate climate, these skills will most likely be wasted. In the right one, there is no ceiling on achievement for women. Jacqueline C. Morby, senior general partner of T.A. Associates, the national venture capital firm, explains.

"It's hard to say what is the road to success," Jacqui said. "It's like the old joke. Mitterand has twenty lovers and one is pregnant, but no one knows which one. Bush has twenty bodyguards and one is a terrorist, but no one knows which one. Yeltsin has twenty economic advisers, and one is good, but no one knows which one. Well, there are twenty women trying to succeed, but no one knows which one it will be."

Jacqui's professional history points out some key factors that helped develop her life's interest in software and developing companies. First she prepared herself well by attending Simmons College School of Management, a highly rated graduate business program conducted in an atmosphere and culture that enhances women's success rate.

Second, Jacqui joined the rapidly growing new industry of venture capital, where women could progress on merit and hard work. When she began in 1978, T.A. Associates was understaffed. It was a perfect opportunity for Jacqui to demonstrate her talents.

"It had a young, aggressive, value system of like people who made it on their own merits. It was competitive inside and outside. People worked long hours, but they could succeed on their own. It wasn't a case of having a degree from a particular school, or having a particular background," Jacqui recalled.

"There was little support at T.A. in 1978. You had to use your ingenuity. You had to figure out on your own what the company valued most. Seventy percent of your time was spent outside the company, so there was little bureaucracy inside. Today, the values are the same. It's a tough environment, but a good one for women.

"I provided real value by finding new ways to find investment opportunities. The secret to success at T.A. was to find good investments, but I didn't have the traditional sources of finding them. There was *no* old-boy network when I came. No one brought me a deal. I looked at magazines, books, and newspapers and made cold calls. I found a wealth of information. I just started doing it because I had to. I had to develop the business on my own, and my way proved to be so successful that it was adopted by the whole firm.

"I also found I could market myself to companies. There are others who did not succeed at T.A. because they couldn't sell themselves. When you want to invest in someone's company, and sit on their board, you have to sell yourself.

"I picked a specialty, software. My strategy was to 'get to the influencers.' I found there were only eight to ten at that time in the industry, and I got to know them. I also used visibility to enhance the reputation of T.A. I learned how to get to know the media; I became friends with them. I helped them with information, and they mentioned me and T.A. in the press. I became known as the software expert at T.A., and when I made calls on companies, I was a known person."

Flexible corporate structure, rainmaking, personal currency, media exposure, little hierarchy, ability to choose her own working style and earn her own rewards, intellectual challenge, directorships—T.A. Associates and Jacqueline Morby were a perfect match.

Unlike Jacqui Morby, Elaine Ullian did not always find a perfect match. She wanted a career teaching eighth-grade civics.

"I owe it all to one nasty man who wouldn't hire me for a teaching job after college," she said. "So I ended up working in the feminist Our Bodies, Ourselves health clinic; me, who never knew until 1970 that a woman could be a doctor!"

But that job didn't last long. Ullian moved out of town, came back, and landed a public sector job in the Massachusetts Department of Public Health. "I was twenty-six years old and they made me the director of the Determination of Need program. All the hospitals had to obtain state permission for their expansion plans. I was called the toughest girl on the street. Likewise, I could hardly wait to get out of that job. So I moved on and worked in administration at the Boston University Medical Center and then at the New England Medical Center.

"I loved my job at New England Medical Center. I never thought about leaving. Someone asked me what I wanted to be one day, and I responded, 'president of Mount Auburn Hospital or Faulkner Hospital.' I thought being president of a small teaching hospital in the Boston community would be great, but I never thought it would happen.

"One day, a headhunter called me at New England Medical Center. I cut him off and said I loved my job and didn't want to leave. He said he was calling about Faulkner. I told him to stay right where he was, and not call anyone else. I put on my sneakers and ran over to his office.

"He told me there was no chance I'd get it. I did not fit the traditional vision of a hospital CEO nor had I followed a traditional career path."

Ullian grinned, remembering. "I got the job."

Ullian was well prepared. The "A Group" in Women in Health Care Management, of which Ullian was a longtime member, set a goal of promoting women as candidates for the top positions in health care and developed a detailed strategy to attack the problem. They developed relationships with headhunters and hospital trustees, gave presentations to industry groups, and raised the public visibility of their members. When a senior executive opening occurred, Women in Health Care Management was ready with several candidates. With the support of other high-powered women in the "A Group," individual candidates were ready to be considered for the tough jobs.

"How did I do it? You have to be flexible. I'm troubled by how we do a number on ourselves. We're too unforgiving. We're too concerned about a vertical career path. We are terrified of being disliked. It's hard, because we're conditioned otherwise. I thought I didn't have a chance at the job, so I took risks in describing my vision for the hospital. I still have to keep remembering that all my decisions may not be popular, but I didn't take this job to be prom queen."

We suspect that if Jacqui Morby and Elaine Ullian were to lose their jobs tomorrow, they'd just move along in the next phase of where their interests lead them. Jacqui Morby's name is synonymous with expertise in the software industry, and even if she were lounging in a beach chair, she'd be researching, writing, investing, speaking, or maybe running her own software company.

Elaine Ullian might be in the chair next to her, doing the same thing in health care. Their self-identity is centered more on what contributions they can make in the areas that interest them than the traditional masculine identity of outward signs of being a good provider or holding a particular title. This comprehensive self-identity is an asset: It makes women stronger, more able to handle the ups and downs of professional life, to weather setbacks. Likewise, the challenge for American corporations is not to put people in narrow career boxes with titles and job descriptions, but to understand more each person's potential and recognize the fact that people change and grow.

A NEW NOTION OF CAREER

Retaining and promoting a woman in the economy of the 1990s does not necessarily lead to rewarding her with a 25-year anniversary gold watch. Longevity is not the measure of success—contribution is. But some companies are still stuck with old notions of seniority and increased-title-advancement. Many women, however, are fundamentally reexamining what it means to be successful in the business world and are suggesting that smart corporate executives will be those who also adopt a new concept about the difference between "job" and "work."

"One is my present title and paycheck," explained an economist. "The other is my real area of interest, my calling, my intellectual pursuit. They are not necessarily the same."

These women state that it is only when managers and executives con-

front outmoded ideas about "careers" that employers will break out of traditional corporate straitjackets and finally create climates of diversity and
inclusion, climates that allow a Jacqui Morby or Elaine Ullian to flourish.

For a variety of reasons, some women approach their work life differently than many men. Socialization, education, family priorities, and institutional barriers are important factors, but there is another, more basic
reason frequently raised by executive women: Many women define careers
differently than men. The corporations and businesses that accommodate
this new definition will be ahead of their competition in attracting female
executive talent.

It is sometimes easier to throw away old concepts if we throw away the
word, as well. So forgoing "career," we suggest MITs (an acronym that
stands for Mission, Interests, and Talents) when describing how a woman
works in her adult life. This term describes how she has used her brain
(and sometimes brawn) over her lifetime to contribute to organizations
and community with reward for her work and accomplishments.

A MIT can be paid or unpaid. Contributions can be measured in many
ways. Rewards can be psychic or monetary. A professional volunteer can
have a MIT, but few corporate executives might accord her the same degree of respect that a high-salaried and titled executive position would.
Such a viewpoint is unnecessarily limiting, as a volunteer may possess excellent leadership and managerial skills and a seasoned executive may
change career direction and become a volunteer without losing her MIT.

A woman in San Diego expressed it best when she said, "My work is
energizing, not draining, so to do more of it is great. What I'm paid or
called is irrelevant to what I do."

A woman with a MIT is a self-reliant executive because her self-
identity can never be taken away from her. A MIT is the totality of an
executive's life and guides her decision making.

"Self-confidence and knowing who you are determines how you
choose each job," said Sally Frame Kasaks. Kasaks turned down a high-
level merchandising position with one of the nation's biggest retailers in
1979 to accept an operations job at half the salary with Ann Taylor. It was
a smart move, as she rose to become CEO of Ann Taylor, president of
Talbot Stores, president and CEO of Abercrombie & Fitch, and then
CEO of Ann Taylor again. Kasaks advises women to take jobs based on
their sense of what is right for them at the time, not on what traditional

career models might dictate. "You have to take control of your own life," she said.

Women's MITs are also likely to be meshed with strong relationships at home or in the community, which at various stages in their life may also impact decision making or loyalty to an employer who does not understand these ties. This does not mean women are any less committed to their profession or have less leadership or motivational ability than men. It *does* mean that women are less fearful of taking breaks along the way.

The old definition of career as "a field for or pursuit of consecutive progressive achievement especially in public, professional, or business life" just doesn't work for many women (or men), although many human resource professionals and executives persist in operating with it. But the old idea of "career" is flawed because fields change often today. Executive skills are easily transferable from one very different working environment to another, as Sally Berger or Dr. Matina Horner have shown.

Transferability is important because work experiences need not be consecutive. Even short breaks are healthy, as many adults will be working for a long time. It's perfectly all right, although still unusual, in a fifty-year career span, to take time off for recharging and regrouping, although some workplace cultures are still resistant to the idea of career breaks.

A female partner in a medium-sized New York law firm, a rainmaker and well respected in her field of family law, told the story of her ill-fated attempt to change the culture at her firm: "I attended a national conference a few years back on the running of law firms, and brought back the new idea of a paid sabbatical program that some firms were introducing. My partners were lukewarm, but they told me to go ahead and organize it for us. So I wrote the policy, got it approved by everyone, and watched while all the men who were eligible to take the sabbatical declined.

"Finally, six years later, when I was eligible, I took it," she said. "I arranged for others to handle my cases, I notified my clients, I found a substitute for new clients, and then I took three months off. I spent a while in Maine with my husband, and then went to India with a friend, and to Africa on an 'Earthwatch' program. It was exactly what I wanted to do, and it really cleared out my brain.

"When I came back, I prepared a whole report for my partners on what I did, how it worked, and how I handled my clients. Even though they know I have the report, few have asked for it. Now it is several years later, and not one other partner has taken the paid sabbatical, even though the firm has plenty of money to fund it, and some of my male partners have teenage children or other family situations where three consecutive months off would be valuable.

"Frankly, I think they are so caught up in the notion of being irreplaceable, and so afraid that if they turn their work over to someone else that person will steal their clients, that they can't do it."

Her experience is not isolated. A survey of one senior-level women's business and professional group by Dr. Suzyn Ornstein of Suffolk University's School of Management and Dr. Lynn Isabella of the Darden School at the University of Virginia pointed up the differences between how men and women view their work and identity. Far more women described critical career events as "confirmatory," those that affirmed their self-image, while men chose the "milestones," or specific levels of accomplishment, as most significant. Similarly, more than twice the percentage of women than men described their careers in relation to other personal qualities, such as self-esteem or intellectual growth, while most men saw their career as a means to an end. Women feel that "who they are as a person" is more important than certain levels of success, explained Dr. Ornstein. Employers who match the structures and rewards of work to those motivations will earn the loyalty of executive women.

It is no accident that Jacqui Morby and Elaine Ullian made it to the top of their fields without encountering major roadblocks; they found the right employer. Morby described the absence of a glass ceiling in her company: "I never ran into it because I provided real value and the organization was open and looked at everyone in the same way."

Ullian had a similar story to tell. "If my goal were to be president of Massachusetts General Hospital, I would have hit the glass ceiling badly. But it wasn't. Women have to ask themselves [if they] really want to go through it. You don't need to do that. Find the right culture."

Ullian's interest in medical administration began with the feminist movement's focus on health care for women in the early 1970s, and she has continued that emphasis, building the world famous Faulkner Breast Center and the Faulkner Center for Reproductive Medicine. Four of her six vice presidents are women, and she is unstinting in her attention to promoting other women in the health care field.

Elaine Ullian never worried about a career but always had a MIT. "I could sell mascara at Filene's and feel good about it," she said. But being the chief executive officer of a dynamic hospital is much more rewarding. "I know this sounds hokey, but I pinch myself every day I come here!"

Whether Ullian ends up at the cosmetic counter at Filene's or Massachusetts General Hospital, her concept of what constitutes achievement centers more around her own attitude about the job at hand than on any external status symbol. Critics might well argue that Robert Stempel achieved little for General Motors despite his promotion to chairman, or that Fred Joseph's career at Drexel Burnham and John Gutfreund's career at Salomon Brothers were less than outstanding. Career achievement is often regarded as moving to the top status level, but being at the top doesn't guarantee success or respect. Undoubtedly there are individuals who earned far less at those same companies who made real contributions to the enterprises. Both men and women fall into the trap of being impressed with titles as a measure of achievement. The truth is that an individual with a solid business background, a track record as an active and serious professional, or impressive community contributions can be highly effective in many settings—as manager, corporate director, or even ambassador, perhaps—but without a title, many individuals assume there is no presumption of achievement.

Thinking of MITs instead of careers can make the difference for women who have a discouraging view of the benefits of senior executive status or leadership positions in the business community. Striving for the top spots is not about a new title, line on the résumé, longer work day, or more money. Leadership status is just another piece in a woman's total MIT, giving her the power and resources to change the debate, to restructure old structures, and to tilt the outcome for other women. It is well worth the effort, say top executive women.

Corporate leaders who understand and appreciate MITs instead of titles alone will be more likely to attract and retain women executives. We cannot believe the paucity of women in The Club is due to any malevolence or predetermined strategy. Many women think it is simply because corporate leaders don't know how to proceed and don't understand what they are doing wrong or why their best efforts still aren't working. Corporate leaders think they are chivalrous and dedicated to developing female talent, but they don't realize that in some cases this very behavior may come across as chauvinistic. They understand the buzzwords (we must all work together to "change the culture,"), but they have yet to learn how to put that mandate into action.

Corporate leaders don't have to change any culture—a difficult, fuzzy notion at best. But they should reexamine old habits, thought processes, automatic reactions, and preconceptions about what it is they *are* doing.

Notice that we put the burden on corporate *leaders*. Corporations, institutions, and associations are not monolithic. They can have a conscience and reputation, as anyone asked to compare Levi-Strauss and Exxon can attest. Corporations can be both profitable and moral when their leaders make moral and ethical decisions. We know that shareholders and stakeholders are interested in more than bottom-line economics. To them, the human capital that corporations are amassing to lead and grow has taken on new importance. The decisions that corporate leaders make about their talent pool are not just day-to-day decisions made in an exercise of rational thought; not to decide is in many cases to decide. Individual employees read the actions and habits of those around them and make their own decisions about their loyalty to the organization. Attitudes of inclusiveness and moral standards are easily discernible by those working with corporate leaders.

Throughout the book we have placed much of the burden of responsibility on executive women themselves (or collaboratively with other women) for gaining membership in The Club. But as *Business Week* suggested, corporate executives need to search their hearts and minds to reexamine why women don't advance in greater numbers. Waiting for the natural flow of demographics or a growing economy to move women along in the pipeline to senior positions won't do it.

The executive women we spoke with across the country rarely used the word *sexism* to describe the attitude of gatekeepers at traditional corporations and professions. "Comfort zone" expresses the dynamic more accurately; some men feel a lack of comfort in entrusting leadership positions in The Club to women. We understand that, as some women are guilty of seeking comfort as well. They express it in their preferences for working environments that are more familiar, more hospitable, and, not coincidentally, probably comprised of large numbers of women. But men and women must work together to reexamine their behaviors and preferences if a true partnership is to result. These behaviors and preferences are part cultural, part institutional, part conscious, part unconscious. Embracing comfort is a reaction to a fear of change, a fear of the unknown. Corporate leaders such as John Macotte express it directly and we admire him for it:

- Facing fear is a major step to managing it and moving past it to unlock solutions to the major barriers blocking women's economic progress in partnership with men.
- Some men fear that the formerly valued two-parent family is now, in reality, just a nostalgic memory from the past. For that reason, their place and level of responsibility in the family and in the office is in flux.
- Some women fear that nothing in their lives can work exactly right without paying the high price of guilt. The perfect standards of the past—as mother, as spouse, as child—may be beyond their grasp.
- Some men fear that in a new age of technology and information, the past model of exercising power by controlling and owning information will no longer work.
- Some men fear that status will no longer be automatically achieved by position or seniority, but by merit and ability to use information.
- Some men and women fear that a partnership cannot work because it requires that old relationships and hierarchies change.
- Partnerships force men and women to learn how to negotiate and accommodate, to accept that a variety of viewpoints may be valid.
- Partnerships force men and women to learn something new, to give up a rigid sense of control and security.
- Partnerships force men and women to admit that fear and need for comfort are unproductive and to learn to face them together with a commitment to change.

COMFORT ZONE INVENTORY

Change begins with an honest examination of the present. It is all very well to tell a company or institution that it is wasting its recruiting money, undervaluing talented executives who may have families, and not utilizing women at the top of the organization. But most corporate leaders are better served with specific guidelines and signposts to underscore changes that they might make. With acknowledgment to Katie Cannon, Ph.D., of Temple University's department of religion, we have adapted a "comfort zone inventory" as a starting point for men and women to use in examining their own institutions.

• Does my company or organization work from the proposition of a zero-sum equation: that every job a female obtains, a man never gets? What strategies have been devised to maximize gains for men when women are given important jobs?

Women recognize a hierarchy of positions and a limited number of job openings in each category. Women are often hired for positions with lower status (public relations, communications, human resources, pediatrics) instead of the most prestigious (sales, engineering, mergers and corporate finance, surgery). Some women's positions are superfluous appendages, soft jobs, mannequin jobs. Men generally do not get these jobs; they rarely are disadvantaged because women hold them.

• Are there quota limits for women?

We will have one woman on the management committee, one woman on the executive committee, one woman on the board of directors. Okay, two, but we'll expand the board to make room for her.

• Is having the right contacts an important factor in initial job placements?

This young man was recommended by a fellow Skull and Bones member. I knew her family from the island where we all summered and agreed to take her on as an intern.

• Is the key to getting a job still a matter of who you know? Formal advancement paths are important, but usually only by passing through the informal route can one reach the executive suite.

We've heard it many times. The chairman of the department recommended that he be given this grant. She served on a board with the chair of the search committee. His roommate from graduate school is now the foreign minister and told him to put his firm on the team list bidding for that construction project. "This is so important," a woman from Cleveland told us. "If you only know people just like you, how do you find others, particularly if it's the others who give the jobs? Homogeneity is not having to deal with difference."

• Does my company or organization depend more on "personality fit" than credentials or achievements (will she "fit" into our family here)?

We are a community in a company, not a family. I am not your sister or daughter; don't play family with me. I am a peer or colleague.

• Within the vortex of groups of directors, senior management, staff, and customers or clients, how can women enter who have considerably less knowledge of how the system works?

We need someone to decode it for us.

• How can women become privy to backstage information that is more accessible to their male cohorts?

Comfort strikes home here, in the high-end suburbs, on the golf course, at the private-club dinners.

• Do men give credence to women's comments in discussions only when it specifically involves women's issues?

Is that all we can talk about? We are spokespersons of our gender but the burden of that is too high. Comfort tells us, "You can't be better than a man about the subject at hand. We want to hear only what your gender thinks."

• If male executives tend to be more interested in executives who will adopt or already share their interests, how can women find models and mentors for subjects related to their interests and experience, subjects that men may know nothing about, care little about, and regard as being of little importance?

The experience and perspective of one gender naturally limit the experiences and perspectives brought to the group to consider or thought to be valued. But as President Linda S. Wilson of Radcliffe College said, "Women represent an important source of renewal. They bring questions, fresh ideas, new and different perspectives on old problems, new energies and new skills. They can learn the existing strategies but they are not blinded by the familiar."

• What can I do to change formal relationships with young women executives to an informal process so that they can benefit from my ties to those in the senior management group who may be able to offer jobs, invitations to events, speaking engagements and so forth?

The old girls and old boys must help others coming along.

• Are the women executives held to the same standards of on-the-job performance or are they evaluated either more severely or more leniently than others?

Women's behavior, anger, and personalities must be kept under wraps. They do not dare transgress unwritten rules; their penalty will be more severe. For example, if men don't show up, it is assumed they are busy or at a more important meeting. Women can't afford to miss a meeting; their absence will be noted, and it will be assumed they are not interested or committed. Leniency is just as bad; men pass women along without making sure they have the skills or contacts to succeed. Then they tighten the rules just as women get to the top and say it was only a coincidence of timing that women came along just as they were doing it.

• How does the company demonstrate its commitment to women?

Demonstrate means the signs must be visible, recognized as substantive, and sincere. One researcher concluded that the strategies considered most effective in promoting women were quotas or numerical goals clearly set at the top of the corporation and carrying the full force of top management. Second, the opening of functional, line management jobs to women was seen as very important. Even the amount of training given to promising executives is an indicator of commitment. Enrollment at the most prominent senior-executive training programs offered by business schools is just 5 percent female, after peaking at 8 percent in the late 1980s.

• Is the company committed to a gender-balanced executive group?

Truth in confronting comfort level would probably result in a "no" answer. But we heard one story about a new CEO of a Fortune 500 company who announced at his first senior staff meeting, "As a worldwide multinational company, our future is imperiled with an all-white male senior executive group. We need an immediate and conscious recognition of the requirement for diversity at all levels of this company."

• What is the current rationale for the underrepresentation of women in the company and on the board?

Emphasize *current* rationale. Every year it changes. "We can't find any." Then the companies send back résumés of those who applied so they won't clog up the human resource files. "We have enough." A certain number is okay, but if there are too many women, the company (department, practice group, organization, profession) will become devalued. "We offered it to her but she turned us down." The executive group did nothing active to recruit her, to tell her she was wanted and why. So she got the message and didn't come. "The salary would be too high because there are so few out there." "It's institutional sexism; it's not *our* fault if there aren't enough qualified women in this area."

• How is the command of language and intellectual knowledge used to rationalize men's monopoly of the most prestigious and highest-paying positions?

Women just aren't plant managers (international currency traders, merger and acquisition specialists, deans of medical schools, insert your own category).

• What standards and practices shroud the gender politics of my company?

Our company has always paid for club memberships for top executives who then take clients golfing. The senior management group lunches together every Friday and we've all known each other since engineering school.

• In order to demonstrate a nonthreatening posture, do my colleagues resort to humorous jokes, frequent smiles, reasonably good performance reviews, and a noncommittal attitude about important issues that divide the executive group?

We do not encourage a culture of candor and openness; good manners and courtesy are valued more than truth telling.

• If bringing in business is part of the criteria for advancement, has the company reexamined "who gets credit" and how credit is recognized? Are diverse styles of operating valued equally? Is teamwork rewarded, or just individual achievement? Have women been offered training and access to avenues where new business might develop and are they supported by senior executives?

• Is the company sensitive to the physical safety of its women?

Have executives reexamined the time and location of work meetings and events and asked female employees and customers how the company can make them feel more comfortable?

• Do company executives, particularly public relations personnel, seek every opportunity to highlight its women executives and are women given opportunities for public exposure that will bring credit to them, the company, and their profession?

• If the company operates globally, are women given special training and an equal opportunity to try international assignments?

• Does the company support the activity of women's professional networks in a visible and enthusiastic manner, knowing that these networks are developing future corporate leaders?

• Does the company encourage its women executives to join mainstream professional organizations of which the company is a member, or does it reserve those memberships for its senior executive group only? Are women who are members backed with corporate contributions and assistance when they are asked to assume leadership positions?

- Have company executives studied the best family-friendly companies and asked experts for advice on how to change existing policies and practices to ensure that all employees are accommodated and allowed to work productively while enjoying a rewarding family life?

- Do senior managers personally know why every highly talented woman derails her career or quits the company?

In one survey, only 7 percent of those women who resigned from a corporation wanted to quit. The rest were frustrated by few opportunities to advance their career and left to join other employers.

- What do we do when we can no longer rely on human resources or an affirmative action policy to circumvent the old-boy social network in attaining jobs monopolized by men?

When faced with decisions at the senior levels, top executives generally exclude the involvement of human resource personnel and affirmative action policies. Those are only relevant at lower levels.

- Is my company headed by a corporate manager whose commitment to intellectual and social ideals is subordinate to the bottom line of the short-term financial statement?

Increasing productivity, earning customer loyalty, achieving rainmaking success, investing in human capital and restoring the social health of our community are necessarily long-term objectives.

- To what extent does the board of directors represent diversity?

Diversity of gender, geography, experience, broad-based leadership competencies, and point of view.

- What changes have been made during the last year to reroute the company's buying power to businesses, firms, bankers, and suppliers that are owned or include women in key positions?

Do we know? Do we care?

- In seeking customers, recognition, or support from institutional investors, how does the company interpret to its many audiences the goal of working to advance women in management and its commitment to social as well as economic improvement?

Few companies, institutions, or professions can remain profitable and grow if one half of society's population is declining economically. Executive women believe that recovery from the economic downturn must begin with recovery from the social recession because the health of American business is inextricably linked to the health of communities and families. Visionary business executives who understand that connection are beginning to communicate it to opinion leaders in the financial world.

The women we talked to throughout the process of writing this book expressed a compelling message. They intuitively expressed understanding of what will be required to achieve productivity and profitability. They made a case for business leadership coupled with a respect for and integration of strong social values critical to lasting economic excellence.

Senior executive women are ready to flex their economic muscle in The Club. They are part of a growing trend of six-figure-income households, estimated to be one in ten by the next century. These influential individuals have enough income to bypass social institutions, choosing private schools for their children and neighborhoods with guards at the gate, or they can use their money and power to influence social and economic policy at the local and national level, demanding a better society for all citizens. The women we spoke with are committed to work for a better society.

Unlike the stereotypical portrait of the superperformer, these senior executive women are involved with traditional women's volunteer activities such as their home-school associations, churches, and community elections. At the same time, they also hold great respect for the mission and core values of their male-dominated business organizations. Deference to the corporate culture and its mores is is not a lack of femininity or a denial of feminist values that are important to executive women. Nor does it mean that these women have accepted the corporate excesses that characterized the eighties Decade of Greed.

In the 1990s Decade of Vision, this dynamic combination of family and work values will enable corporate women to be better poised for leadership positions. Women like Sally Berger, Diane Capstaff, Elaine Ullian, Jacqueline Morby, and others know that the real reward of senior executive status is not limousines and golden parachutes, but the chance to make a difference in their own organizations and community.

Women have stood apart from the business community for years, preferring to influence policy outside the economic arena. Women studied issues, raised money, and made their opinions heard within the comfortable confines of the League of Women Voters, the American Association of University Women, the Nature Conservancy, and home-school associations. But although almost 50 percent of the work force is female, women generally have let men run the chambers of commerce.

Now, however, executive women who have made their mark in the world of capitalism feel it is their moment to lead—or at least share a leadership role. This new breed of female economic leaders will translate its values into the world of commerce. These leaders are no longer ceding leadership positions to men, rationalizing their absence with the notion that the issues of the business world do not concern them. Universal access to health care, literacy, and employment training for the disadvantaged, and energy self-sufficiency for the nation are as much issues for women as the quality of their local public schools. As businesses and their umbrella trade organizations expand their range of issues from those which directly concern their products or marketplace to a broad range of domestic programs affecting all citizens, women are realizing that to influence the debate, they must join the debaters.

They see that in the next wave of social action, the business community will again try to influence events, but unlike in past eras, the business community need not oppose economic programs that will help workers and their families. Likewise, those who advocate social programs need not oppose capitalism, but should work with the business community to design programs that will empower workers and their families in their enlightened self-interest.

In the nineties the focus will be on broad socioeconomic legislation that should allow capitalism to better compete in an international competitive economy. How executives can help move the nation out of its recession, pare the federal budget and trade deficits, and lift future taxpayers out of poverty are questions women are anxious to address.

Perhaps it is because women empathize with other women who are just one husband, job, or major illness away from poverty that they understand the effects of what has happened to the American economy in the past fifteen years. Those women know that even living the high life as a corporate executive does not mean individuals can buy family values, stable relationships, good education, crime-free neighborhoods, or adequate

health care. They are concerned that the living status for families has declined as fast as the gap between the rich and the poor has expanded.

These concerns are humanistic. Many women envision a system combining a free-market concern for liberty, individualism, and economic productivity with a broader social concern for community, responsibility, and
economic sufficiency.

It is essential that executive women add their voices to the debate.
Just as women have moved into positions of power in the business community, business leaders are gradually moving toward values that reflect a
concern beyond the bottom line. In an elegant, antebellum hotel nestled
in the Blue Ridge mountains of Virginia, one hundred chief executives—
all male—who comprise the Business Council listened attentively in 1991
as a panel of experts challenged them to expand their social commitments
to embrace issues of housing, transportation, preschool programs for poor
children, and nutrition aid. The power of this group, perhaps The Ultimate Club, to influence the nation's economy and the decision making of
elected officials is "little short of awesome," according to a business journal
that monitors them. Despite the fact that these business leaders were discussing important issues, the presence of women in the Business Council
might have added a valued dimension.

The power of these chief executive officers is replicated in every community, where companies use their money and power either to bring about
change or enforce the status quo. Enlightened companies are those that
are the moral leaders. Like the John Hancock Company, Stride Rite, and
others, they can lead by example, with innovative family-care programs
for employees. This is in stark contrast to a major national defense contractor that silenced employees for suggesting a review of defense spending
or a New York financial investment firm that reacted sharply when one of
its female stockbrokers advocated women for board membership on publicly held corporations.

We see a direct connection between the presence of more women in
corporate leadership positions and the success of American businesses. If
corporations and institutions, particularly those that deal with broad
masses of society, are to be effective in what they do, they must reflect
society, the marketplace in which they operate. Therefore they must include women and women's values. Corporations that are successful have a
connection *with* society, not isolation *from* it. They must look like the

community in which they operate, and its executives must understand the importance of adopting community values.

Women must be leaders in The Club if its members will determine how the next generation of workers and families will fare economically.

If that sounds like a feminist call to action, it is.

A NEW MODEL OF FEMINISM

It would be easy to believe that the few businesswomen who are leaders in the power structure of the community are nothing more than honorary men in skirts. For men still set the standards of behavior in the business world—educational credentials, career paths, corporate culture, and ethical values. If women are to participate, they presumably have one of two choices: to be equal to men and make it in "a man's world," or to be different than men, succeeding only with accommodations, or not participating at all.

Both points of view have limitations. Executive women who seek only equality find that equality can mean nothing more than accepting the lowest common denominator. The Rev. Suzanne R. Hiatt, one of the first eleven women ordained to the priesthood in the Episcopal church in 1974, called this self-examination the *Animal Farm* scenario. In the last scene of George Orwell's allegory about how revolutions fail, the barnyard animals wait outside while their representatives, the pigs, negotiate with the farmers. After a long wait, the animals peek in the window and see the pigs and the farmers playing cards. To their horror and disgust they realize they can no longer tell the pigs from the farmers.

"Several years ago," Hiatt said, "I did a series of sermonettes for a local television station, meditations broadcast at five A.M. daily, when the station goes on the air, as a public service. After the taping the director told me they were very good; indistinguishable in fact from sermonettes done by Father X, a notorious opponent of women priests. He meant to compliment me—Father X was an articulate man—but I was horrified. When you can no longer tell the women clergy from the men, we, like Orwell's animals, are in danger of a failed revolution."

But the opposite viewpoint isn't helpful either. Women who extol the superiority of female values centered on home, family, and the community (as opposed to what they see as primarily male values of short-term profits, development, and destruction) may feel better about being female, but they make real progress in the mainstream that much more difficult.

The "female as equal" or "female as different" choice is a trap.

The late feminist law professor Mary Jo Frug explained the importance of avoiding generalizations about women. "The first wave of feminist scholarship was concerned with getting women treated like men, and getting men's rights extended to women. But women are not all alike, either. We cannot be simplistic and propose one model for female behavior. Postmodern feminism acknowledges that while women have some commonalities, we also have many differences, including race and class . . . it's not just one 'different voice' we've been ignoring, it's many."

These many different voices can now be heard in the business world, but the women who have reached senior levels in the business world have not simply become men in skirts. Although in some cases they have achieved equal pay and rank with their male peers, it is too late to return to the liberal feminist position that the only thing women seek is equality. That notion would only leave women at status quo. Senior executive women believe that to be a feminist in the business world is not to be assimilated totally, to assume the male norm, to be able to get what a man has. And to be a feminist in the business world is also not to assert the superiority of those characteristics that make women different. To be a feminist in the business world is to be fully integrated into the economic arena, and to make the prevailing culture accommodating of many points of view, chipping away at the constraints of the comfort zone. This new model of feminism brings the women's movement that began in the sixties to its next, and hopefully final, stage.

THE THIRD STAGE: PARTNERSHIP FEMINISM

If most of the prevailing theories of feminism tend to isolate or separate women, putting them in opposition to the prevailing culture as they seek "equality," the next phase is one of partnership, combining traditional feminist thinking with an economic vision.

Partnership feminism, the third stage of the women's movement, espouses a concern for the community combined with pure pragmatism—integrating the feminist values of care and interdependence with the realities of the world of economics and productivity. Partnership feminists aspire to leadership in a capitalist society where neither sex dominates, but where men and women who hold similar values work together. Their goal is to sensitize the professional and business establishments to the notion that partnership is gender-neutral. They see this as possible, because if the clubhouse door is not fully open yet to the talents of partnership feminists, neither is it as tightly closed as before.

Partnership feminists believe the need for change in this third stage of the women's movement is as compelling as it was in the first and second stages. In the first stage, feminists sought equality and broke down barriers that had denied them access to positions of economic power. In the second stage, feminists reasserted their differences and demanded that feminine values be given equal consideration with the prevailing ones. In the third stage, partnership feminists will incorporate their value system into the world in which they work, encouraging men to share those values as well.

In this third stage of the movement, women see a connection between how they view the world and the economic power they wield. They are not unlike ecofeminists, who read the labels on toxic cleaners at the grocery store and recycle paper bags. Partnership feminists have become just as savvy, and are working from their leadership positions in the economic world to bring about change. In Chicago, Sally Berger has turned her revenue-raising skills to help Emily's List, and she has also been working directly with individual female candidates. In Boston, Diane Capstaff has helped make John Hancock a leader in family-centered employee benefits, even in recessionary times.

A few observers of popular culture in America have proclaimed that the women's movement has ended. If all battles haven't been won, most American women are no longer interested in fighting, they claim. They are only partially right. Many women are not interested in fighting because they don't envision goals that benefit society as requiring a war between the sexes. But the need for women to work with each other and with men to achieve those goals is greater than ever.

Anthropologist Mary Catherine Bateson touched upon the ideal of partnership feminism when she wrote in *Composing a Life*, "We must think of sustaining life across generations rather than accepting the short-term purposes of politicians and accountants." Bateson's is a model of human behavior that is win-win—"a way to flourish that will not be at the expense of some other community or the biosphere, to replace competition with creative interdependence." Her vision goes beyond the business community, but her concept is a good place to start.

Partnership feminism accepts the belief that women are the same *and* different. In the nineties, many women have the same biographies as men, with equivalent educational credentials, professional experience, and honors. Most institutions will be open to them, and hopefully few gender-based barriers will remain. Yet differences in communication and cognitive styles, values, socialization, relationships, motivations, psychological development, and personal styles are realities.

But partnership feminism works because differences are fading, as women approach what former Harvard Dean of Education Patricia Albjerg Graham calls "creeping androgyny." On the eve of the twenty-first century men are also ambivalent about the goals of the workplace, and also seek a balanced life. As insurance executive Susan Kiler said, "Some of the issues we face at the senior levels aren't just male-female. There are some great guys in the company who are inclusive, communicate well, and share my values—well, they're not going to make it either, because the 'fit' isn't there. They're not macho enough. We've got to figure out how to open up The Club for them, too."

Susan was echoing the views of Yelena Yershova of Moscow, who, like Sally Berger, Diane Capstaff, and others, is a member of the prestigious International Women's Forum, an association of highly accomplished women around the world. She explained why she welcomes men as partners.

"Everyone is objectively interested in the improvement of women's lives. What husband does not want a wife who is confident in herself and not irritated? What child does not want a kind mother who is not harassed by life, and what boss an energetic and competent woman employee?"

The galvanizing goal of the third stage is economic empowerment, and the challenge to all partnership capitalists is daunting. They are stepping forward in the business community to help reinforce and change the economic infrastructure for others. They know that if women are to be full participants in society at large, they need the power to shape the debate, and sufficient money in their hands to choose their own destiny.

The economic status of many women is fragile, even though they may work. Women are more likely to live in poor housing, and less likely to have health insurance coverage. Many women become poorer as they outlive their husbands; the poverty rate among women over sixty-five is 15 percent, and for older widows living alone 28 percent. Women are twice as likely as men to draw no pensions.

At the lower end of the scale, young women who are poor, abused, often illiterate, and certainly untrained for work are repeating cycles of poverty and dependence. A high school dropout with one or two children who is a female head of household has a cruel 89 percent chance of falling into poverty in the United States today. Twenty percent of all children are growing up in poverty, a 21 percent increase since 1970. One quarter of all babies are now born to single parents. These children face an even bleaker future, as 12 million children lack basic health insurance, and 15 million children have been abandoned by their fathers. These women and their children now comprise over three fourths of all persons living in poverty.

Unlike many industrialized nations against which America competes, the United States has no system of universal health care or child-care programs. The appalling inadequacy of literacy and public education, housing allowances, nutrition and early childhood programs is stalling the American economy, preventing men and women from being productive workers, and their children from envisioning a better future.

But these are not only women's issues, which is why women seek a partnership with men. The health of the American economy and the ability of U.S. citizens to compete globally will depend on tomorrow's workers—the children of today.

Goals such as a universal system of health insurance, early childhood programs, enforcement of child support, improving public education and literacy, and affordable housing will help ensure that parents are more productive workers and families thrive. To achieve these goals, partnership feminists realize the third stage of the women's movement will be played out in the businesses and organizations that influence policy debates on the state and federal level—in The Club. They might agree with artist Joan Erikson, who said, in *Composing a Life*, "I've never been a fighting feminist. But if we don't get into the councils of the mighty, we'll go on having wars. We've got to get the sense of what women stand for represented in the top echelons, because they're gonna kill us all. They just don't have what it takes to make for interdependence and interrelationship."

We've seen how women have progressed to senior executive positions—by rainmaking, by being visible and developing personal currency, by forging relationships in the business community at home and globally, and by assuming leadership positions in mainstream business organizations and corporate boards. We've revealed what they are doing to stamp their own imprint on the business and public world. The values held by these senior executive women mesh perfectly with the opportunities now presented to them at work. By working in traditional corporations and professions, they have more resources and a stronger platform to bring about change than if they were running their own small businesses or acting solely as community volunteers. It is true that the capitalist market system has done more than any other to improve the state of human welfare. But the challenge now is to attain societal and humanistic goals within such a system. The leadership of women will help achieve those goals and move the country assertively into the twenty-first century.

The goals of partnership feminism are long term. They are not only about helping individual women obtain membership in The Club. They are not only about helping improve the status of all women and their families. They are about securing a long-term future for society in which men and women can prosper as equal partners and contributors.

As women have obtained membership in The Club, they are becoming freed of the notion that they have to "go along to get along." They are liberated enough to become instruments of change. It is no longer true that the closer to power and money one gets, the more male is the environment. In a true partnership in The Club, the environment is gender neutral. Ethics and empathy will be as prevalent as efficiency and effectiveness.

Women's experience in the world of work and in The Club will help build the foundation of a new social climate, one in which one's personal experience is as valuable as the rules of society, one in which experiences of injustice and concern for others and a view of the community as a whole rather than a collection of individuals are paramount.

Our culture is beginning a shift toward partnership, toward rights *and* responsibilities, toward growth *and* preservation, toward competition *and* cooperation. The dynamic center of partnership feminism is not occurring in front of television cameras or in marches outside of gates; it is occurring quietly, in the realm of core values and community concerns. Women are building alliances and consensus in The Club about becoming a society of those who care for one another, not a society of the survival of the fittest.

In the future, men cannot function at their optimum alone, any more than women can or desire to do so. Together, these new members of The Club will eliminate the comfort zone and attain the goals of partnership feminism.

Economic empowerment is an imposing concept, but partnership feminists are serious about making it happen. They suggest that when full economic independence for all becomes a reality, there will no longer be a need for a "women's movement." The real coming of age for women will be when they are in a position to bring their skills, talents, vision, and leadership to The Club.

○   ○

THIRTY-EIGHT WAYS TO HELP WOMEN JOIN THE CLUB

A trade association executive who understands the power of collective action urged us to describe some steps that women's professional organizations can take to help more women move into The Club. "Be specific," she said. "We have to share our ideas about what works in the most clear manner!"

The following are the ideas of hundreds of executive women from many professional fields who know the techniques that work in developing female members of The Club. Some of them are self-evident; many groups are using some of them, but few groups have used every technique successfully. The women who suggested the ideas as a basic checklist saw no reason to hide the strategy and action points of women's organizations behind a "women only" facade of secrecy. In fact, they were anxious to share them, not only for the benefit of other women's organizations but also for corporate executives. When they are able to fully understand and enthusiastically endorse the activities of women's professional groups, it is more likely that they will welcome women not as "other" but as full members of The Club.

CHECKLIST FOR WOMEN'S ORGANIZATIONS

Up and Running

1. Direct the mission of the group narrowly; not "special interest" but focused. Keep testing it as conditions change. Some groups are designed solely for the professional advancement of their members but do not take positions on public issues. Others seek to influence the membership, conduct or advocacy position of a particular industry or profession.

2. Look as organized and professional as the most respected business organization in the community. Design and use a specific name, identification, and logo. Have a single address, phone number; develop bylaws and procedures for operating. Develop a directory of members. Establish the dues high enough to conduct the activities of the organization in a first-class manner (subsidizing younger or lower income members if necessary). Hire a professional office manager or staff if possible.

3. Develop a "telephone tree" of members for instant communication purposes. It will be useful for those days when a prominent international visitor arrives in town and the group's members arrange a hastily called lunch or when a legislative alert requires fast action by interested members.

4. Formulate a business plan for the group, with mission statement, goals, strategies, action points, benchmarks, and budget. Ideally, the plan should have one-, three-, and five-year horizons.

5. Strive to keep all members active on committees or task forces. Be inclusive rather than exclusive. Make it easy for members to participate. Delegate decision making and encourage a culture of rewards for decisions made and action taken, rather than second guessing at higher levels. The long-range planning committee should be among the most important.

6. Run programs but set aside time just to brainstorm problems and share observations. Experiment with formats, times, and locations. Invite prominent members of the business community to address the group as well as letting group members share their experiences. Plan and hold a retreat for members.

7. Identify a knowledgeable legislative agent and ask the agent to address the group to teach members about how the legislative and political process relates to the mission and goals of the group. Identify any legislative issues that are relevant to the mission of the group and develop a legislative strategy.

8. Identify outside counsel who specialize in work of the group's industry or profession or who are involved in issues relating to the group's mission. Ask them to brief the group on the legal issues that should be monitored or considered for intervention.

9. Identify the national women's professional group that is a counterpart to the group. Invite national leaders to meet with the group and formulate a relationship that is beneficial to both.

10. Identify the international women's professional group that is a counterpart to the group. Invite international leaders to meet with the

group, or send a delegation from the group to the international meeting, and formulate a relationship that is beneficial to both.

Developing Members

11. Identify group members who have leadership potential and an interest in moving ahead in The Club. Choose several each year for a personal "fast-track" support program. Formulate a development plan for each one to move them into the mainstream business and civic groups in which members of The Club participate.

12. Formulate a strategy to achieve publicity for several members in their own companies or organizations, if the culture of their working environment rewards participation and leadership in extracurricular industry groups.

13. Identify several members who have made significant professional contributions or achievements and feature them in a community-wide publicity campaign. Hire a publicist to design and execute it.

14. Send one or two top officers to leadership and business training programs.

15. Conduct a survey of the companies and professions of members. Identify the services and support that each member can contribute to the objectives of the group (charitable contributions, legal services, publicity, printing, accounting, etc.). Make the services available not only to the group but to other organizations in which members are involved or those targeted for influence by the group.

16. Monitor professional publications, periodicals, and newsletters of other organizations in the field and the general business press. Respond when appropriate in a timely manner with letters to the editor, guest articles, offers for speakers, congratulatory letters, and suggestions for joint programs. Plan a series of op-ed pieces for local trade magazines and newspapers that are read by professionals in the field, written by members. Develop a professional newsletter and mail it to community and opinion leaders as well as the membership. Seek to enlarge the mailing list each year.

17. Establish a mentoring program to match senior-level women with junior-level women.

18. Understand how business is given in the profession and in other fields and formulate a strategy to give business to other women. Learn how credit for new business is allocated. Identify a local directory of women in

business or women-owned businesses; if there is none, develop and print
one. Suggest each member give her personal and professional business to
other women; share information about firms or professional service providers that members are patronizing.

19. Develop links to other women's professional groups for the purpose of sharing business contacts and reciprocating business leads.

20. Develop an advisory team of lawyers, human resource specialists,
psychiatrists, public relations professionals, and others to provide confidential pro bono advice to members in cases of alleged sex discrimination.
Establish a defense fund to assist women who decide to press charges.

21. Compile data regarding civic, community, and business organizations that members support or on whose boards they serve as directors, including the purposes of these organizations and the identity of other directors.
Formulate a plan to support members' participation by publicizing activities
in the newsletter, publicizing achievements or elections of members, and purchasing tickets and attending fund-raising events to support the members.

22. Identify the key executive search firms in the industry or community. Formulate a plan to meet and establish an ongoing relationship with
the appropriate individuals in each firm. Introduce them to those members who have potential for advancement. Invite them to appropriate
functions and keep them informed about group activities and programs.

Outreach to the Community and The Club

23. Join a coalition of women's professional and community organizations. If there is none, help establish one. Assign a member as liaison to
the coalition, share information from the coalition with members, strategize how the coalition can further the group's objectives and the role the
group might play in assisting the coalition.

24. Identify the local corresponding mainstream professional organization of the group. Identify its key members of The Club. Establish a relationship between the group's senior members and the most influential
Club members. Identify the women who are members, directors, and officers of the mainstream group; are they all members of the women's group
as well? Encourage and support additional members of the group to join
and participate in the mainstream organization. Formulate a strategy to
strengthen the relationship between the groups.

25. Identify the primary business or industry reporter for each major news outlet in the community. Develop a mentoring program for selected members to get to know them and continue an ongoing relationship with them. Talk to them even when members do not have stories to give them. Using the telephone tree, identify members who will be willing to be quoted for attribution on various subjects of their expertise when the need arises.

26. Develop a speakers' bureau of members and publicize it.

27. Develop a standard speech for members so they all speak with one voice and message, furthering the group's objectives and mission.

28. Conduct an annual awards ceremony to honor the best corporations or institutions according to standards the group sets. Publicize it well, particularly to corporate leaders. Invite community leaders, political leaders, and the press.

29. Identify key academic institutions and departments and forge links to professors and researchers in the field. Invite them to join the group if appropriate. Understand what they are teaching and researching and see how members can assist them. Formulate a plan of outreach to students in the field or business.

30. Identify key activities, interests, and locations where members of The Club gather for events. Formulate a strategy to join them there, by buying a box at a sporting arena, participating in charity golf tournaments, volunteering for charity committees, buying tickets for political fundraisers or appearing at business symposia.

31. Identify key female legislators. Invite them to the group. Pair them with members. Keep up the relationship with them. Donate money to their campaign at a fund-raiser sponsored by the group and field volunteers at election time.

32. Identify the key committee chairmen and legislative leaders who affect the industry and the issues the group has identified as priorities. Focus on one or two issues of importance and formulate a legislative strategy to implement them. Meet regularly with the legislators.

33. Identify the key administrative department that impacts on the profession or the issues the group is following. Identify the senior official in the department, and invite him or her to the group. Develop a relationship with that individual and key staff members. Meet with them periodically, volunteer group members for advisory task forces, attend administrative hearings.

34. Identify the most effective and influential charities and social ser-

vice organizations in the community. How do they relate to the group's mission? Strategize ways for several members to interact or become involved with the organizations and their opinion leaders.

35. At the appropriate time, seek meetings for the officers with the editorial boards of local media outlets, to advocate a point of view or discuss the objectives of the group.

36. Write a book on a subject of concern to your members, even if the group must hire a ghostwriter. Use the publicity about the book to place members on radio and television talk shows and in the print press, discussing the mission of the group or a particular objective.

37. Compile a resource book of members or other women in the community qualified to serve on nonprofit and corporate boards. Print, publicize, and distribute it.

38. Form an outside committee of lawyers, venture capitalists, accountants, and others who will act as an advisory council for those members who want to pursue an entrepreneurial path. Formulate ways to support start-ups by members, including bringing them business.

PARTNERSHIP GOES TWO WAYS

This list should not be construed as executive women in their professional organizations trying desperately to be noticed and accepted in the mainstream world of business organizations and associations. Many of them are already there, leading The Club. But few of them earned the respect and authority of their professional peers by accident. They joined, worked hard, were recognized, and stepped up to leadership positions when the opportunity arose. Many women's organizations are now in the business of helping duplicate that series of events for other women.

At the same time, concerned executives of companies and business institutions are keeping an eye out for talented women to move up in their organizations, to join their teams, to serve on their boards, to join their business associations or civic organizations, or to introduce them to other women who might be potential business contacts. There is no better place for them to start than with the myriad of existing women's professional organizations. For men in the business community who want to make partnerships happen, executive women offer these suggestions:

1. Identify the women's professional organizations in your industry or business community.

2. Examine the mission of each one. How does it relate to the objectives of your company or the development of your personnel? How does it relate to the mission of the mainstream business organization of your profession?

3. Identify how many of your female executives are members of the group. Why or why not? Should you subsidize the membership dues (or part of it) for your executives?

4. Invite the officers of the group to meet your top executive team at breakfast or lunch. Invite them to address your entire executive group on an appropriate subject.

5. Understand the work of the organization's task forces. Is there any appropriate coordination possible with groups or departments inside your company or organization? Are there executives in your company with particular expertise who might offer to present a program to the organization or assist with a project?

6. Understand the legislative objectives of the organization. Are they compatible with or in opposition to the legislative concerns of your company or mainstream organization? Does that suggest a strategy?

7. What are the partnering relationships you can forge between your mainstream national or international organization and the women's group? Can you help facilitate them?

8. When you have an available position open in a particular department or seek a female candidate for your board of directors, invite the officers of the organization to help you identify suitable candidates.

9. Sharpen your own awareness of the inclusion of women by noticing their participation in every industry committee you serve on, every conference you participate in, every news article you read about your industry or profession, and every charity event you are asked to support. If there are none or only a few, suggest women you have met through the women's professional organizations.

10. Instead of going out to lunch again with your chief financial officer or partner, at least once a month make a point to invite out a woman in your industry or profession whom you have met through the organization. The agenda need be nothing more than "I wanted to get to know you better and catch up with your activities." End the lunch by saying, "How can I help you or your group?"

NATIONAL WOMEN'S PROFESSIONAL ORGANIZATIONS

Advertising Women of New York
153 E. 57th St.
New York, NY 10022
212–593–1950

Alliance of Minority Women for Business
and Political Development
c/o Brenda Alfrod
Brassman Research
PO Box 13933
Silver Spring, MD 20911–3933
301–565–0258

Alliance of Women Bikers
PO Box 484
Eau Claire, WI 54702

Alpha Pi Chi (minority)
PO Box 255
Kensington, MD 20895

American Agri-Women
c/o Sandy Greiner
Rt. 2, Box 193
Keota, IA 52248
515–363–2293

American Agri-Women Resource Center
c/o Marjorie Wendzel
785 N. Bainbridge Center
Watervliet, MI 49098
616–468–3649

American Association of Black Women
Entrepreneurs
909 Pershing Dr., Suite 207
Silver Spring, MD 20910
301–565–0258

American Association of University Women
1111 16th St. NW
Washington, DC 20036
202–785–7700

American Association of Women in
Community and Junior Colleges
Middlesex Community College
100 Training Hill Rd.
Middletown, CT 06457
203–344–3001

American Association of Women Dentists
401 N. Michigan Ave.
Chicago, IL 60611–4267
312–644–6610

American Association of Women Radiologists
1891 Preston White Dr.
Reston, VA 22091

American Business Women's Association
9100 Ward Pkwy.
PO Box 8728
Kansas City, MO 64114
816–361–6621

American Council for Career Women
c/o Joan Savoy
PO Box 50825
New Orleans, LA 70150
504–529–1116

American Council of Railroad Women
Norfolk Southern Corp.
185 Spring St.
Atlanta, GA 30303

American GI Forum Women
c/o Marianne Martinez
9948 S. Plaza, Apt. 1-D
Omaha, NE 68127
402–593–1248

American Medical Women's Association
801 N. Fairfax, #400
Alexandria, VA 22314
703–838–0500

American National Cattle Women
5420 S. Quebec
PO Box 3881
Englewood, CO 80155
303–694–0313

American News Women's Club
1607 22nd St. NW
Washington, DC 20008
202–332–6770

American Society of Mechanical Engineers
Auxiliary
345 E. 47th St.
New York, NY 10017
212–705–7746

American Society of Professional and
Executive Women
1511 Walnut St.
Philadelphia, PA 19102

American Society of Women Accountants
35 E. Wacker Dr., Suite 1068
Chicago, IL 60601
312–726–9030

American Women Composers
1690 36th St. NW, #409
Washington, DC 20007
202–342–8179

American Women in Radio and Television
1101 Connecticut Ave. NW, #700
Washington, DC 20036
202–429–5102

American Women's Clergy Association
214 P St. NW
Washington, DC 20001
202–797–7460

American Women's Society of CPAs
401 N. Michigan Ave.
Chicago, IL 60611
312–644–6610

Amit Women
817 Broadway
New York, NY 10003
212–477–4720

Asian-Indian Women in America
RD 1, Box 98
Palisades, NY 10964
914–365–1066

Association for Women Geoscientists
10200 W. 44th Ave., #304
Wheat Ridge, CO 80033
303–422–8527

Association for Women in Computing
41 Sutter St., #1006
San Francisco, CA 94104

Association for Women in Development
Virginia Tech.
10 Sandy Hall
Blacksburg, VA 24061–0338
703–231–3765

Association for Women in Mathematics
Wellesley College
PO Box 178
Wellesley, MA 02181
617–237–7517

Association for Women in Psychology
c/o Angela R, Gillem, Ph.D.
Haverford College
370 Lancaster Ave.
Haverford, PA 19041–1392

Association for Women in Science
1522 K St. NW, #820
Washington, DC 20005
202–408–0742

Association for Women in Sports Media
PO Box 4205
Mililami, HI 96789
714–733–0558

Association for Women Veterinarians
c/o Chris Stone Payne, DVM
32205 Allison Dr.
Union City, CA 94587
415–471–8379

Association of African-American Women
Business Owners
c/o Brenda Alford
Brasman Research
PO Box 13933
Silver Spring, MD 20911–3933
301–565–0258

Association of American Wives of Europeans
49 rue Pierre Charron
F-75008 Paris, France
1–42560524

Association of Black Women in Higher
Education
c/o Lenore R. Gall
Fashion Institute of Technology
Office of Vice President of Academic Affairs
227 W. 27th St., C-913
New York, NY 10001
212–760–7911

Association of Professional Insurance
Women
PO Box 752
Peckslip Station
New York, NY 10272
212–238–9258

Association of Women in Natural Foods
10159 Brooke Ave.
Chatsworth, CA 91311
818–718–6230

Association of Women Soil Scientists
c/o Marge Farber
PO Box 115
Anram, New York 12502
914–677–3194

Black Women in Publishing
PO Box 6275, FDR Station
New York, NY 10150
212–772–5951

Black Women's Educational Alliance
6625 Greene St.
Philadelphia, PA 19119

Black Women's Network
PO Box 12072
Milwaukee, WI 53212
414–562–4500

Business and Professional Women's Club
2012 Massachusetts Ave. NW
Washington, DC 20036
202–293–1100

Campus Ministry Women
802 Monroe
Ann Arbor, MI 48104
313–662–5189

Caucus for Women in Statistics
c/o Cynthia Struthers
St. Jerome's College
Waterloo, ON, Canada, N2L 3G3
519–888–4801

Coal Employment Project
17 Emory Pl.
Knoxville, TN 37917
615–637–7905

Coalition for Women in International
Development
c/o OEF International
1815 H St. NW, 11th fl.
Washington, DC 20006
202–466–3430

Coalition of Labor Union Women
15 Union Sq. W.
New York, NY 10003
212–242–0700

Comision Femenil Mexicana Nacional
379 S. Loma Dr.
Los Angeles, CA 90017
213–484–1515

Committee of 200
625 N. Michigan Ave., Suite 500
Chicago, IL 60611–3108
312–751–3477

Committee of Women in Asian Studies
Association of Asian Studies
Department of History
State University of New York, Albany
Albany, NY 12222
518–442–4800

Committee on Professional Opportunities
for Women
Biophysical Society
9650 Rockville Pike
Bethesda, MD 20814
202–727–2280

Committee on the Status of Women
American Philosophical Association
Department of Philosophy
University of Delaware
Newark, DE 19716
302–451–1112

Committee on the Status of Women
American Physical Society
335 E. 45th St.
New York, NY 10017
212–682–7341

Committee on the Status of Women
American Sociological Association
1722 N St. NW
Washington, DC 20036
202–833–3410

Committee on the Status of Women in
Economics
American Economic Association
Department of Economics
University of Arizona
Tucson, AZ 85721
602–621–6227

Committee on the Status of Women in
Linguistics
1325 18th St. NW, Suite 211
Washington, DC 20036
202–835–1714

Congressional Club
2001 New Hampshire Ave. NW
Washington, DC 20009
202–332–1155

Consortium of Doctors (minority)
University System
PO Box 20402
Savannah, GA 31404
912–354–4634

Coordinating Committee on Women in the
Historical Profession/Conference
Group on Women's History
c/o Lynn Weiner
527 Clinton
Oak Park, IL 60304
708–386–1829

Cosmetic Executive Women
217 E. 85th St., #214
New York, NY 10028
212–759–3283

Council for Women in Independent Schools
National Association of Independent
Schools
75 Federal St.
Boston, MA 02110
617–451–2444

Council of Women in Business
c/o National Business League (minority)
1629 K St. NW, #605
Washington, DC 20006
202–466–5483

Delta Phi Epsilon Professional Foreign
Service Society
1245 34th St. NW
Washington, DC 20007

Displaced Homemakers Network
1411 K St. NW, Suite 930
Washington, DC 20005
202–628–6767

Eleanor Association
1550 N. Dearborn Pkwy.
Chicago, IL 60610
312–664–8245

Electrical Women's Roundtable
PO Box 292793
Nashville, TN 37229–2793
615–870–1272

Eta Phi Beta (minority business)
c/o Elizabeth Anderson
1724 Mohawk Blvd.
Tulsa, OK 74110
918–425–7717

Executive Women International
Spring Run Executive Plaza
965 E. 4800 St., #1
Salt Lake City, UT 84117
801–263–3296

Federally Employed Women
1400 I St. NW, Suite 425
Washington, DC 20005
202–898–0994

Federated Women in Timber
2543 Mt. Baker Hwy.
Bellingham, WA 98226
206–592–5330

Federation of Organizations for
Professional Women
2001 S St. NW, Suite 500
Washington, DC 20009
202–328–1415

Federation of Woman's Exchanges
231 Brattle Rd.
Syracuse, NY 13203
315–472–2605

Feministas Unidas
2101 E. Coliseum Blvd.
Ft. Wayne, IN 46805
219–481–6836

Financial Women International
500 N. Michigan Ave., #1400
Chicago, IL 60611
312–661–1700

Financial Women's Association of New York
215 Park Ave. S., #2010
New York, NY 10003
212–533–2141

General Commission on the Status and Role
of Women (United Methodist Church)
1200 Davis St.
Evanston, IL 60201
708–869–7330

Graduate Women in Science, Inc.
Sigma Delta Epsilon
PO Box 4748
Ithaca, NY 14852

Hard Hatted Women
PO Box 93384
Cleveland, Ohio 44101
216–961–4449

Hispanic Women's Council
5803 E. Beverly Blvd.
Los Angeles, CA 90022
213–725–1657

Institute of Women Today
7315 S. Yale
Chicago, IL 60621
312–651–8372

International Alliance, an Association of
Executive and Professional Women
8600 LaSalle Rd., #308
Baltimore, MD 21204
301–321–6699

International Association for Personnel
Women
PO Box 969
Andover, MA 01810–0017
508–474–0750

International Association of Physical
Education and Sport for Girls and Women
c/o Ruth Schelberg
50 Skyline Dr.
Mankato, MN 56001
507–345–3665

International Association of Women
Ministers
c/o Rev. Carol S. Brown
579 Main St.
Stroudsburg, PA 18360
717–421–7751

International Association of Women Police
1401 Landwehr Rd.
Northbrook, IL 60062
718–721–6494

International Black Women's Congress
1081 Bergen St.
Newark, NJ 07112
201–926–0570

International Federation of Women Lawyers
186 5th Ave.
New York, NY 10010
212–206–1666

International Federation of Women's Travel
Organizations
4545 N 36th St., #126
Phoenix, AR 85018
602–956–7175

International League of Women Composers
670 Southshore Rd.
Pt. Peninsula
Three Mile Bay, NY 13693
315–649–5086

International Network for Women in
Enterprise and Trade
PO Box 6178
McLean, VA 22106
703–893–8541

International Registry for Religious Wo/men
Artists
1315 N. Van Ness Ave.
Fresno, CA 93728–1937
209–266–3812

International Society of Women Airline Pilots
PO Box 38644
Denver, CO 80238

International Women's Anthropology
Conference
Anthropology Dept.
25 Waverly Pl.
New York University
New York, NY 10003
212–998–8550

International Women's Fishing Association
PO Drawer 3125
Palm Beach, FL 33480

International Women's Forum
1146 19th St. NW, #600
Washington, DC 20036
202–775–8917

International Women's Writing Guild
Box 810, Gracie Station
New York, NY 10028–0082
212–737–7536

Iota Phi Lambda (minority business)
503 Patterson St.
Tuskegee, AL 36088
205–727–5201

Iota Sigma Phi (chemistry)
c/o Dr. Martha Thompson
Oregon Health Sciences University
Dept. of Physiology and Pharmacology
Portland, OR 97201
503–494–8770

Iota Tau Tau (law)
1505 Stovall Circle
Hartwell, GA 30643
404–376–9373

Kappa Kappa Iota (education)
1875 E. 15th St.
Tulsa, OK 74104
918–744–0389

Ladies Professional Bowlers Tour
7171 Cherrydale Blvd.
Rockford, IL 61112
815–332–5756

Ladies Professional Golf Association
2570 Vousin St., #B
Daytona, FL 32114
904–254–8800

Latin American Professional Women's
Association
3516 N. Broadway
Los Angeles, CA 90031
213–227–9060

Leadership Conference of Women Religious
of USA
8808 Cameron St.
Silver Spring, MD 20910
301–588–4955

Mexican American Women's National
Association
1030 15th St. NW, Suite 468
Washington, DC 20005
202–898–2036

Modern Language Association Women's Caucus
English Dept., Box 2000
University of Wisconsin, Parkside
Kenosha, WI 53141

Mothers' Home Business Network
PO Box 423
E. Meadow, NY 11554
516–997–7394

Municipal Bond Women's Club of New York
c/o Bethzaida Cruz
Asch-Dwyer Municipal Services
87 Main St., PO Box 315
Peapack, NJ 07977
908–781–6900

Na'amt USA
200 Madison Ave.
New York, NY 10016
212–725–8010

National Assembly of Religious Women
529 S. Wabash, Rm. 404
Chicago, IL 60605
312–663–1980

National Association for Female Executives, Inc.
127 W. 24th St.
New York, NY 10011
212–645–0770

National Association for Professional
Saleswomen
5520 Cherokee Ave., #200
Alexandria, VA 22312
703–256–9226

National Association for Women in Careers
PO Box 81525
Chicago, IL 60681–0525
312–938–7662

National Association for Women in Education
1325 18th St. NW, #210
Washington, DC 20036–6511
202–659–9330

National Association of Black Women
Attorneys
3711 Macomb St. NW, 2nd fl
Washington, DC 20016
202–966–9693

National Association of Black Women
Entrepreneurs
PO Box 1375
Detroit, MI 48231
313–341–7400

National Association of Collegiate Women
Athletic Administrators
c/o Chris Volez
University of Minnesota
Athletic Dept.
Minneapolis, MN 55455
612–624–8000

National Association of Cuban-American
Women of the USA
2119 S. Webster
Ft. Wayne, IN 46802
219–745–5421

National Association of Insurance Women—
International
1847 E. 15th St.
PPO Box 4410
Tulsa, OK 74159
918–744–5195

National Association of MBA Women
7701 Georgia Ave. NW
Washington, DC 20012
202–723–1267

National Association of Media Women
1185 Niskey Lake Rd. SW
Atlanta, GA 30331
404–344–5862

National Association of Minority Political
Women
6120 Oregon Ave. NW
Washington, DC 20015
202–686–1216

National Association of Minority Women in
Business
906 Grand Ave., #200
Kansas City, MO 64106
816–421–3335

National Association of Negro Business and
Professional Women
1806 New Hampshire Ave. NW
Washington, DC 20009
202–483–4206

National Association of Professional Asian-
American Women
PO Box 494
Washington Grove, MD 20880

National Association of Professional Saleswomen
PO Box 2606
Novato, CA 94948
415-898-2606

National Association of Railway Business
Women
c/o Carmen Taliaferro
2720 Mayfield Rd.
Cleveland Heights, OH 44106
216-321-0971

National Association of Women Artists
41 Union Sq.
New York, NY 10003
212-675-1616

National Association of Women Business
Owners
600 South Federal St., Suite 400
Chicago, IL 60605
212-922-0465

National Association of Women Highway
Safety Leaders
721 Dragoon St.
Mt. Pleasant, SC 29464-3020
803-884-7724

National Association of Women in
Chambers of Commerce
c/o Marie Davis Shope
PO Box 4552
Grand Junction, CO 81502-4552
303-242-0075

National Association of Women in
Construction
327 South Adams St.
Ft. Worth, TX 76104
817-877-5551

National Association of Women Judges
c/o National Center for State Courts
300 Newport Ave.
Williamsburg, VA 23187-8798
804-253-2000

National Association of University Women
1553 Pine Forest Dr.
Tallahassee, FL 32301
904-878-4660

National Association of Women Lawyers
750 N. Lake Shore Dr.
Chicago, IL 60611
312-988-6186

National Bar Association—Women Lawyers
Division
c/o Brenda Girton
1211 Connecticut Ave. NW, #702
Washington, DC 20036
202-291-1979

National Black Women's Consciousness
Raising Association
1906 N. Charles St.
Baltimore, MD 21218
301-727-8900

National Black Women's Political
Leadership Caucus
3005 Bladensburg Rd. NE, No. 217
Washington, DC 20018
202-529-2806

National Coalition of 100 Black Women
300 Park Ave, 2nd floor
New York, NY 10022
212-974-6140

National Coalition of Women's Art
Organizations
123 E. Beutel Rd.
Port Washington, WI 53074
414-284-4458

National Commission for Women's Equality
c/o American Jewish Congress
15 E. 84th St.
New York, NY 10028
212-879-4500

National Conference of Puerto Rico
Women
5 Thomas Circle
Washington, DC 20005
202-387-4716

National Council, Daughters of America
(insurance)
PO Box 154
Harrisburg, OH 43126
614-877-9462

National Council of Administrative Women
in Education
2335 Chatsworth Blvd.
San Diego, CA 92111
619–223–3121

National Council of Career Women
1223 Potomac St. NW
Washington, DC 20007
202–333–8578

National Council of Negro Women
1211 Connecticut Ave. NW, #702
Washington, DC 20036
202–659–0006

National Displaced Homemakers' Network
1625 K St. NW
Washington, DC 20006
202–628–6767

National Federation of Business and
Professional Women's Clubs, Inc., of USA
2012 Massachusetts Ave. NW
Washington, DC 20036
202–293–1100 or 202–393–5257

National Federation of Press Women
Box 99
Blue Springs, MO 64013
816–229–1666

National Foundation for Women Business
Owners
1825 I St. NW, Suite 800
Washington, DC 20006
202–833–1854

National Hook-Up of Black Women
c/o Wynetta Frazier
5117 S. University Ave.
Chicago, IL 60615
312–643–5866

National League of American Pen Women
1300 17th St. NW
Washington, DC 20036
202–785–1997

National Master Farm Homemakers' Guild
c/o Eleanor Straight
RR1, Box 72
Keosauqua, IA 52565
319–293–3266

National Network of Hispanic Women
12021 Wilshire Blvd., Suite 353
Los Angeles, CA 90025
213–225–9895

National Network of Minority Women
in Science
c/o American Association for Advancement
of Science
Directorate for Education and Human
Resource Programs
1333 H St. NW
Washington, DC 20005
202–326–6670

National Network of Women in Sales
710 E. Ogden Ave., Suite 113
Naperville, IL 60563
708–369–2406

National Organization for Women
1000 16th St. NW, Suite 700
Washington, DC 20036
202–331–0066

National Osteopathic Women Physicians
Association
c/o Marlene Wager D.O.
Grosvenor Hall #351
Athens, OH 45701
614–593–2259

National Pork Council Women
c/o National Pork Producers Council
PO Box 10383
Des Moines, IA 50306
515–223–2600

National Sorority of Phi Delta Kappa
(education)
8233 S. Martin Luther King Dr.
Chicago, IL 60619
312–783–7379

National Women Bowling Writer's
Association
8061 Wallace Rd.
Baltimore, MD 21222
410–284–6884

National Women's Political Caucus
1275 K St. NW, Suite 750
Washington, DC 20005
202–898–1100

National Women's Studies Association
c/o Deborah Lewis
University of Maryland
College Park, MD 20742–1325
301–405–5573

Newswomen's Club of New York
15 Gramercy Pk.
New York, NY 10003
212–777–1610

9 to 5, National Association of Working
Women
614 Superior Ave. NW, Rm 852
Cleveland, Ohio 44113
216–566–9308

Ninety-Nines—International Women Pilots
Will Rogers Airport
PO Box 59965
Oklahoma City, OK 73159
405–685–7969

North American Network of Women Runners
PO Box 719
Bala-Cynwyd, PA 19004
215–668–9886

Older Women's League
730 11th St. NW, Suite 300
Washington, DC 20001
202–783–6686

Organization of Chinese American Women
1300 N St. NW, Suite 100
Washington, DC 20005
202–638–0330

Organization of Pan Asian American Women
PO Box 39128
Washington, DC 20016

Priests for Equality
PO Box 5243
West Hyattsville, MD 20782
301–779–9298

Professional Women in Construction
342 Madison Ave., #451
New York, NY 10173
212–687–0610

Professional Women Photographers
c/o Photographics Unlimited
17 W. 17th St., No. 14
New York, NY 10011
212–255–9678

Professional Women's Appraisal Association
8383 E. Evans Rd.
Scottsdale, AZ 85260
602–998–4422

Republican Women of Capitol Hill
160B Longworth House Office Building
Washington, DC 20515
202–224–3004

Religious Network for Equality for Women
475 Riverside Dr., Rm. 812-A
New York, NY 10115
212–870–2995

Rockette Alumnae Association
c/o Fern Weizner
908 N. Broadway
Yonkers, NY 10701
914–423–3636

Roundtable for Women Food-Beverage-
Hospitality
145 W. 1st St., #A
Tustin, CA 92680

Roundtable for Women in Food Services
425 Central Park West
New York, NY 10025
212–865–8100

Rural American Women
50002 Old Jeanerette Rd.
New Iberia, LA 70560
318–367–3277

Ruth Jackson Orthopaedic Society
c/o Carole Murphy
222 S. Prospect Ave., #127
Park Ridge, IL 60068
708–698–1632

Section for Women in Public Administration
1120 G St. NW
Washington, DC 20005
202–393–7878

Section of Women in Legal Education of AALS
c/o American Association of Law Schools
1201 Connecticut Ave. NW, #800
Washington, DC 20036
202–296–8851

Sigma Delta Epsilon, Graduate Women in
Science
111 E. Wacker Dr., #200
Chicago, IL 60601
312–616–0800

Society for Women in Philosophy
c/o Peg Walsh
Bradford College
Dept. of Humanities
Bradford, MA 01835
508–372–7161

Society for Women in Plastics
PO Box 775
Sterling Heights, MI 48078–0775
313–949–0440

Society of Women Engineers
345 E. 47th St., Rm 305
New York, NY 10017
212–705–7855

Society of Women Geographers
1619 New Hampshire Ave. NW
Washington, DC 20009
202–265–2669

Sociologists for Women in Society
c/o Ms. Carla Howery
American Sociological Association
1722 N St. NW
Washington, DC 20036
202–833–3410

Southern Baptist Women in Ministry
2800 Frankfort Ave.
Louisville, KY 40206
502–896–4425

Status of Women in the Economics
Profession (AEA)
c/o Dr. Nancy Gordon
Congressional Budget Office
Second and D Streets SW, Rm. H2–418A
Washington, DC 20515
202–226–2669

Stuntwomen's Association of Motion Pictures
202 Vance
Pacific Palisades, CA 90272
213–462–1605

Task Force on Equality of Women in Judaism
838 5th Ave.
New York, NY 10021
212–249–6100

Tradeswomen, Inc.
PO Box 40664
San Francisco, CA 94140
415–821–7334

Unitarian Universalist Women's Federation
25 Beacon St.
Boston, MA 02108
617–742–2100

WAVES National
c/o Berenice George
PO Box 6064
Clearwater, FL 34618
813–447–0865

Whirly-Girls (International Women
Helicopter Pilots)
PO Box 584840
Houston, TX 77058–8484
713–474–3932

Woman's National Farm and Garden
Association
c/o Ms. William Slattery
PO Box 608
Northville, MI 48167
313–348–9175

Woman's Organization of the National
Association of Retail Druggists
666 W. Willow Glen St.
Addison, IL 60101
708–628–1729

Women Airforce Service Pilots WWII
PO Bos 9212
Ft. Wayne, IN 46899
219–747–7933

Women and Foundations/Corporate
Philanthropy
141 5th Ave., 7-S
New York, NY 10010
212–460–9253

Women and Mathematics Education
c/o Charlene Morrow
Mt. Holyoke College
302 Shattuck Hall
S. Hadley, MA 01075
413–538–2608

Women Band Directors National
Association
345 Overlook Dr.
W. Lafayette, IN 47906
317–463–1738

Women Chemists Committee
American Chemical Society
115 16th St. NW
Washington, DC 20036
202–872–4456

Women Church Convergence
c/o Loretto Staff Office
590 E. Lockwood Ave.
St. Louis, MO 63119
314–962–8112

Women Construction Owners and
Executives
PO Box 883034
San Francisco, CA 94188
415–467–2140

Women Educators
c/o Renee Martin
College of Education's Allied Professions
The University of Toledo
Toledo, OH 43606–3390
419–537–4337

Women Executives in Public Relations
PO Box 20766
New York, NY 10025–1516
212–721–9661

Women Executives in State Government
2000 M St., #730
Washington, DC 20036
202–293–7006

Women for Racial and Economic Equality
198 Broadway, Rm. 606
New York, NY 10038
212–385–1103

Women for Wine Sense
P.O. Box 2098
Yountville, CA 94599

Women Grocers of America
1825 Samuel Morse Dr.
Reston, VA 22090
703–437–5300

Women in Advertising and Marketing
11100 Whisperwood Lane
Rockville, MD 20852
301–493–5808

Women in Aerospace
6325 Rolling Mill Pl., No. 102
Springfield, VA 22152
703–866–0020

Women in Agribusiness
PO Box 10241
Kansas City, MO 64111

Women in Broadcast Technology
c/o Susan Elisabeth
2435 Spaulding St.
Berkeley, CA 94703
510–540–8640

Women in Cable
c/o PM Haeger & Assoc.
500 N. Michigan Ave., #1400
Chicago, IL 60611
312–661–1700

Women in Cell Biology
c/o Dr. Mary Lou King
University of Miami R-124
Dept. of Anatomy and Cell Biology
1600 NW 10th Ave.
Miami, FL 33101
301–496–7531

Women in Communications
2101 Wilson Blvd., Suite 417
Arlington, VA 22201
703–528–4200

Women in Energy
c/o Kim Fresher
555 N. Kensington
LaGrange Park, IL 70525
708–352–3746

Women in Film
6464 Sunset Blvd., #900
Hollywood, CA 90028
213–463–6040

Women in Fire Service
PO Box 5446
Madison, WI 53705
608–233–4768

Women in French
Department of Foreign Languages
Ball State University
Muncie, IN 47306
317–285–1374

Women in Government
c/o Joy Stone
1101 30th St. NW, Suite 500
Washington, DC 20006
202–625–3479

Women in Government Relations
1325 Massachusetts Ave. NW, #510
Washington, DC 20005–4171
202–347–5432

Women in Housing and Finance
655 15th St. NW, #300
Washington, DC 20005
202–639–4999

Women in Information Processing
Lock Box 39173
Washington, DC 20006
202–328–6161

Women in International Security
Center for International Studies
University of Maryland
School of Public Affairs
College Park, MD 20742
301–403–8109

Women in Literature and Life Assembly
National Council of Teachers of English
1111 Kenyon Rd.
Urbana, IL 61801
217–328–3870

Women in Management
2 N. Riverside Plaza, Suite 2400
Chicago, IL 60606
312–263–3636

Women in Mining International
1801 Broadway St., Suite 400
Denver, CO 80202
303–298–1535

Women in Municipal Government
National League of Cities
1301 Pennsylvania Ave. NW
Washington, DC 20004
202–626–3000

Women in Production
347 5th Ave., #1008
New York, NY 10016–5010
212–481–7793

Women in Sales Association
8 Madison Ave.
PO Box M
Valhalla, NY 10595
914–946–3802

Women in Scholarly Publishing
c/o Marilyn Campbell
Rutgers University Press
109 Church St.
New Brunswick, NJ 08901–1242
908–932–7396

Women in Science Committee
c/o New York Academy of Sciences
2 E. 63rd St.
New York, NY 10021
212–838–0230

Women in the Arts Foundation
1175 York Ave., Apt. 2G
New York, NY 10021
212–751–1915

Women Life Underwriters Confederation
1126 S. 70th St., #S-100
Milwaukee, WI 53214
800–776–3008

Women Make Movies
225 Lafayette St., #207
New York, NY 10012
212–925–0606

Women Marines Association
140 Merengo, No. 605
Forest Park, IL 60130
708–366–6408

Women of the Motion Picture Industry,
International
c/o Lili Beaudin
PO Box 900
Beverly Hills, CA 90213
213–203–4083

Women Officials
National Association of County Officials
440 1st St. NW
Washington, DC 20001
202–393–6226

Women Outdoors
55 Talbot Ave.
Medford, MA 02155

Women World War Veterans
Morgan Hotel
237 Madison Ave.
New York, NY 10016
212–684–678

Women's Alliance for Theology, Ethics and
Ritual
8035 13th St., Suites 1, 3, 5
Silver Spring, MD 20910
301–589–2509

Women's All-Star Association (bowling)
c/o Pearl Keller
29 Garey Dr.
Chappaqua, NY 10514
914–241–0365

Women's Aquatic Network
PO Box 4993
Washington, DC 20008
202–789–1201

Women's Army Corps Veterans Association
PO Box 5577
Ft. McClellan, AL 36205

Women's Campaign Fund
1601 Connecticut Ave. NW, Suite 800
Washington, DC 20009
202–234–3700

Women's Caucus
American Public Health Association
1015 15th St. NW
Washington, DC 20005
202–789–5600

Women's Caucus
National Education Association
1202 16th St. NW
Washington, DC 20036
313–373–1800

Women's Caucus
Speech Communications Association
5105 Backlick Rd., Suite E
Annandale, VA 22003
703–750–053

Women's Caucus for Art
Moore College of Art
20th The Parkway
Philadelphia, PA 19103
215–854–0922

Women's Caucus for Modern Languages
c/o Emily Toth
Louisiana State University
Dept. English—Women's Studies
Baton Rouge, LA 70803

Women's Caucus for Political Science
c/o Karen O'Connor
Emory University
Dept. of Political Science
Atlanta, GA 30322
404–727–6572

Women's Caucus of the Endocrine
Society
University of Maryland School of Medicine
Dept. of Physiology
655 W. Baltimore St.
Baltimore, MD 21201
301–328–3851

Women's Caucus: Religious Studies
American Academy of Religion
2529 Elm St.
Youngstown, OH 44505
216–742–1625

Women's Classical Caucus
c/o Prof. Barbara McManus
5 Chester Dr.
Rye, NY 10580
914–698–5798

Women's Council of Realtors of the National Association of Realtors
430 N. Michigan Ave.
Chicago, IL 60611
312–329–8483

Women's Council on Energy and the
Environment
PO Box 33211
Washington, DC 20033
202–822–6755

Women's Direct Response Group
224 7th St.
Garden City, NY 11530
516–746–6700

Women's Issues, Status and Education
(American Association for Adult and
Continuing Education)
c/o Ellen Ironside
Meredith College
Raleigh, NC 27607
919–829–8353

Women's Jewelry Association
11 2nd Ave.
New Hyde Park, NY 11040
516–326–1369

Women's Legal Defense Fund
200 P St. NW, #400
Washington, DC 20036
202–887–0364

Women's National Book Association
160 5th Ave., #604
New York, NY 10010
212–675–7805

Women's National Democratic Club
1526 New Hampshire Ave. NW
Washington, DC 20036
202–232–7363

Women's National Farm and Garden
Association
2230 Quail Lake Rd.
Findlay, OH 45840
419–422–2466

Women's Network
National Conference of State Legislators
1560 Broadway, Suite 700
Denver, CO 80202
303–830–2200

Women's Overseas Service League
c/o Colonel Doris M. Cobb
7400 Crest Way, #917
San Antonio, TX 78239
512–654–8296

Women's Professional Racquetball Association
153 S. 15th St.
Souderton, PA 18964
215–723–7356

Women's Professional Rodeo Association
Rt. 5, Box 698
Blanchard, OK 73010
405–485–2277

Women's Rights Committee (American
Federation of Teachers)
c/o Human Rights Dept.
555 New Jersey Ave. NW
Washington, DC 20001
202–879–4400

Women's Tennis Association
133 1st St. NE
St. Petersburg, FL 33701
813–895–5000

Women's Transportation Seminar-National
808 17th St. NW, #700
Washington, DC 20006–3953
202–223–9669

NOTES

INTRODUCTION

p. xiii. *Project:* Our project was interdisciplinary. As historians, we wanted to tell the story of women, to let their own narrative speak to the experience of other women. Carolyn Heilbrun has warned that we must document the experience of women and we agree. Economic historians who will chronicle this era will be missing a story if they omit the vision of women and the voices of those who have held leadership roles in our business institutions. See Carolyn Heilbrun, *Writing a Woman's Life* (New York: Ballantine Books, 1988).

As journalists, we were asking questions that were different than what other reporters might have asked. We wanted to know if the language of the economic world and the language of feminism shared any common words, values, or ideas.

As social scientists, we wanted to investigate the difference between the sexes in the business world. Can women reconcile these differences if they think their professional success will only come in male environments, assuming male models, following rules of the game set by men?

Finally, as "business anthropologists," we were observing successful women whose values and opinions we respected. We conducted soft research, uncovering common themes and language of women in senior positions that allowed us to draw conclusions about the nature and challenge of their professional activities and goals. As business anthropologists, we knew that we were looking at a unique tribe. We could have written an entire book on the topic from the perspective of just one woman—our own Iacocca or Trump, as it were. Instead, we self-selected a broad cast of women whose thoughts we wanted to share, women whom we felt had something of value to communicate to the businesses and professions willing to hear them and to other women. For as women speak, so do they empower others. See Ursula LeGuin, "Bryn Mawr Commencement Address," in *Dancing at the Edge of the World* (New York: Grove Press, 1989).

p. xiv. *Behavior:* Betty Lehan Harragan, *Games Mother Never Taught You: Corporate Gamesmanship for Women* (New York: Warner Books, 1977).

Techniques: Nathaniel Stewart, *The Effective Woman Manager: Seven Vital Skills for Upward Mobility* (New York: John Wiley & Sons, Inc., 1978); Margaret Fenn, *In the Spotlight: Women Executives in a Changing Environment* (Englewood Cliffs, N.J.: Prentice-Hall, 1980); Helen J. McLane, *Selecting, Developing and Retaining Women Executives: A Corporate Strategy for the Eighties* (New York: Litton Educational Publishing, Inc., 1980); Alice G. Sargent, *The Androgynous Manager* (New York: AMACOM, 1981); Nancy Lee, *Targeting the Top: Everything a Woman Needs to Know to Develop a Successful Career in Business, Year After Year* (Garden City, N.Y.: Doubleday & Co., Inc. 1980); Ann McKay Thompson and Marcia Donnan Woods, *Management Strategies* for Women or Now That I'm Boss, How Do I Run This Place? (New York: Simon & Schuster, 1980); Peggy Van Hulsteyn, *What Every Business Woman Needs to Know to Get Ahead* (New York: Dodd Mead & Co., 1982); Margaret Hennig and Anne Jardim, *The Managerial Woman: The Survival Manual for Women in Business* (New York: Pocket Books, 1976); Jinx Melia, *Breaking into the Boardroom* (New York: G.P. Putnam's Sons, 1986); Melody Sharp Quarnstrom, *Getting on Top* (Los Angeles: Price Stern Sloan Inc., 1988); Jo Foxworth, *Boss Lady: An Executive Woman Talks About Making It* (New York: Hawthorn Books, Inc., 1979).

"Why Women . . . ": Jacyn Fierman, "Why Women Still Don't Hit the Top," *Fortune,* July 30, 1990. The story didn't get much better two years later. See Anne B. Fisher, "When Will Women Get to the Top?," *Fortune,* September 21, 1992, p. 45.

Naysayers: Sarah Hardesty and Nehama Jacobs, *Success and Betrayal: The Crisis of Women in Corporate America* (New York: Franklin Watts, 1986); Tara Roth Madden, *Women v. Women* (New York: AMACOM, 1987); Kathleen Hirsch, "Women vs. Women," *Boston Globe Magazine,* May 20, 1990; Edith Gilson with Susan Kane, *Unnecessary Choices: The Hidden Life of the Executive Woman* (New York: William Morrow and Co., 1987); Susan Fraker, "Why Women Aren't Getting to the Top," *Fortune,* April 16, 1984; Colette Dowling, *The Cinderella Complex: Women's Hidden Fear of Independence* (New York: Pocket Books, 1981); Mary Ann Mason, *The Equality Trap: Why Women Shouldn't Be Treated Like Men* (New York: Touchstone Books, 1988); Barbara Bools and Lydia Swan, *Power Failure* (New York: St. Martin's Press, 1989).

p. xv. *Popular backlash:* Ruth Sidel, *On Her Own: Growing Up in the Shadow of the American Dream* (New York: Viking Penguin, 1990); Susan Faludi, *Backlash: The Undeclared War Against American Women* (New York: Crown Publishers, Inc., 1991); Nancy Gibbs, "The War Against Feminism," *Time,* March 9, 1992, p. 50.

CHAPTER 1: OPENING THE CLUBHOUSE DOOR

p. 1. *Tom Peters:* Tom Peters, "The Best New Managers Will Listen, Motivate, Support," *Working Woman,* September 1990, p. 142.

45 percent: U.S. Department of Labor, Women's Bureau, "Facts on Working Women," No. 89–4, December 1989, p. 1.

54 million: Sylvia Nasar, "Women's Progress Stalled? Just Not So," *New York Times,* October 18, 1992, p. F1.

40 percent: Daphne Spain, "Women's Demographic Past, Present and Future," paper presented for the Radcliffe Conferences on Women in the 21st Century, Defining the Challenge: Emerging Needs and Constraints, Cambridge, Massachusetts, December 1–3, 1988; Margaret H. Marshall, "Not by Numbers Alone: A New Decade for Women in the Law," *New England Journal of Public Policy,* Spring/Summer 1990.

p. 2. *34 percent:* Nancy J. Perry, "If You Can't Join 'Em, Beat 'Em," *Fortune,* September 21, 1992, p. 58. But business schools are beginning to become alarmed at trends that suggest this number may represent peak enrollments. At Northwestern's Kellogg School, women constituted just 27 percent of the class entering in the fall of 1992, a ten-year low; at the UCLA's Anderson School, which had an enrollment of 40 percent women in 1985, the figure was down to 30 percent in 1992. Reasons for the drop in enrollment range from a desire to combine work and family life to an expectation that despite an M.B.A. degree, women will still face the glass ceiling. Gilbert

Fuchsberg, "Female Enrollment Falls in Many Top M.B.A. Programs," *Wall Street Journal*, September 25, 1992, p. B1; Alison Leigh Cowan, "For Women, Fewer M.B.A.'s." *New York Times*, September 27, 1992, p. F4.

6.1 million: Anne B. Fisher, "When Will Women Get to the Top?," *Fortune*, September 21, 1992, p. 47.

41 percent: Anne B. Fisher, "When Will Women Get to the Top?," *Fortune*, September 21, 1992, p. 45.

Glaringly underrepresented: U.S. Department of Labor, "A Report on the Glass Ceiling Initiative," 1991; and Korn/Ferry International and UCLA's John E. Anderson Graduate School of Management, "Korn/Ferry International's Executive Profile 1990: A Survey of Corporate Leaders," 1990. For example, women represent just 8.6 percent of dentists, 7.6 percent of engineers, and 3 percent of top executives, according to one analysis. Sylvia Nasar, "Women's Progress Stalled? Just Not So," *New York Times*, October 18, 1992, p. F1. The percentage of female officers in the country's fifty largest companies shot up to 5.1 percent in 1992, report researchers. "Bits," *Director's Monthly*, December 1992, p. 13.

500: "Slow Progress," *Wall Street Journal*, December 17, 1991, p. 1.

Top jobs: "Few Women Found in Top Public Jobs," *New York Times*, January 2, 1992, p. 11.

10 percent: A 1992 survey noted that the progress of women in the federal government has been so slow that women are likely to be underrepresented in the top jobs for more than the next twenty-five years. U.S. Merit Systems Protection Board, "A Question of Equity: Women and the Glass Ceiling in the Federal Government," Washington, D.C., 1992; "'Glass Ceiling' for Women," *News-Press*, October 29, 1992, p. A8. See also Statement of Honorable Constance Berry Newman, director, Office of Personnel Management, before the Committee on Governmental Affairs of the U.S. Senate, October 23, 1991.

$20,656: Sylvia Nasar, "Women's Progress Stalled? Just Not So," *New York Times*, October 18, 1992, p. F1. See "The Gender-Wage Gap," *Working Woman*, January 1993, p. 43. Female bank tellers and statistical clerks earned 92 percent of a male wage in 1991, but female physicians, lawyers, and financial managers still lagged, at 54, 75, and 59 percent of male salaries, respectively.

College graduate: Susan Faludi, *Backlash: The Undeclared War Against American Women* (New York: Crown Publishing Co., Inc., 1991), p. xii; "Unequal Equals," *News Press*, November 14, 1991, p. A13.

Four times: Reuters, "Women-Owned Firms Show 57% Increase," *Boston Globe*, October 3, 1990, p. 67.

30 percent: Reuters, "Women-Owned Firms Show 57% Increase," *Boston Globe*, October 3, 1990, p. 67. The 30 percent figure has received great media attention, but the real number may be 9 percent. There were 5.4 million women-owned businesses filing IRS tax returns in 1991, but only 618,000 had more than one employee.

"Glass ceiling:" See Carol Hymowitz and Timothy D. Schellhardt, "The Glass Ceiling," *Wall Street Journal*, March 24, 1986, sec. 4, p.1; Jean R. Haskell, "Through the Glass Ceiling? A New

Look at Women in the Corporate World" (Philadelphia: Haskell Associates, 1990); Ann M. Morrison, Randall P. White, Ellen Van Vestor, and the Center for Creative Leadership, *Breaking the Glass Ceiling: Can Women Reach the Top of America's Largest Corporations?* (Reading, Mass.: Addison-Wesley Publishing Co., Inc., 1987); Patti Doten, "Beyond Corporations' 'Glass Ceiling,'" *Boston Globe*, August 31, 1989, p. 79; U.S. Department of Labor, "A Report on the Glass Ceiling Initiative," 1991; Susan B. Garland, with Lisa Driscoll, "Can the Feds Bust Through the 'Glass Ceiling'?," *Business Week*, April 29, 1991, p. 33; Albert R. Karr, "Labor's Martin Is Out to Break 'Glass Ceiling,'" *Wall Street Journal*, August 9, 1991, p. B1; Knight-Ridder Newspapers, "'Ceiling' Blocks Women, Minorities, Study Says," *Providence Journal*, August 9, 1991, p. A1; Ruth E. Fitch, "The Glass Ceiling in Need of Shattering," *Boston Business Journal*, June 24, 1991, p. 18; Cathy Taylor, "Through the 'Glass Ceiling,'" *ADWEEK*, March 18, 1990, p. 18; Cindy Skrzycki and Frank Swoboda, "Breaking the Corporate 'Glass Ceiling,'" *Washington Post*, June 14, 1991, p. 6; Peggy Simpson, "How Lynn Martin's Career Will Affect Yours," *Working Woman*, October 1991, p. 86.

p. 5. *Prominent:* For example, Marion Wright Edelman of the Children's Defense Fund would surely be considered a member of the Washington "Club" in the Clinton-Gore administration, and yet she holds no cabinet or top executive post. Through her distinguished work as head of the Fund, she has influenced many individuals who will be setting economic and social policy for the country.

p. 6. *Secret lore:* R. Richard Ritti and G. Ray Funkhouser, *The Ropes to Skip and the Ropes to Know* (Columbus, Ohio: GRID, Inc., 1977), pp. 2–3.

Is open: The profile of prominent opinion and community leaders in other cities shows that women are gaining membership in The Club. While Kathy Whitmire was mayor of Houston (1981–91), women held the offices of police chief, district chief of county hospitals, superintendent of schools, president of the chamber of commerce, and president of the University of Houston. In Colorado, in 1991, the state treasurer, state attorney general, secretary of state, eight of Denver's thirteen city council chairs, and the heads of the Colorado Association of Commerce and Industry, the Greater Denver Chamber of Commerce, and the Greater Denver Corporation for Economic Development were all women. Patricia Aburdene and John Naisbitt, *Megatrends for Women* (New York: Villard Books, 1992), p. 9.

p. 7. *Who Rules . . . :* Boston Urban Study Group, *Who Rules Boston?* (Boston: The Institute for Democratic Socialism, 1984).

Similar: The chamber is "one business voice among many" (p. 45); the Greater Boston Real Estate Board "fills an unusual niche in the Boston power structure" (p. 52); The Boston Municipal Research Bureau's "chairmen and board members have been drawn from the city's business elite" (p. 54); "When the Massachusetts Business Roundtable speaks, people listen" (p. 58); Associated Industries of Massachusetts is "the single largest business association in the state . . . a very effective player in Massachusetts politics" (p. 61); the Massachusetts High Technology Council is "a commanding presence in the state's political arena" (p. 61); the Massachusetts Taxpayers Foundation "speaks with a quiet, but powerful voice for the blue-chip business community" (p. 64), *Who Rules Boston?* (Boston: The Institute for Democratic Socialism, 1984).

p. 9. *2466:* Karen Ball, "Study: Less Than 3% of Fortune 500 Top Jobs Go to Women," *Boston Globe*, August 26, 1991, p. 13. Accurate figures are difficult to agree upon. A report from the Department of Labor showed that among 90,000 federal contractors, women accounted for 25 percent of the total officials and managers in 1991, up from 18 percent in 1981. However, the category of "officials and managers" is so broadly defined that it includes heads of clerical pools and janitorial services. See Albert R. Karr, "Progress Is Reported in Labor Agency's Effort to Crack Corporate 'Glass Ceiling,'" *Wall Street Journal*, August 12, 1992, p. A8. When senior-level managerial positions are counted, the percentage of women in 1991 drops to less than 5 percent. See Anne B. Fisher, "When Will Women Get to the Top?," *Fortune*, September 21, 1992, p. 46. Another study of women "officers" in Fortune 50 companies showed the percentage to be 5.1 percent. "Women Officers Make Big Gains in Corporations," *Wall Street Journal*, September 8, 1992, p. A1.

Men: In the eight years of his presidency, Ronald Reagan appointed 385 federal judges, of whom only 31 were women.

Okin: Christina Robb, "A Tough, Brilliant Study of Justice and How Gender Affects It," *Boston Globe*, December 15, 1989, p. 74.

p. 10. *Allen:* Jolie Solomon, "Taking a Stand," *Boston Sunday Globe*, July 21, 1991, p. 45.

Feminism: There are many excellent books about the origin of modern-day feminism and its many variations. See Flora Davis, *Moving the Mountain, the Women's Movement in America Since 1960* (New York: Simon & Schuster, 1991); Nancy Cott, *The Grounding of Modern Feminism* (New Haven: Yale University Press, 1987); Betty Friedan, *The Feminine Mystique*, with new introduction and epilogue (New York: Dell, A Laurel Book, 1974); Betty Friedan, *It Changed My Life: Writings on the Women's Movement* (New York: Norton, 1985); Betty Friedan, *The Second Stage* (New York: Summit Books, 1986); Wendy Kaminer, *A Fearful Freedom: Women's Flight from Equality* (Reading, Mass.: Addison-Wesley Publishing Co., Inc., 1990); Elizabeth Spelman, *Inessential Woman: Problems of Exclusion in Feminist Thought* (Boston: Beacon Press, 1988). The most comprehensive source for books, periodicals, papers, oral history, photographs, letters, and unpublished materials about women's history, including feminism, is the Arthur and Elizabeth Schlesinger Library on the History of Women in America at Radcliffe College, Cambridge, Massachusetts. The authors acknowledge with gratitude the collection and staff of this distinguished library.

p. 13. *Frug:* Professor Frug was one of a group of feminist legal theory scholars. See Tamara Lewin, "Feminist Scholars Spurring a Rethinking of Law," *New York Times*, September 30, 1988, p. B9. Among Frug's works are "Securing Job Equality for Women: Labor Market Hostility to Working Mothers," *Boston University Law Review* 59, page 55 (1979), and "Re-Reading Contracts: A Feminist Analysis of a Contracts Casebook, 1985," *American University Law Review* 1065 (1985).

16 percent: Paula Kamen, "Feminism, a Dirty Word," *New York Times*, November 23, 1990, p. A15. See also Wendy Kaminer, *A Fearful Freedom: Women's Flight from Equality* (Reading, Mass.: Addison-Wesley Publishing Co., Inc., 1990).

40 percent: Edith Gilson, with Susan Kane, *Unnecessary Choices: The Hidden Life of the Executive Woman* (New York: William Morrow and Co., 1987).

p. 14. *Stripes:* Feminist classifications now fit all points of view. Generally, gender feminists seek an androgynous culture in which maternal responsibility for children is eliminated, since it only serves to oppress women and perpetuate gender biases. Radical or cultural feminists focus on the biological-based domination of women by men, and reject the goal of equal treatment in a patriarchal culture. This "big picture" feminism reexamines the very assumptions of modern-day culture, from faith in technological progress to militarism. (Battered women's shelters and equal pay initiatives are only bandages on a fundamentally flawed society, they would assert.) Even traditional religious views have been complemented by a feminist spirituality movement, celebrating the relationship between women and nature. Socialist feminists may agree with their radical sisters that capitalist patriarchies, with their primarily male values and power structure, are undesirable, but they are not as discouraged about the future. They maintain the cultures that developed because of the socialization of men and women in time can be changed toward some form of an egalitarian state. But there are also those who have criticized the woman-as-different or female-as-nurturer schools of thought, saying that gender issues are not a matter of difference or socialization but of power.

p. 24. *Fear power:* See Xandra Kayden, *Surviving Power, The Experience of Power—Exercising It and Giving It Up* (New York: The Free Press, 1990).

Horner: The fear of success may have been replaced by an ever more exhausting circle of high expectations and guilt. While professional accomplishment and femininity were once viewed as mutually exclusive, now many women simply feel overburdened by the stresses of work and family. See Matina Horner, "The Changing Challenge, From Double Bind to Double Burden," *New England Journal of Public Policy*, Spring/Summer 1990, p. 47.

Not worried: Contrast executive women portrayed in such books as Liz Roman Gallese, *Women Like Us* (New York: William Morrow and Co., 1985), and Edith Gilson, with Susan Kane, *Unnecessary Choices: The Hidden Life of the Executive Woman* (New York: William Morrow and Co., 1987).

Different view: In a longitudinal study of AT&T managers, research scholars Ruth Jacobs and David McClelland observed that men and women seemed to view power differently. Upper-level women managers more often described power as a resource that could be shared with others, but upper-level male managers viewed power as a way to control others. Nancy Kressin, "Moving Up the Corporate Ladder," *Radcliffe News*, Summer 1992, p. 7.

p. 25. *More power:* Actually, as Elizabeth Spelman argues, the use of less power shows more power: "To tolerate your speaking is to refrain from exercising the power I have to keep you from speaking. In tolerating you I have done nothing to change the fact that I have more power and authority than you do. And of course I don't have to listen to what you say." Elizabeth V. Spelman, *Inessential Woman: Problems of Exclusion in Feminist Thought* (Boston: Beacon Press, 1988), p. 182.

Negotiators: Dana Jack and Rand Jack, "Women Lawyers: Archetype and Alternatives," in *Mapping the Moral Domain*, Carol Gilligan, Janie Ward, Victoria Taylor, and Jill McLean, eds. (Cambridge: Harvard University Press, 1988). Phyllis Bonanno, corporate staff vice president of WARNACO, Inc., described her experience as a U.S. trade representative: "Women negotiators don't have to put their egos on the line all the time. If there was a woman in another trade delegation, she and I could go off and resolve the problems." Contrast this with the old advice to act more like a man and be tough, e.g., Melody Sharp Quarnstrom, *Getting on Top* (Los Angeles: Price Stern Sloan, Inc., 1988).

Thinking smart: Liz Roman Gallese, "Why Women Aren't Making It to the Top," *Across the Board*, August 1991, pp. 19–22.

1990 study: Russell Reynolds Associates, Inc., "Men, Women and Leadership in the American Corporation," November 1990; and Lori Hough, "Study Reports Women More Adept as Leaders," *Boston Business Journal*, January 7, 1991, p. 14.

p. 28. *Pressure:* See Caryl Rivers, "The Affirmative-Action Gender Gap," *Boston Globe*, September 9, 1991, p. 15.

p. 29. *Right industry:* Contrast the usefulness of that advice to what many women believe, that career progress is due to factors outside a woman's control or simply a matter of luck. See Jacqueline Landau and Lisa Amoss, "Myths, Dreams and Disappointments: Preparing Women for the Future," in *Not as Far as You Think: The Realities of Working Women*, Lynda L. Moore, ed. (Lexington, Mass.: D.C. Heath and Co., 1986).

p. 30. *Large:* Some women conclude that the entire male business culture is hostile to women, as if the culture itself is a unified, monolithic institution rather than a collection of individual managers with varying degrees of skill. Negative headlines that feature large companies such as Texaco only help perpetuate this notion. See Allanna Sullivan and Arthur S. Hayes, "Woman Gets $6.3 Million in Sex-Bias Case," *Wall Street Journal*, September 27, 1991, p. B3.

Flatter: In many large companies, traditional "command and control" styles of management are giving way to cross-departmental teams, centrarchies, and informal work structures for free-agent problem solvers. See Robert B. Reich, *The Work of Nations* (New York: Knopf, 1991); Conall Ryan, "Where Values and People Are Portable," *New York Times*, August 18, 1991, p. F11; Robert M. Tomasko, "Redefining the Corporation," *PRISM* (Cambridge, Mass.: Arthur D. Little, Inc., 1990), pp. 33–49; Rosabeth Moss Kanter, "The New Managerial Work," *Harvard Business Review*, November/December, 1989; Rosabeth Moss Kanter, *When Giants Learn to Dance: Mastering the Challenges of Strategy, Management and Careers in the 1990's (New York: Simon & Schuster, 1989)*; Anne Jardim and Margaret Hennig, "The Last Barrier: Breaking into the Boys' Club at the Top," *Working Woman*, November 1990.

p. 31. *Enrollments:* One think tank predicted a "female meritocracy/gerontocracy unlike anything we have ever seen before," as the number of well-educated women begins to exceed the number of men. Women have been outnumbering men attending higher educational institutions since 1979, not only at the bachelor degree level, but at the masters and doctorate level as well. Southport Institute for Policy Analysis, "Memorandum," Southport, Connecticut, April 4, 1991.

Adelman: James J. Kilpatrick, "Well-Qualified Women Still Don't Make the Top in Business," *News-Press*, September 17, 1991, p. A12; David Stipp, "The Gender Gap," *Wall Street Journal*, September 11, 1992, p. B8.

CHAPTER 2: RAINMAKING: THE ENTRY TO THE CLUB

p. 33. *Hauser:* Amy Dockser Marcus, "Women Lawyers, Despite Success, Say Sex Bias Hurt Their Careers," *Wall Street Journal*, December 4, 1989, p. B9.

p. 34. *Hale and Dorr:* Joan Vennochi, "A New Order in the Law Trade," *Boston Sunday Globe*, February 17, 1991, p. A85.

p. 35. *Koch:* David Margolick, "At the Bar," *New York Times*, December 7, 1990, p. B7.

Peat: Alison Leigh Cowan, "Peat Says It Will Cut 300 Partners," *New York Times*, January 14, 1991, p. C1.

Richards: Thomas F. O'Boyle, "Fear and Stress in the Office Take Toll," *Wall Street Journal,* November 6, 1990, p. B1.

Revenues: For an in-depth analysis, see David Maister, "Profitability: Beating the Downward Trend," *American Lawyer,* July/August 1984, pp. 6–9.

p. 36. *Similar:* Rainmaking credit occurs at every step in the process. For example, designer Alice, an employee of ABC Designs, conceives an exciting one-piece spring dress in cotton jersey. It is adopted by Beverly Dress Company (bringing Alice a big sale). Bloomingdale's buyer Charlotte orders it in quantity for spring (bringing Beverly a big sale). The dress is fabricated and assembled by Deborah's factory in Miami (bringing Deborah a big sale), after the contract was drawn up by lawyer Evelyn (bringing her a new client) and the necessary trademark work done for the design and label by consultant Frances (bringing her a new client). Banker Grace and venture capitalist Helen have lent money to Beverly Dress Company to finance the production (bringing them new fees). The dresses are shipped to Bloomingdale's by Irene's Trucking Company (bringing her a new client). The dresses are promoted with a television advertising spot conceived by Jane (bringing her agency new business) and placed by Kristin (earning her a commission). The customers respond, the dresses fly out of the store, requiring reorders all through the spring and eliminating the need for any markdowns. Charlotte has her best season ever. The gross margin on this dress alone made her department the most profitable in Bloomingdale's and earned her a promotion to senior buyer and a private lunch with the chairman.

p. 39. Law Journal: Emily Couric, "Women in the Large Firm: A High Price of Admission?," *National Law Journal,* December 11, 1989.

p. 40. *Marshall:* Margaret H. Marshall, "Not by Numbers Alone: A New Decade for Women in the Law," *New England Journal of Public Policy,* Spring/Summer 1990. See also Cynthia Fuchs Epstein, *Women in the Law* (New York: Basic Books, 1981); Brad Hildebrant and Jack Kaufman, "The Two-Tiered Partnership," *National Law Journal,* November 28, 1983; Deborah Graham, "Rainmaking: The Next Major Hurdle for Women," *Legal Times,* May 19, 1986, pp. 9–19; Phyllis Weiss Haserot, *The Rainmaking Machine* (New York: Garland Publishing, (1989); John Sansong, "First, Kill All the Lawyers," *Washingtonian,* November 1990, pp. 132–43.

Accountant: According to *Accounting Today,* an average of 46 percent of staffers at the Big Six public accounting firms are female, yet only 4.9 percent of the partners are. Mary Granfield, "Why Accounting Doesn't Add Up," *Working Woman,* January 1993, p. 16.

p. 45. *AICPA:* American Institute of Certified Public Accountants, "Upward Mobility of Women, Special Committee Report to the AICPA Board of Directors," New York, March 1988.

p. 46. *Sinay:* A survey unveiled at the 1992 American Women in Radio and TV convention found that women occupy only 26 percent of the top five managerial jobs at TV stations. More important, they are absent from the rainmaking slots that lead to a station's top post, that of general manager. While 42 percent of the program director jobs are held by women, only 18 percent of news directors and 16 percent of general sales managers are women. Only 7 percent of general managers are women. William Mahoney, "Women on the Move," *Electronic Media,* June 15, 1992, p. 1.

p. 53. *Whitman:* Aida K. Press, "Making It in the Corporate World, an Interview with Marina Whitman," *Radcliffe Quarterly,* June 1983, p. 11.

p. 56. *Love:* Carol Stocker, "Operating with Love," *Boston Globe*, June 27, 1990, p. 61.

p. 64. *Styles:* Dr. Mildred S. Myers, "Leadership and Language Styles: Do Men and Women Really Differ?," presented at the annual conference of the American Planning Association, New Orleans, Louisiana, March 25, 1991.

Measures: There is evidence that women sell themselves short in performance reviews, giving themselves lower ratings and taking the blame for things. Burke Stinson of AT&T explains why AT&T offers assertiveness-training classes and workshops for women: "Women place a greater value on a sense of community and not the individual," he said, quoted in the *Wall Street Journal*. Presumably it did not occur to AT&T that women's sense of priorities may have equal value to one that extolls individual achievement and credit. "Labor Letter," *Wall Street Journal*, July 21, 1992, p. A1.

CHAPTER 3: VIVE LA DIFFÉRENCE?

p. 68. *Look and are:* See Paula Cronin, "Women in Business, How Far Have They Come?," *Radcliffe Quarterly*, June 1983, p. 8.

p. 69. *Treated:* Simone deBeauvoir, *The Second Sex*, translated and edited by H. M. Parshley (New York: Knopf, 1953).

p. 70. *Helgesen:* Sally Helgesen, *The Female Advantage: Women's Ways of Leadership* (New York: Doubleday/Currency, 1990); Jacyn Fierman, "Do Women Manage Differently?," *Fortune*, December 17, 1990.

p. 71. *Jardim:* Anne Jardim and Margaret Hennig, "The Last Barrier: Breaking into the Boys' Club at the Top," *Working Woman*, November 1990.

Rosener: Judy B. Rosener, "Ways Women Lead," *Harvard Business Review*, November/December 1990, p. 301.

Carol: Carol R. Goldberg, "Ways Men and Women Lead," *Harvard Business Review*, January/February 1991, p. 160.

Myers: Dr. Mildred S. Myers, "Leadership and Language Styles: Do Men and Women Really Differ?," paper presented at the American Planning Association, New Orleans, Louisiana, March 25, 1991.

p. 73. *Barrow:* Donald G. McNeil, Jr., "Should Women Be Sent into Combat?" *New York Times*, July 21, 1991, p. E3; for a humorous rejoinder, see Maureen Dowd, "When Men Get a Case of the Vapors," *New York Times*, June 30, 1991, p. E2.

Biological: Christine Gorman, "Sizing Up the Sexes," *Time*, January 20, 1992, p. 42; Malkah T. Notman, M.D., and Carol C. Nadelson, M.D., "A Review of Gender Differences in Brain and Behavior," in *Women and Men, New Perspectives on Gender Differences* (Washington, D.C.: American Psychiatric Press, 1991).

p. 74. *"Something other:"* See Rosabeth Moss Kanter, *Men and Women of the Corporation* (New York: Basic Books, 1977); Rosabeth Moss Kanter with Barry A. Stein, *A Tale of "O": On Being*

Different in an Organization (New York: Harper & Row, 1980); Anne Wilson Schaef, *Women's Reality: An Emerging Female System in a White Male Society* (New York: Harper & Row, 1981).

p. 76. *Panel:* Even in polyglot New York, the opinion of outsiders seems not to matter. In March 1992, the Manhattan Institute and the Citizens Union held a four-hour conference on "Rethinking New York" and all twelve speakers were white males. "No blacks, no women, no Hispanics, no Asians and no apologies," noted a subsequent editorial. Joyce Purnick, "Including Them Out," *New York Times*, March 26, 1992, p. A14. But exclusion happens everywhere. A financial services executive from Tulsa said, "The mayor appointed a Committee on the Future of Tulsa. Men chair it and men chair all the task forces. And then they think the businesswomen of this city will buy into their recommendations? They ought to think again."

Subordinate: The business community is not the only offender. The American political system and American Catholic bishops send a clear message that women are unsuitable to be presidents and priests, with no reasonable rationale. Anna Quindlen, "Ms President," *New York Times*, April 19, 1992, p. E11.

p. 79. *Violence:* Dr. Rosalind Miles of England explains the underlying trait of violence in men in her book *Love, Sex, Death and the Making of the Male:* "All *violence is sexual* in the most basic meaning of the word, determined by sex as breasts or testes are. Women may get angry, threaten and scream, lash out in fury or seek murder and revenge. Only men habitually prey on those weaker than themselves, stalk the night in search of the lonely victim, hunt one another in packs, devise initiation rituals, exquisite tortures, pogroms and extermination camps, delight in Russian roulette, running the gauntlet, chicken and all the world's neverending games of fear, pain and death." (New York: Summit Books, 1991) p. 105.

Gender: The fact that most consistently correlates with fear of crime is femaleness. Marilyn French, *War on Women* (New York: Summit Books, 1992), p. 197. A growing number of companies are helping to pay for courses that teach female employees how to ward off male assailants. See Sarah Lubman, "Firms Offer Workers Self-Defense Classes to Combat Perils of Long Hours of Travel," *Wall Street Journal*, January 19, 1993, p. B1.

Koop: Jan Hoffman, "When Men Hit Women," *New York Times Magazine*, February 16, 1992, p. 25. Domestic violence is the leading cause of injury and death to American women; each year 6 million women are beaten by the men they live with. Jane E. Brody, "Personal Health," *New York Times*, March 18, 1992, p. B8.

p. 82. *Children:* A Boston University research group showed that verbally, parents treat little boys and girls very differently. By the age of thirty-two months, little girls hear twice as many diminutives—affectionate words like kitty or dollie in place of cat or doll—as boys. Elizabeth Mehren, "Parents Give Gender Clues in How They Talk to Kids," *News-Press*, May 21, 1992, p. D4.

Passivity: Carol C. Nadelson, "Women in Leadership Roles: Development and Challenges," in *Adolescent Psychiatry*, Sherman C. Feinstein, ed., vol. 14. (Chicago: University of Chicago Press, 1987); see also Malkah T. Notman and Carol C. Nadelson, *Women and Men, New Perspectives on Gender Differences* (Washington, D.C.: American Psychiatric Press, 1991).

Self-esteem: American Association of University Women, "Shortchanging Girls, Shortchanging America," January 1991; Marlee Miller, ed., "An Ounce of Prevention," in *Outlook, American Association of University Women*, Fall 1991, p. 5; Suzanne Daley, "Girls' Self-Esteem Is Lost on

Way to Adolescence, New Study Finds," *New York Times*, January 9, 1991, p. B1; Diane Helman and Phyllis Bookspan, "Why No Female Bert & Ernies on Sesame?," *Providence Journal-Bulletin*, July 29, 1992, p. A9; Gloria Steinem, *Revolution from Within* (Boston: Little, Brown & Co., 1992).

Nadelson: Carol C. Nadelson, "Women in Leadership Roles: Development and Challenges," in *Adolescent Psychiatry*, Sherman C. Feinstein, ed., vol 14 (Chicago: University of Chicago Press, 1987), p. 36.

p. 83. *Horner:* Matina S. Horner, Margaret Cuninggim Lecture, Vanderbilt University, Nashville, Tennessee, November 10, 1988.

p. 84. *Remarks:* Some women don't understand the fuss over titles and forms of address and just accept that language is by its form sexist, with use of "generic he" ("prior to *his* presentation, the speaker expects an introduction"), "generic man" ("evidence of *man's* existence goes back millions of years"), titles (chairman, businessman, policeman, statesman), and the trivialization of positions (actress, waitress, lady lawyer, seamstress for tailor, and cook for chef). Other women believe that eradicating sexism in all areas of the social culture starts with the elimination of any sexist language that reinforces women's subordinate position. For a fuller discussion see Susan Mura and Beth Waggenspack, "Linguistic Sexism: A Rhetorical Perspective," in *The Rhetoric of Western Thought*, 3rd ed., James L. Golden, Goodwin F. Berquist, and William E. Coleman, eds. (Dubuque, Iowa: Kendall-Hunt Publishing Co., 1983).

p. 85. *California court: Sail'er Inn* v. *Kirby*, 5 Cal. 3d., p. 20, 1971; see also Dawn-Marie Driscoll and Barbara J. Rouse, "Through a Glass Darkly: A Look at State Equal Rights Amendments," *Suffolk University Law Review*, vol. 7, no 5 (Fall 1976); Betty Friedan, *The Feminine Mystique* (New York: Dell Books, 1963); "Twenty Years Toward Justice," NOW Legal Defense and Education Fund 1990 Annual Report; Sara M. Evans, *Born for Liberty* (New York: The Free Press, 1989).

p. 86. *Structured:* See Kate Millet, *Sexual Politics* (New York: Ballantine, 1969).

Building: Robert Campbell, "Why Tall Buildings Are Held in Low Esteem These Days," *Boston Sunday Globe*, February 10, 1991, p. A39.

p. 90. *Gilligan:* Carol Gilligan, *In a Different Voice: Psychological Theory and Women's Development* (Cambridge: Harvard University Press, 1982). For another view of gender difference and its relation to power, see Catharine A. MacKinnon, *Feminism Unmodified, Discourses on Life and Law* (Cambridge: Harvard University Press, 1987).

p. 91. *Study:* Dana Jack and Rand Jack, "Women Lawyers: Archetype and Alternatives," in *Mapping the Moral Domain*, Carol Gilligan, Janie Ward, Victoria Taylor, and Jill McLean, eds. (Cambridge: Harvard University Press, 1988).

Another study: Gerard J. Clark, Michael Rustad, and Thomas Koenig, "Life After Law: A Comparison of Male and Female Suffolk Alumni Who Left the Law," *Advocate*, Spring 1992, p. 40. See also Judy Klemesrud, "Women in the Law: Many Are Getting Out," *New York Times*, August 9, 1985. For an examination of how women judges fare in a male-constructed legal system, see Judith Resnik, "On the Bias: Feminist Reconsiderations of the Aspirations for Our Judges," *Southern California Law Review*, vol. 61:1877, 1988.

Theorists: Jean Baker Miller, *Towards a New Psychology of Women* (Boston: Beacon Press, 1976); Nancy Chodorow, *The Reproduction of Mothering: Psychoanalysis and the Sociology of Gender* (Berkeley: University of California Press, 1978); Sara Ruddick, *Maternal Thinking* (New York: Ballantine Books, 1989).

p. 95. *Glass walls:* See Julie Amparano Lopez, "Study Says Women Face Glass Walls as Well as Ceilings," *Wall Street Journal*, March 3, 1992, p. B1.

CHAPTER 4: DEVELOPING PERSONAL CURRENCY

p. 100. *Interaction:* Deborah Tannen, *You Just Don't Understand: Women and Men in Conversation* (New York: William Morrow and Co., 1990).

The story: Jean Gogolin, "Micho in Motion: City Hall's Woman at the Top," *Boston Magazine*, December 1980, pp. 179–234.

p. 102. *Constituencies:* See Warren Bennis, *On Becoming a Leader* (Reading, Mass.: Addison-Wesley Publishing Co., Inc., 1989), for more discussion on these qualities; also David Finn, "Public Invisibility of Corporate Leaders," *Harvard Business Review*, November/December 1980.

p. 105. *Fifties and sixties:* Winifred Breines, "Young, White and Miserable: Female in the Fifties," *Bunting Institute Colloquium*, Cambridge, Massachusetts, December 5, 1990.

Preoccupation: See Susan Brownmiller, *Femininity* (New York: Linden Press/Simon & Schuster, 1984); Ruth Sidel, *On Her Own: Growing Up in the Shadow of the American Dream* (New York: Viking Penguin, 1990); Carol Kleinman, "Old Bias Lurks in Workplace," *Providence Journal*, August 5, 1991, p. A8; Joanne Lipman, "Sexy or Sexist? Recent Ads Spark Debate," *Wall Street Journal*, September 30, 1991, p. B1.

p. 107. *Expression:* Contrast: "You have only one chance to make a first impression. Dresses are out." Paula Cronin, "How to Dress for Success in the Corporate World," *Radcliffe Quarterly*, June 1983, p. 9.

p. 108. *Beauty:* Emily Mitchell, "The Bad Side of Looking Good," *Time*, March 4, 1991, p. 68; Maureen Dowd, "Yes, but Can She Make Them Swoon?," *New York Times*, May 26, 1991, p. E3. See also Naomi Wolf, *The Beauty Myth, How Images of Beauty Are Used Against Women* (New York: William Morrow and Co., 1991).

Haltom: Christopher Conte, "Labor Letter," *Wall Street Journal*, May 21, 1991, p. 1.

p. 109. *Hopkins:* Deborah L. Jacobs, "Getting Mad, Then Getting Even," *New York Times*, July 1, 1990, P. F21; Tamar Lewin, "Accountant Wins Suit on Sex Bias," *New York Times*, December 6, 1990, p. A13; Daniel Seligman, "Price Waterhouse Gets a Partner," *Fortune*, June 18, 1990, p. 133.

p. 110. *Carli:* Alison Bass, "Talking to Men, a Bold Woman Just Can't Win," *Boston Globe*, January 7, 1991, pp. 33–34.

p. 111. " . . . *constituencies:*" Marilyn Swartz Lloyd, "Women, Leadership and Power," *New England Journal of Public Policy*, Spring/Summer 1990, p. 193.

*Atmosphere:*American Association of University Women, "Shortchanging Girls, Shortchanging

America," January 1991; Sandy Hill, "Researchers Find Subtle Biases Favor Boys in Science Classes," *Boston Sunday Globe*, July 12, 1991, p. 81; Renee Graman, "Growing Up Invisible," *Boston Globe*, February 19, 1992, p. 69; Barbara Kantrowitz, "Sexism in the Schoolhouse," *Newsweek*, February 24, 1992, p. 62.

In one study on self-esteem, researchers from the University of Illinois tracked high school valedictorians and salutatorians. Upon entering college, about equal numbers of women and men stated they considered themselves above average in intelligence, but by sophomore year, only 4 percent of the women did, as opposed to 22 percent of the men. The reason for such a decline in confidence on the part of women suggested that the experience they received in a coeducational college was markedly different than the experience men received. Mary S. Hartman, dean of Douglass College of Rutgers, suggested that women can obtain many of the advantages of a women's college education if they ask tough questions about the experience offered at coeducational institutions: Are there special programs for women? Are awards and scholarships distributed equally between men and women? How many tenured female faculty members do they have? Are female faculty members being sought in areas in which they are underrepresented? Mary S. Hartman, "Mills Students Provided Eloquent Testimony to the Value of Women's Colleges," *Chronicle of Higher Education*, July 5, 1990, p. A40.

Women's colleges: Dorothy W. Cantor and Toni Bernay, with Jean Stoess, *Women in Power: The Secrets of Leadership* (Boston: Houghton Mifflin Co., 1992), p. 205.

Krupnick: Edward B. Fiske, "Lessons," *New York Times*, April 11, 1990, p. B8; Deborah Tannen, "Teachers' Classroom Strategies Should Recognize That Men and Women Use Language Differently," *Chronicle of Higher Education*, June 19, 1991, p. B1; Anthony Flint, "Boosting 'Co' in Coeducation," *Boston Globe*, February 13, 1992, p. 1.

p. 112. *McKenna:* Margaret A. McKenna, "Providing Access to Power: The Role of Higher Education in Empowering Women Students," *New England Journal of Public Policy*, Spring/Summer 1990, p. 33.

Diminished: Susan Chira, "Bias Against Girls Is Found Rife in Schools, with Lasting Damage," *New York Times*, February 12, 1992, p. 1.

McKenna: Margaret A. McKenna, "Providing Access to Power: The Role of Higher Education in Empowering Women Students," *New England Journal of Public Policy*, Spring/Summer 1990.

p. 113. *Tannen:* Deborah Tannen, *You Just Don't Understand: Women and Men in Conversation* (New York: William Morrow and Co., 1990); Barbara Gamarekian, "Men. Women. Talk Talk Talk. Hear? No," *New York Times*, June 19, 1991, p. B8.

p. 114. *Double standard:* See Ann M. Morrison, Randall P. White, Ellen Van Vestor, and the Center for Creative Leadership, *Breaking the Glass Ceiling: Can Women Reach the Top of America's Largest Corporations?* (Reading, Mass.: Addison-Wesley Publishing Co., Inc., 1987).

p. 115. *Geis:* Alison Bass, "Studies Find Workplace Still a Man's World," *Boston Globe*, March 12, 1990, p. 39.

p. 118. *Television:* Joseph R. Dominick, *The Dynamics of Mass Communications* (New York: McGraw-Hill Publishing Co., 1990); Warren K. Agee, Phillip H. Ault, Edwin Emery, *Introduction to Mass Communication* (New York: HarperCollins Publishers, Inc., 1991).

p. 119. *Rarely seen:* William Hoynes and David Croteau, doctoral candidates at Boston College, conducted a study of 865 different broadcasts over 40 months. David Nyhan, "Taking 3 TV Icons to the Woodshed," *Boston Sunday Globe*, June 24, 1990, p. A5. The media activist group Women Are Good News has criticized PBS for featuring less than 15 percent women on public affairs programs. Robin Pogrebin, "Women Get a Word in Edgewise," *Working Woman*, August 1992, p. 15.

89 percent: Martin A. Lee, Letter to the Editor, *Wall Street Journal*, January 16, 1992, p. A13.

Clerical: It shouldn't come as a surprise that television presents a primarily male picture, according to a 1990 report by Women in Film and the National Commission on Working Women. For example, most television families are headed by two parents, but single-parent households on television are as likely to be headed by men as by women. Andrea Adelson, "Study Attacks Roles of Women in Television," *New York Times*, November 19, 1990, p. B3; "Women at Work," National Commission on Working Women, Women's Work Force Network of Wider Opportunities for Women, Winter/Spring 1991, p. 2.

13.3: Warren K. Agee, Phillip H. Ault, and Edwin Emery, *Introduction to Mass Communication* (New York: HarperCollins Publishers, Inc., 1991), p. 176.

1991 study: A 1991 study of coverage of women in the nation's top news magazines by Unabridged Communications, a survey firm, found low coverage of women. The month-long study of *Newsweek*, *Time*, and *U.S. News & World Report* showed that references to women, who are 52 percent of the U.S. population, averaged 13 percent. Men received 87 percent of the coverage. Female reporter bylines were highest in *Newsweek* at 37 percent and lowest in *U.S. News & World Report* at 29 percent, but female bylines did not correlate with a higher number of references to female sources in the copy. M. Junior Bridge, *The Invisible Majority* (Alexandria, Va.: Unabridged Communications, October 1991).

p. 120. *"Why Women. . . . "* Jacyn Fierman, "Why Women Still Don't Hit the Top," *Fortune*, July 30, 1990.

Phyllis: Phyllis S. Swersky, "Another View of the Facts of Life," *New England Journal of Public Policy*, Spring/Summer 1990, p. 75.

Life: Claudia Glenn Dowling, "The Testing of Dory Yochum," *Life*, August 1990, pp. 54–62.

p. 121. *Lewent:* Joseph Weber, "I am Intense, Aggressive and Hard-Charging," *Business Week*, April 30, 1990, p. 58.

Audience: Newspapers are reaching an elite audience, as opposed to the general mass audiences of television and magazines. As of 1988, approximately 63 million copies of morning and evening newspapers found their way into American homes and offices. Readers are more likely to be older (73 percent of those between ages fifty and sixty-four), educated (75 percent of those who have attended college), and married (73 percent). Joseph R. Dominick, *The Dynamics of Mass Communications* (New York: McGraw-Hill Publishing Co., 1990).

11 to 12 percent: A study by the Women, Men and Media Project at the University of Southern California indicates that only 11 to 12 percent of page-one references are to women. George Dean of Connecticut, president of 50/50 by 2000, an organization working to elect women to public office, believes that the paltry number of references generally reflects the disappointing percentages of women in leadership positions in government, business, higher education, and international affairs. But as women are beginning to emerge in these fields, he noted, increasing coverage of women will result. George A. Dean, "Gender Bias in the News," *Christian Science Monitor*," May 2, 1991, p. 3.

Buresh: See the important study, Nurses of America, "Who Counts and Who Doesn't in News Coverage of Health Care" (New York: Nurses of America, 1991).

p. 122. *Articles*: We did not analyze all the articles in each of these papers, but chose representative articles of general interest that we concluded would appeal to and be read by a member of The Club in any given community. We assumed that our composite Club member received the *Journal* and *Times* each day, and also subscribed to the primary daily newspaper in his or her community. The articles spanned a period from October 2, 1991, to January 30, 1992. Because the *News-Press* was a smaller paper that primarily relied on wire service stories, its business coverage generated by local reporters was modest. Most of its twenty-four stories (13.19 percent of the total surveyed) appeared on Sunday or in its special "Business Monday" section. We analyzed seventy-two stories from the *New York Times* (39.56 percent) and eighty-six stories from the *Wall Street Journal* (47.25 percent).

The purpose of the study was to determine how frequently business reporters use women as sources of information about business and economic news—instances in which women are presented as authorities in their field to a business readership. How often was the full extent of women's professional stature and expertise visible in news coverage, or were women still relegated to the woman-as-executive feature story? A secondary question was whether the presence of women journalists affected the gender of sources sought and subjects covered on the business pages. Can we assume that as more women make their way up the professional ladder in journalism, that the coverage of women will increase?

Categories:

Subject	Frequency	Percent
Individual industry	56	30.77
Workplace issues	13	7.14
International business	15	8.24
Stock market	26	14.29
Individual companies	32	17.58
Economy/money	28	15.39
Legislation	12	6.59
Total	182	100.00

business reporters: A woman's byline appeared on 30.8 percent, men on 66 percent, and six stories contained a byline that did not connote the sex of the author. A woman reporter wrote most of the stories in the *News-Press* at 70.8 percent; she appeared to be the primary reporter assigned to cover business news. Women reporters handled 20.8 percent of the stories in the *Times*, and 27.6 percent of the stories in the *Journal*.

The fact that women were the authors of fifty-six of the business articles did not make any major difference in the representation of women executives as sources in the stories. In stories that contained a male byline, women accounted for 11.8 percent of the sources; in stories that women clearly authored, the percentage of women sources increased slightly, to 17.6 percent.

Newspaper	Male	Female	Un-ID	Total
News-Press	96	12	1	109
N.Y. Times	309	41	18	368
Journal	434	71	25	530
Total	839	124	44	1007

Author	Male Source		Female Source		Un-ID	
Female	244	78.2%	55	17.6%	13	4.2%
Male	552	83.5%	78	11.8%	31	4.7%

p. 123. *Silent:* Patricia M. Flynn, now dean of the Graduate School of Business at Bentley College, found out just how silent women can be. Flynn, one of only six female deans of graduate business schools in the United States, is an economist who is noted for her research on industrial employment. As the city of Lowell, Massachusetts, was being hailed in 1984 as a mill town revitalized into a high-technology center, a public-private partnership model for the nation, Flynn's research warned that Lowell was flirting with future disaster by its dependence on just one industry. By 1991 her prediction had come true and Flynn received national recognition for her work. Even the prestigious publication *The Economist* featured a story on the decline of Lowell and the researcher who predicted it, saying, "she was right." She? Dean Flynn wrote to *The Economist,* "For the record, *she* is Patricia M. Flynn, professor of economics at Bentley College, Waltham, Massachusetts." "She Has a Name," *Economist,* October 19, 1991, p. 8.

"Sampling:" New York Times, November 5, 1991, p. C1; *Wall Street Journal,* January 13, 1992, p. B1; January 30, 1992, p. B1; December 17, 1992, p. B1; February 11, 1993, p. B1; February 19, 1993, p. B1. It is worth mentioning that the *News-Press* was not guilty of any such one-sided gender opinion samplings, perhaps because Gannett papers evaluate their reporters on "mainstreaming," or the degree to which their stories mirror the diversity of the area's readership.

p. 126. " . . . *Glass ceiling* . . . ": Patti Doten, "Beyond Corporations' 'Glass Ceiling,'" *Boston Globe,* August 31, 1989, p. 79; Sandra L. Balzer, "The Glass Ceiling," *Boston Globe,* September 10, 1989, p. 15.

p. 127. *Salhany:* "A View from Atop Twentieth," *Broadcasting,* January 21, 1992, p. 57.

p. 128. *"Kitty . . . ":* Barbara Carton, "Kitty She Ain't," *Boston Globe,* January 3, 1991, p. 57.

p. 131. *Trudy's style:* Beth Wolfensberger, "Starting Over," *New England Business,* vol. 13, no. 2 (February 1991):15–17.

p. 136. *Iacocca:* Lee Iacocca, with William Novak, *Iacocca: An Autobiography* (New York: Bantam Books, 1984).

Conley: Jane Gross, "Female Surgeon's Quitting Touches Nerve at Medical School," *New York Times*, July 14, 1991, p. 12; Frances Conley, M.D., "Women and Academic Medicine: Is There Room at the Top," The Maurine and Robert Rothschild Lecture, The Arthur and Elizabeth Schlesinger Library on the History of Women in America, Radcliffe College, Cambridge, Massachusetts, October 23, 1991.

p. 137. *Stone:* Michael Abramowitz, "One Woman v. Her Law Firm," *Washington Post*, October 14, 1991, p. D13.

p. 139. *Fischette:* Chris Reidy, "Facing Down Continental," *Boston Globe*, May 21, 1991, p. 53.

CHAPTER 5: FORGING FRIENDSHIPS: A BUSINESS REALITY

p. 140. *Hennessey:* Alice E. Hennessey, "Climbing the Corporate Ladder," *Radcliffe Quarterly*, June 1983, p. 17.

p. 144. *Required Behavior:* See Lisa A. Mainiero, *Office Romance: Love, Power and Sex in the Workplace* (New York: Rawson Associates, 1989).

p. 148. *Breaking into:* Nearly half of the 1980 women graduates of the Wharton School at the University of Pennsylvania thought they would rise higher than they did in the corporate world. "Never underestimate the power of the boys' club," reported one. Katherine Ann Samon, "Great Expectations," *Working Woman*, July 1991, p. 68.

The Oak Room: See Marcia Cohen, *The Sisterhood, The True Story of the Women Who Changed the World* (New York: Simon & Schuster, 1988).

p. 151. *Haven:* Randall Rothenberg, "As Club Breaks Bread, a Tradition Crumbles," *New York Times*, May 4, 1991, p. 12.

" . . . *discriminatory* . . . ": Yale Club Admits Women; Irate Alumni Bar the Door," *New York Times*, April 15, 1991, p. 8; "Yale's Skull and Bones Votes to Admit Women," *Providence Journal-Bulletin*, July 25, 1991, p. D12.

p. 152. *Buckley:* Jodi Wilgoren, "Bonesmen Sue to Ban Women from Class of '92," *Boston Globe*, September 7, 1991, p. 21.

" . . . *certain trust* . . . ": Nancy Marx Better, "Another Vote on Girls in an Old-Boy World," *New York Times*, May 12, 1991, p. F23.

" . . . *explain it* . . . ": Phyllis Theroux, "Man and Animal at Yale," *New York Times*, September 25, 1991, p. A15.

p. 153. *Varies by city:* Alan Farnham, "The Mystique of Private Clubs," *Fortune*, June 4, 1990, p. 170; Sonia L. Nazario, "Gentlemen of the Club," *Wall Street Journal*, March 24, 1986, p. D21.

p. 155. *Laws:* Coalitions of women's professional organizations, civil rights groups, and progressive elected officials are advocating changes in laws that would make it illegal for private clubs with more than 100 members and where business is transacted to discriminate against women and minorities. Norma G. Blumenfeld, "Why Do Clubs Still Exclude Women and Blacks?," *New York Times*, April 25, 1992, p. 15.

p. 163. *Johnson:* Hope Lampert, *True Greed: What Really Happened in the Battle for RJR Nabisco* (New York: New American Library, 1990), p. 6.

p. 164. *Poling:* Deirdre Fanning, "Office or Golf Course, the Game Is the Same," *New York Times,* October 14, 1990, p. F25.

Thompson: Pat Baldwin, "Women Execs Try Power Play by Mastering the Game of Golf," *Dallas Morning News,* November 1, 1992, p. H1.

p. 165. *"Very critical . . . ":* "Welcome to the Woman-Friendly Company," *Business Week,* August 6, 1990, p. 49.

5.4 million: William C. Symonds, "Is Sex Discrimination Still Par for the Course?" *Business Week,* December 24, 1990, p. 56; Barbara Carton, "Golf, Women and Office Politics," *Boston Globe,* June 19, 1991, p. 41.

8 million: Patricia Aburdene and John Naisbitt, *Megatrends for Women* (New York: Villard Books, 1992), p. 48.

Research study: Hill, Holliday, Connors, Cosmopulos, "Profile of Women Golfers," March 15, 1990 (paper).

Golf tournament: Patrick M. Reilly, "Magazines in U.S., at 250 Years, Devise New Ways to Do Business," *Wall Street Journal,* October 7, 1991, p. B6.

p. 166. *Burning Tree:* "Keeping Women Subpar," *Boston Globe,* December 30, 1990, p. 12. The Beltway seems to do everything in excess. The Annual Congressional Golf Tournament was described by one member as a "feeding frenzy," in which members stuffed prizes ranging from crystal to CD players to splits of champagne into their "donated" $400 golf bags. "Congress Holes Out," *Wall Street Journal,* October 7, 1991, p. A14.

Only 20: Kate Ballen, "Women's Work Is on the Links," *Fortune,* June 3, 1991, p. 13.

p. 167. *" . . . playground . . . ":* Sally Greenberg, "Private Club Discrimination," *WBA Newsletter,* February/March 1991, p. 2.

Yorba Linda: "Re-examining Golf's Discriminatory Policies," *Golf for Women,* January/February 1991, p. 93.

Shoal Creek: Dave Gould, "The Debate Over Country Club Bias After Shoal Creek," *Wall Street Journal,* June 11, 1991, p. 20; Jaime Diaz, "Shoal Creek Decision Puts Sport on a New Course," *New York Times,* January 14, 1991, p. B12.

Watson: "Watson Cites Club Bias as He Quits, *New York Times,* December 1, 1990, p. 29; Tom Watson, "The American Way of Golf," *New York Times,* June 17, 1991.

Course is Open: See Jim Donaldson, "Women, Golf: No Common Link," *Providence Journal-Bulletin,* June 29, 1991, p. B1, explaining the message that courses send to women by excluding them. Contrast the sport of tennis, once as inhospitable as golf. For example, at the prestigious Longwood Cricket Club in Chestnut Hill, Massachusetts, 113 years after its founding and 16 years after it allowed its female members to vote, the club elected Chris Creelman, a forty-three-year-old investment adviser its first female and fortieth president. Bud Collins, "Longwood Points Hallowed Past in New Direction," *Boston Globe*, January 11, 1991.

p. 168. *Each other's ideas:* Contrast what many women have experienced, even after they have broken through the glass ceiling: "the interruption factor." See Nan Robertson, *The Girls in the Balcony, Women, Men and The New York Times* (New York: Random House, 1992).

CHAPTER 6: THE COSTLY WAR OVER SEX DISCRIMINATION

p. 169. *Worthen:* Fay Goodman Cohen and Carla McCulloch Okigwe, "Bitter Memories," *Radcliffe Quarterly*, September 1990, p. 24.

p. 170. *Cunningham:* See Allan Sloan, *Three Plus One Equals Billions* (New York: Carroll & Graf Publishers, Inc., 1983). For another version of the controversy, see Mary Cunningham, with Fran Schumer, *Powerplay: What Really Happened at Bendix* (New York: Linden Press/Simon & Schuster, 1984).

p. 171. *Obvious place:* Lisa A. Mainiero, *Office Romance: Love, Power and Sex in the Workplace* (New York: Rawson Associates, 1989).

Reports: Ellen Kapp, "Dangerous Liaisons," *Working Woman*, February 1992, p. 59.

" . . *sanctuary* . . . ": ABC News "Primetime Live," March 5, 1992.

p. 172. *Polling data:* Forty-two percent of federal workers surveyed in 1981 and 1988 said they experienced sexual harassment in the previous two years; a 1989 *National Law Journal* survey of 900 female attorneys revealed that almost two thirds of the women reported experiencing some form of sexual harassment and a 1992 study conducted by the Ninth U.S. Circuit Court of Appeals found that 60 percent of women lawyers practicing in that circuit had been sexually harassed. Five ABC News polls during the Thomas-Hill hearings found one third of all women said they had been sexually harassed at work. The National Association of Female Executives, in a poll of 1,300 of its members, found 53 percent said they were sexually harassed by people with power over their jobs or careers; but 64 percent didn't report the incident. Even three of four female United Methodist ministers reported incidents of sexual harassment, often by other members of the clergy and sometimes at church socials. Chris Black and Larry Tye, "Victims Find Task of Proof Daunting," *Boston Globe*, October 9, 1991, p. 15; Amy Dockser Marcus, "Women Lawyers, Despite Success, Say Sex Bias Hurt Their Careers," *Wall Street Journal*, December 4, 1989, p. B9; Junda Woo, "Sexual Harassment Is Found in Study of Federal Courts in 9 Western States," *Wall Street Journal*, August 5, 1992, p. B5; Mark Baker, "Sexual Shock and the Emergence of the New Man," M, February 1992, p. 70; Christopher Conte, "Labor Letter," *Wall Street Journal*, October 15, 1991, p. 1; Ari L. Goldman, "Religion Notes," *New York Times*, December 1, 1990, p. 31.

Sexual harassment is not limited to the United States. In Japan, 82 percent of women said they have been subjected to harassment; in a 1986 survey, 84 percent of Spanish women workers reported that sexual remarks or jokes were made to them on the job. See International Labor Office, "Combating Sexual Harassment at Work," Geneva, Switzerland, 1992, a comprehensive United Nations report based on surveys in twenty-three nations.

p. 173. *State of mind:* Researchers report that women with profeminist attitudes were more likely to indicate they had experienced sexual harassment and feminists were more likely than traditional women to agree that unwanted sexual advances were not a woman's fault. Linda Brooks and Annette R. Perot, "Reporting Sexual Harassment," *Psychology of Women Quarterly* 15 (1991):31–47.

One study: Maxine Arnold Hatcher, "The Corporate Woman of the 1990's," *Psychology of Women Quarterly* 15 (1991):251–59.

p. 174. *A court: Barnes* v. *Costle,* 561 F2d 983, 1977, a decision of the U.S. Court of Appeals for the District of Columbia. For a comprehensive discussion of the evolution of the law prohibiting sex discrimination to include sexual harassment, see Fred Strebeigh, "Defining Law on the Feminist Frontier," *New York Times Magazine,* October 6, 1991, p. 28; Catharine A. MacKinnon, *Sexual Harassment of Working Women* (New Haven: Yale University Press, 1979), and Flora Davis, *Moving the Mountain, the Women's Movement in America Since 1960* (New York: Simon & Schuster, 1991).

Guidelines: 29 CFR Ch. XIV, Part 1604, ss 1604. 11. See Elaine Frost. "Sexual Harassment In the Workplace," *Women Lawyers Journal 71,* No. 3 (Spring 1985).

Vinson: Meritor Savings Banks, FSB., v. *Vinson,* 106 S. Circuit 2399 (1986).

Professions: Women who tried to become firefighters, police officers, and join the military also suffered severe abuse. See Wendy Kaminer, *Fearful Freedom: Women's Flight from Equality* (Reading, Mass.: Addison-Wesley Publishing Co., Inc., 1990), p. 109.

p. 175. *Nude pinups:* Tamar Lewin, "Nude Pictures Are Ruled Sexual Harassment," *New York Times,* January 23, 1991, p. A11; Amy Dockser Marcus and Ellen Joan Pollock, "Judge Rules Against Pinups in Workplace," *Wall Street Journal,* January 23, 1991, p. B2; Susan Tifft, "A Setback for Pinups at Work," *Time,* February 4, 1991, p. 61. This case raises the constitutional question about the fine line between free speech and sexual harassment. See Arthur S. Hayes, "Pinup Case Splits Free-Speech Activists," *Wall Street Journal,* April 29, 1992, p. B12.

"reasonable woman": Ellison v. *Brady,* CA 9, No. 89–15248, January 23, 1991.

$6.7 million: Freada Klein, *The 1988 Working Woman Sexual Harassment Survey* (Cambridge, Mass.: Klein Associates, Inc., 1988). The survey concluded it was thirty-four times more expensive to ignore the problem of sexual harassment than to try to prevent it. See also "Dr. Benedek Speaks," *Washington Psychiatric Society Newsletter,* Washington D.C., February 1991; Lynn Hecht Schafran, "The Harsh Lessons of Professor Hill," *New York Times,* October 13, 1991, p. F13. Sexual harassment also results in job loss and other traumas and is a possible trigger for depression in women, according to the American Psychological Association. Judy Mann, "Our Culture as a Cause of Depression," *Washington Post,* December 7, 1990, p. B3.

Surveys: "The Case of the Hidden Harassment," *Harvard Business Review,* March/April 1992, p. 23.

p. 176. *One survey:* Alan Deutschman, "Dealing with Sexual Harassment," *Fortune,* November 4, 1991, p. 48.

Nervous: Charges of sexual harassment filed at the EEOC nearly doubled in the decade of the eighties; pregnancy discrimination complaints soared from 58 in 1980 to more than 4,000 in 1985, and sex discrimination complaints rose nearly 30 percent in those years. Susan C. Faludi, "Women Lost Ground in 1980s, and EEOC Didn't Help," *Wall Street Journal,* October 18, 1991,

p. B4. After the Clarence Thomas hearings, sexual harassment charges filed with the EEOC increased to 1,244 in the first quarter of 1992, from 728 the prior year. "Labor Letter," *Wall Street Journal*, February 25, 1992, p. A1.

p. 179. *Make a fool:* Once a harasser is exposed, the press often takes over the job of ridiculing him. Victor Kiam, owner of the New England Patriots and the chief executive officer of Remington Products, made a bad situation worse when *Boston Herald* sports reporter Lisa Olson was allegedly harassed by several Patriots players in the team's locker room in 1990. Instead of apologizing for their behavior and dealing swiftly with any offending players, Kiam allegedly called Olson a "classic bitch." After the National Football League investigated the incident and fined the team and the players, and even after Kiam's company found itself the object of a boycott by female consumers, Kiam did it again. At an all-male sports banquet four months later, Kiam made an inappropriate joke at Olson's expense. Reporters were quick to make Kiam and the joke a major newspaper story, calling Kiam a joke himself, and demanding his head. Dan Shaughnessy, "Patriots Owner Is a Laughingstock," *Boston Globe*, February 7, 1991, p. 45.

p. 182. *Senators:* Early in 1992, U.S. senator Brock Adams of Washington, long regarded as sympathetic to women's issues, announced he would not run for reelection the day after the *Seattle Times* published a lengthy report of allegations of sexual harassment by several women that spanned several years. The women were not named in the press reports, leading to a debate in some circles about the fairness of a U.S. senator being disadvantaged by anonymous complaints. Senator Bob Packwood of Oregon faced similar complaints after he was safely reelected to his Senate seat, prompting deliberation about whether he could have been defeated if those who had come forward with the charges had done so earlier, in time for media coverage prior to election day.

p. 183. *Put up with:* It is worth noting the tone of Conley's letter to the dean at Stanford, as she tries to both alert him to the environment at the Medical School while defusing the conflict that the problem had created for both of them. Dr. Conley describes a working culture experienced by many women:

"There is a pervasive behavioral gender insensitive environment at Stanford Medical School that has been there for as long as I've been affiliated with the institution, and undoubtedly will persist for a long time to come. Many women are aware of these gender insensitive behavioral characteristics. And while we may not necessarily like them, for the most part we endure them with good grace, lots of humor, and by developing thick skins. They are truly a part of that environment we have chosen to work in, and we know we cannot effect immediate change. We learn from our tormentors, work for our tormentors, in many instances we love, admire and respect our tormentors. The world we accept is one of dichotomy: the ability to respect a particular peer, but at the same time knowing that some of his behavior is not correct. I believe that most of us are willing to continue our dichotomous existence if the gulf does not widen, and if there is tangible evidence on the part of leadership that there is commitment to and active pursuit of evolutionary change leading to a reduction in the dichotomy."

p. 185. *Evaluations:* Nancy O'Mara Ezold v. *Wolf, Block, Schorr and Solis-Cohen*, Civil Action No. 90–0002, U.S. District Court for Eastern District of Pennsylvania, November 27, 1990. See Janet L. Fix, "A Woman's Case, a Nation's Issue," *Philadelphia Inquirer*, December 3, 1990, p. C1.

Partner: See Milo Geyelin and Wade Lambert, "Law Partnership Can Be Awarded as Remedy in Discrimination Case," *Wall Street Journal*, March 18, 1991, p. B8; "Victory in Sex-Bias Suit Would Only Do So Much," *New York Times*, August 21, 1992, p. A21.

p. 186. *1993:* Ezold has said she will now appeal the decision to the U.S. Supreme Court. "Lawyer Denied a Rehearing in Sex-Bias Suit Against Firm," *New York Times,* February 5, 1993, p. B9.

p. 188. *Researchers:* See Tara L. L'Heureux and Janet L. Barnes-Farrell, "Overcoming Gender Bias in Reward Allocation," *Psychology of Women Quarterly* 15 (1991): 127–39.

p. 189. *The judge: Contardo* v. *Merrill, Lynch, Pierce, Fenner & Smith, Inc.,* Civil Action No. 86–1081-S, U.S. District Court, District of Massachusetts, December 14, 1990. See Elsa C. Arnett, "Ex-Broker Wins Sex-Bias Suit," *Boston Globe,* December 15, 1990, p. 21.

p. 191. *Business:* Contardo's story has one silver rainmaking lining. While her lawsuit was proceeding, she made contact with an executive woman in another state who had successfully pursued a major sex discrimination claim. The woman was unfailingly supportive of Contardo, telling her that when she won her suit, she must do the same for other women plaintiffs who were discouraged and isolated. When Contardo called to tell her of her victory, the woman asked for a copy of the decision and her business card. "I've just received a settlement from my suit and I'd like you to invest it for me," she said. "An old family friend handles my other investments and I can't change that account, but I'm happy for you to manage this portion." Contardo was pleased and understood about the family friend, but not when she heard the account was being managed from another Merrill Lynch office. It didn't take long for her new client to agree that rewarding corporate wrongdoers with the business of women was totally inappropriate and family friend or not, she changed all her accounts to Contardo at Smith Barney.

p. 192. *Wall Street firm:* Women hold 40 percent of the jobs at Wall Street's ten largest securities firms, but they make up just 4 percent of all partners and managing directors. At Goldman Sachs & Co., Wall Street's most successful investment banking firm, just 4 of 146 partners in 1991 were women and at the New York Stock Exchange that same year only 2 of 26 directors were women. Goldman Sachs was severely rebuked by a federal judge for not providing documents in a sex discrimination lawsuit filed by Joanne Flynn, a thirty-eight-year-old former Goldman Sachs vice president. Goldman Sachs has also been sued for $18 million by Rita M. Reid, forty, who alleged that the firm denied her a partnership and fired her after fourteen years. Elizabeth Sobol, one of just four women among Kidder, Peabody & Co.'s managing directors in 1989 and head of the firm's utility finance department, resigned from the firm and sued Kidder in 1991, accusing the firm of paying her less than her male peers. Edith Wulack, fifty-one, a former vice president at Bear, Stearns & Co., won her lawsuit for sex and age discrimination against the firm in 1990, alleging that she was passed over for partnership in favor of younger males. See Laurie P. Cohen, William Power, and Michael Siconolfi, "Financial Firms Act to Curb Office Sexism with Mixed Results," *Wall Street Journal,* November 5, 1991, p. A1; Michael Siconolfi and William Power, "Goldman Sachs Is Dogged by Charges of Discriminating Against Two Women," *Wall Street Journal,* November 20, 1991, p. B5; Michael Siconolfi, "Woes of a Senior Wall Street Woman: Why Is My Bonus Thinner Than His?," *Wall Street Journal,* November 29, 1991, p. B8; Ellen Joan Pollock and Randall Smith, "Jury Awards Damages Against Bear, Stearns & Co. for Sex and Age Discrimination," *Wall Street Journal,* January 26, 1990, p. B7; Meryl Gordon, "Discrimination at the Top," *Working Woman,* September 1992, p. 68.

Boycott: Economist and novelist John Kenneth Galbraith may have been predicting the future in his scene in *A Tenured Professor,* in which his hero, a professor and successful investor, schemes ways in which to force corporations to act ethically and responsibly:

"As food manufacturers were required to list the ingredients of the marmalades and cookies they sold and drug companies the chemicals in their medicines, so, in plausible continuity, corporations would be asked to list the percentage of women in their executive ranks. A tag or sticker on the product would convey this information, and female consumers, those now known to be largely in control of the expenditures from family budgets, would be asked to withhold patronage from any product without one.

"Companies employing fewer than five thousand people, they decided, would be exempt, the tag or sticker on their products could so state. As a further step, those with more than five thousand employees and publicly traded stock would be asked to provide similar information on their annual reports for the benefit of women investors. Women, not men, were the ultimate beneficiaries of rather more than half of all the revenues from invested funds. The great New York investment houses would also be asked to provide their ratios of female to male executives in companies whose stock, bonds or junk bonds they were about to sell." (Boston: Houghton Mifflin Co., 1990), p. 105.

p. 193. *Polsby:* Kateri Butler and Gloria Ohland, "Making the Case Against Discrimination," *LA Weekly,* January 18–24, 1991, pp. 22–25.

p. 195. *Supported:* On April 9, 1991, the FOPW announced the formation of a Legal Fund to help professional women fight harassment, discrimination, and lack of ethics in the workplace, and decided to support the cases of Maureen Polsby and Margaret Jensvold. The FOPW represents more than 20,000 women belonging to over thirty professional groups.

p. 196. *Lawsuit:* Polsby's attempt to have her complaint about retaliation heard in court was rejected by the U.S. Court of Appeals for the Fourth Circuit, which said that the civil rights laws do not cover retaliatory acts against *former* employees (*Polsby* v. *Chase,* 970 F.2d 1360, 4th Cir. 1992). This does not mean the court's decision is right; three other circuits have interpreted "employee" to include a "former employee."

Jensvold: Complaint for Injunctive and Monetary Relief, *Margaret Jensvold, M.D.* v. *Louis W. Sullivan, M.D.,* December 3, 1990.

p. 198. *Paper:* Margaret F. Jensvold, M.D., "Workplace Sexual Harassment: The Uses of and Misuse and Abuse of Psychiatry," *Psychiatric Annals,* December 1992.

p. 199. *Young-Horvath:* Violet Young-Horvath, "Statement for Press Conference Regarding Sex Discrimination Against Women Researchers at NIH," December 3, 1990.

Nussbaum: Bruce Nussbaum, *Good Intentions* (New York: Atlantic Monthly Press, 1990), p. xiii.

Senior: Women fill only 16.4 percent of the senior executive positions at NIH. Despite the fact that women now make up 40 percent of all medical students, there is only one woman dean among all American medical schools, whose faculties are 79 percent male. Ann Armbruster, "Closing the Medical Gender Gap," *Working Woman,* September 1992, p. 63.

p. 200. *Caucus:* The Congressional Caucus for Women's Issues was founded by the women members of Congress in 1977 as a bipartisan legislative service organization dedicated to promoting women's economic and legal rights. The Caucus serves as a resource on women's issues and as an advocate on behalf of women's rights, and has almost 170 members of Congress included in its ranks. Congresswomen Patricia Schroeder and Olympia Snowe, cochairs of the Caucus, introduced the Women's Health Equity Act (WHEA), a package of twenty-two separate bills designed to improve the status of women's health in the areas of research, services, and prevention.

Jensvold: Margaret Jensvold, "Statement of Margaret F. Jensvold, M.D.," December 3, 1990.

Ramey: Estelle Ramey, "Statement of Estelle Ramey, M.D.," December 3, 1990.

p. 201. *NIH history:* Anne C. Roark, "Research Office for Women's Health Answers Complaint of Bias in Research," *Los Angeles Times,* November 29, 1990, p. A5. In June 1990 the General Accounting Office reported that NIH had made little progress toward including women in clinical trials.

Heart: Gina Kolata, "Study Finds Bias in Way Women Are Evaluated for Heart Bypass," *New York Times,* April 16, 1990, p. A15; Susan Okie, "Study: NIH Slow to Include Women in Disease Research," *Washington Post,* June 19, 1990, p. A10. The 1981 Physicians' Health Study on aspirin and heart disease included not one woman among its 22,071 subjects. Ann Armbruster, "Closing the Medical Gender Gap," *Working Woman,* September 1992, p. 63.

$8 million: Kateri Butler and Gloria Ohland, "At Risk: Is America's Health-Care System Endangering Women?," *LA Weekly,* January 18–24, 1991, pp. 20–26.

p. 202. *Depression:* Malcolm Gladwell, "Women and Depression: Culture Called a Key Factor," *Washington Post,* December 6, 1990, p. A1.

70 percent: Ann Armbruster, "Closing the Medical Gender Gap," *Working Woman,* September 1992, p. 63.

Cost considerations: Andrew Purvis, "A Perilous Gap," *Time,* Fall 1990 (special issue entitled "Women: The Road Ahead"), p. 67.

$10 billion: Ann Armbruster, "Closing the Medical Gender Gap," *Working Woman,* September 1992, p. 63.

$25 million: "Women have suffered from the intrinsic masculinity of science," said Sandra Raymond, the founding executive director of the National Osteoporosis Foundation. Address to the International Women's Forum Conference, September 26, 1992, Denver, Colorado.

Six: Letter to President George Bush from Congresswomen Patricia Schroeder and Olympia Snowe, December 5, 1990. The National Academy of Sciences is not much better. In the last twenty years, the percentage of women elected to the academy has averaged only 5 to 10 percent of the total. "It's an old club, elected by its own members," said one female academy member. "Men just tend to know each other better than they do women." Natalie Angier, "Academy's Choices Don't Reflect the Number of Women in Science," *New York Times,* May 10, 1992, p. 14.

Rapidly: Bernadine Healy, the first woman director of the NIH and a self-proclaimed feminist, opposed the WHEA and also lobbied against overturning the ban on fetal tissue research. See Eleanor Clift, "Body Politics," *Working Woman,* September 1992, p. 61. But the NIH has begun a "Women's Health Initiative," a $500 million, ten-year study of women's health issues. By contrast, the NIH spent $800 million in 1991 on AIDS research alone. Patricia Aburdene and John Naisbitt, *Megatrends for Women* (New York: Villard Books, 1992), pp. 136, 143.

Fallen prey: Speech of Senator Brock Adams in the U.S. Senate, March 31, 1992.

Disruptive: Speech of Senator Orrin Hatch in the U.S. Senate, March 31, 1992.

p. 203. *Occupations:* Carolyn Shaw Bell, "Shortchanging the Sexes," *Boston Globe*, March 31, 1992, p. 40.

NIH supports: Christopher Farrell and Michael J. Mandel, "Industrial Policy," *Business Week*, April 6, 1992, p. 72.

CHAPTER 7: INTERNATIONAL REALITY

p. 205. *3 percent:* Nancy J. Adler, "Women in International Management: Where Are They," *California Management Review*, vol. 26, no. 4 (Summer 1984):78.

80 percent: Jolie Solomon, "Women, Minorities and Foreign Postings," *Wall Street Journal*, June 2, 1989, p. B1; Nancy J. Adler, "Expecting International Success: Female Managers Overseas," *Columbia Journal of World Business*, Fall 1984.

p. 209. *Relationships:* Marlene L. Rossman, *The International Businesswoman of the 1990s* (New York: Praeger Publishers, 1990), p. 28.

p. 210. *12.3 million:* "Women-Owned Businesses Gaining," *News-Press*, April 6, 1992, p. 20; "Study Finds Sharp Rise in Firms Owned by Women," *Wall Street Journal*, March 31, 1992, p. B2. Texas business owner Dr. Mary Jordan-DeLaurenti is amazed by the media hype on this statistic, and warns that women-owned businesses are not the fastest-growing segment of the economy when you look at numbers of *enterprises* with employees, annual receipts, amount of business with the federal government, or even when compared with minorities. "What is so great about 618,000 businesses hiring as many people as 500 businesses? If it were 618,000 male-owned businesses would they be bragging?" Dr. Mary Jordan-DeLaurenti, speech presented to International Women's Forum, San Antonio, Texas, May 1, 1993.

1950s: See Marvin Centron and Owen Davies, *American Renaissance* (New York: St. Martin's Press, 1990).

Investments: Lester C. Thurow, "Losing Leadership at Home," *Boston Globe*, February 12, 1992, p. 58.

Citicorp: "World Business," *Wall Street Journal*, September 20, 1991, pp. R8–R9.

Foreigners: Robert Reich, *The Work of Nations* (New York: Knopf, 1991), pp. 6, 136. In 1969, American companies produced 82 percent of the nation's television sets, 88 percent cars, and 90 percent of its machine tools. Now, even in new markets such as semiconductors, the American share of the market has shrunk from 85 to 15 percent from 1980. Richard Rosencrance, "Must America Decline?" *WQ*, Autumn 1990, p. 68.

p. 211. *Blurred:* Robert Reich, *The Work of Nations* (New York: Knopf, 1991), pp. 120, 129.

" . . . *advantage* . . . ": Robert Reich, Address to WGBH-TV Overseers annual meeting, May 14, 1992, Cambridge, Massachusetts.

Integration: Marvin Centron and Owen Davies, *American Renaissance* (New York: St. Martin's Press, 1990), p. 342. If there are bright spots on the horizon, it may be in the emergence of major markets. Europe will continue to gain stature as a major economic entity, with 337 million people and a buying power of over $4 trillion—a market almost as large as the United States and Japan combined, although smaller than the North American Trading Area. Another 500 million people in the rest of Europe, the former Soviet Union, and the Middle East present new market opportunities as well. Marlene L. Rossman, *The International Businesswoman of the 1990s* (New York: Praeger Publishers, 1990), p. 67. Some American exports are gradually becoming competitive, due to lower costs of production, a declining dollar, low inflation, lower interest rates, and smaller wage increases for American workers. At the same time, greater numbers of American companies have learned how to export their products and services. Among 220 businesses surveyed, 45 percent said they exported goods in 1991, up from 36 percent in 1990, and export orders have been expanding overall at an annual rate of better than 9 percent. Exports to lesser developed countries have grown faster, at an annual rate of 14 percent. These signs barely register in the positive column, as exports only account for one tenth of the gross national product. But international business opportunities are broader than just exports; U.S. firms are engaged in a full range of international business ventures, from licensing to joint ventures and offshore operations. Michael Selz, "Hiring the Right Manager Overseas," *Wall Street Journal,* February 27, 1992, p. B2. Sylvia Nasar, "World's Appetite for U.S. Products Is Still Increasing," *New York Times,* November 11, 1991, p. 1; James Beeler, "Exports: Ship 'Em Out," *Fortune,* Spring/Summer 1991 (special issue entitled "The New American Century"), p. 58.

83 percent: Mariann Jelinek and Nancy J. Adler, "Women: World-Class Managers for Global Competition," *Academy of Management Executive,* vol. 2, no. 1 (February 1988):15.

p. 212. *Three times:* Gilbert Fuchsburg, "As Costs of Overseas Assignments Climb, Firms Select Expatriates More Carefully," *Wall Street Journal,* January 9, 1992, p. B1.

40 percent: Michael G. Harvey, "The Executive Family: An Overlooked Variable in International Assignments," *Columbia Journal of World Business,* vol. no. 20, 1 (Spring 1985). Managers who go abroad without cross-cultural training have a failure rate ranging from 33 to 66 percent. Arthur M. Whitehill, "America's Trade Deficit: The Human Problems," *Business Horizons,* January/February 1988, p. 22. See also Sue Shellenbarger, "Family Support Keeps Expatriates in the Fold," *Wall Street Journal,* August 20, 1992, p. B1.

One quarter: Michael Selz, "Hiring the Right Manager Overseas," *Wall Street Journal,* February 27, 1992, p. B2.

Hairdressers: Robin Pascoe, "Employers Ignore Expatriate Wives at Their Own Peril," *Wall Street Journal,* March 2, 1992, p. A12.

p. 215. *Questions:* Gilbert Fuchsburg, "As Costs of Overseas Assignments Climb, Firms Select Expatriates More Carefully," *Wall Street Journal,* January 9, 1992, p. B1.

Whitehill: Arthur M. Whitehill, "America's Trade Deficit: The Human Problems," *Business Horizons,* January/February 1988, p. 19.

Nationals: Joann S. Lublin, "Foreign Accents Proliferate in Top Ranks as U.S. Companies Find Talent Abroad," *Wall Street Journal,* May 21, 1992, p. B1; "Firms Woo Executives from 'Third Countries,'" *Wall Street Journal,* September 16, 1991, p. B1.

p. 218. *Livingston:* Cambio International, "American Women as Global Managers," Boston, Massachusetts, 1992.

p. 219. *38 percent:* The Fund for the Feminist Majority, "The Feminization of Power: An International Comparison" (pamphlet), Washington, D.C., p. 1.

Robinson: See Betty Fussell, "A Bloody Miracle," *Lear's*, April 1992, p. 68.

Leave: "Worldwide Policies," *News-Press Business*, April 27, 1992, p. 17; "U.N. Reports on 'World's Women,'" *Wall Street Journal*, June 24, 1991, p. A11.

52 percent: The Fund for the Feminist Majority, "The Feminization of Power: An International Comparison" (pamphlet), Washington, D.C., p. 4.

p. 220. *Major:* "Women's Rights in Britain," *Wall Street Journal*, October 29, 1991, p. A19.

One survey: The Institute of Management survey indicated that women make up only about 3 percent of all senior managers and the old-boy network remained the single biggest obstacle to the advancement of women in the workplace. Associated Press, "'Old Boy Network' Blocks Women," *News-Press*, November 4, 1992, p. A9; Trudy Coe, "The Key to the Men's Club, Opening the Doors to Women in Management" (London: The Institute of Management, 1992).

Gap: "Britain's Pay Gap for Women," *Wall Street Journal*, October 20, 1992, p. A17.

France: "French Women Pioneers in EC," *Wall Street Journal*, September 23, 1991, p. A10.

Germany: Shlomo Maital, "A Long Way to the Top," *Across the Board*, December 1989, p. 7.

Kanter: Peter Costa, "A Conversation with Rosabeth Moss Kanter," *Harvard Gazette*, May 17, 1991, p. 5.

p. 221. *Hungary:* Teddie Weyr, "Hungary Women on Fast Track," *Providence Journal-Bulletin*, July 1, 1991, p. A8; "Women's Role Opening Hungary," *Wall Street Journal*, June 20, 1991, p. A11.

p. 222. *Generations:* Elderly women are having the worst time of it. In Moscow, 70 percent of the newly unemployed are women between the ages of forty-five and fifty-five. Katrina vanden Heuvel, "Women of Russia, Unite!" *New York Times*, September 12, 1992, p. 15.

Locked: According to a global United Nations study, women perform 66 percent of all work, but receive only 10 percent of all income and own less than one percent of all material assets. Martha N. Ozawa, ed., *Women's Life Cycle and Economic Insecurity* (Westport, Conn.: Praeger Publishers, 1989).

One percent: Kumiko Makihara, "Who Needs Equality?," *Time*, Fall 1990 (special issue entitled "Women: The Road Ahead"), p. 35.

Resign: Ross Laver, "Forfeiting a Career," *Maclean's*, November 18, 1991, p. 50.

Marrying: "Japan's Women Gaining Power, Changing Nation," *News-Press*, December 29, 1991, p. 18A; Ross Laver, "Forfeiting a Career," *Maclean's*, November 18, 1991, p. 50.

p. 223. *Status quo:* Flora Lewis, "Ms. Doi's Advantage," *New York Times,* October 10, 1990, p. A15.

*Dissatisfied:*Yumiko Ono, "Women's Movement in Japan Isn't Moving Very Fast," *Wall Street Journal,* June 6, 1991, p. A1.

New law: Kathryn Graven, "Sexual Harassment at the Office Stirs Up Japan," *Wall Street Journal,* March 21, 1990, p. B1.

Discourage: Tim W. Ferguson, "An Outsider/Insider's Watchful Eye on Japan U.S.A. Inc.," *Wall Street Journal,* February 19, 1991, p. A27.

85 percent: "Women Feel Bias in Japan," *Wall Street Journal,* August 8, 1991, p. A8.

Hiring away: Some Japanese firms have already moved American women into top positions, at least in the United States, even though they will have Japanese men reporting to them. "An American Woman Heads Sumitomo Unit," *New York Times,* October 8, 1991, p. D4.

p. 224. *Willing:* Sony may not be typical or she may be unusually lucky. As more and more Japanese companies do business in the United States, there is increasing publicity about charges that the companies discriminate against American managers. Peter T. Kilborn, "U.S. Managers Claim Job Bias by the Japanese," *New York Times,* June 3, 1991, p. 1; "Panel Targets Complaints of Bias at Japanese Firms," *Providence Journal-Bulletin,* August 19, 1991, p. 8; Claude Lewis, "Japan's Barbs of Bias," *Providence Journal-Bulletin,* August 24, 1991, p. A13.

Pacific Rim: Marlene L. Rossman, *The International Businesswoman of the 1990s* (New York: Praeger Publishers, 1990), p. 61; Louis Kraar, "Iron Butterflies," *Fortune,* October 7, 1991, p. 143; "Gains for Women in Philippines," *Wall Street Journal,* February 13, 1992, p. A16.

p. 225. *Latin America:* Marlene L. Rossman, *The International Businesswoman of the 1990s* (New York: Praeger Publishers, 1990), p. 80.

CHAPTER 8: THE POWER OF COLLABORATION

p. 228. *Member:* As quoted in Elizabeth Graham Cook, "Women, Power and Partnership," *New England Journal of Public Policy,* Spring/Summer 1990.

p. 231. *Forty:* Elizabeth Graham Cook, "Women, Power and Partnership," *New England Journal of Public Policy,* Spring/Summer 1990, p. 99. The authors are grateful for the survey research conducted by Cook on the members of the Women's Economic Forum for her article.

p. 232. *Award:* The public award led to more publicity for the Tobin School and its principal, Janet Short, as the group knew it would. Short received an honorary degree from Regis College in Weston, Massachusetts, and was featured in a lengthy Sunday magazine article (Peter Anderson, "A Portrait in Bravery," *Boston Globe Magazine,* May 4, 1989). A subsequent television drama, "A Matter of Principal" was based on her life, in which Loretta Swit of "M*A*S*H" fame played Short.

p. 233. *United Way:* Some felt it was time to change the image of United Way, as reflected in the description contained in *Who Rules Boston?* (Boston: The Institute for Democratic Socialism, 1984): "The irony is that the United Way is dominated by the same corporations and a corporate mentality that are largely responsible for many of the area's social and economic problems in the first place" (p. 74). Attention to United Way was not coming just from this group. "In a nation where tens of millions of women now work outside the home, questions about why Girls Scouts get less than Boy Scouts from the United Way are being raised by more and more career women." "United No More," *Foundation News*, November/December 1989. The inquiry was timely. In Boston, a poor person was three times as likely to be female as male, according to the city's leading foundation. "In the Midst of Plenty—a Profile of Boston and Its Poor," Boston Foundation, Boston, Massachusetts, 1989, p. 9.

p. 234. *Connection:* The Forum members' values reflected the importance of combining the pleasures of friendship along with the pursuit of success and power. See Grace Baruch, Rosalyn Barnett, and Caryl Rivers, *Lifeprints: New Patterns of Love and Work for Today's Women* (New York: New American Library, 1983).

p. 235. *Male system:* She was experiencing what Anne Wilson Schaef so effectively described as two different worlds. Anne Wilson Schaef, *Women's Reality: An Emerging Female System in a White Male Society* (New York: Harper & Row Publishers, 1981).

One Forum: Elizabeth Graham Cook, "Summary of Study Findings—June 1989" (paper), p. 8.

p. 236. *248,000:* Liz Roman Gallese, "A New Focus for Women's Groups," *New York Times*, January 1, 1992, p. F23.

Ericson: "Women in Corporate Firms," *Architecture*, October 1991, p. 85.

p. 237. *North Florida:* "Exchange," *International Alliance*, December 1990, pp. 1–4.

p. 239. *Concerns:* "International Business Engrossing to Network Women from Two Continents," *International Alliance*, June 1992, p. 1.

p. 240. *San Diego:* Jordan Bonfante, "Lady Power in the Sunbelt," *Time*, March 19, 1990, p. 21.

New York: "Spotlight on the Forums," *Connection*, Fall/Winter 1990, p. 4.

p. 241. *Baltimore:* "Exchange," *International Alliance*, December 1990, pp. 1–4.

Special issue: The origins of the *Journal* are described in Dawn-Marie Driscoll, "Editor's Note," *New England Journal of Public Policy*, Spring/Summer 1990, p. 8.

Public policy: See Kitty Dukakis and Vivian Li, "Women and Economic Empowerment," *New England Journal of Public Policy*, Spring/Summer 1990, p. 195.

Private sector: See Carol R. Goldberg, Aileen P. Gorman, and Kathleen Hanson, "Issues in the Corporate Workplace," *New England Journal of Public Policy*, Spring/Summer 1990, p. 65; Margaret A. McKenna, "Providing Access to Power: The Role of Higher Education in Empowering Women Students," *New England Journal of Public Policy*, Spring/Summer 1990, p. 33.

Empowerment: See Sister Therese Higgins, "Reaching Tomorrow's Hispanic Leaders," *New England Journal of Public Policy*, Spring/Summer 1990, p. 25.

Collective action: See Dawn-Marie Driscoll, "The Third Stage: An Economic Strategy," *New England Journal of Public Policy*, Spring/Summer 1990, p. 179; Sheryl R. Marshall, "Women and Money: Getting Money and Using It," *New England Journal of Public Policy*, Spring/Summer 1990, p. 239; Cathleen Douglas Stone, "Women and Power: Women in Politics," *New England Journal of Public Policy*, Spring/Summer 1990, p. 157.

Adult literacy: See Brunetta R. Wolfman, "Moving into the Economic Mainstream," *New England Journal of Public Policy*, Spring/Summer 1990, p. 15.

Child care: See Evelyn Murphy, "A Feminized Work Force, a Humanized Workplace," *New England Journal of Public Policy*, Spring/Summer 1990, p. 203.

Maternity: See Mary Jane Gibson, "Employment Leave: Foundation for Family Policy," *New England Journal of Public Policy*, Spring/Summer 1990, p. 209.

Health care: See Dolores Mitchell, "Health Care: An Economic Priority," *New England Journal of Public Policy*, Spring/Summer 1990, p. 229.

Freedom: See Susan Estrich, "Women, Politics, and the Nineties: The Abortion Debate," *New England Journal of Public Policy*, Spring/Summer 1990, p. 149.

Creative career: See Carol B. Hillman, "Women as Managers: Myths and Realities," *New England Journal of Public Policy*, Spring/Summer 1990, p. 83; Margaret H. Marshall, "Not by Numbers Alone: A New Decade for Women in the Law," *New England Journal of Public Policy*, Spring/Summer 1990, p. 107; Phyllis S. Swersky, "Another View of the 'Facts of life,'" *New England Journal of Public Policy*, Spring/Summer 1990, p. 75.

Gender assumptions: See Dell Mitchell, "The Boardroom: Still a Fraternity?," *New England Journal of Public Policy*, Spring/Summer 1990, p. 91; Matina Horner, "The Changing Challenge: From Double Bind to Double Burden," *New England Journal of Public Policy*, Spring/Summer 1990, p. 47.

Response: "Money and Power Women Goals?," *Boston Globe*, May 8, 1990, p. 45. The book was hailed as "cogent, well argued, in some cases moving and in a number of instances, pathbreaking." The feedback most valued by the authors, however, was a personal letter from a subscriber in Florida, Edris Bradford Kelley, who wrote, "I do know that each of the articles made me feel better prepared and less frightened of the future. By the end of the day, with all of this information in my head, I was able to lift myself out of the doldrum and say to myself, 'Isn't it great to be a female?' In my opinion, this special issue should be required reading for every female who is not part of the mollusk family."

p. 242. *Rivals:* Tara Roth Madden, *Women vs. Women, the Uncivil Business War* (New York: AMACOM, 1987); Tracy, Laura, *The Secret Between Us: Competition Among Women* (Boston: Little, Brown & Co., 1991).

Hirsch: Kathleen Hirsch, "Women vs. Women," *Boston Sunday Globe Magazine*, May 7, 1990, p. 20.

Problem: Group support helps women solve their own problems as well. Networking and mentoring are important elements in the process of self-empowerment. Marcia Chellis, *Ordinary Women, Extraordinary Lives* (New York: Viking Penguin, 1992).

p. 244. *Power-building:* Bella Abzug described it this way: "Women will change the nature of power rather than have power change the nature of women." Bella Abzug, "A Challenge to Women, the Politics of Gender," Lowell Lecture Series, Suffolk University, Boston, Massachusetts, April 18, 1990.

Mikulski: Senator Barbara Mikulski, address to International Women's Forum, Washington, D.C., October 24, 1991.

p. 247. *"edge . . . ":* George A. Dean, "NOW, the Leading Edge," *USA Today,* January 13, 1992, p. A12; for a comprehensive look at NOW, see Jane Gross, "Does She Speak for Today's Women?," *New York Times Magazine,* March 1, 1992, p. 16.

p. 248. *Kanter:* Rosabeth Moss Kanter, "The New Managerial Work," *Harvard Business Review,* November/December 1989, p. 89.

" . . . web": Sally Helgesen, *The Female Advantage, Women's Ways of Leadership* (New York: Doubleday, 1990).

p. 249. *Support groups:* Actually, women's voluntary societies have a long tradition of developing a cooperative professional behavior style among women, in the days before any traditional professional field was open to them. See Anne Firor Scott, *Natural Allies, Women's Associations in American History* (Urbana: University of Illinois Press, 1992), and Arlene Kaplan Daniels, *Invisible Careers: Women Civic Leaders from the Volunteer World* (Chicago: University of Chicago Press, 1988).

Elements: John P. Kotter, "What Leaders Really Do," *Harvard Business Review,* May/June 1990, p. 104.

p. 250. *Cultures:* For an examination of the relationship between adaptive corporate cultures and economic performance, see John P. Kotter and James L. Heskett, *Corporate Culture and Performance* (New York: The Free Press, 1992).

p. 252. *Fourteen:* "Commerce and Growth," *News-Press,* April 19, 1992, pp. 38–52.

p. 253. *" . . . radical bill":* Thomas Duffy, "Bill Requires Education to Fight Sexual Harassment at Work," *Beverly Times,* March 20, 1992, p. 1.

p. 254. *Roberts:* See Lynn Hecht Schafran, "Issues and Models for Judicial Education About Gender Bias in the Courts," *Court Review,* vol. 26, no. 3 (Fall 1989):38, and Norma J. Wikler, "Water on Stone," *Court Review,* vol. 26, no. 3 (Fall 1989):13.

p. 256. *" . . . abortion . . . ":* The American Bar Association, the 370,000-member national association of attorneys, also took a neutral position on abortion until its 1992 convention in San Francisco. Alice Richmond, former president of the Massachusetts Bar Association and an advocate of reproductive freedom for women, introduced the resolution allowing the ABA to lobby for state and federal legislation assuring abortion rights and against those restricting abortion. The resolution was approved by the ABA's House of Delegates 276–168 and by the membership in a 659–340 vote. Gail Appleson, "Abortion Rights Vote Ratified at ABA," *Boston Globe,* August 12, 1992, p. 3.

CHAPTER 9: THE IMPRINT OF WOMEN: THE PUBLIC CLUB

p. 261. *picture:* The Supreme Court decision in *Webster* v. *Reproductive Health Services*, 109 S. Ct. 3040 (1989) gave state legislatures an open invitation to enact statutes and regulations regarding abortion.

p. 262. *themselves:* Women are also becoming more highly educated. Gene Koretz, "America's Neglected Weapon: Its Educated Women," *Business Week*, January 27, 1992, p. 22.

Hagen: See also Margery Guest, "Vote for a Woman! Any Woman? Yes!," *Philadelphia Inquirer*, February 27, 1992, p. A19.

p. 263. *Children:* These statistics about the plight of America's children are becoming well known. See also David E. Rosenbaum's thoughtful essay, "The Paralysis of No-Pain Politics," *New York Times*, August 19, 1992, p. E1.

p. 264. *Kentucky:* "Women Win State Legislative Elections in Record Number," *Women's Political Times*, Winter 1992–93, p. 2. See also Robin Toner, "Women in Politics Gain, But Road Is a Long One," *New York Times*, February 25, 1991, p. A6. George Dean notes that gender imbalance across the Old South is pervasive. Women represent 52 percent of the population but only 2.6 percent of the U.S. House of Representatives from the South.

Brundtland: William E. Schmidt, "Who's in Charge? Women, No Doubt," *New York Times*, May 22, 1991, p. A4.

A study: Gwen Ifill, "Female Lawmakers Wrestle with New Public Attitude on 'Women's Issues,'" *New York Times*, November 17, 1991, p. 14.

Connecticut: Although men and women leaders were similar on many issues, the greatest difference was in support for gay rights legislation (67 percent women strongly agree vs. 12 percent men), the ability of minors to obtain an abortion without parental consent (67 percent women vs. 41 percent men), and family leave (76 percent women disagreed that family leave legislation would hurt business vs. 21 percent men). The biggest gender differences in leadership style between men and women in state government occurred in their managerial style. Men were more likely to prefer a small group of two to three top staff members as a working group (77 percent) while women were more likely to expand their working group to include department heads and line staff (73 percent). Women were more likely to see the purpose of working groups as reaching consensus (47 percent) as compared to men, who preferred working groups to be a place where information was exchanged (73 percent). All of the male respondents indicated they'd inform their staff of their final decisions, while nearly half of the female respondents indicated staff would be involved in the final decision. Catherine A. Havens and Lynne M. Healy, "Do Women Make a Difference?," *Journal of State Government*, vol. 64, no. 2 (April–June 1991), Lexington, Kentucky, The Council of State Government.

p. 265. *Brown:* Amanda Troy Segal, "Corporate Women," *Business Week*, June 8, 1992, p. 76.

Survey: Debbie Howlett, "Women Hold Record Number of State Cabinet Jobs," *USA Today*, April 8, 1992, p. A10.

p. 268. *$6 million:* See R. W. Apple, Jr., "Steady Local Gains by Women Fuel More Runs for High Office," *New York Times*, May 24, 1992, p. E1; Richard L. Berke, "Women Discover the

Political Power of Raising Money for Their Own," *New York Times*, May 31, 1992, p. E3; Stephen Labaton, "Women's Group Looks to Political Races of '94," *New York Times*, December 20, 1992, p. 13. At the 1992 Democratic National Convention, Emily's List raised $750,000 for Democratic female Senate candidates in one night. Chris Black, "Women, with Help From Women, Fill Campaign Coffers," *Boston Globe*, August 10, 1992, p. 1.

Richards: Connie Koenenn, "Setting Priorities for Emily's List," *Los Angeles Times*, October 9, 1991, p. 12.

p. 269. *Women's Campaign Fund:* Jill Abramson, "Women's Anger About Hill-Thomas Hearing Has Brought Cash into Female Political Causes," *Wall Street Journal*, January 6, 1992, p. A16.

p. 270. *Wall Street:* Mary Billard, "Wall St. Dems Find Little to Like in 1992," *New York Times*, March 1, 1992, p. 33.

p. 271. *Kanter:* Rosabeth Moss Kanter, "Women Lend One Another a Helping Hand," *HBS Bulletin*, February 1993, p. 22.

Gallup: "Civic Values Survey, Analysis of Men and Women on Questions Related to Running for Public Office," the George H. Gallup International Institute, Princeton, N.J., May 13, 1991.

Woods: "Women on the Warpath," *Economist*, November 23, 1991, p. 25.

p. 272. *Dean:* George A. Dean, "A Bipartisan Approach to Equal Representation," address at Wellesley College, Wellesley, Massachusetts, March 21, 1990.

Reform: See "A Reform Wish List," *Christian Science Monitor*, December 15, 1991, p. 7.

p. 273. *40 percent:* William E. Schmidt, "Who's in Charge? Women, No Doubt," *New York Times*, May 22, 1991, p. A4.

p. 275. *Male domain:* Celinda Lake, "Challenging the Credibility Gap," *Notes from Emily*, June 1991, pp. 1–4.

CHAPTER 10: THE IMPRINT OF WOMEN: WORK AND FAMILY

p. 278. *Rodgers:* Barbara Presley Noble, "A Corporate Collaboration for Care," *New York Times*, September 27, 1992, p. F27.

Overburdened: Marilyn French, *The War Against Women* (New York: Summit Books, 1992), p. 19.

Balancing: In a 1990 poll, 57 percent women said that a life combining career, marriage, and children was the ideal. For 53 percent women, the ideal marriage was one of shared responsibilities, in which both partners work and share housekeeping. Bickley Townsend and Kathleen O'Neil, "American Women Get Mad," American Demographics, August 1990, p. 29.

p. 279. *Higher:* Fran Sussner Rodgers and Charles Rodgers, "Business and the Facts of Family Life," *Harvard Business Review*, November/December 1989, p. 122. A Boston Bar Association survey found that senior women attorneys were less likely to be married than men (38.9 percent vs. 80.4 percent) and for women practicing sixteen years or more, 55.6 percent reported having no children while only 5.4 percent of men reported having no children. See David Davis, et al., "Preliminary Report of the Boston Bar Association Study of the Role of Gender in the Practice of Law," Litigation Sciences, Inc., February 1988.

Vieira: "Did Meredith Vieira Expect Too Much?," *Working Woman*, September 1991, p. 40.

Handle both: Toni Messina, "Having It All," 18 *M.L.W.*, vol. 18, no. 88, p. B1; Cathy Trost, "Women Managers Quit Not for Family But to Advance Their Corporate Climb," *Wall Street Journal*, May 2, 1990, p. B1.

p. 280. *Attitude:* Phyllis Swersky, "Another View of the Facts of Life," *New England Journal of Public Policy*, Spring/Summer 1990, p. 78. An important part of attitude is guilt. Many women who have successfully balanced the demands of home and work have overcome self-defeating behaviors borne out of guilt arising from unrealistic expectations of parenting. See Barbara J. Berg, *The Crisis of the Working Mother* (New York: Summit Books, 1986).

p. 281. *Okin:* Steve Curwood, "Scholar Studying Gender, Justice Finds Inequality Begins in the Family," *Boston Sunday Globe*, January 14, 1990, p. 90; Christina Robb, "A Tough, Brilliant Study of Justice and How Gender Affects It," *Boston Globe*, December 15, 1989, p. 74.

p. 283. *Age thirty-five:* Janice Castro, "Watching a Generation Waste Away," *Time*, August 26, 1991, pp. 10–12.

p. 284. *"New individualists":* Paul Leinberger and Bruce Tucker, "The Sun Sets on the Silent Generation," *New York Times*, August 4, 1991, p. F11.

" . . . *good girl* . . . ": This sentiment is rising among professional women across the country and in many cases leading to a renewed activism. Catherine S. Manegold, "No More Nice Girls," *New York Times*, July 12, 1992, p. 25.

p. 285. *Three:* Fran Sussner Rodgers and Charles Rodgers, "Business and the Facts of Family Life," *Harvard Business Review*, November/December 1989, p. 122.

" . . . *on strike* . . . ": There was a "Women's Strike Day" on August 26, 1970, the fiftieth anniversary of the suffrage victory.

One fourth: Kenneth Labich, "Can Your Career Hurt Your Kids?," *Fortune*, May 20, 1991, p. 48. The labor force participation by mothers of children under age three rose to 54.5 percent in 1991, and among women with children under age eighteen, 67.2 percent were in the work force. Many of these women have spouses, but there were 5.8 million single working mothers in 1991, 2 million of whom had incomes of only $10,000 to $20,000. Sue Shellenbarger, "Work & Family," *Wall Street Journal*, February 2, 1992, p. B1; "Increasing the Quantity and Quality of Child Care," *Ford Foundation Letter*, vol. 21, no. 2 (Summer 1990):1; Celia W. Dugger, "Tiny Incomes, Little Help for Single Mothers," *New York Times*, March 31, 1992, p. A1.

99 percent: Susan Faludi, *Backlash: The Undeclared War Against American Women* (New York: Crown Publishers, Inc., 1991), p. xiii.

Resource: Sylvia Ann Hewlett, *When the Bough Breaks: The Cost of Neglecting Our Children* (New York: Basic Books, 1991).

p. 286. *2020*: Jonathan Rauch, "Kids as Capital," *Atlantic*, August 1989, p. 57.

Hundred: Jonathan Rauch, "Kids as Capital," *Atlantic*, August 1989, p. 59.

p. 287. *Affordable*: See Victor R. Fuchs, "Economics Applies to Child Care Too," *Wall Street Journal*, April 2, 1990, p. 12.

p. 288. *1995*: "Embracing Our Future—a Child Care Action Agenda," Boston, The Boston Foundation Carol R. Goldberg Seminar on Child Care, 1992, p. 16.

Two Thirds: "Embracing Our Future—a Child Care Action Agenda," Boston, The Boston Foundation Carol R. Goldberg Seminar on Child Care, 1992, p. 40.

Expense: "Embracing Our Future—a Child Care Action Agenda," Boston, The Boston Foundation Carol R. Goldberg Seminar on Child Care, 1992, p. 22; Sue Shellenbarger, "Work & Family," *Wall Street Journal*, January 7, 1992, p. B1.

"Latch key": Michelle Seligson and Dale B. Fink, *No Time to Waste—An Action Agenda for School-Age Child Care* (Wellesley, Mass.: Wellesley College Center for Research on Women, 1989).

Small: Barbara Marsh, "Firms Offer Parents Help Caring for Kids," *Wall Street Journal*, September 5, 1991, B1.

Referral: Of America's 6 million employers, only one tenth of one percent provide any child-care services at all, *including* referral. Susanne Gordon, "Helping Corporations Care," *Working Woman*, January 1993, p. 32.

p. 289. *Morale*: Sue Shellenbarger, "Work & Family," *Wall Street Journal*, January 20, 1992, p. B1.

$3 billion: "Embracing Our Future—a Child Care Action Agenda," Boston, The Boston Foundation Carol R. Goldberg Seminar on Child Care, 1992, p. 28.

Employers: Honeywell Space Systems Group estimates every dollar it spends on child care and after-school care programs returns $2.50 in increased retention and productivity; Union Bank in California conducted a study that showed the bank actually saved money despite a huge investment in a child-care center. General Electric found that many of its employees would consider changing jobs for better family benefits. When GE added family leave, part-time work, and flexible schedules, 1,500 employees used the benefits the first year. Claudia H. Deutsch, "More Care for the Corporate Kids," *New York Times*, June 9, 1991, p. F23; Carl M. Cannon, "Employers Find On-Site Child Care Is an Investment with Big Payoffs," *Providence Journal-Bulletin*, August 14, 1989, p. A12; Sue Shellenbarger, "GE Unit Sees Advantage in More Family Benefits, *Wall Street Journal*, February 12, 1992, p. B1.

Mommy Track: The words actually came from a headline writer, reporting on an article in the *Harvard Business Review* that discussed a two-track career path for women. Felice N. Schwartz, "Management Women and the New Facts of Life," *Harvard Business Review*, January/February 1989, p. 22.

Enraging: Barbara Presley Noble, "Round Two on the Mommy Track," *New York Times*, February 23, 1992, p. F23; Phyllis Segal, "Recruitment Traps in the 90's: Tales of Glass Ceilings, Mommy Tracks and Lawyers' Lives," luncheon address, Large Law Firm Recruitment Conference, New York City, April 5, 1991.

Days lost: American Civil Liberties Union, Equal Rights Advocates, National Women's Political Caucus, National Organization for Women, and NOW Legal Defense and Education Fund, "Letter to the Editor," *Harvard Business Review,* May/June 1989, p. 194.

p. 290. *Chosen career:* American Bar Association, Young Lawyers Division, National Survey of Career Satisfaction/Dissatisfaction, Chicago, American Bar Association, 1980; American Bar Association, Young Lawyers Division, The State of Legal Profession 1 (1990); Gerard J. Clark, Michael Rustad, and Thomas Koenig, "Life After Law: A Comparison of Male and Female Suffolk Alumni Who Left the Law," *Advocate,* Spring 1992, p. 40.

"Law firms . . .": Joan Vennochi, "Verdict: Insensitive," *Boston Globe,* April 25, 1991, p. 1.

p. 291. *". . . 'linkage' . . .":* In Santa Monica, California, developers of new office complexes are asked to provide on-site child-care centers or help support such centers elsewhere. Other cities have copied this approach.

p. 292. *". . . law . . .":* Chapter 521 of the Acts of 1991.

Studies: Fran Sussner Rodgers and Charles Rodgers, "Business and the Facts of Family Life," *Harvard Business Review,* November/December 1989, p. 125; Renee Graham, "Parent Care: A Role Reversal of Love and Necessity," *Boston Globe,* August 23, 1990, p. 1.

200: "Labor Letter," *Wall Street Journal,* May 23, 1989, p. A1.

Siblings: See Margaret Moorman, *My Sister's Keeper* (New York: W.W. Norton & Company, Inc. 1992).

p. 293. *40 percent:* "Parental Leave: Would It Be Just Another Middle-Class Benefit?" *Wall Street Journal,* May 12, 1992, p. 1.

England: Joann S. Lublin, "Hope for Curse of the Working Mummy," *Wall Street Journal,* November 16, 1987, p. 30.

p. 295. *Labor:* Under Labor Department interpretation of its regulations, an employer may not adjust the compensation of salaried employees who want to leave for part of the day; it must either pay a full day's salary for less than a full day of work or forbid people from taking less than a full day's leave. This policy impacts on students, retirees, and those with medical needs as well as employees with families. Linda Froehlich, "The Labor Department Is Anti-Family," *Wall Street Journal,* August 7, 1992, p. A12.

Trust: Sue Shellenbarger, "Employers Try to See If Family Benefits Pay," *Wall Street Journal,* April 3, 1992, p. B1; Gail Davison, "Changing times," *HBS Bulletin,* December 1990, p. 31.

Few men: Few men use family-leave time. Kodak offers employees up to seventeen weeks of unpaid time off. Since 1987, 42 men and 624 women have taken it, despite the fact that 75 percent of Kodak's employees are men. Carol Lawson, "When Baby Beckons, Why Is Daddy at Work? Just Ask His Employer," *New York Times,* May 16, 1991, p. B1. Few men even use paternity-leave benefits when a child is born, fearing financial concerns and reflecting deeply entrenched male stereotypes about acceptable activity. Shari Rudavsky, "New Fathers Reluctant to Take Time Out," *Washington Post,* July 7, 1992, p. A3.

More men: A survey of DuPont Pharmaceuticals' male employees showed that 56 percent of men expressed interest in flexible work options in 1991, up from 37 percent of men five years earlier. "Males Seek Flexible Work Schedules," *MMR,* August 19, 1991, p. 9.

Share: One survey of 244 companies showed 45 percent of employees refusing to move because of family ties or spouse's employment, up from 30 percent in 1986. Sue Shellenbarger, "Work & Family," *Wall Street Journal,* August 16, 1991, p. B1. Men handle most of the grocery shopping in 17 percent of all households; one study found that men are responsible for most home chores, including meal planning, in one out of six homes. Joanne Lipman, "Mr. Mom May Be a Force to Reckon With," *Wall Street Journal,* October 3, 1991, p. B6.

25 percent: Cathy Trost and Carol Hymowitz, "Careers Start Giving in to Family Needs," *Wall Street Journal,* June 18, 1990, p. B1.

Part-time: Including job sharing. Most of the job-sharing teams are women. Maureen McLellan, "Two for One," *This Week's Working,* Supplement to the *Middlesex News,* August 11–17, 1991, p. 1.

p. 296. *Bailyn:* Kathleen Hirsch, "A New Vision of Corporate America," *Boston Globe Magazine,* April 21, 1991, p. 16; Carol Hymowitz, "Trading Fat Paychecks for Free Time," *Wall Street Journal,* August 5, 1991, p. B1.

Commitment: Research shows women as a group are still widely seen as lacking in career commitment. Sue Shellenbarger, "Work & Family," *Wall Street Journal,* April 22, 1992, p. B1; see also Meredith K. Wadman, "Mothers Who Take Extended Time Off Find Their Careers Pay a Heavy Price," *Wall Street Journal,* July 16, 1992, p. B1.

More hours: Juliet B. Schor, "The 30-Hour Work Week!" *Providence Journal-Bulletin,* August 2, 1991, p. A11; Suzanne Gordon, "Work, Work, Work," *Boston Globe Magazine,* August 20, 1989, p. 16; Maureen Sayres Van Niel, "Needed: A New Track for Men and Women," *Boston Globe,* June 20, 1989, p. 28.

p. 297. *Questioning:* Claudia Deutsch, "The Fast Track's Diminished Lure," *New York Times,* October 6, 1991, p. F25. Even many men are moving toward a middle ground of balancing a quest for status and material goods with a need to be more in control of their own time and activities, according to a survey by Yankelovich Clancy Shulman. "For Men, Dark Thoughts Overtake Idealism," *Adweek,* June 29, 1992, p. 36.

p. 298. *Militancy:* Sue Shellenbarger, "More Job Seekers Put Family Needs First," *Wall Street Journal,* November 15, 1991, p. B1.

p. 299. *Brumfield:* Remarks made at the Women's Program Forum, "At Home and in the Workplace," New York City, December 1989.

p. 300. *Collaboration:* IBM and other blue-chip companies collaborated to establish a nationwide network of programs and facilities to care for children and elderly relatives of employees. Gail Fitzer-Schiller, "Major Firms Join in Plan to Give Care," *Boston Globe,* July 10, 1992, p. 73;

Diane E. Lewis, "A New Direction for Child Care," *Boston Globe*, July 13, 1992, p. 11; Tamar Lewin, "11 Companies Join on Family Project," *New York Times*, September 11, 1992, p. A10; Susan Shellenbarger and Cathy Trost, "Partnership of 109 Companies Aims to Improve Care Nationwide for Children and the Elderly," *Wall Street Journal*, September 11, 1992, p. A20; Barbara Presley Noble, "A Corporate Collaboration for Care," *New York Times*, September 27, 1992, p. F27.

p. 301. *$5.6 billion:* Ron Winslow, "Infant Health Problems Cost Business Billions," *Wall Street Journal*, May 1, 1992, p. B1. It is not just infant health problems that are impacting on corporate costs. Peter Magowan, the chairman of Safeway, Inc., states that the corporate community has a huge stake in making sure that health care spending is brought under control nationally, as health care spending is now the equivalent of 45 percent of net corporate profits. Peter Magowan, "A Great Prognosis for 'Play or Pay,'" *Wall Street Journal*, March 26, 1992, p. A15.

CHAPTER 11: THE IMPRINT OF WOMEN: MEMBERS OF THE BOARD

p. 303. *1950s:* Janice E. Stultz, Ph.D., "Madam Director," *Directors & Boards*, Winter 1979, p. 8.

Forty-six: Marilyn Hoffman, "Women in the Boardroom," *Christian Science Monitor*, June 10, 1982, p. 15.

60 percent: Julie Amparano Lopez, "Once Male Enclaves, Corporate Boards Now Comb Executive Suites for Women," *Wall Street Journal*, January 22, 1993, p. B1. See also Diane E. Lewis, "Survey: Women Gain at N.E. Corporations," *Boston Globe*, January 15, 1991, p. 49.

p. 304. *Sisco:* Clare Ansberry, "The Board Game," *Wall Street Journal*, March 24, 1986, p. D29.

58 percent: Diane E. Lewis, "Survey: Women Gain at N.E. Corporations," *Boston Globe*, January 15, 1991, p. 49.

133: "Women on Boards," *Wall Street Journal*, June 16, 1992, p. A1.

481: "Women on Boards," *Wall Street Journal*, June 16, 1992, p. A1.

A third: A 1991 survey by the Corporate Board Resource Committee of the Boston Club. According to Directorship, a Connecticut consulting firm, at least ten of the fifty largest industrial companies have no female directors. Alison Leigh Cowan, "The New Wave Director," *New York Times Magazine*, April 1, 1990.

7.5 percent: Andrea Shalal-Esa, "Women, Minorities Penetrating 'Ceiling,'" *Boston Globe*, August 12, 1992, p. 68.

Golfer: Fox Butterfield, "Role of a Man and $13 Million in Rhode Island's Bank Crisis," *New York Times*, January 3, 1991, p. 1. Shareholders can sometimes learn about their directors from company reports, such as the fact that Centennial Bancorp's Harry Rubenstein missed half the board meetings due to vacation travel and General Builders Corporation's only unaffiliated director William G. Harding missed the only full board meeting of the year. "Outrages," *Issue Alert*, May 1991, p. 5.

Orr: Ronald Rosenberg, "Top Executives Have Formulas for Finding Right Directors," *Boston Sunday Globe,* February 3, 1985, p. A81.

p. 305. *Scott:* Michael Quint, "Bank Directors Face Rising Risks," *New York Times,* March 26, 1992, p. C1.

"Parsley . . . ": Arthur Fleischer, Jr., Geoffrey C. Hazard, Jr., Mariam Z. Klipper, *Board Games, the Changing Shape of Corporate Power* (Boston: Little, Brown, 1988), p. 3.

Choosier: Timothy D. Schellhardt, "Willing Directors Are Hard to Find," *Wall Street Journal,* July 22, 1992, p. B1.

Thrift: Kenneth H. Bacon, "Bank Directors May Be Getting New Guidelines," *Wall Street Journal,* July 21, 1992, p. C18.

p. 306. *$32,352:* Michelle Osborn, "Boardroom's Hefty Perks Draw Fire," *USA Today,* June 7, 1991, p. B1.

Contributions: RJR Nabisco directors received fees of $50,000 a year, private jet service around the world, and VIP treatment at sporting events. Four directors received generous salaries and Nabisco endowed the Juanita Kreps Chair at Duke University and funded an ethics program at Georgetown where another director was a trustee. Hope Lampert, *True Greed: What Really Happened in the Battle for RJR Nabisco* (New York: New American Library, 1990), p. 9. In many companies, employee-matching programs for charitable donations applies to directors' contributions as well, and corporate contributions go to causes espoused by directors.

Payouts: For example, E.F. Hutton directors wrote themselves checks totaling $2,192,500 as they closed up E.F. Hutton. Mark Stevens, *Sudden Death: The Rise and Fall of E.F. Hutton* (New York: New American Library, a Division of Penguin Books USA Inc., 1989), p. 295.

Legal: See Arthur Fleischer, Jr., Geoffrey C. Hazard, Jr., Mariam Z. Klipper, *Board Games, the Changing Shape of Corporate Power* (Boston: Little, Brown and Company, 1988).

p. 307. *Political:* John Pound, "After Takeovers, Quiet Diplomacy," *Wall Street Journal,* June 8, 1992, p. A10.

Savings and Loans: See Michael A. Robinson, *Overdrawn: The Bailout of American Savings* (New York: Penguin Books USA, 1990); Martin Mayer, *The Greatest-Ever Bank Robbery: The Collapse of the Savings and Loan Industry* (New York: Charles Scribner's Sons, 1990).

85 percent: Wendy Hower, "Women Offered Few Seats in Boardroom," *Boston Business Journal,* November 11, 1991, p. 1. Interlocking directorates are still common. In 1985 the Bank of Boston's twenty-three directors sat on the boards of sixty companies. Jan Wong, "Interlocks a Concern, Often Controversial," *Boston Sunday Globe,* February 3, 1985, p. A80.

Resource: Catalyst's resource is the oldest, but other women's groups followed, including the Financial Women's Association of New York. See Dell Mitchell, "The Boardroom, Still a Fraternity?" *New England Journal of Public Policy,* Spring/Summer 1990, p. 91.

p. 308. *Other CEOs:* See Felice N. Schwartz, "'Invisible' Resource: Women for Boards," *Harvard Business Review,* March/April 1980.

Crises: See Ashok S. Kalelkar and John F. Magee, "Corporate Management of a Major Crisis," *Prism*, Second Quarter 1990, p. 63.

Social responsibility: For example, Time Warner tried to argue the First Amendment when it ran into controversy over the rap entertainer Ice-T's violent, and race-obsessed lyrics in "Cop Killer." Others argue the media conglomerate failed to exercise even the minimum standards of corporate responsibility in accepting "Cop Killer" and other equally objectionable songs. After all, it makes decisions every day to accept or reject recordings for distribution. Time Warner directors finally became personally involved, concerned that the company not put shareholders' investments at risk by unnecessarily damaging the company's image. Johnnie L. Roberts, "Time Warner Directors May Bar Release of Certain Music," *Wall Street Journal*, July 24, 1992, p. B1.

Fellow CEO: Robert Comment, "Wimpy Directors Likely Result of Proxy Reform," *Wall Street Journal*, December 4, 1990, p. A18.

Vehicle: James A. White, "Business Roundtable, Calpers Declare a Truce Over Director Questionnaire," *Wall Street Journal*, November 19, 1990, p. B7A.

p. 309. *Qualification:* Another qualification mentioned as important is the status as a trophy spouse of a distinguished CEO. We do not think such experience is relevant. Alison Leigh Cowan, "The New Wave Director," *New York Times Magazine*, April 1, 1990.

p. 310. *Pension funds:* The estimated assets of pension funds in 1991 was $2.5 trillion, making them a significant force.

General Motors: James A. White, "GM Bows to California Pension Fund by Adopting Bylaw on Board's Makeup," *Wall Street Journal*, January 31, 1991, p. A4.

p. 311. *Other companies:* Timothy D. Schellhardt, "More Directors Are Recruited from Outside," *Wall Street Journal*, March 20, 1991, p. B1.

Ratio: The average ratio of outsiders to insiders has risen from two to one in 1980. Joann S. Lublin, "More Chief Executives Are Being Forced Out by Tougher Boards," *Wall Street Journal*, June 6, 1991, p. 1.

300: John Pound, "After Takeovers, Quiet Diplomacy," *Wall Street Journal*, June 8, 1992, p. A10.

Diversity: "Even as a stockholder with only 20 shares I wanted to be proud of my company," wrote one investor. Mel London, "Deconstructing the Annual Report," *New York Times*, April 19, 1992, p. F11.

Salaries: Kevin Salwen, "Shareholder Proposals on Pay Must Be Aired, SEC to Tell 10 Firms," *Wall Street Journal*, February 13, 1992, p. 1.

20 percent: Kate Ballen, "Stockholders Get Listened To," *Fortune*, May 20, 1991, p. 12.

Rule changes: John Pound, "After Takeovers, Quiet Diplomacy," *Wall Street Journal*, June 8, 1992, p. A10; Kate Ballen, "Stockholders Get Listened To," *Fortune*, May 20, 1991, p. 12.

Consumer Activism: The social investing movement encompasses nearly $500 billion worth of assets invested according to some type of ethical screen as of the fall of 1989, according to the Interfaith Center on Corporate Responsibility. Although most investors are men, at least one half of the socially responsible investors are women. See Elizabeth Judd, *Investing with a Social Conscience* (New York: Pharos Books, 1990).

Maquiladora: These are addressed to companies that operate in Mexico, to promote fair work practices, protect the environment, create a safe work environment, and provide an adequate standard of living. "New Social Policy Initiative: The Maquiladora Standards," *Issue Alert*, May 1991, p. 3.

Eisner: "Executive Pay—Up, Up, and Away," *Issue Alert*, May 1991, p. 1.

Millions: Amanda Bennett, "Hard Times Trim CEO Pay Raises," *Wall Street Journal*, April 17, 1991, p. R1. The combined annual compensation of the dozen CEOs who accompanied President Bush to Japan in 1991 was $25 million or an average of more than $2 million each. By comparison, Japanese chief executives are paid $300,000 to $400,000 a year on average and pay a much higher tax rate. Jill Abramson and Christopher J. Chipello, "High Pay of CEOs Traveling with Bush Touches a Nerve in Asia," *Wall Street Journal*, December 30, 1991, p. A1. In the middle 1970s, CEOs earned about 34 times the pay of the average worker; by the late 1980s they earned 109 times that average. Paul A. Gigot, "Executive Pay—an Embarrassment to Free Marketers," *Wall Street Journal*, January 10, 1992, p. A8. Some executives are feeling the pressure and agreeing to pay cuts. Carol Hymowitz, "More Employees, Shareholders Demand That Sacrifices in Pay Begin at the Top," *Wall Street Journal*, November 8, 1990, p. B1.

p. 312. *Restructurings:* See General Motors, Goodyear Tire and Rubber, General Public Utilities Corporation, Digital, to name a few. John Pound, "After Takeovers, Quiet Diplomacy," *Wall Street Journal*, June 8, 1992, p. A10; Steve Lohr, "Pulling Down the Corporate Clubhouse," *New York Times*, April 12, 1992, p. F3; Joann S. Lublin, "More Chief Executives Are Being Forced Out by Tougher Boards," *Wall Street Journal*, June 6, 1991, p. 1.

Specific needs: See Janice E. Stultz, Ph.D., "Madam Director," *Directors & Boards*, Winter 1979.

p. 313. *Kreps:* Marilyn Hoffman, "Women in the Boardroom," *Christian Science Monitor*, June 10, 1982, p. 15. Without overstating the importance of the remark and concluding that women make a profound difference, it is interesting to note that when Ross Johnson proposed a leveraged buyout to the RJR Nabisco board, reportedly only Kreps had doubts, saying, "Isn't it a shame to break the company apart?" Hope Lampert, *True Greed: What Really Happened in the Battle for RJR Nabisco* (New York: New American Library, 1990), p. 2.

p. 314. " . . . *interlocking* . . . ": The issue of heads of companies who sit on each other's boards and compensation committees is gaining more attention. See Alison Leigh Cowan, "Board Room Back-Scratching?," *New York Times*, June 2, 1992, p. C1.

p. 315. *Symbolize:* See Janice E. Stultz, Ph.D., "Madam Director," *Directors & Boards*, Winter 1979.

Own women: The cost of not paying attention can be high. For example, Corning had a reputation for recruiting women, but it was not retaining them. Between 1980 and 1987, one out of every seven female professionals resigned (and one out of every six minorities) while only one out of every fourteen white males resigned. Corning estimated that replacing the women and minorities who left cost it $2 million a year. Elizabeth Judd, *Investing with a Social Conscience* (New York: Pharos Books, 1990), p. 14.

Sewell: Louis B. Fleming, "More Firms Welcome Women on Board at the Directors' Table," *Los Angeles Times,* April 24, 1983, p. 19.

Face: Investors do not always look just to the return on their investment in assessing the value of a company. An accounting professor at Yeshiva University conducted a survey that asked shareholders what corporations should spend money on. The results were surprising: shareholders wanted corporations to direct more money to cleaning up plants and stopping environmental pollution and making safer products. Higher dividends ranked third on the list. According to the professor, this suggests that corporations must integrate corporate awareness of social, ethical, and environmental issues at all levels of the corporation. Marc J. Epstein, "What Shareholders Really Want," *New York Times,* April 28, 1991, p. F11.

Positive: See Wendy Hower, "Women Offered Few Seats in Boardroom," *Boston Business Journal,* November 11, 1991, p. 1.

Environments: Entrepreneurs are forming kitchen cabinets of directors who are paid in stock options and token fees and who bring skills and resources to the chairman that might not be available in senior executive ranks. Barbara Marsh, "More Small Firms Are Employing Outside Directors," *Wall Street Journal,* June 11, 1991, p. B2. Even labor unions are noticing that women are a larger percentage of their membership and are supporting women on their boards. Ann Hagedorn, "Teamsters Grapple with Democracy at their Government-Run Convention," *Wall Street Journal,* June 28, 1991, p. B8.

CHAPTER 12: A VISION OF THE FUTURE: THOUGHTS FOR CORPORATE AMERICA

p. 319. *Mascotte:* Amanda Troy Segal, "Corporate Women," *Business Week,* June 8, 1992, p. 78.

p. 321. *"A Group":* Carol Stocker, "The A Group," *Boston Globe,* January 14, 1992, p. 25.

p. 323. *MITs:* Many women are seeking to live their values outside a male-dominated work environment, sacrificing prestige, money, and security to pursue their own long-term interests. See Susan Wittig Albert, Ph.D., *Work of Her Own* (New York: G.P. Putnam's Sons, 1992). Corporations are missing the opportunity. See Felice N. Schwartz, "Women as a Business Imperative," *Harvard Business Review,* March/April 1992, p. 106.

p. 324. *Definition: Webster's New Collegiate Dictionary* (Springfield, Mass.: G & C Merriam Company), 1976, p. 168.

p. 325. *Survey:* S. Ornstein, and L. A. Isabella, "Making It to the Top: Challenges of Personal and Professional Career Management." Presentation to The Boston Club, February 12, 1991, Boston, Massachusetts.

p. 326. *Doing wrong:* In one poll of women executives, 70 percent saw the male-dominated corporate culture as an obstacle to their success. Amanda Troy Segal, "Corporate Women," *Business Week,* June 8, 1992, p. 74.

p. 327. *"Change the culture":* Changing culture does not produce changes in behavior; changing the rewards and recognitions does. Peter F. Drucker, "Don't Change Corporate Culture—Use It," *Wall Street Journal*, March 28, 1991, p. A14.

Shareholders: The corporation has an independent interest in maintaining itself so as to generate earnings for present and future shareholders and, according to some, to perform certain corollary functions within society beyond enhancing per share earnings. Employees and bond holders have contractual claims, shareholders have fiduciary claims, and a community's relationship to the corporation is addressed by a complex tangle of local, state, and federal laws. Ralph C. Ferrara, "The Institutional Investor and Corporate Ownership," *Director's Monthly*, July 1992, p. 1. All of this suggests that the quality of executives representing the company, making short- and long-term decisions and planning its future strategy is a critical component to evaluating a company's long-term prospects.

Business Week: "How to Create Gender-Blind Companies," *Business Week*, June 8, 1992, p. 122.

p. 329. *Informal:* Bette Woody, "Corporate Policy and Women at the Top," Working Paper No. 211, Wellesley College, Center for Research on Women, 1990, p. 8.

"fit": At the top of corporate hierarchies, political power and inertia play more important roles in determining CEO succession than individual characteristics. Bette Woody, "Corporate Policy and Women at the Top," Working Paper No. 211, Wellesley College, Center for Research on Women, 1990, p. 7.

p. 330. *Wilson:* Linda S. Wilson, Testimony at Oversight Hearing on Sexual Harassment in Non-Traditional Occupations, Subcommittee on Employment Opportunities, Committee on Education and Labor, U.S. House of Representatives, June 25, 1992.

p. 331. *Quotas:* Bette Woody, "Corporate Policy and Women at the Top," Working Paper No. 211, Wellesley College, Center for Research on Women, 1990, p. 14.

5 percent: Anne B. Fisher, "When Will Women Get to the Top?," *Fortune*, September 21, 1992, p. 45.

Gender-balanced: At Pitney Bowes, 35 percent of promotions must go to women. At Baxter International, bonuses are linked to the number of women who are promoted. "Women in Management," *Economist*, March 28, 1992, p. 17.

p. 333. *7 percent:* "Women in Management," *Economist*, March 28, 1992, p. 17.

Senior levels: Managers may need to be reminded about women. A poll of 201 chief executives revealed that only 16 percent believe it is "very" or "somewhat" likely that they will be succeeded by a female CEO in the next *decade*. Anne B. Fisher, "When Will Women Get to the Top?," *Fortune*, September 21, 1992, p. 44.

p. 334. *Six-figure-income:* Malcolm S. Forbes, Jr., "Tremendous Trend," *Forbes*, September 2, 1991, p. 23.

Difference: We heard many stories to substantiate this difference. One that we like particularly is about Muriel Siebert, the first female member of the New York stock Exchange, a former New York State Superintendent of Banking and the founder of Muriel Siebert & Co. In addition to her own personal foundation, she has started a program in her firm by which half the commissions buyers pay for stocks or bonds from a new issue will go to charity. "The money downtown is vast, almost lewd," she said, noting that Wall Street executives can give much more than they do to charity. Fred R. Bleakley, "Broker's Generosity Generates Business, Worries Wall Street," *Wall Street Journal*, July 7, 1992, p. C1.

p. 336. " . . . *awesome*": Laton McCartney, *Friends in High Places, the Betchtel Story: the Most Secret Corporation and How It Engineered the World* (New York: Ballantine Books, 1988), p. 106.

p. 337. *Hiatt:* The Rev. Suzanne R. Hiatt, address to the trustees and faculty of Regis College, Weston, Massachusetts, May 20, 1988.

p. 338. *Frug:* Tamara Lewin, "Feminist Scholars Spurring a Rethinking of Law," *New York Times*, September 30 1988, p. B9.

Third Stage: Dawn-Marie Driscoll, "The Third Stage: An Economic Strategy," *New England Journal of Public Policy*, Spring/Summer 1990. We are also mindful of the danger of generalizing any time we speak of feminism, and are sensitive to the criticism that our view of feminism is not just white middle-class Western, but from our experience in an industrialized capitalist country as well. We do not presume to speak for or about the experience of all women, but we argue that to improve the economic status of all women, we have to start with the place that has the greatest power to affect change, The Club. See Elizabeth V. Spelman, *Inessential Woman: Problems of Exclusion in Feminist Thought* (Boston: Beacon Press, 1988). We agree with Eleanor Holmes Norton who said that women's greatest challenge is to liberate half the world, across race and class lines. This dynamic must begin with educated professional women, she said. Women's liberation cannot just consist of what our sage friend John Hoving of Washington, D.C., calls the Gloria Steinem syndrome, a movement "only for sparkling people." Our movement may begin with businesswomen, but it is for *all* women.

Partnership: Riane Eisler compares a partnership model with a dominator model, one that is based on ranking, backed by fear or force, and characterized most usually by men dominating women. Riane Eisler, *The Chalice and the Blade* (San Francisco: Harper & Row, 1987).

Concern: James O'Toole describes a similar concept, "humanism," a system combining capitalism's concerns for liberty and economic efficiency with socialism's concerns for community and economic security. See James O'Toole, "Triumphant Capitalism?," *Aspen Institute Quarterly*, Winter 1991.

p. 339. *Observers:* Susan Faludi, *Backlash: The Undeclared War Against American Women* (New York: Crown Publishers, Inc., 1991), p. 240.

Bateson: Mary Catherine Bateson, *Composing a Life* (New York: Atlantic Monthly Press, 1989), p. 239.

p. 340. *Graham:* Patricia Albjerg Graham, "The Cult of True Womanhood: Past and Present," in All of Us Are Present, The Stephens College Symposium, Women's Education: The Future; Eleanor M. Bender, Bobbie Berk, Nancy Walker, eds.; Stephens College, 1983.

Yershova: "Gaya and the Women's Forum," *VIP*, Moscow, 1991, p. 53.

Poorer: Renee Loth, "A Baby Boomer Wants Her Peers to Get Noisy," *Boston Sunday Globe*, July 21, 1991, p. A2.

p. 341. *89 percent:* Margaret C. Snyder, "Growth of Mother-Centered Families," *New York Times*, December 28, 1991, p. 12.

Children: Sylvia Ann Hewlett, "Devaluing the Innocents," *Providence Journal*, July 20, 1991, p. 12.

Erikson: Mary Catherine Bateson, *Composing a Life* (New York: Atlantic Monthly Press, 1989), pp. 230–31.

p. 342. *Ethics:* Professor Fran Burke of Suffolk University's School of Management suggests adding "a second set of E's," evaluation, empathy, and ethics, to the traditional E's of economy, efficiency, and effectiveness and proposes that the second group will promote heightened productivity. Fran Burke with Amy Black, "Improving Organizational Productivity: To Efficiency, Effectiveness and Economy, ADD ETHICS," *Public Productivity Review*, September/October 1990.

INDEX

DATE DUE

The Library Store   #47-0107